PHILOSOPHY AND THE MATERNAL BODY

Philosophy and the Maternal Body is one of the first full-length studies to properly consider the relationship between philosophy and the maternal body. Michelle Boulous Walker investigates one of the key questions in contemporary feminist theory: how are we to understand the silence of the feminine voice in Western thought?

Philosophy and the Maternal Body gives a new voice to the mother and the maternal body which have often been viewed as silent within philosophy. Michelle Boulous Walker clearly shows how some male theorists have appropriated maternity and suggests new ways of articulating the maternal body and women's experience of pregnancy and motherhood. Drawing on rich examples such as Plato's allegory of the cave, the "productive man" of Marx's philosophy, Sigmund Freud and Melanie Klein's writing and the psychoanalytic and feminist insights of Julia Kristeva and Luce Irigaray, the author calls into question some of the ways in which women have been traditionally constructed as silent in relation to philosophy. This book also draws upon the work of Louis Althusser and Jean-François Lyotard – figures often overlooked in feminist theory – and clearly shows how their work bears importantly on the significance of the maternal body. Throughout, Michelle Boulous Walker questions the assumption that silence must necessarily mean the absence of language and presents highly and compelling new strategies for understanding how silence operates.

Philosophy and the Maternal Body is an invaluable study of the crucial significance of the maternal body in philosophy and is essential reading for all those in gender studies, feminist philosophy, psychoanalytic studies and literature.

Michelle Boulous Walker is Senior Lecturer in Philosophy at the University of Queensland.

PHILOSOPHY AND THE MATERNAL BODY

Reading silence

Michelle Boulous Walker

London and New York

First published 1998
by Routledge
11 New Fetter Lane, London EC4P 4EE

Simultaneously published in the USA and Canada
by Routledge
29 West 35th Street, New York, NY 10001

Typeset in Garamond by
Ponting–Green Publishing Services, Chesham, Buckinghamshire
Printed and bound in Great Britain by
Creative Print and Design (Wales), Ebbw Vale

British Library Cataloguing in Publication Data
A catalogue record for this book is available
from the British Library

Library of Congress Cataloguing in Publication Data
Walker, Michelle Boulous, 1959–
Philosophy and the maternal body: reading silence/
Michelle Boulous Walker.
p.   cm.
Includes bibliographical references and index.
1. Feminist theory.   2. Motherhood.   I. Title.
HQ1190.W34   1998
305.42'01—dc21   97–30381

ISBN 0–415–16857–0 (hbk)
ISBN 0–415–16858–9 (pbk)

FOR JOSEPHINE AND JAMES

a dilemma that regularly besets and vexes feminist studies – will we be mothers or daughters? The mother's daughter or the father's? Can we be both at once? Mothers of daughters, of sons? Indeed, how many permutations of these positions are possible? And what is politically at stake in each? Can they be altogether avoided? What does mother mean? What does daughter mean? Is there a paradigm other than the familial one from which we can more productively or at least comfortably speak and write, live?

(Michèle Longino Farrell, *Performing Motherhood: The Sévigné Correspondence*)

CONTENTS

CONTENTS

ACKNOWLEDGEMENTS

In the acknowledgements to his Wellek Lectures (published as *Peregrinations: Law, Form, Event*, New York: Columbia University Press, 1988) Jean-François Lyotard speaks of the difficulty of describing or locating the function of one's translator. I think that what he says about this function is a fitting tribute not only to one's translator but also to one's reader. Let me repeat, with some degree of infidelity, Lyotard's gesture here: "[reading] … is a tiresome and difficult task, a kind of 'rewriting' that makes [one] co-responsible for these texts. There is not yet any accepted name for this function, which falls between translator and co-author … let's call it co-writer. To thank [this person] would be very little. One does not clear oneself of a gift of language." Acknowledging that it is very little I nonetheless thank Anne Freadman. For a variety of other reasons I would also like to thank the following people: Anthony Ashbolt, Christine Barron, Max Deutscher, Alice Jardine, Gregorio Kohon, Valli Shaio Kohon, Sabine Sielke, Alec Waskiw, my sisters Suzanne and Patricia, my brother Russell, and my father James. Finally, I would like to thank the *Australasian Journal of Philosophy* for permission to use material that appears in revised form in chapter one.

INTRODUCTION

In this book I ask questions about the silencing of women. I focus much of my early discussion on the terrain of Western philosophy, looking at specific texts written by men. I suggest that within these texts we can discern a masculine imaginary that works to silence women in quite specific ways. My claim, throughout this work, is that women are silenced most effectively by their association with maternity. The maternal body operates as the site of women's radical silence. My concern with the maternal body pre-dates this book in a significant way. The death of my own mother forced me to confront a number of painful issues that were eventually to find their way into my philosophical work. Initially this surfaced as a desire for feminist theory itself. Later this evolved into a theoretical exploration of the maternal in discourses such as Marxist feminism. Marxist feminism was to serve as an initial site of contact with questions of both the mother and the maternal.[1]

Throughout this book I uncover the strategies that comprise the complex process of silencing, strategies such as exclusion, repression, denial and foreclosure. The specific claim that I elucidate is that the maternal body occupies the site of a radical silence in the texts of Western philosophy, psychoanalytic theory and literature. Read symptomatically, these texts reveal a masculine imaginary that speaks for the maternal. Along with this, I discuss the complex nature of silence itself. I argue that silence is an inappropriate concept for understanding women's relation to philosophy if it is understood merely in opposition to speaking or voice. I disrupt the oppositional relation between silence and language, via a discussion of non-productive poetic language practice, and then go on to explore how subjectivity can be rethought in ways that make it possible to theorise women's voice. I conclude the work by concentrating on writing by women that challenges the authority of traditional philosophical texts, suggesting that this writing forces us to reconsider the spatial logics that typically assign women to a position exterior to symbolic speech.

The book is divided into two parts: "Reading Silence" and "Speaking Silence". In the first part I begin in chapter one by investigating the silencing of woman's voice in philosophy, arguing that this needs to be understood as something more than a simple exclusion. The spatial logic separating inside

1

and outside is inadequate for understanding the complex philosophical processes that assign women to silence while simultaneously placing them at the very heart of its domain. Here I discuss the work of Luce Irigaray and Michèle Le Doeuff and show how, even though their ideas on women and rationality seem to conflict, they both draw our attention to the peculiar spatial logic that philosophy operates in its relation to women. In the second chapter I use Irigaray's work on the repressed maternal body and Le Doeuff's exploration of metaphor and the imaginary as two different yet compatible models of reading to pursue the way the masculine imaginary silences women. I link these with Louis Althusser's strategy of symptomatic reading in order to discern the repressed moments of certain philosophical texts; the symptomatic silences or readable absences which reveal that a structure of denial is at play. This chapter serves to shift my discussion of silencing away from a concern with exclusion toward the question of denial. I begin with a reading of Plato's work suggesting that his phantasy of self-engendering is a denial of the maternal body. I show how Plato's conscious denial of the body is unconsciously exceeded by various references to bodily fluids – metaphors that implicate Plato within a masculine desire for self-generation. From Plato I shift to Althusser, whose symptomatic reading practice I employ to read the silences, repressions and denials of his own work. Chapter three enacts another theoretical displacement. Here I shift terrain away from the questions of silencing structured by exclusion, repression and denial, in order to ask what psychoanalysis has to offer diagnostically to this ongoing discussion. My analysis of psychosis provides an alternative model for thinking about the masculine imaginary and its recurrent theme of self-generation. I re-work the psychoanalytic category of foreclosure to explain how this imaginary surfaces in a most ruthless way. In the process I look at psychoanalysis as Freud's own psychotic foreclosure of the mother, re-read his *fort-da* in terms of a masculine psychotic desire to master and replace the mother, and conclude with a discussion of Schreber's psychotic text. After analysing the implications of Schreber's phantasies of self-generation (and Freud and Lacan's refusal to register these), I turn to Julia Kristeva's notion of the abject in order to ask some preliminary questions about writing and the maternal body. In chapter four I seek in Jean-François Lyotard's notion of the *différend* another way of asking questions about silence. Here I argue that even though Lyotard's work is useful for foregrounding the question of silence that it silences, in its turn, questions pertaining to women. At this point I introduce some of Luce Irigaray's work on sexual ethics. I suggest that she provides us with an alternative philosophy, one that insists upon voicing, rather than silencing, the concerns of women. In chapter five I return to the theme of self-genesis and its relation to the masculine imaginary. I argue that we need to question the logic that constructs the world as a society of self-generating (masculine) bodies, a world where the re-productive maternal body is replaced by the productive masculine one. The productive man of Marx's philosophy is a subject quite familiar to humanist thought. He is a self-created, self-conscious subject who is considered to be very much in control of himself and his external world. In fact he gains this control and mastery of the external world *through* his productive labour. I am interested in what this particular subject means for feminism. While I am interested in exploring how Marx constructs this subject, I am equally interested in finding those moments when Marx's productive man exceeds his own logic. Productive labour may well be the foundation of Marx's man, but there are moments when the body exceeds this logic in a kind of eruptive (and unproductive) play. We can identify a possible subject beyond the productive implications of Marx's self-made man. I am interested in pursuing the notion of a poetic subject, one which disinvests from the cumulative logic of production. Julia Kristeva's work is instructive here. She offers an alternative reading of Marx (with the help of Freud) which focuses on the poetic or excessive in his work, the non-productive practices. I use her non-productive language practice as an alternative to Marx's productive logic. I find it a useful way of thinking about subjects which are not self-produced. Her discussion of non-productive language practice allows me to radicalise my discussion of silence because it displaces the dichotomy between language and silence. Her poetic practices refer to an unquiet silence that inhabits and disrupts language.

The second part of the book, "Speaking Silence", begins with chapter six in which I look at Kristeva's alternative to the productive subject. The negativity of her poetic subject displaces Marx's self-produced man. Here the illusion of identity dissolves in the face of a powerful and heterogeneous negativity. I discuss the emphasis that Kristeva places on the sensuous, embodied nature of subjectivity, investigating her ideas about the agency of bodily and textual crisis. I place this work in the context of her overriding concern with the avant-garde, arguing that while her poetic subject offers an enticing alternative to Marx's productive man, ultimately it still refers to men. I go on to investigate the links between poetic language and the maternal *chora* in her work asking whether this offers us a way of rethinking subjectivity through either the bodies or writing of women. I suggest that it does not because the maternal occupies an exclusively metaphorical site that precludes reference to women. I follow this with feminist responses to Kristeva, arguing that we can reorient her questions toward women. Using Susan Rubin Suleiman's work on women and the avant-garde for inspiration I begin this discussion with an exploration of woman's body as the site of a radical agency. I explore how woman is silenced as a hysterical body in pain. Using a phenomenological notion of the body in crisis as a starting point, i.e. a body in an unliveable, contradictory state, I look at how woman's hysterical silence is pitted against man's abject voice; how man's abjection is productive (of literature, himself, etc.) while woman's hysteria is silent. I ask whether this hysterical silence – suffered through the body in crisis – might be viewed as a kind of non-productive practice that speaks woman's desire. The body in crisis is read as a radical state of sensuous contradiction. A textual practice of writing the body issues from this contradictory state

3

offering the possibility of both agency and voice for women. In chapter seven I respond to Kristeva's reduction of the maternal to metaphor by collecting work on the mother. I gather together writing by women in the mode of a Symposium where (contra Plato) women are present and speak. My aim here is to begin the preliminaries toward a philosophy amongst women rather than one about them. I begin by asking questions about the role of the maternal metaphor in feminist work, suggesting that we be cautious of adopting it as an emblem of defiance without considering, at length, the many ways that it may be appropriated or disarmed by phallocentric thought. I go on to suggest that it is important politically, aesthetically and ethically for women to adopt the maternal, despite the considerable risks of doing so. I follow this with an investigation of women's writing on the mother, focusing on the possibility or desirability of theorising the *real* mother in the work of Hélène Cixous, Melanie Klein, Julia Kristeva, Iris Marion Young, Adrienne Rich and Luce Irigaray. In this chapter I allude to an ambiguity in Kristeva's work by indicating the moments where she focuses on the sensuous, embodied processes of pregnancy and motherhood over and against the maternal as metaphor. I conclude with a discussion of what I call Irigaray's labial logic, suggesting that her bilabial trope manages to displace the dichotomous relations between reference and metaphor, self and other, speaking and silence. I argue that her labial logic shifts us away from a concern with the symbolic as *the* speaking position toward a discussion of the difference that women's voices make. In the final chapter there is a special emphasis on writing that seeks to capture the sensuous mother–daughter bond. Here I use the complex relationality between mother and daughter to question those *real* mother accounts that either subsume the mother beneath a theoretical concern with the child or sustain an oppositional division between mother and child. Following this I question what is at stake in Kristeva's rather Oedipal claim that women's writing is repetitive, that it imitates masculine transgressions without producing anything new. I trace the conceptual elisions between reproduction and repetition in the work of three writers, Sigmund Freud, Simone de Beauvoir and Gilles Deleuze, investigating the ways in which reproduction comes to be figured as repetition-as-same. I argue that in their work the maternal body occupies the site of similitude and identity. Returning to Kristeva I suggest that her depiction of women's writing as derivative reinforces an Oedipal scenario where women are reduced to the status of daughters who faithfully desire to reproduce their fathers' words. Against this I gesture toward writing by women that displaces this masculine coupling. I complete the chapter with a discussion of the attempt, in Irigaray's work, to theorise mothers and daughters as speaking subjects who do more than simply repeat the same.

I conclude the book by returning to a question that runs throughout the work, the question of the place of women's writing. Here I return to the spatial metaphors with which I began in chapter one, arguing that women's writing can not be located by means of a simple inside/outside spatial logic. I argue that the mother–daughter bond disrupts any attempts (Lacan's included) to locate women's writing, language or speech as simply outside symbolic law. I offer the work of Kristeva and Irigaray as alternatives for rethinking the space of the symbolic, suggesting that women's writing performs, by its audacious styles, the (re)production of new symbolic spaces in which woman's desire can be spoken. I conclude that Irigaray's work on gesture and speech serves as a provisional model for understanding and appreciating the (sexual) difference that women's writing makes.

Throughout the book I am confronted by the problem of identification. Writing a philosophical work *on* women's silence means that to a significant degree women have become the object of my inquiry. This makes it difficult, at times, to decide whether to identify with or distance myself from my object. As feminist scholars *we* may choose to incorporate a collective "we" into our theoretical discourse. I have done so at times. The collective "we" does have some problems though. In chapter eight I indicate that "we" is the standard or predictable mode of address used in the manifesto and that as a critical discourse it leaves something to be desired. My own text hovers, therefore, between *we* and *they*. I have retained these inconsistencies in order to allow for local judgements to be made concerning suitable modes of address.

Part I

READING SILENCE

1

SPEAKING SILENCE

Woman's voice in philosophy[1]

The exclusion of "woman" is ... consubstantial with the philosophical ... Plato's *Phaedrus* does not say that women must be excluded
from the dialectical enterprise. But with Zeus in love with Ganymede
serving as an example, it is clear that this is not women's business.
(Michèle Le Doeuff, "Women and Philosophy", p. 6)

So some speak and others are silent.
(Luce Irigaray, *Speculum of the Other Woman*, p. 257)

How does a woman begin a philosophical work, if not by saying something
about woman's voice in philosophy? I shall consider how this voice has been
excluded from the philosophical domain, and I shall argue that the exclusion
of woman's voice can be understood as a question of silencing. Philosophy
excludes women by silencing them, either by refusing them entry, or by refusing to listen to those who have, through whatever means, managed to gain
access to its privileged domain. Luce Irigaray and Michèle Le Doeuff investigate the systematic silencing of both woman and women from the discourse
of Western philosophy. They understand silence as involving an absence of
women's voices from the dialogues that constitute the philosophical enterprise as a tradition. In *Speculum of the Other Woman* Irigaray retraces the steps
leading to this silencing of woman. Her careful readings of the metaphors that
structure philosophical texts from Plato to Freud highlight a systematic exclusion of woman from the production of philosophy. Plato's parable of the cave,
the fecund womb from which all Western philosophy derives its inspiration,
is for Irigaray the metaphor that initiates this silencing of woman. It is both an
ideological and a rhetorical device that structures femininity as the marginal
and unacknowledged support of the philosophical enterprise. The silencing
of woman from the traditional project of philosophy interests Le Doeuff in as
much as she argues that it is tied up with the construction of femininity. She
claims that philosophy creates that which it excludes. She sees philosophy as
tied up with "the formal idea that discourse must involve exclusion or discipline, that inadmissible modes of thought cannot be undefined."[2]

9

Reading silence

For Irigaray, woman's exclusion from the project of philosophy is complete. The equation of rationality with masculinity is totalised in her account, and she argues that this equation allows no voice for the feminine Other. Le Doeuff's position is less emphatic. Woman's exclusion from philosophy is only partial and rationality is far from a wholly masculine domain. In practical terms, this places Irigaray and Le Doeuff in seemingly antagonistic positions. Irigaray goes on to champion the cause of *speaking otherwise*, of speaking beyond or outside the masculine logic of philosophical reason, while Le Doeuff opts for transforming philosophical rationality in accord with its own potential; that is, of extending philosophy beyond its own self-enclosure precisely by adopting a non-hegemonic form of reason. We might say that the two positions fall loosely within the alternatives of (for Le Doeuff) speaking with, or (for Irigaray) speaking against philosophy.[3] While these seem useful descriptions for the moment I suggest that they are a gross simplification of the problem I am addressing; in the course of this chapter I shall show why this is so.

In order to make some sense of the complexity of these perspectives, I want to spend some time rehearsing the particular arguments of these two women philosophers. I shall do this by looking at what they have to say about philosophy, about exclusion, and about the spatial logics and metaphors that philosophy adopts in order to effect this exclusion. But before I go on to elaborate Irigaray's and Le Doeuff's respective positions, it will be useful to say a few words about silence. Let me start by asking what the question of silencing is. A simple version of this problem might be that if women are located outside a privileged domain, they do not have the opportunity to speak inside it. In this sense, silencing involves a sort of spatial logic. By this I mean that silence and voice are differentiated each according to their status as either *inside* or *outside* a domain. Now, if we assume that the discourse of philosophy establishes itself by de-limiting its legitimate boundaries, then we need to ask who legitimately speaks (and is heard) from within that space.

However, it may well be misleading to take this as an analysis of the difficulty of dialogue between women and philosophy. For by reducing the question of silencing to the (imaginary?) relation between women and philosophy, we foreclose any discussion of how the categories of both *woman* and *women* are at least partially constructed *within* philosophy's domain. And this is to some extent the concern of Le Doeuff's and Irigaray's work. In particular, Irigaray argues that philosophy (along with other discourses) partially establishes "woman" in the very act of exiling her to the place of the Other.[4] If woman, or indeed women, do occupy this site beyond philosophy's realm, then it must be inappropriate to speak of a possible dialogue. Moreover this notion of dialogue (and hence the conjunction "woman *and* philosophy") would be premised on a simplification of what it means both to speak and to listen. However, if we suppose that women are able to speak within philosophy's domain, then the question of silencing might be less a prohibition against speech than a refusal to listen. What I mean by this is that women may well speak, may be able to speak, but may never be heard. Philosophy, in this scenario, would be repeating the masculine gesture of turning a deaf ear toward the ever-nagging woman.

Speaking inside philosophy's domain might not necessarily entail dissent. For, as we will later see with Le Doeuff, the voices of women inside philosophy have historically been the voices of faithful disciples or (as Elizabeth Grosz puts it) dutiful daughters – the women who knew their sacred duty as keepers of the father's or lover's wisdom.[5] So women may well speak from inside philosophy, and may well be heard, but yet remain effectively silenced if all they mouth is determined by the ventriloquist's art. What, then, would it mean to speak *outside* philosophy's domain? Speaking outside seems to suggest speaking in a language wholly incomprehensible from the standpoint of sound philosophical reasoning. Silencing, then, is no simple matter. Not speaking, or not being permitted to speak are only two possible prohibitions that constitute women as mute. The effective silencing of women, as I have suggested, also involves the refusal of philosophy to listen, i.e. a blank denial of their claim to subjectivity. This is important because if we are able to understand silencing as a complex series of strategies aimed at denying women their role as philosophical subjects, then we are better equipped to counteract these with our own complex interventions and excursions into the philosophical domain. It is for these reasons that I see the question of silencing as a kind of theoretical hinge upon which feminist strategies might be secured.

Luce Irigaray: speaking otherwise – woman as the place of philosophy

Luce Irigaray's celebration of speaking otherwise seems to occupy a terrain outside philosophy's inner sanctum. Her attack on the self-styled importance of philosophy's truth is enacted from the uncharted territory beyond the fortress walls. She speaks from the place of the Other – perhaps a logical impossibility? – where philosophy's constructed images, metaphors, and truth of woman find no sympathetic ear. This is true both stylistically and institutionally, for a great deal of Irigaray's work comes from her not inconsiderable connections, affiliations and allegiances beyond the strictly academic pursuit of philosophy. (It should be noted, having said this, that she is currently associated with the Centre National de la Recherche Scientifique in Paris.)

Irigaray's work is emblematic of those feminists who call for a gesture of indifference toward philosophy rather than a transformation of its inner logic, which is a good characterisation of Le Doeuff's work. I am interested in Irigaray's work because it offers a radical rethinking of how philosophy effects the silencing and exclusion of women.[6] Rather than rehearsing the familiar theme of "woman as outside" philosophy, she suggests something much more interesting. We might say that Irigaray's contribution to the contemporary debates around these questions is to show, through a series of carefully detailed and close readings of Plato's texts, that woman is most effectively silenced through her construction as silent foundation or mute *interiority* of philosophy.[7] She is the silent, unacknowledged *place* of philosophy, its empty/subjectless interiority. What this suggests is that the spatial logic organising the opposition inside/outside is far too simplistic to describe woman's relation to philosophy as she simultaneously occupies both an exterior position outside philosophy (in that she is to a large extent excluded from its institutional practice) and an interior position inside philosophy (by metaphorically constituting its empty/silent interiority). Irigaray introduces us to these complex manoeuvres by reading Plato's parable of the cave with its pronouncements on the philosopher's journey. In *Speculum of the Other Woman* she argues that Plato's writing enacts the silent prescription for Western metaphysics.[8] At one and the same time Plato's work constructs the maternal body, and then proceeds to appropriate it for its own ends. The maternal body operates here as a metaphor indicating the silent place of philosophy.

In Plato's world woman is not a subject who speaks.[9] (Or at least one who speaks for herself.) She remains silent, reduced to the mute passivity of her reproductive role.[10] She is the unacknowledged place or grounding substance from which the masculine subject draws his reserves and resources. Woman (as *hystera*) is paradoxically the silence that guarantees (masculine/philosophical) speech.[11] She is the receptacle of speech, its possibility, though not its articulation. Irigaray claims that woman as receptacle is "not designated as such" (p. 306) in speech, and that as the matrix or foundation of discourse she cannot be expressed or represented. This disavowal goes hand in hand with the representation of the father as the absolute speaking being. So woman is silenced in Plato's world by being designated as the place of philosophy. Her (maternal) body is figured, made metaphor. She is the stage or theatre upon which the aspiring philosopher will gesture toward his journey to truth (*alētheia*). She is his stepping-stone, and as such the foundation (though unacknowledged) of his spiritual quest. Plato's great achievement is to silence woman by making her the material of metaphor. He figures her and in so doing disfigures her as mute matrix. She is the receptacle, the womb that holds men prisoners, the immanence of embodiment, the maternal.

Irigaray uncovers the many layers of Plato's texts. Within his desire to displace, to make metaphor, she reads a simultaneous desire to appropriate and distance the maternal body. Plato's cave displaces the womb (the *hystera*) figuring it as the prison-house of mankind.[12] It is the philosopher's task to break free from the magic and illusion of the womb, the false security of bodily immanence. So begins the philosopher's journey. Plato opens the parable of the cave in the seventh book of *The Republic* thus:

imagine men to be living in an underground cave-like dwelling place, which has a way up to the light along its whole width, but the entrance is a long way up. The men have been there from childhood, with their neck and legs in fetters, so that they remain in the same place and can only see ahead of them, as their bonds prevent them turning their heads.

(514a–b)

The cave operates here as figure, metaphor and displacement. Irigaray writes:

Already the prisoner was no longer in a womb but in a cave – an attempt to provide a figure, a system of metaphor for the uterine cavity. He was held in a place that was, that meant to express, that had the sense of being like a womb. We must suppose that the womb is reproduced, reproducible, and reproductive by means of projections.

(p. 279)

She argues that Plato contains woman by projecting her as his receptacle. Within philosophy the theme of woman as receptacle is a common one.[13] Irigaray argues that it is an all-consuming phantasy – the phantasy of woman reduced to a contained and immobilised volume. It is a phantasy, however, that co-exists with the masculine fear of the excessive possibilities of this volume, i.e. the open container or the overflowing fluid.[14] In Plato's *Timaeus* we read of this mother/receptacle. He writes:

Wherefore, the mother and receptacle of all created and visible and in any way sensible things, is not to be termed earth, or air, or fire, or water, or any of their compounds, or any of the elements from which these are derived, but is an invisible and formless being which receives all things and in some mysterious way partakes of the intelligible, and is most incomprehensible.[15]

It is worth noting at this point that Irigaray passes over Plato's statement that the mother "in some mysterious way partakes of the intelligible". I think that it would be useful to read this as a tension in Plato's work, i.e. one of those rare moments when woman or the body occupies a more proximate relation with the soul or the intelligible. What are we to make of Irigaray's silence on this matter? This question will come up again in chapter two so I will return to it and address it then.

Plato's philosophical journey entails a theatrics that transmutes the womb/receptacle analogically into a scene of masculine fantasy. Woman's body becomes a projection screen in the service of the philosophical quest. In this scenario woman *is* the theatre of representation. A theatre directed (in

13

obstetric fashion) by Plato's persistent probe. Irigaray writes of the "so-called virginity and muteness of that back of the matrix/womb which a man, an obstetrician, turned round, backward and upside down in order to make it into the stage, the chamber, the stronghold of representation" (p. 263). The philosopher as an obstetrician forcibly extracts the prisoner from the immanence of his prison/womb.[16] And this, we learn from Plato, involves a difficult delivery. "And if one were to drag him thence by force up the rough and steep path, and did not let him go before he was dragged into the sunlight, would he not be in physical pain and angry as he was dragged along?" (*The Republic* 515e–516).[17] Irigaray paraphrases Plato's story this way:

> It may be imagined – in fact you have already been told – that this same "someone" has first twisted the chained man round, turning him away from the farthest wall of the cave, so as to direct his gaze, his head, his body, toward the statues and the fire, and also toward the opening of the grotto: thus imprinting the man with a rotational movement that anticipates his exit from this chamber, this room or womb … No doubt the prisoner, the child is made to twist around before he is pushed out, but there is no twisting of the theatre of representation from which, as such, he cannot so easily escape. Even by means of philosophical fiat. The instructor conducts the operation in this way "as if" the enclosure of the cave were the womb … And he, or they, seem to have forgotten the staging or at least he – the scriptwriter – claims to disguise the part it plays.
>
> (pp. 279–80)

Obstetrician, philosopher, script-writer, director? Where does this lead us? Away from the immanence of the mother and toward the transcendence of the father. "This steep rocky ascent along which an obstetrician and then a philosophy teacher have dragged the child, the adolescent, the young man, ends at last in the crowning glory of the Idea" (p. 298). The movement toward essence is simultaneously a movement away from the senses. Plato writes:

> The realm of the visible should be compared to the prison dwelling, and the fire inside it to the power of the sun. If you interpret the upward journey and the contemplation of things above as the upward journey of the soul to the intelligible realm, you will grasp what I surmise since you were keen to hear it … in the intelligible world the Form of the Good is the last to be seen, and with difficulty.
>
> (*The Republic* 517b)

While the philosopher's journey involves this transcendent movement away from the immanence of the body and senses it is more than a little interesting to note how fundamental *bodily movement* is to this enterprise. At one point

Plato seems to equate the body with the soul, arguing that it is in the process of turning (i.e. movement) that the soul takes flight. He writes:

> It is as if it were not possible to turn the eye from darkness to light without turning the whole *body*; so one must turn one's whole *soul* from the world of becoming until it can endure to contemplate reality, and the brightest of realities, which we say is the Good.
>
> (518c–d)

Bodily movement does not function as a metaphor for the journey of the soul, it is rather its precondition. I think that, once again, Irigaray fails to register the significance of this tension in Plato's work. In bringing our attention to Plato's denial of the maternal, she neglects the critical moments when his text exceeds its own (internal) logic. However, I shall address this issue in the following chapter.

For Irigaray the rational movement toward essence, Idea and truth is a movement that attempts to erase any trace or sign of the mother. Now what is important for our purposes here is that Irigaray insists on the masculinity (i.e. the sexual specificity) of this movement. She argues that it is based on denial in that it depends upon, and yet represses, its debt to the maternal body. Rationality consists in a process of transcending its material/maternal origin and this places the entire philosophical enterprise between itself and this (unacknowledged) debt. Because of this we can no longer simply portray philosophy and its repressed other as spatially *distinct* regions, i.e. one inside, one outside. We must realise that philosophy's other – and here Irigaray refers to the maternal body, the feminine, or more problematically woman – occupies a place internal to philosophy's own logic. (With Le Doeuff, we might say that woman is above all the internal enemy.)

Michèle Le Doeuff: woman as enclosed space/ interiority

We might be permitted to say that Irigaray's call for women to speak otherwise falls largely upon deaf ears when it comes to the French philosopher Michèle Le Doeuff. Le Doeuff is more than a little suspicious of those philosophies which self-consciously place themselves beyond the gravitational pull of (sound) philosophical reasoning. Before I go in to her criticisms, though, I will say something about Le Doeuff's intellectual itinerary; that is, something about the kind of philosopher she is. While she is well known outside France for her writing on women and philosophy, we can reduce her work to these concerns only at the risk of silencing her significant work on the history of philosophy and the history of science which coalesce around her notion of *l'imaginaire philosophique* – the philosophical imaginary. Very simply, we could say that her researches into the philosophical imaginary are tantamount to a critical inquiry into the nature of philosophy itself; its observations, its methodology and its endless quest for self-foundation.

Le Doeuff currently researches at the Centre National de la Recherche Scientifique in Paris (the same institution as Irigaray) and has previously taught at the École Normale Supérieure (Fontenay-aux-Roses). Her work is much less ambiguously positioned within philosophy than is Irigaray's – whose intellectual concerns span literature, psychology, linguistics and psychoanalysis. Le Doeuff is avowedly "French" in her manner of philosophy. In conversation with Raoul Mortley she states "[mine] is … the French way of philosophising not to separate philosophical reasoning from knowledge of the history of philosophy, or acquaintance with the classics".[18] We might add to this that Le Doeuff's work shares a common French preoccupation with the literary, for as Mortley himself reminds us "The Literary conscience weighs heavily in French philosophy; the link between the two disciplines is thought to be natural and important" (p. 2). In his "Translator's Note" to *The Philosophical Imaginary*, Colin Gordon places Le Doeuff in an ambiguous relation to the contemporary fashion of French philosophy. He contends that while "Politically and affectively, Le Doeuff belongs to the generation of May 1968: stylistically, she is an unseasonable classicist."[19] For Gordon, Le Doeuff's work can best be understood as emerging from the French tradition of critical epistemology, philosophical work with links to the Lumières, Koyré and Bachelard. What distances her most from her contemporaries, he suggests, is that her philosophical work "is singularly bare of the period's usual fashionable impedimenda" (p. vii). Gordon's depiction of Le Doeuff's intellectual concerns may well shed light on the *reasonable* quality of her work i.e. why it appears less foreign in more traditional philosophical terms. The fact that she seemingly rejects the infinite play of the postmodern gesture may well endear her to her English-speaking readership.[20] The *serious* quality of her work is more or less alluded to when Gordon suggests that Le Doeuff pits herself against the postmodern times.[21]

Given what I have so far decided to say about Le Doeuff, it is probably not surprising that I have chosen to compare her with Irigaray. Superficially, the picture that emerges seems something like this. On the one hand we have Le Doeuff, an institutional philosopher whose traditional concerns, intellectual itinerary, stylistic moderation and ethical priorities situate her on terrain distinct from Irigaray's whose philosophical qualifications are questionable, whose intellectual itinerary suggests a refusal to choose, whose stylistic qualities verge on the excessive and whose ethical priorities are avowedly political. But let me just say, at this point, that what I have *not* said about Le Doeuff is more telling than what I have. Indeed this is her argument about philosophy itself.

Le Doeuff's answer to the (perennial) question: *What is philosophy?* is probably a good place to begin our discussion of the really challenging perspectives her work offers us today. In "The Shameful Face of Philosophy", the preface to *The Philosophical Imaginary*, Le Doeuff writes:

> Whether one looks for a characterization of philosophical discourse to Plato, to Hegel or to Bréhier, one always meets with a reference to the rational, the concept, the argued, the logical, the abstract. Even when a certain coyness leads some authorities to pretend that they do not know what philosophy is, no agnosticism remains about what philosophy is not. Philosophy is not a story, not a pictorial description, not a work of pure literature.
>
> (p. 1)

Le Doeuff goes on to argue that if one goes looking for a *pure* form of philosophy, one cannot find it.

While I will return to the question of images in a moment, I shall first say a little about Le Doeuff's views on the disciplinary nature of philosophy. This is relevant to my concerns here because it touches upon the strategies that philosophy employs to exclude certain things. Philosophical discourse, Le Doeuff informs us, is a discipline:

> that is to say a discourse obeying (or claiming to obey) a finite number of rules, procedures or operations, and as such it represents a closure, a delimitation which denies the (actually or potentially) indefinite character of modes of thought; it is a barrage restraining the number of possible (acceptable) statements.
>
> (p. 114)

So the disciplinary nature of philosophy bears testimony to its exclusive (or indeed repressive) mode of operation. "The simple fact that philosophical discourse is a discipline is sufficient", for Le Doeuff, "to show that something is repressed within it" (p. 114). And while she suggests that rhetoric, seductive discourse, inconclusive syllogisms, analogical reasoning and arguments from authority are now or have at some time historically been excluded from the supposedly pure practice of philosophy, she contends that what is excluded can in no real sense be determined or defined because of its imprecise, indeterminate or vague status. Now this brings us back to the question of images, for Le Doeuff's notion of the philosophical imaginary is precisely about those images or metaphors "that philosophy labours to keep at bay" yet which are, paradoxically, essential for the philosophical enterprise. Le Doeuff reflects on "strands of the imaginary operating in places where, in principle, they are supposed not to belong and yet where, without them, nothing would have been accomplished" (p. 2). Her argument about these images – this philosophical imaginary – is that they are inseparable from the pure or theoretical speculations of the philosophical text. They cannot be considered purely literary embellishments or pedagogical or heuristic devices as, without them, the text cannot signify. She contends that: "the imaginary which is present in theoretical texts stands in a relation of solidarity with the theoretical enterprise itself (and with its troubles) that it is, in the strict sense of the phrase, at work in these productions" (p. 6).

Le Doeuff's reference to the "shameful face of philosophy" alludes to the fact that philosophy is unable to recognise its dependence upon the images or metaphors that it plunders from an imaginary outside. Elsewhere she speaks of this as the "internal scandal" of philosophy, its inability to fathom its own inclusory and exclusory devices.[22] What is interesting about this is that she goes on to argue that philosophy's externalised other, although historically contingent, is often associated with the feminine, or more significantly women. And it is at this point that Le Doeuff's argument becomes crucial for our discussion. While she points out that the feminine is not universalised within philosophical texts, i.e. that it varies culturally and historically, she adds that nonetheless it circulates within the context of common, that is to say non-philosophical, phallocratic prejudices. Throughout her work Le Doeuff weaves the threads of imagery and metaphor (in her notion of the philosophical imaginary) along with her discussion of women's exclusion from the philosophical enterprise. I shall explore these themes firstly by looking at Le Doeuff's reading of woman as enclosed space in the philosophical imaginary, and then by asking some questions about how this forces us to rethink the familiar inside/outside scenario of woman's relation to philosophy. In so doing I shall draw out the implications of Le Doeuff's work on exclusion for the questions of silencing I initially raised. In the process I hope to provide a common ground from which Irigaray and Le Doeuff might speak.

Le Doeuff's exploration of the philosophical imaginary finds a particular feminist intonation in her chapter on "Pierre Roussel's Chiasmas". Here she traces an elision of woman and interiority in the text of an eighteenth-century physician whose concerns slip curiously from medicine to moral philosophy. The text in question, *Système physique et moral de la femme*, published in 1777, is read in conjunction with some contributions to a contemporary one, *Le Fait féminin*, edited by Évelyne Sullerot and published in 1978.[23] The fact that just over two hundred years separates these is cause for (feminist) concern when Le Doeuff exposes their ideological function of assigning woman the place of a mute interiority. I should point out that Le Doeuff does not attempt to reduce the structural complexities or specificities of these texts to one simple statement about femininity, but rather that she discovers the echo of an imaginary femininity embedded in a philosophical tradition that can only be labelled phallocratic.

Roussel's text charts an imaginary cartography of the female body, a virtual hystericization of woman's body as (sexual) text. He writes: "so that woman is not woman merely in virtue of one place, but rather is so in every aspect from which she is regarded" (Roussel, cited in Le Doeuff, p. 141). Through a com-

plex series of denials and displacements, a spatial logic Le Doeuff calls chias-
matic, Roussel assigns femininity to every part of woman's body. While this
also includes her spatial and moral aptitude, it curiously does not include the
one signifier of sexual difference we would normally ascribe femininity to.

> Thus, Roussel sees sexual difference in every element of women's
> lives and bodies, but holds that there is one bone in the body which
> admits of no sexual difference: namely the pubis. Silence as to the
> literal meaning, a void at the centre; metonymic proliferation every-
> where else.
>
> (p. 140)

Roussel goes on to construct woman's body as a totalised interiority, a self-
enclosed void devoid of external relationality. The moral and philosophical
implications of Roussel's text exceeds its narrowly defined *scientific* status.
From this image of self-enclosure Roussel extrapolates woman's character as
non-functional. "Woman never enters into an operational relation with the
world (her soft body prevents this); she has no effective actions, only graceful
gestures … Her physiognomy expresses quite generally a zero level of alert-
ness to exteriority" (p. 158).

Le Doeuff finds striking parallels in some of the contributions to Sullerot's
collection. Here (sociobiological) references abound attesting to the activity
and exteriority of the male (even *in utero*) as against the passivity and interiority
of the self-enclosed female. "From the beginnings in foetal life, 'masculinity'
is a thing of drama, conflict, struggle, danger, openness to influence, relation
to an Other, while 'femininity' is tranquil, immobile unfolding of the inherent, self-enclosure in the same" (p. 165). For Le Doeuff, this echoes Roussel's
imaginary universe, where woman remains enclosed, at home, "already a house-
wife" (p. 167).

In a further essay entitled "Long Hair, Short Ideas" (previously translated
and published in English in a slightly different version as "Women and Philosophy".[24] Le Doeuff shows how these spatial mappings of woman as enclosed interiority work elsewhere in conjunction with the opposition passivity/
activity. In Rousseau's *Émile*, Hegel's *Philosophy of Right* and Comte's *Système
de politique positive*, we can read a philosophical anti-feminism that systemati-
cally positions women beyond the universal and philosophy, i.e. beyond
subjectivity toward (and here let me quote Hegel) "a placid unfolding, the
principle of which is the undetermined unity of feeling" (*Philosophy of Right*
pp. 263–4). What emerges from this is an equation of femininity with a
passive interiority, an empty space; with the corollary of masculinity as an
active exteriority. And the very interesting thing that happens after that is
that the philosophical enterprise is granted equal exterior status. Now this *is*
interesting because elsewhere Le Doeuff hints at the self-contained, insular
character of philosophy: "But in so far as the activity of separation, of

division, is philosophically creative (the field is created by its exclusions), philosophy creates itself in what it represses and, this object of repression being essential to it, is endlessly engaged in separating, enclosing and insularizing itself" (p. 115). It is worth noting that Le Doeuff does not comment on this echo between the concepts of femininity and philosophy, i.e. she does not register the paradoxical elision of these supposedly antagonistic principles. I think that we need to ask when and how philosophy and femininity are (structured as) similar.

Clearly the question of philosophy's *space* is no simple matter. It would seem that philosophy actively externalises itself at the same time as constructing the space of its own containment. Philosophy is both actively externalised and passively self-contained; a structure folding in on itself in a manner reminiscent of Roussel's hysterical woman. Just as we have found in Irigaray's work, Le Doeuff's readings of these characteristic texts of Western philosophy suggest the inadequacy of thinking about woman's relation to philosophy in terms of inside and out. Once again we must say that this spatial alternative is too simplistic as woman simultaneously inhabits philosophy's (empty) interiority while remaining exterior to the practices that would confer subjectivity and voice upon her. In light of this we need to rethink woman's exclusion from/in philosophy. An alternative way of addressing this problem might be to consider whether woman may be silenced by being or becoming philosophy's (unacknowledged) centre; its internal enemy (p. 115).

I shall now focus on what Le Doeuff has to say about the relationship between women and philosophy; what strategies philosophy has adopted for silencing women (and denying them the philosopher's journey), and what might be done, in feminist terms, about this. We can summarise Le Doeuff's position with reference to the following terms: permissiveness, amateurism and fidelity. Let me start with the question of permissiveness. Philosophy, we learn, has never totally excluded women from its domain; there is indeed a handful of privileged women who, before the eighteenth century, were known as philosophers, or perhaps known *through* philosophers. The obvious examples are Hipparchia, Héloïse, Elizabeth de Paladin and Sophie Volland. Now what is permissive here is not, as one may think, these philosophising women, but rather philosophy (or philosophers) itself. The fact that philosophy has not crudely excluded all women at all times, hints at a certain permissiveness on its part. Here the permissiveness of philosophy works to obscure a more subtle prohibition against women philosophising. Permissiveness, Le Doeuff contends, often provides "a more revealing indicator than the crude practice of exclusion" (p. 102). Views about women's capacity to philosophise fall generally into two categories, and Le Doeuff argues that the first of these does not really surface until the mid-eighteenth century. The first view, then, suggests that women really are unfit to philosophise (for reasons too numerous to canvas here), while the second is a subtle and perhaps ultimately more effective position. It need not legislate against women philosophising for at this time the educational practices are organised in such a manner as to make it virtually impossible for women ever to do so (p. 103).

For Le Doeuff, the permissive gesture of a Peter Abélard permitting an Héloïse to study (privately) grammar and dialectic masks a more subtle system of prohibitions and discouragements. The question of the private nature of tuition is quite important, for as Le Doeuff points out, what this small band of philosophising women did share was that their love for philosophy was, in each case, mediated through their love for a particular philosopher. Le Doeuff extends this discussion with various references to the erotico-theoretical transference circulating between female disciple and male philosopher. This amorous transference is, of course, modified from the psychoanalytic concept of transference, and is crucial for our understanding of the erotics of the pedagogical relation. For Le Doeuff it is: "equivalent to an absence of any direct relationship of women to philosophy. Only through the mediation of a man could women gain access to theoretical discourse" (p. 104). It would seem, then, that the radical exclusion of women from philosophy is all the more effectively executed by establishing the necessity of a male mediator – a philosophical protector, if you like – who ultimately bars women from any direct access to the institution or practice of philosophy itself. Now what is really interesting about this question of transference (as anyone who has read their Plato will know) is that it is by no means a purely heterosexual phenomenon. Le Doeuff argues that men, too, succumb to the love of an admired master or professor; that a certain erotic or amorous spark helps pave the way for the aspiring philosopher's journey. She describes it this way:

> In fact, you – Tom, Dick and Harry – who were at the Sorbonne or prepared the *agrégation* with me, did you really act any differently from Hipparchia? Was it not only too easy sometimes to sense – in the knotting of a tie, in a hairstyle or some such fad – the symbol of allegiance to some cult figure?
>
> (pp. 105–6)

Historically, and we might be tempted to say even today, men have been able to bypass this transferential relation, by sublimating or inflecting the love component onto the institutional framework of philosophy itself. Now, until relatively recently, this has not been an option for that rare species, the "philosophising woman". And this, in fact, brings me to Le Doeuff's next point which is the danger of amateurism for women in philosophy.

It is clearly the case that the women I have already referred to were condemned to an amateur relationship with philosophy and thus were unable to transcend or sublimate the dynamics of the transferential relation with their philosopher lovers. Le Doeuff argues that while we may be tempted to dismiss this situation today, when women seemingly do have institutional access to the study of philosophy, that we would be missing the point, for women today are not yet in a position that would effectively negate the amateur role.[25] This is, in a sense, related to the final point – the question of fidelity. While we can say that women do indeed have access to philosophy today, that their exclusion is by no means a straightforward or crude affair, we might ask what roles they play (or assume) once there? Le Doeuff argues that there is something like a sexual division of labour within philosophy and that women (predictably?) play the dutiful and subservient roles of faithful admirer or faithful commentator to the masters' sacred texts.[26] There is a kind of theoretical adulation of the faithful female admirer that places women in quite subservient and traditionally phallocentric roles.[27] The relation goes something like this: woman, incapable of philosophising herself, plays faithful admirer to man, the philosopher who (for reasons too numerous to go into here) is sorely in need of (someone's) admiration. Le Doeuff argues that this fidelity most often manifests itself in the faithful commentaries that comprise the classic works on the history of philosophy.

> Who better than a woman to show fidelity, respect and remembrance? A woman can be trusted to perpetuate the words of the Great Discourse: she will add none of her own … How could a woman manhandle a text, or violate a discourse? The vestal of a discourse which time threatens to eclipse, the nurse of dismembered texts, the healer of works battered by false editions, the housewife whom one hopes will dust off the grey film that successive readings have left on the fine object, she takes on the upkeep of the monuments.
>
> (p. 125)

Assuming this role of fidelity is perhaps the final in a series of subtle prohibitions and discouragements that ultimately work to exclude or silence women in a manner far more insidious (and difficult to combat) than the overt misogyny of the eighteenth- and nineteenth-century philosophical world views. Taken together, permissiveness, amateurism and fidelity form a powerful barrier to women as philosophical subjects. And this is ironically enacted by simultaneously placing them both inside and outside the magisterial philosophical realm. It is perhaps philosophy's master stroke to silence and exclude women most effectively by allowing them entry to the inner sanctum of the classical texts as sacred guardians and dutiful daughters of their fathers' and lovers' truth.

Now if the exclusion of women from/in philosophy is such a subtle affair it leaves us with the question of how, and from where, woman can speak? And it is at this point that the differences between Irigaray and Le Doeuff become pronounced. For Le Doeuff rejects what she characterises as the irrationality of Irigaray's position. Speaking from the place of otherness, i.e. speaking otherwise, is, for Le Doeuff, no place to speak at all. Although she does not name it as such, Irigaray's strategy is, for Le Doeuff, a hopeless project, in that it is produced by the very rationality that it seeks to subvert. It is a fantasy-product of philosophical reason:

> As soon as we regard this femininity as a fantasy-product of conflicts within a field of reason that has been assimilated to masculinity, we can no longer set any store by liberating its voice. We will not talk pidgin to please the colonists … However, that is exactly what is expected of us.
>
> (p. 116)

For Le Doeuff there are alternatives beyond the impasse of speaking from inside or outside philosophical reason. She argues that we need not accept the metaphysical option this false alternative offers; that there are possibilities that exist in the project of transforming or salvaging philosophy that would be lost if one were to opt for its total abandonment.

> From which position, then, do we speak? … Today it is possible to think of rationality otherwise than in a hegemonic mode – possible, but not easy or straightforward … this is not to pronounce the extinction of the philosophical enterprise but rather to evoke a mediation which still remains difficult to conceptualize.
>
> (pp. 117–18)

Le Doeuff's own work is instructive here. Rather than constructing philosophy against a backdrop of its metaphysical *other* she follows alternative possibilities, choosing instead to involve herself with projects that are recognisable as philosophy while simultaneously lending themselves to feminist work. By thinking of the philosophical enterprise as comprising "genres" (such as the "history of philosophy", etc.) she is able to displace the logic of space which functions to exclude feminist work; a logic that repeatedly attempts to position feminist work outside of traditional philosophical concern. I think that by working with this notion of genre she also manages to unsettle a familiar and similarly political binary, the Anglo-American/continental divide. An appreciation of philosophical work in terms of various genres thus provides Le Doeuff with the opportunity to open out the field of legitimate philosophical inquiry. It allows her to experiment with a variety of non-traditional concerns, priorities, methodologies and writing styles.

Le Doeuff is deliberately vague about the form of a future philosophy, though hints that it lies somewhere in the direction of a rationality that can cope with its own limitations and incompleteness. She asks: "Is it possible to make philosophy, or philosophical work, abandon its wish to be a speculation which leaves no room for lack of knowledge, to make it accept its intrinsic incompleteness and create a non-hegemonic rationalism…?" (p. 126).[28] While Le Doeuff is reticent to chart or legislate upon this future direction, she is adamant that a move in the general direction that she is indicating would mean a radical displacing of the contemporary impasse between women and philosophy: "The fact remains that this change is likely to alter the interlocking of the 'philosophical' and the 'feminine', for it is now possible to cease wishing to mask the incomplete nature of all theorization" (p. 118). Her own work rehearses the "incomplete" nature of this philosophy that she alludes to, relying, as it does, on the essayistic form;[29] the only format, she concludes, that does not "close a question reductively before it has even been posed" (p. 2). In an attempt to avoid the closure of a self-enclosing and self-foundational philosophy, Le Doeuff concludes: "that the future of a philosophy that is no longer anti-feminist is being performed somewhere in the region of Brechtian drama, which ... produces unfinished plays which always have a missing act and are consequently left wide open to history" (p. 118). I would say, then, that Le Doeuff's project entails opening or extending philosophy beyond its own self-imposed self-enclosure;[30] that is to say, voicing the repressions that philosophy as a discipline has silenced. And here the voices of women are crucial, because, as Le Doeuff suggests, there is a necessary relationship between the masculine imaginary and the exclusion of women. Philosophy's repressions are bound up with the silencing of women's voices. And yet, as Le Doeuff also shows, it is not enough just to have women speaking from philosophy's domain if all they manage to do is mimic its (masculine) voice.

Le Doeuff's project refuses the general form of exclusion that has become such a central part of rationality, at least in so far as it has been practised in the West. She distances herself from Irigaray when she claims that such an attack on this exclusive form of reason can be carried out only from within rationality itself. It is the somewhat paradoxical stance of using philosophy against itself. "I shall oppose this mystification [and exclusion of woman] by the paradox that a *practical application of philosophy* is necessary in order to oust and unmask the alienating schemas which philosophy has produced" (p. 101). So while Irigaray reduces rationality to a masculine speaking position, Le Doeuff defends it, at least in its future potential, as a more inclusive practice. She defends it because she believes that the history of philosophy demonstrates certain examples of a rationality that can and indeed does accept its limits. Her comments on the exploratory logic of Roger Marin illustrate a philosophical position that positively engages with these limits (cf. *L'Imaginaire philosophique*, pp. 133–4). For Le Doeuff there is no speaking position outside rationality. Speaking otherwise can be interpreted by her only as a fantasy-product, an irrationality itself produced from the reason it imagines itself to oppose.

Le Doeuff's position is quite convincing and useful, I think, for thinking through the complexities of woman's relation with philosophy. Her analysis provides a strategic intervention within the philosophical domain. By reclaiming rationality (in its non-hegemonic and non-misogynistic manifestations) for feminist philosophy, she provides women with a way out of the impasse of speaking in the wilderness; of speaking to the perennially deaf ear of her masculine counterpart. Her project of transforming philosophy from "within" is admirable in that it assumes no fixed position for women either in or outside philosophy. As Meaghan Morris has argued, the value of Le Doeuff's position is that it is, in itself, a rejection of all general positions. She writes that what we learn from Le Doeuff is possibly that:

> the setting up of *general* "positions" on the relations between femininity, rationality, and philosophy, when conceived of as a general problem, may not always or necessarily matter very much … Le Doeuff disengages from the debate which assumes that stable relationship between "feminism" and "philosophy" needs to be established (fixed as contestation *or* cooperation, refusal *or* practice).[31]

Having said this I would like to add that I remain just a little uneasy about the effects of Le Doeuff's own speaking position. Perhaps I can voice my concerns this way: if Le Doeuff is concerned to open the arena of philosophy to those very voices that she herself claims to have been silenced by a rationality unable to confront its own limitations, then is she not in danger of enacting a silencing of her own when she dismisses voices, such as Irigaray's, as fanciful products of an over-imaginative rationality? To be fair I must point out that she anticipates such an accusation, though I am not fully convinced that she satisfactorily addresses this anxiety. She claims: "it would be too easy to say that my present discourse is being conducted from the standpoint of philosophy, that it is yet another colonizing discourse, and that femininity is no more allowed to express itself here than in the texts of Hegel" (p. 116). Le Doeuff needs to say more than this. She needs to take this (potential) criticism more seriously and spell out how and why her own project escapes the colonising gesture of rational thought. I am concerned that Le Doeuff's project of salvaging rationality runs the not inconsiderable risk of silencing those who refuse her belief that reason is in fact gender-neutral. Le Doeuff works against herself when, in the final analysis, her own voice enacts a closure of those discourses, such as Irigaray's, attempting to speak in logics other than the dominant rationality of the logos. What is worrying about this is that a potentially exciting dialogue between two women is foreclosed. Having said this I must point out that Le Doeuff provides the preliminaries toward an "exchange" with Irigaray when in *Hipparchia's Choice* she speaks of her hesitations with such a feminism of difference being just that, hesitations rather than polemic. She writes:

> But to hesitate is not to produce a polemic and this fact should be noted. It seems to me that we felt we should let those things be said, basically, "just in case" – just in case something important arose from

this current of thought which did not appear likely to have any worrying negative consequences whatever the case.

(pp. 224–5)[32]

Now it may be that Le Doeuff's comments against the allegedly irrationalist
tendency of theorists such as Irigaray are better and more generously understood as criticisms that expose what she believes to be the masculine fantasy
supporting any belief in a uniquely *feminine* voice. That is, they are criticisms
that provide the possibility for a future engagement with Irigaray, rather than
being statements that work to silence her and others like her. If this is the
case, then I would be delighted to see this engagement develop into something more closely resembling a philosophical encounter.

I am sure that a dialogue between Irigaray and Le Doeuff would be invaluable for the kind of non-hegemonic philosophy that Le Doeuff herself champions. I say this in the knowledge that her own "dialogue" with another French
feminist philosopher, Simone de Beauvoir, has radically altered the way that
many of us, outside France, today think through the shifting relations between women and philosophy.[33] To call for such a dialogue, though, may be
somewhat naive. Le Doeuff's project of a philosophy without borders ironically positions itself against those analyses that tend to re-establish borders by
characterising philosophy as a closed domain of masculine privilege.[34] Le Doeuff
seems to read Irigaray in this way. Irigaray's project of *speaking otherwise* can be
read by Le Doeuff only as "speaking pidgin" much to the delight of those
philosophical colonists who would have women remain unheard. Whether
such a criticism of Irigaray's work is just remains to be determined. While it is
relatively easy to focus on these apparent differences between Irigaray and Le
Doeuff, I think that in the long term it is more useful to ask how their projects
might be brought together in order to further our interrogation of woman's
silence. Rather than continuing to focus on the possible antagonisms between
them I would like to suggest that their work can be used together, that their
projects are not incompatible in practice. I think, for example, that Irigaray's
work on the silent maternal body can be mobilised in conjunction with Le
Doeuff's work on the imaginary. Le Doeuff's imaginary effectively provides
us with a way of reading philosophy. In so doing it also offers us a way of
thinking about the fundamental question of what it means to read. Irigaray's
emphasis on the maternal inflects this question toward the silent body of
woman, forcing us to think through the complex relations between philosophy, reading and silence. So in the following chapter I shall pursue two models of reading. Irigaray's discussion of the repressed (maternal) body will provide
one; Le Doeuff's exploration of metaphor and the imaginary the other.

2

PHILOSOPHY

Reading denial

In the previous chapter I argued that Irigaray and Le Doeuff offer us insights into how complex the question of silencing actually is. Irigaray does this by drawing our attention to the repressed maternal body, while Le Doeuff opens the question of silencing through her examination of philosophy's metaphors and images. She shows how a certain reading can uncover things that philosophy says without actually saying them. In this chapter I shall continue this discussion. I shall use their work to read the silent spaces in philosophy. By silent spaces I mean the places where the discipline of philosophy actually covers over something. We have already learnt from Irigaray and Le Doeuff that silencing does not entail a simple sense of absence, that it actually involves something we might more appropriately refer to as a readable absence. If we think of this in terms of speech we could say that silence entails a spoken yet unheard voice. Now this readable absence or unheard voice is structured by a logic of repression. Repression is a process that is closely tied to denial, and it is this that I shall investigate (or read) here.

Le Doeuff argues that philosophy (because it is disciplinary) is structured by denial. Denial is central to my concerns for it opens the whole question of silencing out onto more complex terrain than the question of exclusion would allow. The processes of denial enact a silencing by attempting to cover over or repress troubling voices. Not surprisingly we find that what is repressed is often associated with woman – her voice, her body, her sexuality. Once again Le Doeuff makes this point clearly. If we are at all concerned to hear woman's voice in philosophy we need to be able to listen to or read this denial, this repression. In order to achieve this we need a practice that will help us to articulate the repressed moments that exist in tension with philosophy's more obvious statements. This methodology involves reading philosophy against itself, a strategy that makes it reveal what at least superficially seems hidden. Irigaray and Le Doeuff both practise their own styles of reading denial. In this chapter I shall say a little more about these as well as introduce Louis Althusser's strategy for teasing out these repressed moments. His symptomatic reading is another example of how we can give voice to the silences in a text. Now what Irigaray, Le Doeuff and Althusser share is a certain indebtedness to psychoanalytic reading practices, and I shall say more about what this entails later on.

In this chapter I shall argue that denial works hand in hand with a philosophical phantasy of self-generation. What I mean by this is that denial surfaces at those moments when philosophy or philosophers imagine themselves to be capable of magically reproducing themselves without maternal help. In fact their self-engendering bodies act as a denial of the maternal and of mothering in general. It is my belief that it is common to find the phantasy of self-engendering whenever we attempt to read the repressions and denials of the philosophical discipline. This seems to suggest that the question, or more correctly questions, of silencing touch up against a specific masculine imaginary. This imaginary is structured by a desire to displace the maternal in order to speak both in and from the mother's place.

Returning to the repressed: Plato's bodily fluids

I shall begin the process of reading philosophy's denials by returning to Plato. In the previous chapter I showed how Irigaray's reading of Plato alerts us to the strategies he adopts in order to silence woman by constructing her as the mute foundation of Western thought. I find Irigaray's argument very convincing and yet I am interested in the fact that she seems to simplify Plato's position somewhat. There are passages in Plato where an ambivalence is in play. The denial of the body that Irigaray so carefully reads is momentarily disrupted. At this time we are able to discern a tension in Plato's text, a tension which ironically re-inscribes the (repressed) body. Irigaray fails to register or comment on these points of tension. I contend that Plato's texts speak against themselves, and that if we listen very carefully to his work we can hear philosophy (unconsciously) affirming what it (consciously) denies. Plato rejects the body, and yet (simultaneously) tells us how necessary it is. To begin with Plato reminds us how to escape the (sensuous) bonds of our bodily prison:

> whenever one tries through dialectic, and *without any help from the senses* but by means of reason to set out to find each true reality and does not give up before apprehending the Good itself with reason alone, one reaches the final goal of the intelligible as the prisoner escaping from the cave reached the final goal of the visible.
>
> (*Republic*, 532a–b emphasis added)

The study of dialectic enables the soul to take flight from the senses. At this stage Plato's separation of body and soul seems straightforward. And yet in another passage Plato arguably describes the soul in terms of the body. Here the soul seems to be appropriating the movement of the body. He writes:

28

the capacity to learn and the organ with which to do so are present in every person's soul. It is *as if* it were not possible to turn the eye from darkness to light without turning the whole *body*; so one must turn one's whole *soul* from the world of becoming until it can endure to contemplate reality, and the brightest of realities, which we say is the Good.

(518c–d emphases added)

We could say that in this passage Plato constructs the body and soul in an analogical relation. We could even go so far as to suggest that the body's movement functions here as a necessary precondition for comprehending the journey of the soul. By establishing the eye as a relay point Plato shifts from soul to body and back again to soul enacting a metonymic displacement of one term to the next. What is important here is that Plato tells us that the process of learning involves a turning; it is an embodied movement.

Education then is the art of doing this very thing, this *turning around*, the knowledge of *how the soul can most easily and most effectively be turned around*; it is not the art of putting the capacity of sight into the soul; the soul possesses that already but *it is not turned the right way* or looking where it should. This is what education has to deal with.

(518d emphases added)[1]

I am suggesting that the movement of turning that Plato refers to here should be read as a tension in his text. Movement activates the eye as a relay switch, so that when Plato speaks of turning, and he does so often, we can read this as a positive inscription of the body (and its analogical or even at times equivalent status with the soul) not merely as a "metaphorical" turn of phrase. Let us begin with one of Plato's descriptions of dialectic. For him it is a characteristic movement toward philosophy, and involves: "turning a soul from a kind of day that is night to the true day, being the upward way to reality which we say is true philosophy" (521c). And further: "It gently draws the eye of the soul, which is really buried in a kind of barbaric mire, and leads it upwards, using the sciences we have described as assistants *(synerithroi)* and helpers *(symper-iagogoi)* in the process of *turning the soul around*" (533d emphasis added). Dialectic fulfils an intelligible law, and is itself a journey:

The deliverance from bonds and *the turning around* from the shadows to the images and the firelight, and then the way up out of the cave to the sunlight, and there the continuing inability to look at living creatures and plants and the light of the sun but only at divine images of them in water and shadows of actual things – no longer at shadows of images thrown by another source of light which is itself

29

an image as compared to the sun – the practice of every study we have described has this *power to rouse the best part of the soul and lead it upwards* to the contemplation of that which is the best among the existents, *just as* then the clearest sense in the body was driven to the contemplation of the brightest things in the physical and visible world.

(532b–d emphases added)

Plato's desire to transcend the body, to leave it behind in the philosopher's spiritual quest, might not be as straightforward as it initially appears. In the previous passages we have seen how the body actually functions as a necessary template in providing the movement required by the soul. In fact the journey is impossible without this turning of the soul. It would seem that the body and its movements or gestures are fundamental to this journey, though it is only at best ambiguously acknowledged. So, while Plato will endeavour to distance himself from the corporeal, he will inadvertently remain in a proximate relation with it by animating the soul with the body's gestures.

The question of movement that I have linked to the phrases indicating *turning* in Plato's work requires further discussion. It is important to note that in the original Greek, Plato utilises different terms that invariably have been translated by the one English verb, to turn. It could be said that this dilutes my argument somewhat. And perhaps it does. However, I am willing to continue this line of thought because each original Greek verb indicates motion (arguably of a bodily kind). Plato's texts build and develop a series of complex analogies between the soul and those bodies capable of motion. To further complicate this issue, it is worth noting that while Greek philosophers long before Plato made motion a fundamental attribute of the soul – by analogy with living bodies – they also depicted the soul as a source of motion, in an attempt to *differentiate* it from living bodies. Given this, it is less than clear how motion is to be understood in Plato's work, and I can argue my case only from the perspective of one interested in demonstrating how unsettling the whole question of motion or movement is in relation to any simplistic body/soul divide.

In the *Phaedrus* Plato alerts us to the importance of the body as an initial prompt toward spiritual flight. He has Socrates explain in his second speech how physical love (or love of physical beauty) can serve to arouse our passions toward the higher and more spiritual love of truth. "When a man sees beauty in this world and has remembrance of true beauty, he begins to grow wings" (*Phaedrus* 249). Plato's discussion of how we grow wings is entirely sensual:

when a man recently initiated, who has looked upon many of the great realities, sees a god-like countenance or physical form the beauty of which is a faithful imitation of true beauty, a shudder runs through him … As he gazes there comes over him a reaction from the shudder, *an unusual fever and perspiration*. Once he has received the emanation of beauty through his eyes, he grows warm, and through the perspiration that ensues, *he irrigates the sprouting of his wing.* When he is quite warm, the outer layers of the seedling unfurl – parts which by reason of their close-drawn rigidity had for a long time prevented anything from blossoming. *As nourishment streams upon it* the stump of the wing begins to swell and grow from the root upward as a support for the entire structure of the soul, fully developing the wing which every soul possessed in the past.

(*Phaedrus* 251 emphases added)

Bodily fluids are the essential lubricant enabling the divine wings of the soul to sprout. Plato tells us that the body and its functions awaken (or irrigate) the dormant seed of the soul's winged potential. Now it seems to me that in this instance Plato's bodily fluids enact a similar textual function to his eye. They both serve as relay points capable of switching the text back and forth between body and soul, providing the movement or play necessary for the text to unsettle any clear distinction between literal and metaphorical senses of the body.[2]

For Plato there are two possible paths that the soul may take once arousal has occurred, and he equates these with the black and white tendencies of the soul. He tells us that the soul is divided into three parts – one black horse, one white horse and one charioteer. The black horse is the carnal, lustful part of the soul that threatens to drag the higher, noble (white) tendency of the soul toward the base and worldly. When Plato's lover of beauty gazes upon the object of his desire, his soul is caught between these competing tendencies and the charioteer (the third reigning part of the soul) is called upon to mediate between the two. If the black horse wins, and the lover gives in to the pleasures of carnal lust, the wings of the soul will not develop. However, if restraint wins out, and the white horse and charioteer urge the lover to transcend the immanence of this bodily act, the wings of the soul will sprout forth in glory. Plato's notion of the divided soul is interesting for a number of reasons. By thinking of the soul as itself divided between rational and irrational or physical and spiritual tendencies, he displaces the weight of the body–soul distinction. It is no longer the body that stands in as the sole corrupting influence. The soul is itself the site of a conflictual tension between opposing principles. What is also of interest is that the irrational tendency of the soul is actually used to positive advantage by its rational counterpart. The desire inspired in the black horse by physical beauty, if carefully contained by an expert charioteer, is translated to the white horse where it becomes transformed into a profound desire for spiritual beauty. In this way physical, bodily desire serves as the initial impetus enabling the philosopher's journey toward truth.

Now while physical love may act as an important spur to spiritual love, Plato elsewhere tells us quite clearly that only spiritual love is legitimate. In the *Symposium* he has Pausanias tell us that physical love is associated with

Common Aphrodite and spiritual love with Heavenly Aphrodite. According to Pausanias:

> There can be no doubt of the common nature of the love which goes with Common Aphrodite; it is quite random in the effects which it produces, and it is this love which the baser sort of men feel. Its marks are, first that it is directed towards women quite as much as young men; second, that in either case it is physical rather than spiritual; third, that it prefers that its objects should be as unintelligent as possible, because its only aim is the satisfaction of its desires, and it takes no account of the manner in which this is achieved ... In all this it partakes of the nature of its corresponding goddess, who is far younger than her heavenly counterpart, and who owes her birth to the conjunction of male and female. But the Heavenly Aphrodite to whom the other Love belongs for one thing has no female strain in her, but springs entirely from the male, and for another is older and consequently free from wantonness. Hence those who are inspired by this Love are attracted towards the male sex, and value it as being naturally the stronger and more intelligent.
>
> (*Symposium* 181)

What we learn from this, if we keep in mind what we have already understood from the *Phaedrus*, is that physical love serves a purpose. It inspires us toward the higher and more noble desire for the pursuit of wisdom. If it is subdued and channelled in that direction, physical love need not be seen as wholly evil. Indeed it is a necessary precondition for love of the spiritual. However physical love in this instance is understood only as love between two males. It is a desire for the body of another man that stimulates the philosopher's desire for knowledge, not desire for the body of a woman. Further on in the *Symposium* Socrates recounts this truth to us, telling us that he has learnt it (ironically) from a woman, Diotima:[3] "there are some whose creative desire is of the soul, and who long to beget spiritually, not physically, the progeny which it is the nature of the soul to create and bring to birth" (208). The desire for knowledge is depicted here as a form of spiritual parentage. It is a process of men giving birth to children of the soul, and is, once again, prompted by man's desire for the beauty of other men:

> By intimate association with beauty embodied in his friend, and by keeping him always before his mind, he succeeds in bringing to birth the children he has long desired to have, and once they are born he shares their upbringing with his friend; the partnership between them will be far closer and the bond of affection far stronger than between ordinary parents, because the children that they share surpass human

children by being immortal as well as more beautiful. Everyone would prefer children such as these to children after the flesh.

(209)

So the philosopher, whose body is indisputably masculine, gives birth to his children of the soul. He does this in spiritual communion (and with the help of bodily fluids) with his male beloved. This communion, although initially stimulated by physical desire, is displaced onto the intellectual terrain of philosophical thought. Once there the lover of wisdom is required to discipline and in some senses deny his initial lustful and bodily desires. So philosophy becomes synonymous *with* discipline; it is a practice of bodily restraint or denial, a self-discipline and self-governing that preaches control and self con-straint.[4]

In Plato's work, self-constraint functions as a kind of silence in that it covers over the desire to displace the mother. Silence speaks from the depth of his denial, and in so doing renders audible (and legible) the body he attempts to transcend. Plato's body surfaces as a readable absence. By listening in a par-ticular way we can hear what he actually does not intend us to hear. Ironically we hear this body via Plato's insistent and intriguing use of the eye as a media-tion (or relay point) between body and soul. The eye functions in his texts to shift or slide his discussion back and forth between body and soul. As such it translates or glances between them. Plato's eye is a relay that allows his text to look in both directions at once. Working at cross purposes, the eye enables his text to unsettle the distinction between literal and metaphorical discussions of bodily gesture.

This slippage between literal and metaphorical references to the body may well be characteristic of the philosophical imaginary. In a moment I shall investigate how a similar slippage occurs in the work of a modern philoso-pher, Louis Althusser. It is curious that Althusser's work is very much con-structed around the metaphor of the eye and that seeing (or not seeing) provides the movement necessary for this slippage to occur. It could be that Plato's metaphors inaugurate a genealogy that links him to his twentieth-century counterpart. Plato's eye may well be reflected in his distant philosophical pupil, but in order to follow the slippages of this eye we need to think more carefully about how we are to read, so without further hesitation I shall turn to a discussion of Althusser's particular practice of reading.

Symptomatic reading

The strategy I have adopted from Irigaray, in order to read Plato so far, has much in common with what the French philosopher Louis Althusser calls symptomatic reading, and I want to say something about it now. Althusser's practice involves reading the text against itself. It is a strategy designed to make it say more than it consciously intends to say. There are obvious similarities with Le Doeuff's practice of reading the imaginary of philosophy. Indeed Althusser's symptomatic reading can be used to bring many of Irigaray's and Le Doeuff's concerns together.

Le Doeuff's imaginary and Althusser's symptomatic reading are both concerned with the silences constructed by the text itself. Each practice reads the metaphors and images mobilised by philosophy in a way that reveals what the text unconsciously represses. Metaphors or images are understood as the point in the text where the (artificial) distinction between reality and fiction breaks down. They are for this reason points of great interest, as they indicate the excessive moments when the text speaks its silences in disguised form. Althusser's work on reading has been influential on the generation of French intellectuals following him. I think that Le Doeuff's preoccupations bear a certain indebtedness to his practice, though to my knowledge she never explicitly states this. (In fact she actively distances herself from her "contemporary" counterparts). While her work on the imaginary resembles Althusser's revolution in reading, it does something extra with this. It makes the significant gesture of consciously raising the question of sexual difference. Le Doeuff's reading is very much a reading of sexual difference, i.e. its inflection within the philosophical imaginary.

I think that Le Doeuff's notion of the imaginary can be mobilised in an interesting way. I intend to use it to focus on what Althusser denies in his own work, even while he is talking about denial. His practice of symptomatic reading is invaluable for revealing repressed moments and yet it arguably participates in a repression of its own. We can read the metaphors that structure Althusser's work as instances of Le Doeuff's imaginary, specifically instances of a masculine imaginary. By focusing on some key metaphors we can actually turn Althusser's practice back toward his own texts. I am interested in doing this because it seems a good opportunity to examine how the practice of reading what is repressed might itself be implicated in the guilt of repression. Speaking about repression may well be a subtle way to deflect attention from what is actually being repressed.

Althusser's symptomatic reading is a double reading that brings together Marx and Freud. On the one hand, it takes its cue from Marx's own reading of classical economy, by identifying the blanks and silences of a text as symptomatic absences of its own structuring logic. On the other hand, it mobilises these silences in order to read what, according to Freud, cannot be said, i.e. it reads what the text represses in its attempt to construct itself as unified and complete. In *Reading Capital* Althusser introduces psychoanalysis as first and foremost a practice of reading.[5] His grasp of psychoanalysis as reading is largely mediated through Lacan whose "exemplary lesson" organises his reading of Freud (n. 1, p. 16).[6]

Reading with the eye

Symptomatic reading correlates elements that are often seen in opposition. Just as theory and practice are brought together, so too are silence and voice.

For Althusser the non-vision of a text (its silences) is a function of its vision (what it voices). Oversight, non-vision, silence are all absences that concern what is present (i.e. sight, vision, voice). "Non-vision is therefore inside vision, it is a form of vision and hence has a necessary relationship with vision" (*Reading Capital* p. 21). When we read symptomatically, then, we compare a text with itself, its non-vision or silence with its vision or voice. In Althusser's words we attempt: "To understand this necessary and paradoxical identity of non-vision and vision with vision itself ... [in order] to make us see what the ... text itself says while not saying it, does not say while saying it" (pp. 21–2). Althusser speaks of the field of the problematic as what structures the silences of the text. This field organises the possibilities of the text, as a field of vision and in so doing creates in this same gesture the field of non-vision or impossibility, the silences and exclusions. What the problematic refuses becomes the repressed, unconscious of the text.

Now I think that it is worth commenting that Althusser's concept of the problematic is reliant upon the eye, and its ability both to see and not to see, in order for the field (philosophy?) to forbid and repress any (theoretical) reflection on what it has excluded. It seems to me that Althusser's problematic and his practice of symptomatic reading mobilise the eye as a significant site. It functions as a pivotal space or relay switch shifting our gaze between what is simultaneously visible and invisible, what is present and excluded. Now this is not to say that it serves the same purpose as it does in Plato's text but rather that its presence signifies a tension in each, the point at which the text "divulges the undivulged event" (p. 28). In Althusser's text the eye is the locus both of sight and oversight (of vision and non-vision). It is the privileged metaphor that mobilises the whole practice of reading symptomatically. The eye both produces and represses the readable absence as an "undivulged absence" which will manifest itself as a "fleeting presence" within the "visible field of the existing problematic", but only (we must infer) to a trained eye under "very special critical circumstances" (p. 27). For the problematic structures these possibilities precisely as impossibilities. The readable absences:

> are necessarily invisible in the field of the existing theory, because they are not objects of this theory, because they are forbidden by it ... the invisible is the theoretical problematic's non-vision of its nonobjects, the invisible is darkness, the blinded eye of the theoretical problematic's self-reflection when it scans its non-objects, its nonproblems without seeing them, in order not to look at them.
>
> (p. 26)

For Althusser the eye does not see and is blind to the invisible or excluded moment of the text or field. But it is important to stress that this is an active "not seeing", a peculiar vision that produces the "undivulgeable absence". So a symptomatic reading is one which is motivated by what is repressed in the text, one which seeks to see/articulate what the text cannot: "it divulges the undivulged event in the text it reads, and in the same movement relates it to *a different text*, present as a necessary absence in the first" (p. 28). In sympto-matic reading "the *second text* is articulated with the lapses in the first text" (p. 28).

My use of Althusser's reading practice remains tactical. I appropriate it, turning its "gaze" toward Althusser's own texts in an attempt to voice the silences and repressions of his own problematic, a problematic squarely situ-ated in the field of the masculine imaginary. The space of this imaginary is the space of repression. It is the site of a textual denial of the maternal body which is enacted at the precise moment of the text's production. Both Althusser and Plato inhabit this imaginary. They both enact this denial as a means of ensur-ing their own (self)production.

Before going on to say more about Althusser I shall pause in order to retrace some of the steps I have already undertaken. It seems to me that there are a few aspects of my discussion so far that need to be noted. It is a curious fact that the eye occupies or signifies two distinct places in the texts I have been read-ing. In Plato the eye functions as the site of a tension. As such we might think of it as a *symptom* alerting us to something ambiguous in his work. In Althusser the eye functions more as a *diagnostic* tool, a strategy enabling us to read the repressed voice of the text. Two things are happening here; let me address the first. I suggest, at this stage, that a double ambiguity is at work. The eye is ambiguously symptom and diagnosis, and as such marks the place of ambigu-ity itself. The eye functions as the site of ambiguity, an ambiguity that is as silent as the eye itself. The silence of the eye brings me to my next point, for it is another curious thing that (in Althusser) the eye enables us to read (or hear?) the repressed *voice* of the text.

Reading with innocence and guilt

Althusser's discussion of reading relies heavily upon the alternative metaphors of innocence and guilt. He describes reading as a guilty practice, one that reveals what usually remains hidden. Now this is interesting, because I am suggesting that his own writing (and reading) involves the other guilty prac-tice of evacuating the maternal body. So what we have here is a curious collec-tion of crimes. I accuse Althusser of the guilt of denying (concealing) the maternal body (a crime with murderous implications) at the same time as he willingly admits that guilt structures the very act of reading. Does this suggest that reading/revelation is somehow structured by, rather than opposed to, the guilt of denial? And does the proximity of these crimes amount to something other than juxtaposition – to coincidence, for example? Indeed it may be that the anaclitic relation between the crimes of reading and denial harbours its own mystery. In Althusser's guilty claim to reveal he conceals.

If we think about what Le Doeuff has to say about metaphor in her notion of the philosophical imaginary, we can focus on some of the revealing rhetorical devices that structure Althusser's discussion of reading. His obsession with reading as a guilty act demands some consideration. In Althusser's text we read of "subtle murder", of "innocence" and "guilt". Reading symptomatically, with this against his other work, I want to repeat that Althusser's texts enact the guilt of the mother's denial. He writes: "as there is no such thing as an innocent reading, we must say what reading we are guilty of" (p. 14).[7] Althusser's philosophical reading is:

> a guilty reading, but not one that absolves its crime on confessing it. On the contrary, it takes the responsibility for its crime as a "justified crime", and defends it by proving its necessity. It is therefore a special reading which exculpates itself as a reading by posing every guilty reading the very question that unmasks its innocence, the mere question of its innocence: *what is it to read?*
>
> (p. 15)

In order to read Althusser's texts as guilty of murderous intent I am aware of a certain guilt of my own. I defend the "justified crime" of my motivated reading with the confession that I seek to speak (construct?) what Althusser's texts themselves cannot consciously voice, the murderous denial of the maternal body. I am guilty of a reading that seeks to undo the repression of this denial.

> Our admission of this crime is deliberate, we shall fetter ourselves to it, anchor ourselves in it, cling fiercely to it as the point which must be hung on to at all costs if we hope to establish ourselves on it one day, recognizing the infinite extent contained within its minute space.
>
> (p. 30)

A lengthy passage from Althusser sets the scene for my following discussion of reading, guilt and murder. Here a certain (empirical) reading is guilty of killing off (sexual?) difference:

> This play on words plays on a difference it kills: at the same time it *spirits away the corpse.* Let us look at the name of *the victim of this subtle murder.* When empiricism designates the essence as the object of knowledge, it admits something important and denegates it in the same instant: it admits that the object of knowledge is not identical to the real object, since it declares that it is only a part of the real object. But it denegates what it has admitted, precisely by reducing this difference between two objects, the object of knowledge and the real object, to a mere distinction between the parts of a single object: *the real object.* In the *admission*, there are two distinct objects, *the real*

object "which exists outside the subject, independent of the process of knowledge" (Marx) and *the object of knowledge* (the essence of the real object) which is quite clearly distinct from the real object. In the denegation, there is no longer more than *one object*: the real object. Hence we are within our rights in concluding that the true play on words has deceived us as to its site, its support (*Träger*), the word which is its ambiguous seat. The true play on words is not a play on the word "*real*", which is its mask, but on the word "*object*". It is not the word "*real*" which *needs to be interrogated in connexion with the murder*, but the word "*object*"; the *difference* of the *concept* of object *must be produced to deliver it from* the fraudulent unity of the *word* "object".

(p. 40 emphases added)

The problem of the object is central here. But how are we to understand this? I think that Althusser's discussion alerts us to the fact that two objects – the real object and the object of knowledge – are reduced to one. This reduction *is* the murder; it *is* the guilty crime. Let us continue by reading yet another of Althusser's texts. It was in November of 1980 that Louis Althusser murdered his wife. We could symptomatically read Althusser's obsession with innocence and guilt, with murder, against the text of a dead woman's body. Or would this be an over-zealous play on words that "plays on a difference it kills" (Althusser/Althusser's texts?) "Let us look at the name of the victim of this subtle murder", Hélène Rythmann. Althusser's second text, his dead wife's body, can indeed be read as the murder of *sexual* difference. This is a reading that does not allow us to "spirit away the corpse."

If I read Althusser's crime as a "murder mystery" that repeats in its very gesture the *uncanny* return of the repressed, i.e. the violent denial of the mother's body, what then is my relation to guilt? "I am guilty if I reveal what ought to have been kept secret," I am also guilty "if I refuse the demand it makes on me to 'get in', to penetrate all the way to the bottom of the mystery." Is it, then, a crime to reveal the crime? Is the feminist reader guilty of revealing what should and must remain repressed (or concealed)? What is the status of this reading as interrogation (revelation)?[8]

Louis Althusser: a world without women

In her essay "Ideology Against Women",[9] Monique Plaza argues the following:

When Althusser defends a strategy against the capitalist state, when he analyzes positivism in philosophy, he doesn't occupy just a position as professor or committed intellectual. He defends his social position as a man, which totally blinds him to the sex–class antagonisms and oppression in which he participates. This is far more a crime of theory against women than it is a crime of revisionism. The murder of a woman is within the continuum of the discursive negation of women. It is, perhaps the Althusserians would say, an ideology in action. In fact, I agree: ideology against women is not just a matter of words; it is also a matter of death.

(p. 75)

Without reducing the complexity of Althusser's life to a singular and self-evident truth, I shall take up Plaza's suggestion by reading his second text, the murder of his wife, in conjunction with his first text, his philosophy; a philosophy which denies material existence to the role of woman. In doing this I think we can return to Althusser's problem of the object. The murder of his wife can be seen as the object (the sexual difference) that is eclipsed by Althusser himself. As Plaza suggests, we need to unravel this reduction by showing that Althusser's work is itself implicated in this crime.

Some of Althusser's metaphors are implicated in his crime. They operate, within his text, as points of denial. At the same time they rehearse a desire for self-engendering. His writing rehearses an obsession with the theme of reproduction. His depiction of the state as an ensemble of self-generating structures finds parallel expression in his belief in man's ability to give birth to himself. In his celebrated essay "Ideology and Ideological State Apparatuses" (ISAs) he describes the process whereby the state reproduces itself through ideology.[10] The repressed sexuality of Althusser's discussion betrays here an unspoken desire to probe the logic of a self-generating universe. Read in conjunction with his essay on "Freud and Lacan",[11] Althusser's "ISAs" reproduces a philosophy of birth in which the mother plays no role.

The basis of Althusser's argument in "Freud and Lacan" is that Freud gives birth to himself in the act of giving birth to his brain child, psychoanalysis. Freud is depicted as the original father, the self-generating origin from which all others flow. Althusser poses the question: "Who, then, was Freud, simultaneously the founder of analytic theory and the inaugurator, as Analyst number one, self-analysed, original Father, of the long line of practitioners who claim their descent from him?" (p. 217). His essay opens with a discussion of the birth of science. "In the history of Western Reason", he argues, "every care, foresight, precaution and warning has been devoted to births." Science, drawn into the confines of the family drama, is depicted as the (boy) child of an established and identifiable patriarch: "When a young science is born, the family circle is always ready for astonishment, jubilation and baptism. For a long time, every child, even the foundling, has been reputed the son of a father" (p. 195). The genealogical lineage of science is disrupted when, in the nineteenth century, Freud and his science of the unconscious are born without paternal aid. It is not that Freud and his science are illegitimate in the sense of having no lawful father, but rather that they have no father at all.

39

While Althusser seems uninterested in the fact that Freud seemingly has no mother, he is obsessed by the fact that, as a fatherless child, Freud gives birth to himself. Freud's enigmatic birth haunts him throughout his life. Unable to turn to any recognisable father for help, he labours in solitude with the birth of his own child, psychoanalysis.

Althusser speaks of the need for "an authentic return" to Freud. A return which rehearses the desire for origins; a compulsive repetition of the source. For him it is Lacan who inaugurates this search. Lacan's return to Freud rehearses this desire for origin and site. It is "a return to Freud to seek out, distinguish and pin-point in him the theory from which all the rest, both practical and technical, stems by right" (p. 199). But in his return to Freud, Lacan refuses to confront the horror of birth, the impure passage of non-science to science. His return to Freud is rather, a return to the mature, magically generated Freud unfouled by the muddy afterbirth of youth.

> Lacan does not return to Freud as Husserl does to Galileo or Thales, to capture a birth at its birth – i.e. to achieve that religious philosophical preconception, purity, which like all water bubbling up out of the ground, is only pure at the very instant, the pure instant of its birth, in the pure passage from non-science to science. For Lacan, this passage is not pure, it is still impure: purity comes after the still "muddy" passage (the invisible mud at its past suspended in the newborn water which pretends transparency, i.e. innocence). A return to Freud means: a return to the theory established, fixed and founded firmly in Freud himself, to the mature, reflected, supported and verified theory, to the advanced theory that has settled down in life (including practical life) to build its home, produce its method and give birth to its practice. The return to Freud is not a return to Freud's birth: but a return to his *maturity*.
>
> (p. 200)

Freud's youth, suffering as it does from *pre*conceptions, is of little interest to Lacan, who sees in the maturity of Freudian theory the true birth of the unconscious. Lacan is able to recognise the significance of this birth through his association with another newly born science, Saussurian linguistics. Freud is midwife at a skilful delivery announcing the arrival of a truly revolutionary child. From the theatre of psychoanalysis he simultaneously delivers psychologism from its terrible burden. Rationally conceived, psychoanalysis gives birth, in turn, to Freud, the mature Freud, who emerges fully grown from his own brain child. In a parody of the birth of Athene from Zeus' head, Freud springs forth fully armed for battle in order to campaign for the embattled realm of the unconscious.

Althusser's discussion of Freud's birth becomes even more interesting when we read it in conjunction with his essay on ideology. While the focus of "ISAs"

40

is the self-generating structures of the state, there is a supplementary argument within it linking Althusser to Freud. Here Althusser identifies with
Freud, arguing indirectly that, just as Freud gives birth to a theory of the
unconscious, so too does he give birth to a theory of ideology. For Althusser,
the unconscious and ideology are both reproductive structures. In the case of
the unconscious what is reproduced, apart from Freud, is the individual, the
conscious self emerging from the unconscious. In the case of ideology what is
reproduced, apart from Althusser, is the state, the relations of production. In
"ISAs" Althusser pursues his obsession with self-generating structures. The
essay investigates the process whereby the state or social formation reproduces
the existing relations of production. While reproduction remains his focus, its
sexual nature has been repressed, leaving a theory of the state which generates
itself through the mysterious intervention of ideology.

"How", Althusser asks, "is the reproduction of the relations of production
secured?" To answer this he invokes the classical Marxist base–superstructure
model where the base (the economic infrastructure) is distinguished from the
superstructure (the politico-legal and ideological levels). He speaks of a "re-
ciprocal action" of the superstructure which is erected on the base. "Like every
metaphor", he argues, "this metaphor suggests something, makes something
visible" (p. 135). What becomes visible is, for Althusser, the self-generating
structures of the state. He argues that it is at the level of the superstructure that
the relations of production are reproduced. In classical Marxist theory the
superstructure contains both state power and state apparatuses. He distinguishes, however, between repressive and ideological state apparatuses. The
repressive state apparatuses (the government, administration, army, police,
courts and prisons) use force to reproduce the political conditions of the
relations of production. This allows the ideological state apparatuses (ISAs –
religion, education, family, media, arts, etc.) to reproduce the relations of
production which are, for Althusser, capitalist relations of exploitation. While
his argument is retold here only in schematic form it is important to note that
what is of interest is not so much the validity of his thesis, but rather the
significance of the metaphors and imagery employed. Althusser devises a
philosophy of the state as a self-generating structure. But the level of abstraction to which he rises forecloses any discussion of the sexual nature of reproduction. In a move similar to that in "Freud and Lacan", he evacuates the role
of the mother from what is arguably an obsessive probe into the reproductive
process.

Althusser goes on to identify with the "self-made" Freud. He argues that his
theory of ideology resembles, in crucial ways, Freud's theory of the unconscious. Just as Freud's theory of the unconscious negates pre-Freudian beliefs
concerning the illusion of the dream, so too does Althusser's theory of ideology negate pre-Althusserian beliefs concerning the negative determination of
ideology. What links the two is the fact that neither has a history: "our proposition: ideology has no history, can and must ... be related directly to Freud's

proposition that the *unconscious is eternal*, i.e. that it has no history" (p. 161). For Althusser, the "organic link" between Freud and himself is the eternal nature of their offspring. Through ideology and the unconscious they gain a certain immortality. Now what is important here is Althusser's identification with Freud. Linked to him through the eternal structures of ideology and the unconscious, Althusser imagines (phantasises) himself a similarly self-styled man. In the process of giving birth to the concepts of ideology and the unconscious, Althusser and Freud give birth to themselves.

Returning to the scene of the crime

In Althusser's texts the metaphors of denial act in conjunction with a privileging of the father as reproductive site. Althusser is thoroughly obsessed with the actual reproduction of people, events and structures. He exhibits an almost obstetric desire to probe the logic of his self-generating universe. Here patrilineal descent is taken to its (il)logical conclusion in an attempt to position the father as reproductive locus. There is a homo-erotic quality to Althusser's work. His desire to identify with Freud borders on a neurotic obsession for proximity. But what is really interesting about Althusser's work is that it actually provides us with a way of thinking about denial as a socially produced structure rather than the guilty crime of an individual man. By reading Marx with Freud (and Lacan) Althusser draws our attention to this social/cultural dimension of repression and denial. Freud's interrogation of psychic denial is contextualised, literally placed in its cultural context by Althusser. What may be read as individual denials are thus re-read as the repetitious encodings of a masculine imaginary. Accordingly, philosophy can be read as a discipline which erects itself upon the social structures of repression and denial.

Althusser's practice of symptomatic reading also allows us to distinguish between intention and reading effect. As a consequence, the *murderous* denial of philosophy is understood as a textual or metaphorical denial enacted in a disciplinary sense, not necessarily as the intention of an individual writer. However, the neat and convenient separation of reading effect and intent spirits away the troublesome body of woman. And indeed this brings us back to Althusser's problem of the object. Reduced to metaphor, she is yet again silenced, exiled to the marginal realms of philosophical discourse. In this sense my text is complicit with philosophy's murderous crime. In speaking of murder metaphorically (emblematically), am I not guilty of enacting a double silencing?

Once again it is Althusser who serves as a key figure in this dilemma. The murder of his wife is the crime, the lived ideology, that refuses to be spirited away. It is the text that demands we pay attention to the actual body of (a) woman; and one that inconveniently poses a dilemma for my own reading practice. If I am arguing that murder be understood here as a metaphor, a textual strategy enacted by the discipline of philosophy, then what am I to make of the "coincidence" of Althusser's crime? I seem to be confusing the text with the man, and this is a crime in itself, from the standpoint of a reading practice which resists this kind of reduction. There is indubitably a tension between these irreducible readings. In the first instance I am reading metaphorically, while in the second I am reading referentially (literally). My crime (or guilt) is associated with the naive gesture of reading referentially, of reading too literally, and thus confusing metaphor (or reading effect) with a dead woman's body. My own reading produces a slippage between ideology and the *real* bodies of women. It falters somewhere between metaphor and referent.

The slippage between real and metaphoric murder is addressed by two very different writers, Virginia Woolf and Luce Irigaray. I would like to look at what they have to say about this because it helps to illuminate how silencing and this slippage are connected. Let us begin with Woolf. In two carefully crafted passages of *A Room of One's Own* she raises the problem of murder, both metaphorical and real. Let us read these together.

I began idly reading the headlines. A ribbon of very large letters ran across the page. Somebody had made a big score in South Africa. Lesser ribbons announced that Sir Austen Chamberlain was at Geneva. *A meat axe with human hair on it had been found in a cellar.* Mr Justice — commented in the Divorce Courts upon the Shamelessness of Women. Sprinkled about the paper were other pieces of news. A film actress had been lowered from a peak in California and hung suspended in mid-air. The weather was going to be foggy. The most transient visitor to this planet, I thought, who picked up this paper could not fail to be aware, even from this scattered testimony, that England is under the rule of a patriarchy. Nobody in their senses could fail to detect the dominance of the professor. His was the power and the money and the influence. He was the proprietor of the paper and its editor and sub-editor. He was the Foreign Secretary and the Judge. He was the cricketer; he owned the racehorses and the yachts. He was the director of the company that pays two hundred per cent to its shareholders. He left millions to charities and colleges that were ruled by himself. He suspended the film actress in mid-air. *He will decide if the hair on the meat axe is human; he it is who will acquit or convict the murderer, and hang him, or let him go free.* With the exception of the fog he seemed to control everything. Yet he was angry.

... what still remains with me ... was the poison of fear and bitterness which those days bred in me. To begin with, always to be doing work that one did not wish to do, and to do it like a slave, flattering and fawning, not always necessarily perhaps, but it seemed necessary and the stakes were too great to run risks; and then the thought of that one gift which it was death to hide – a small one but dear to the possessor – *perishing and with it my self, my soul* – all this became like a rust eating away the bloom of the spring, destroying the tree at its heart.[12]

Woolf couples a subtle yet quite powerful reference to the mutilation and murder of women, with an equally incisive description of the cultural murder of women's minds and souls. In each case she reminds us of the overarching power of patriarchy; the structural logic that acts and then sits in judgement upon such action against women. The chill of the "meat axe with human hair" resonates with Woolf's "thought of that one gift which it was death to hide". In her depiction woman perishes both literally and metaphorically. She writes: "perishing and with it *my self, my soul*" (pp. 48–9).

Let us turn now to what Irigaray has to say about this slippage between the murder of self and soul:

> Vengeance is practised, outside of laws or rights, in the form of aggressions that may or may not be preconcerted. Thus a sort of international vendetta is set up, present more or less everywhere, which disorients the female populace, the groups and micro-societies which are in the process of being formed. *Real murders take place as part of it, but also (insofar as they can be distinguished) cultural murders, murders of minds, emotions and intelligence.*[13]

At first glance Irigaray's point seems clearly germane to my discussion, and yet it is a little disconcerting to discover that in this passage she is actually referring to murder *amongst* women. She argues that because women are deprived of rites and social institutions, they "are left to polemicize and settle their accounts privately", and that murder (real or otherwise) is one of the consequences of this lack of (social/institutional/symbolic) repression. Now this really complicates our discussion of murder. Not only is there a difficulty in talking about its coincidence as both real and metaphoric, there is the difficult realisation that women are somehow implicated in this as well. Irigaray alerts us to the fact that possibly the most silent aspect of these murders is that men ultimately (but not always) leave the crime to women themselves; (thus murder becomes suicide). By denying them symbolic representation or voice within patriarchal society, men create a state amongst women where murder (real or otherwise) may be the only possible act of vengeance. She argues that to a large extent men bypass this "primitive" society because they have access to judicial institutions (the official sacrificial rites of symbolic representation) in the form of laws and rights.

It is interesting, for our purposes, that Irigaray goes on to compare women, in this regard, with intellectuals. "Some intellectuals", she writes, "lack judicial status too" (p. 15). Women and intellectuals are alike in that neither is "rewarded for what they bring to the functioning of society" (pp. 15–16).[14]

What can this curious coupling of women and intellectuals possibly offer our discussion of murder and silencing? Perhaps we can say that because intellectuals do share a close relationship with women, that they may have a great stake in denying or repressing this fact. The intellectual may repress his identification with woman (and her lot) in order to phantasise himself as a more powerful and acknowledged member of the (patriarchal) social contract. Perhaps the intellectual will unconsciously even go so far as to kill off woman (metaphorically, theoretically, though not always) in some vain attempt to annul this relation. Indeed, perhaps patriarchy thrives by encouraging the intellectual to do just this, enacting the sacrifice in its place. Think about Althusser and the coincidence of his crimes as we return, once more, to Irigaray: "Unwaged at the site of its production, subject to a sacrificial misunderstanding (recognition often comes only with old age or after death), intellectual work entails a social disfunctioning. What's more, as victims, intellectuals turn into instigators of sacrifices" (p. 15).

There is another way of thinking about this coupling of women and intellectuals. I think that it is more interesting, and useful for our purposes, to recognise that Irigaray is actually making a point here about the non-essentialist nature of silencing and oppression. Her analysis provides us with a way of thinking through the complexities of silencing without resorting to strict essentialist categories. The intellectual may stand in, or occupy, the position of woman. From this perspective, the site of femininity is what is really at stake. Irigaray's gesture is useful for a number of reasons. It allows us to think about the complexity of Althusser's analysis and positioning. At one and the same time Althusser silences and is himself silenced by the murder of woman. As intellectual he is both instigator and sacrificial victim of the patriarchal crime. Using Irigaray's logic we could say that in murdering woman Althusser, as intellectual, attempts to murder himself. Indeed his former student, Maria-Antonietta Macciocchi, explains it this way. She writes: "By killing Hélène, in a final grip of love and hate, he sent to the tomb the Mother ... he had protected from persecution, and also the only voice that could prolong his own. He really wanted to silence himself forever."[15] Feminists such as Somer Brodribb have rightly criticised Macciocchi for reducing the murder of his wife to a metaphor for Althusser's *self-destruction*.[16] However Macciocchi's explanation warrants some consideration. Rather than dismissing the identification the intellectual makes between himself and woman, it would be preferable to ask why and under what circumstances this may be possible. Could this tell us anything about the masculine imaginary?

Irigaray's coupling of women and intellectuals makes it necessary for us to think about femininity as a position constructed by this masculine imaginary, a position that may well at times be occupied by those other than women. In saying this I am not retreating from a belief that women are in fact murdered and silenced by men. I am simply saying that we need to consider the ways in which the signifier *woman* may at times operate as a location rather than an unproblematic sexual identity. Accordingly, I insist that we hover between signifier and referent. Having said this I want to return to Macciocchi: "He really wanted to silence himself forever." Her explanation is, no doubt, to some extent fitting; it does help us to think through the possible connections between the intellectual and woman. And yet … We cannot reduce Althusser to the place of the intellectual without simultaneously reducing the complexity of his case. As I have been arguing throughout this chapter, we need to comprehend both Althusser's actions and his philosophy in light of the masculine imaginary.

Let me illustrate my point with the following passage:

> I am suddenly standing, in a dressing-gown, at the foot of my bed in my apartment in the Ecole Normale. The light of a grey November day – it was Sunday the 16th, around nine in the morning – came from the left, from the very tall window, framed for a very long time past by some very old red Empire curtains tattered with age and scorched by the sun, to light the foot of my bed.
> *In front of me: Hélène, lying on her back, also in a dressing-gown.*
> *Her pelvis is resting on the edge of the bed, her legs splayed on the moquette on the floor.*[17]
>
> (emphasis added)

This is taken from Althusser's autobiographical account and explanation of the strangling of Hélène Rythmann. In *"L'Avenir dure longtemps" suivi de "Les Faits": Autobiographies* he seeks to undo the silence imposed upon him after the "event". Now I want to emphasise the ironic use of silence here. *L'Avenir dure longtemps* is Althusser's attempt to voice the "truth" of this murder, a voice that he claims was silenced by psychiatric restraint. Are we to accept Althusser's claim, keeping in mind our discussion of the intellectual as marginal other? If so we ironically lift the silence (yet again) on the one who silenced (for all time) the voice of Hélène; i.e. we allow Althusser to speak through Hélène's silence, her silence being the structuring possibility of his voice.

In his review of *L'Avenir dure longtemps* John Sturrock sums up the situation in the following way:

> Althusser is at pains to reassure us that what he is making is no more than the statement in his own defence which he wasn't allowed to make at the time, because no charge was laid against him. Instead, he was discreetly diagnosed as being in too chaotic a mental state to answer for his act, and consigned to what he calls the "tombstone of silence", of psychiatric restraint. Coming from a man who, unlike his irrevocably muted victim, is now free to break his silence, this metaphorical "tombstone" is hard to take.[18]

We can only agree. *L'Avenir dure longtemps* brings us back to the painful realisation that, however metaphorical our discussion of murder may be, in the final instance the (dead) bodies of real women function as enabling mechanisms for masculine texts.

I think that the "coincidence" of Althusser's textual/"real" murder produces a reading that is symptomatic of a certain feminist insistence, a reading that is motivated by the life-and-death necessity of interrogating the tension between women's lived experiences and the textual construction of these by men. Symptomatic reading, as I intend it here, is thus a strategy aimed at exploring the coincidence produced when reading refuses to be reduced to either the referential or metaphorical mode. The feminist gesture of this reading involves a refusal to smooth over the contradictions involved in attempting to read both ways. It is a political reading motivated by the harsh reality of women's silent bodies. By risking the unfashionable gesture of reading referentially I am attempting to speak *from* the body of woman. And I shall insist on the disturbance that this referential reading produces. This insistence, a feminist recuperation of nagging,[19] celebrates the infidelity involved in refusing to be bound by any one reading.

The political difference of such a feminist reading is premised upon the refusal to remain faithful to any discourse or discipline that supports itself with, and speaks from, the unacknowledged body of woman. Political difference is associated here with demanding that we speak, however tastelessly, of the mute and mutilated bodies of women that litter the history of the philosophical enterprise.[20] While I acknowledge that there is a problem involved in saying that murder is coincidentally both metaphor and referent, I contend that it is this problem that alerts us to the overdetermined (to bring us back to Althusser and Freud) nature of this crime, and that it is more than emblematic of women's experience within patriarchal culture. My reading is thus motivated by a desire to exploit the ambivalence or infidelity of adopting seemingly contradictory reading styles. In this it involves a playful gesture that makes tensions, contradictions and problems both the focus and product of inquiry. It is a reading that explores these tensions through the interventions of theoretical, political and psychoanalytic practice.

Althusser's problematic: silencing and exclusion

I shall conclude my discussion of Althusser by returning to my notion of a readable absence. I have argued that his symptomatic reading provides us with a practice of locating these absences (what Althusser himself calls "fleeting presences", *Reading Capital* p. 26). Now it seems to me that Althusser's concept of the problematic, the field that structures both the visible and invisible (the presence and absence) of the text, is a very useful way of thinking about exclusion and silencing in general. Indeed we can re-read Le Doeuff's comments on exclusion in light of what Althusser has to say about the peculiar spatial logic structuring the problematic.

We must remember that Althusser stresses the necessary relation structuring the problematic, i.e. the coincidence of both the invisible and visible, or for our purpose, silence and voice. The invisible does not lie outside the field (or terrain) of the problematic, but is rather an integral component of its internal space, its structural possibility. The very notion of the problematic acts to displace the spatial alternatives of inside and out, because what is excluded (or absent) lies precisely *within* the theoretical field. In this sense external limits are internal. In a lengthy passage Althusser speaks of "a certain relation of necessity" existing between the included visible and excluded invisible:

> In the development of a theory, the invisible of a visible field is not generally *anything whatever* outside and foreign to the visible defined by that field. The invisible is defined by the visible as *its* invisible, *its* forbidden vision: The invisible is not therefore simply what is outside the visible (to return to the spatial metaphor), the outer darkness of exclusion – but the *inner darkness of exclusion*, inside the visible itself because defined by its structure. In other words, the seductive metaphors of the terrain, the horizon and hence the limits of a visible field defined by a given problematic threaten to induce a false idea of the nature of the field, if we think this field literally according to the spatial metaphor as a space limited by *another space outside it*. This other space is also in the first space which it contains as its own denegation; this other space is the first space in person, which is only defined by the denegation of what it excludes from its own limits. In other words, all its limits are *internal*, it carries its outside inside it.
>
> (pp. 26–7)

It is tempting to pause at this stage in order to ponder the uncanny spatial parallels existing between this "other space" which Althusser designates as "the first space in person", and the (paradoxical) space of the maternal body, the body whose "limits are *internal*", who carries "its outside inside it." Are we to think of the problematic as a concept literally pregnant with meaning? I am not certain but I do think Althusser's problematic offers fertile terrain for such speculation. Indeed Althusser is himself perplexed by the proliferation of spatial metaphors littering his text. In a comment marginalised to the space of a footnote he writes:

> The recourse made in this text to spatial metaphors (field, terrain, space, site, situation, position, etc.) poses a theoretical problem: the problem of the validity of its *claim* to existence in a discourse with scientific pretensions. The problem may be formulated as follows:

why does a certain form of scientific discourse necessarily need the use of metaphors borrowed from non-scientific disciplines?

(n. 8, p. 26)

I do not think that it is important that we answer Althusser's question now. (Really, this is the question that Le Doeuff's work constantly seeks to address.) I do, however, think that it is much more interesting at this point to look at how Althusser's construction of the problematic literally "opens up" the question of silencing. The problematic allows us to comprehend woman's voice in philosophy as an integral invisibility, an internal limit not unlike Le Doeuff's notion of an internal enemy. Woman's voice is that invisible or silent space occupying the theoretical domain of the problematic, the silences "that *sound hollow* to an attentive ear" (p. 30). The problematic poses a different logic from the exclusive one of either inside or out. It suggests a topology wherein silence is enacted as a structuring possibility of philosophy itself. The process of denial works very much in this manner. It involves a silencing that is far more serious than a simple logic of exclusion. With the structure of denial we are dealing with voices that speak from an excluded place internal to that logic.

3

READING PSYCHOANALYSIS

Psychotic texts/maternal pre-texts

My discussion so far has shifted terrain from an initial concern with the mechanisms of exclusion that structure the discipline of philosophy, to an elaboration of silencing as repression and denial. In this chapter I shall ask more specifically what psychoanalytic theory may be able to offer to this discussion. I intend to establish this by reading silence through the structure of psychosis. Placed in this context psychosis has an instrumental value. I shall use it as a (psycho)analytical instrument in order to further tease out the problem of silence. I do not intend to reduce silence to a particular psychosis or conversely to suggest that it is emblematic of all psychoses. I am more interested in appropriating and rewriting psychosis from its psychoanalytic frame in order to demonstrate that it can be useful as a further strategy for reading silence. Psychosis enables us to hear repressions and denials in a way that arguably throws more light on the structure of the masculine imaginary. Introducing psychosis allows me to do a number of things. Firstly, it transforms my ongoing discussion of silence. By reading silence through the structure of psychosis we shift our conceptual terrain away from exclusion, repression and denial, toward a psychoanalytic exploration of the mechanism of foreclosure. (I shall say more about the specific mechanism of foreclosure and its structural relation with the masculine imaginary later in the chapter.) Secondly, it allows me to raise the problem of silence in the work of Julia Kristeva. Toward the end of this chapter I shall introduce some Kristevan themes that will be elaborated in later chapters of the book. In particular I shall examine Kristeva's notion of the abject in order to discover what she has to say about the possible links between silence, psychosis and writing. Finally, I intend to use psychosis as a way of reading (and voicing) a masculine desire (*for* the mother – *to be* the mother) that generates certain literary works.

I shall begin, however, by looking at what psychoanalysis has to say about psychosis; I intend to do several things with this. I want to use (psychoanalytic) theory to read certain texts. A theory of psychosis will function here as a reading strategy, as another way of reading the symptomatic silences of the masculine imaginary. I shall also use a theory (or reading) of psychosis to ask questions about the discipline (or practice) of psychoanalysis itself. In a sense, this amounts to a gesture of psychoanalysing psychoanalysis, an immanent critique that involves reading Freud beyond or against himself. Psychosis functions here as an enabling metaphor, a way of reading (beyond?) the repressions and denials of disciplinary exclusion.

Reading Freud

Freud's occulting of the mother in the Oedipus complex ... could be viewed as an individual phenomenon. But is it not more useful to see this blindness in so astute an analyst as the manifestation in him of a perversion – repression of the mother – which lies at the root of Western civilization itself?[1]

But in any case if Oedipus does not solve the riddle, then the riddle is no longer a riddle; it remains an enigma ... And men will have to imagine other ways to deal with the fact that they, men, are born of women.[2]

For Freud the Oedipal struggle represents "the child's great cultural achievement – the instinctual renunciation" of the mother.[3] This symbolic separation from the maternal body involves a repression that returns in the guise of a quest for origins. In a sense it finds expression in the child's desire for the resolution of his enigmatic birth. The virtual eclipse of the mother from this Oedipal drama is a situation which (coincidentally) parallels the eclipse of the mother in Freud's own writing.[4] This seems extraordinary, as many have observed, for a man who was obsessed with the collection of mother goddess statues. Freud's quest for origins, perhaps represented in this ensemble of archaic mother images, is displaced from his writings where we find little evidence of concern with the maternal. According to Julia Kristeva, "one looks in vain to Freud's case studies for insight into mothers and their problems. It might seem as though maternity were a remedy for neurosis which *ipso facto* eliminated the need for a woman to seek that other remedy, psychoanalysis."[5] Freud's silence on the question of mothers has interesting consequences for the development of his own brain child psychoanalysis. Psychoanalytic theory emerges as a motherless infant from Freud's own fertile mind. In the previous chapter we saw how Althusser grasped the self-generating implications of Freud's intellectual endeavour. Althusser's discussion of Freud as "the founder of analytic theory and the inaugurator, as Analyst number one, self-analysed, original Father, of the long line of practitioners who claim their descent from him",[6] captures Freud's birth phantasy, and then proceeds to use it as a general model of masculine production.

Psychosis: foreclosing the mother

Psychosis can be understood in a number of ways. The far end of the spectrum indicates those suffering from such extreme states as schizophrenia, manic depression and paranoia, as well as a range of hypochondriacal, obsessional and narcissistic disorders.[7] While these states identify individuals with distinctive psychological pathology, I shall argue that psychosis represents a much broader state; it constitutes the parameters of so-called normal masculine

51

identity. This understanding of "normal" psychosis is defined by a masculine desire to be, or stand in for, the mother. It enables us to read the major texts of our patriarchal culture as psychotic texts, i.e. not as deviant or abnormal works, but more poignantly, as "normal" masculine ones. This psychotic confusion with the mother goes beyond transgressive or liminal states. It is encoded in the symbolic framework of "normal" patriarchal culture. There are various activities which inscribe this masculine desire to replace the mother; writing is one. Psychotic man, self-made and self-produced, contextualises this desire within the canon of symbolic law – in the mythologies, philosophies and literatures that combine to create cultural life.

Freud's work is rather pessimistic about the possibility of treating "classic" psychosis because such patients lack the libidinal transference to the analyst that is essential for "cure". He argues that psychotic patients are not able to be reached as they have failed to insinuate themselves within the Oedipal drama. As a consequence they are disconnected from the continuity of generational succession. This lack of Oedipalisation means that the psychotic repudiates castration and thus fails to succumb to symbolic law. Fails to be *inside* that law. Because of this, the psychotic has an altered relation to what we loosely·term reality. For Freud psychosis represents a "disturbance in the relations between the ego and the external world".[8] Thus it is a question not so much of a loss of reality but more essentially of "*a substitute for reality*".[9] Later, Lacan will repeat this when he speaks of the problem lying "not in the reality that is lost, but in that which takes its place".[10] The psychotic's withdrawal from reality often distinguishes him from his neurotic counterpart. Neurosis is thought to represent a repression of reality (a state that may well characterise the silencing gesture we have so far explored) while psychosis is the result of *foreclosing* that reality. While neither Freud nor Lacan argues for an absolute break between the two, there is a tendency within psychoanalytic literature to assume a certain separateness. Indeed Lacan himself speaks of "the minimal split, which is certainly justifiable between neurosis and psychosis".[11]

To understand the distinction between repressed (neurotic) and foreclosed (psychotic) reality we must first turn to the question of castration. Freud argues that the child's discovery of his mother's castration effectively separates him from his dependence upon her body. Once this dependence is severed it becomes part of his relation to the symbolic order or paternal law. The mother's lack thus operates as a powerful reminder of paternal authority. Julia Kristeva defines castration as the transfer of semiotic maternal fusion to symbolic paternal law.[12] Symbolic law stands between the newly emerging subject and its desire to return to the maternal body. This separation (signified through the threat of castration) subjects the child to what Lacan terms the Name-of-the-Father (*nom-du-père*). But when the paternal metaphor fails, the threat of castration is no longer there. At such times castration becomes either repressed or more significantly foreclosed. That is, the subject is forced into either a neurotic or psychotic identification with the mother. An identification that, for Freud and Lacan, lies outside the symbolic realm.

The neurotic repression of castration involves a simultaneous affirmation and denial. As seen in the case of fetishism the neurotic both accepts and refuses the horror of maternal castration. (That is, he is simultaneously both inside and outside symbolic law.) In this way he both separates and remains fused to the maternal body. The fetish, which acts as a substitute for the maternal phallus, mediates the contradiction between affirmation and denial. Reality (i.e. maternal castration) is thus repressed, disavowed, though not totally denied. In the case of the psychotic, repression becomes a rejection, a foreclosure or refusal of maternal castration. Freud speaks of *Verwerfung*, a process that precedes neurotic repression (*Verdrangung*).[13] Unlike repression *Verwerfung* does not involve an oscillation between affirmation and denial. Rather it is a rejection of castration, a refusal to register its existence. According to Freud, "this really involved no judgement upon the question of its existence, but it was the same as if it did not exist".[14]

In his later work Lacan takes up Freud's notion of *Verwerfung* which he calls *forclusion*.[15] Foreclosure (*Verwerfung/forclusion*) is understood as a psychotic rejection of "reality". In place of castration there exists a gap or hole, a refusal to register. This forces the psychotic to fashion an alternative reality in order to patch what, in effect, never took place. Serge Leclaire, a disciple of Lacan's, argues that repression figures analogically as a "rent" or "tear" in the psychic fabric, while foreclosure represents a gap (*béance*) or "primal hole" that has never existed, one that can only be at best patched.[16] For the psychotic this patch takes the form of a ruthless identification *with* the mother; a belief that one *is* in fact the mother. This distinction between psychotic foreclosure and neurotic repression is described by François Roustang in terms of divided and dissociated processes: "In the case of the neurotic, thoughts circulate between the ego and the other; for the psychotic, the ego vanishes because it is no longer anything but the other's thoughts, and the unconscious other has no thoughts of its own, other than those that inhabit the egoless consciousness."[17] Rather than speaking, the psychotic is "spoken". The ego disappears, as the process of foreclosure has failed to register the "truth of castration" that in "normal" psychic function becomes repressed and exists as the discourse of the Other. Lacan argues that the discourse of the Other is in fact the unconscious, and that the subject's condition is dependent upon what unfolds there.[18] Accordingly, the psychotic is egoless as there exists nothing within the unconscious (i.e. no repressed truth of castration) that it can mirror. For Lacan what ultimately separates psychosis from the structure of neurosis is the foreclosure of the Name-of-the-Father in the place of the Other, and the resultant failure of the paternal metaphor.[19] The foreclosed paternal metaphor thus constitutes the pathology of the psychotic. The threat of castration is expelled and appears in the realm outside the subject in the form of hallucination. It is banished from the symbolic order, the realm of law, authority and signification.

Lacan refers to this realm outside the subject as the *Real* (a term, however, that is not to be confused with reality). The Real exists outside symbolisation, and consists of what has been foreclosed. In this sense the Real describes "that which is lacking in the symbolic order, the ineliminable residue of all articulation, the foreclosed element, which may be approached, but never grasped: the *umbilical cord* of the symbolic".[20] Unlike the neurotic, who is apparently caught in a dialectic of affirmation and denial, the psychotic forecloses castration only to hallucinate it in the murky realm of the Real.[21]

Theoretically these distinctions between psychosis and neurosis seem useful, however in practice they appear to dissolve. Phobia, the imaginary crossroad between psychosis and neurosis, indicates the slippery nature of this division, verging as it does on the point of psychosis.[22] Freud speaks of the undecidability of the neurotic/psychotic cleave refusing to legislate definitively on their distinction. He writes that in neurosis, as in psychosis, "there is no lack of attempts to replace a disagreeable reality by one which is more in keeping with the subject's wishes".[23] In *The Loss of Reality in Neurosis and Psychosis*, Freud suggests that the distinction between the two is, in fact, a temporal one. Martin Thom has pointed out that here Freud is arguing that there is a *deferral* on the part of the neurotic to withdraw from and foreclose reality. Neurotic behaviour is, according to Freud, a second-stage phenomenon and represents the "loosening of the relation to reality".[24] Because of this temporal element the type of reality foreclosed here is quite different. This loosening of reality takes place at an earlier stage in psychosis. In the second stage of psychosis there exists a process of remodelling, an active refashioning of an alternative reality, a raiding of phantasies. While this phantasmic element is common to both neurotic and psychotic processes, Thom argues that "there is nevertheless this difference between the two, a difference that Freud defines temporally".[25]

So the psychoanalytic discussion of psychosis, elaborated in relation to neurosis, serves to establish it as an identifiable, albeit complex, phenomenon. Psychoses are recognisable pathological states situated outside the parameters of so-called healthy or normal behaviour. This description, however, is based upon an intuitive denial. Freud registers this when he fails to accord psychosis a unique and identifiable identity outside of time. This deferral on his part (a latter-stage neurosis?) sows an appreciable seed of doubt in our ability to exile psychosis from the realm of (normal) symbolic exchange. Indeed, as Melanie Klein has shown, there exist observable resemblances between the phantasies of young children and psychotic patients.[26] Psychosis, in this sense, represents identifiable phases of early (normal) childhood experience.

I think that the psychotic identification with the mother, the attempt to *be* the mother, raises significant questions that are related to the nature of the masculine imaginary. If we suppose that psychosis does to some degree constitute the "normal" function of the masculine psyche then we could argue that what is in fact foreclosed is not the threat of castration, the paternal metaphor, but rather the mother. What returns in the Real as hallucination is the maternal function, the ability to give birth. It is the mother's procreative ability that is foreclosed, repudiated, and this returns as a psychotic hallucination of one's own ability to give birth to oneself. Widespread phantasies of male birth might then appear as psychotic renderings of this (normal) masculine desire. In foreclosing the mother the (psychotic) male weaves an alternative and more acceptable reality for himself. If we return to Leclaire's metaphor we might ironically add to this that the "primal hole" in the material (matter/mother) which signifies foreclosure is in fact a psychotic rendering of the mother. This gap (*béance*) which "would never have been anything other than the substance of a hole" is thus "filled" by the psychotic's "hallucination". In the light of this we can view Freud's articulation of the Oedipal complex (and psychoanalytic theory itself) as an elaborate psychotic hallucination. In foreclosing the mother, Freud gives birth to himself in the form of his own brain child, i.e. psychoanalysis. This refusal to register the mother might well explain her conspicuous absence from his work. In a psychotic identification with the maternal body Freud appropriates, and stands in for, the generative principle. There is no great mystery why Althusser identifies with the psychotic Freud, the father who provides him with the model of masculine self-sufficiency.

"Fort-da" as the compulsion to repeat

I shall continue my discussion of the normal parameters of psychosis (i.e. psychosis as a structuring logic of the "normal" masculine imaginary) by looking at what Freud has to say about the apparently normal psychic tendency he calls the *repetition compulsion*. The repetition compulsion is characterised for Freud by the child's attempt to separate from the mother, to master her absence and in so doing master himself. Freud argues that the repetition compulsion is part of normal psychic development. Drawing parallels between this and psychotic behaviour, I shall argue that the pathological psychoses are in fact implicated in normal psychic development. That is to say that the playful mastery typical of the repetition compulsion is, in a sense, another expression of the psychotic desire to replace and become the mother. If this is so, a barrier between normal and psychotic behaviour becomes even less sustainable. A question remains, however, as to whether the repetition compulsion links psychosis to normal psychic development or normal *masculine* psychic development. If it is the latter, then Freud's discussion of the little boy who plays at losing his mother may well be inadequate as a model for human psychic development. It could be another instance of Freud's desire to universalise from (a limited?) masculine experience of the world. His discussion of this "thrown away" mother might then be part of his larger unconscious desire to eliminate questions of sexual difference altogether. Freud's discussion of the repetition compulsion centres around his observations of a small boy at play. In his attempt to explain the puzzling behaviour of the child, Freud hypothesises that his games involve the desire to master the absence of his mother. Freud describes the game thus:

> This good little boy, however, had an occasional disturbing habit of taking any small objects he could get hold of and throwing them away from him in a corner, under the bed, and so on, so that hunting for his toys and picking them up was often quite a business. As he did this he gave vent to a loud long-drawn-out "o-o-o-", accompanied by an expression of interest and satisfaction. His mother and the writer of the present account were agreed in thinking that this was not a mere interjection but represented the German word "fort" [gone]. I eventually realized that it was a game and that the only use he made of any of his toys was to play "gone" with them.[27]

After some time Freud discovers a variation on this theme. With the help of a wooden reel, which has a string attached to it, the child completes this ritual:

> What he did was to hold the reel by the string and very skilfully throw it over the edge of his curtained cot, so that it disappeared into it, at the same time uttering his expressive "o-o-o-o". He then pulled the reel out of the cot again by the string and hailed its reappearance with a joyful "da" [there]. This, then, was the complete game in itself.[28]

Freud interprets the "*Fort-da*" game as the child's renunciation of instinctual satisfaction. The young boy masters his mother's absence by re-enacting her disappearance and reappearance with the help of his toys. While Freud notes that the return ("*da*") of objects serves to please the child, he points out that the game also exists as the staging of a disappearance ("*fort*") only.[29]

Freud argues that the "*Fort-da*" game allows the child to move from a passive acceptance of the mother's absence to an active role in controlling her presence/absence in a symbolic form.[30] By repeating the experience with the aid of a signifier standing in for the mother (i.e. toy or reel) the child rehearses a masterful control of her being. Not merely an active control of her presence/absence, but also, as Freud notes, a vengeful act:

> Throwing away the object so that it was "gone" might satisfy an impulse of the child's, which was suppressed in his actual life, to revenge himself on his mother for going away from him. In that case it would have a defiant meaning: "*All right, then, go away! I don't need you. I'm sending you away myself.*"[31]

It is the repetition of an act, whether pleasurable or not, that gives the child the ability to master undesirable circumstances. By displacing experience on to the symbolic realm, the little boy learns to actively fashion his own reality. Activity and mastery become the means whereby the child reproduces his self.

The "*Fort-da*" game can be described in terms of foreclosing the mother. Rather than representing a sole desire to master her absence, however, we could say that Freud's repetition compulsion also involves an elaborate series of acts aimed at coping with her presence. As such it might better be described as more "*Fort*" than "*da*", more "gone" than "here". Indeed Thom draws a similar conclusion: "In fact the *Fort* game (and one should perhaps resolve to call it this) represents more than a response to privation and does not have as its aim the reappearance of the mother."[32] In a marginal note Freud reveals that the small boy (who is in fact his grandson Ernst) *loses* his mother at the age of 5.[33] His mother dies and literally goes away. Freud tells us that the child interestingly displays no grief. One might suspect that the child had already dealt with his mother's loss by replacing her with himself. This may be so but nonetheless one must ask why Freud exiles the *real* mother of the "*Fort-da*" story to the silent margin of his own text.

Luce Irigaray's discussion of Freud's "*Fort-da*" is instructive. She claims that the child (Ernst) could not be a girl, that a girl's gestures would not be the same.

> In the absence of her mother, a girl's gestures are not the same. She does not play with a string and reel symbolizing her mother, for her mother's sex is the same as hers and the mother cannot have the objective status of a reel. The mother's identity as a subject is the same as hers.[34]

Irigaray's basic claim here is that girls and boys enter language in different ways. She suggests that the gestures that accompany their entry into language are also different. She writes:

> it is by a gesture of the hand and arm, together with the pronuncia-tion of some syllables, that the small boy enters the symbolic uni-verse, by mastering the absence of his mother ... He searches for his mother with his arms and his mouth. And with his ears perhaps? Sounds vibrate in his mouth and resonate in his ears. It is almost as though, in some way, he becomes speech, he speaks to himself.
>
> (pp. 131–2)

According to Irigaray girls will adopt gestures more in keeping with continu-ity and sameness between their mother's bodies and their own:

> The *fort-da* is not the gesture by which they enter language. It is too linear, too analogous with the in-out movement of the penis or of

masturbation [*son substitut manuel*], or with the mastery of the other in the form of an object; also, too angular a movement. Girls enter language without taking in anything (except empty space). They do not speak around an introjected object, male or female, but rather *with* (sometimes in) a silence and with, in any case, the (m)other. They can find no replacement for her ... Woman always speaks *with* the mother; man speaks in her absence.

(pp. 133–4)

With Irigaray's discussion in mind, I shall suggest once again that the game of "*Fort-da*" traces a similar gesture to what I have been referring to as the psychotic foreclosure of the mother. While the compulsion to repeat would seem to fall within the boundaries of castration and thus "normal" symbolic functioning, nevertheless it does enact a foreclosure of a psychotic type. Again I would argue that what is foreclosed here is not the paternal metaphor, but more obviously the mother. I want to explore the terrain of psychosis and masculine desire by going on now to look at one of Freud's famous psychotic cases, Judge Daniel Paul Schreber. I am particularly interested in Schreber's psychosis because it seems to provide us with a link between the psychotic (masculine) imaginary and writing. Schreber's text offers us a highly stylised account of the psychotic state. It presents, perhaps more clearly than most, the fundamental link between psychosis and the desire to give birth. It is an engrossing account not only of a generalised desire to give birth, but more specifically, perhaps, of a masculine desire to take the place of the maternal body and reproduce in its absence.[35]

Schreber: the self as psychotic text

The question of what is foreclosed in psychosis arises in relation to Schreber's case. Freud's early work on psychosis relies heavily upon a reading of Schreber's memoirs. His analysis of Schreber's condition goes on to form the basis of his psychoanalytic theory of psychosis. Following Freud's lead, Lacan interprets Schreber's condition as a psychotic foreclosure of the paternal metaphor and the threat of castration. That is to say he accepts wholeheartedly the Oedipal explanation offered by Freud. Schreber's delusional reality is thus one that he fashions in order to patch up the gap in reality that psychotic foreclosure entails. Schreber falls prey to a spiralling series of psychotic identifications as he fails to register the *truth* of castration. I want to challenge this analysis and read Schreber's case as a foreclosure of something other than the paternal metaphor. Indeed I intend to read it as a foreclosure of the mother which results in a desire to become her, to take her place. In this reading Schreber's memoirs are an extreme example of what I have been describing as the psychotic text of the (normal) masculine imaginary. As such it is a text against which we might read more generally patriarchal culture. Another way of saying this is to suggest that it represents a *pre-text* of masculine desire.

Freud's analysis of Schreber's case is decisive for the history of psychoanalytic understandings of psychosis. It was published in 1911, and outlines an inverted Oedipal theory of unconscious homosexual desire. In it he argues that Schreber's psychosis stems from a passive homosexual desire for his father, which later becomes manifest in a series of metonymic displacements. Schreber's physician and God will later stand in for his father, becoming the objects of his homosexual wishes. Freud contends that Schreber's condition results from his inability to deal with his (unconscious) homosexual longings. The threat of castration implied in this passive "feminine" desire throws Schreber into a state of anxiety, culminating in his repudiation of paternal law. Schreber effectively forecloses the threat of castration. He forecloses reality and replaces it with an elaborately conceived reality of his own. Freud's analysis repeatedly stresses Schreber's psychosis as a struggle against castration. The significance of this cannot be overstated as psychoanalysts since him have largely accepted this along with its Oedipal implications. In so doing, they have themselves unwittingly foreclosed the possibility of alternative explanations. Most significantly they have foreclosed any real discussion of the role of the mother, a gesture which compulsively repeats Freud's own stance. Schreber's psychosis is thus understood in terms of an Oedipal drama in which the mother plays no role.

I have suggested that Lacan's discussion of psychosis closely resembles Freud's own position. His belief in the foreclosure of the paternal metaphor upholds Freud's Oedipal interpretation of psychotic functioning. It is significant, not only for its rehearsal of Freudian themes, but more importantly for its dismissal of alternative readings of Schreber that challenge these. In his analysis Lacan makes reference to a reading of Schreber's case by Ida Macalpine. The work to which he refers, written in fact in collaboration with Richard Hunter, is an elaborate critique of Freud's analysis published in the early 1950s. Lacan's objection to Macalpine's thesis is essentially that she refuses the "truth" of Freud's Oedipal theory. Presumably he accuses Hunter of this sin as well, though the repression of his name remains an enigmatic symptom of the text. Lacan seems outraged by Macalpine's insistence upon birth phantasies at the expense of sound Oedipal interpretations. Macalpine's great sin lies in searching beyond Oedipus for the riddle of psychosis. Her discussion of birth phantasies and associated delusions displays a perversion unwarranted in serious psychoanalytic endeavour. Lacan's case against her rests largely upon what he regards as an illegitimate move whereby Macalpine apparently inserts the verb "to deliver" into the English translation of Schreber's text. He writes:

> Now the word "to deliver" is indisputable as a translation, for the simple reason that there is nothing to translate. I looked again and again at the German text. The verb was *simply forgotten* by either the

59

author or the compositor, and Mrs Macalpine, in an effort to make sense of the translation, has, unknown to herself, restored it.[36]

Lacan's highly ironic comment, "simply forgotten", warrants some discussion. It is a curious fact that Lacan chooses to focus on a technical point about translation when he admonishes Macalpine for her unseemly insertions. He makes quite a fuss about Macalpine introducing the verb "to deliver" in to Schreber's text, arguing that the verb was simply never there in the first place. Now it seems to me that this is something of a displacement on his part because in focusing on this he rather cunningly refuses to address the really significant issue that is at stake. He refuses to ask himself whether or not Schreber's text actually motivates Macalpine's idiosyncratic reading. In so doing he closes off a productive line of inquiry. He forecloses or fails to register the numerous ways in which Schreber's text might not only permit Macalpine's insertion but in fact actively authorise it.

Macalpine and Hunter do construct a convincing argument based upon allusions to birth found within Schreber's text. They contend that the projection of unconscious homosexual desire in fact constitutes only a symptom, not a cause, of his dis-ease. It is causal neither phenomenologically nor aetiologically.[37] They argue that Freud's selective reading of Schreber's memoirs leads him to disregard evidence of procreation phantasies that exist within the text. In foregrounding the elements of persecution within Schreber's psychosis, Freud ignores the significance of somatic delusions. Macalpine and Hunter believe Schreber's hypochondriacal (somatic) delusions to be hallucinatory expressions of pregenital procreation phantasies. They argue that his somatic hallucinations share a complementary relationship with his psychic delusions, thus forming a connection between the earlier and later phases of his psychosis.[38] Macalpine and Hunter point out that when Freud does make reference to Schreber's procreation phantasies, he does so in order to cite them as proof of Schreber's unconscious homosexual desire. That is, they are seen to derive logically from the prior expression of Schreber's homosexual attachment. Macalpine and Hunter find similar conclusions in their search of the psychoanalytic literature relating to pregnancy phantasies. In each case procreative phantasies in men are considered as dependent upon the existence of passive homosexual desire and are thus explained by the anxiety induced by the threat of castration.[39] Macalpine and Hunter consider homosexual desire to be a secondary phenomenon in Schreber's case. They believe it remains dependent upon the primary phantasy of procreation which necessitates his transformation into a woman. The desire to give birth thus constitutes the core of Schreber's psychotic identification with the maternal body.

Memoirs of My Nervous Illness is the text in which Schreber gives birth to his psychotic self. It attests to the obsessional nature of his desire to procreate, and is filled with intricate discussions of reproduction. The *Memoirs* chronicle Schreber's attempt to live through the delusions associated with his desire. In them we find two distinct phantasies which merge into a single desire to give birth. In the first instance, Schreber imagines himself to be the chosen one who will re-populate humanity after a world calamity. Believing that the end of the world has arrived, Schreber thinks God has chosen him to renew mankind. This is a popularly rehearsed theme in mythology, where legends tell of a being who procreates from himself in order to re-establish humanity.[40] In this stage of Schreber's illness he imagines himself to be performing a time-honoured ritual. The phantasy invoked here is one of male procreation, and it is this phase of Schreber's condition that marks his most delusional state.[41] Schreber's second yet related phantasy is the belief that he is turning into a woman. In this phase of his illness Schreber experiences a series of somatic hallucinations; bodily sensations which he attributes to the process of *unmanning*. In the *Memoirs* he describes the experience of "the (external) male genitals (scrotum and penis) being retracted into the body and the internal sexual organs being at the same time transformed into the corresponding female sexual organs" and goes on to say "I have myself twice experienced (for a short time) the miracle of unmanning on my own body".[42] Schreber's psychotic identification with the maternal body finds further expression in his association with the Virgin Mary.

> Something like the conception of Jesus Christ by an Immaculate Virgin – i.e. one who had never had intercourse with a man – happened in my own body. Twice at different times ... I had a female genital organ, although a poorly developed one, and in my body felt quickening like the first signs of life of a human embryo: by a divine miracle God's nerves corresponding to male seed had been thrown into my body; in other words fertilization had occurred.[43]

Freud interprets Schreber's immaculate conception as a homosexual desire directed toward God, who stands in metonymically for his father – literally *God the father*. Schreber's discussion of unmanning is interpreted as a castration, yet as Macalpine and Hunter point out, to interpret it as such is to deny (or foreclose?) the basic procreative desire upon which it rests.

Schreber's process of unmanning involves the gradual transformation of his body into that of a woman's. It is a process designed to offer him a reproductive female body, one from which he can give birth. In Freud's theory of castration the woman's body is viewed as a mutilated and impotent male body. Schreber's unmanning, however, represents a psychotic desire to appropriate the *potent* and creative maternal body. As such it is a repudiation of psychoanalytic truth; one which raises questions for how we are to understand castration. Schreber's unmanning displaces the Oedipal drama from its position of so called universal truth. Macalpine and Hunter argue that Schreber's "homosexual" desires toward his physician and God should be understood in light of this. If Schreber believes himself to be transformed into a potent female body, then his desire toward these men is not the desire of a castrated or emasculated male.[44]

In the *Memoirs* Schreber describes how his body is diminishing in size, "approximating the size of the female body".[45] He describes also how unmanning brings with it a softening of his masculine features. "I myself received the impression of a female body, first on my arms and hands, later on my legs, bosom, buttocks and other parts of my body."[46] Elsewhere, he writes "When I exert light pressure with my hand on any part of my body I can *feel* certain string or cord-like structures under the skin; these are particularly marked on my chest where the woman's bosom is, here they have the peculiarity that one can feel them ending in nodular thickenings."[47] These cord-like structures are also described in "the gradual filling of my body with nerves of voluptuousness (female nerves)"[48] and are associated with Schreber's belief in his ability to conceive and give birth.

Macalpine and Hunter argue that Schreber falls ill when his desire to give birth becomes all-consuming.[49] After repeated miscarriages and stillbirths Schreber and his wife are unable to gain their much desired family. Schreber speaks of the time after his first illness as a happy period "marred only from time to time by the repeated disappointment of our hope of being blessed with children".[50] Indeed Freud suggests that Schreber may have "formed a fantasy that if he had been a woman he would have managed the business of having children more successfully".[51] Yet, as Macalpine and Hunter point out, he goes on to interpret this as yet another passive homosexual desire, the desire to be the woman for the man.[52]

Macalpine and Hunter's discussion of Schreber is a useful corrective to the overarching Oedipal implications of Freud's analysis. The focus upon birth phantasies as the centre of psychosis provides an insightful re-reading of Schreber's text. Yet their belief in the archaic nature of procreative phantasies leaves the question of the specific relation of masculinity to psychosis unposed. Macalpine and Hunter argue that archaic birth phantasies exist in both men and women. However, what they fail to ask is whether such phantasies are experienced or expressed differently by the two. For example, whether significant differences (i.e. differences in meaning) are placed upon such phantasies by men and women. It is possible that birth phantasies in women are experienced in a radically different manner, and that the violent foreclosure of the maternal body effected in masculine psychosis is lacking from their experience. Female birth phantasies might effect an identification with the maternal body, one that does not aim at the mother's foreclosure. If this is so then the question must be posed: do women experience psychotic states, or is psychosis (as I have been describing it here) a peculiarly masculine phenomenon?

Schreber's psychosis is fundamentally a masculine form of the desire to give birth. In his somatic hallucinations we observe a hysterical identification with the potency of the maternal body. Irigaray puts it this way:

Schreber, like Ernst [the child in Freud's *fort-da*] played with gestures, with words, with his image in the mirror, to compensate for the absence of his mother ... instead of becoming fully man, especially in his symbolic creativity, [he] becomes woman, or tries to take on the virginal sex of his wife, distancing himself from her and putting himself in the hands of the medical profession.[53]

Schreber becomes the mother, and in so doing, displaces her. This psychotic desire finds material expression in his *Memoirs* which issue forth as progeny of his deluded state. In writing, Schreber gives birth not only to his text, but more importantly, to himself. He reproduces himself in an act of intellectual creativity:

> my unmanning will be accomplished with the result that by divine fertilization offspring will issue from my lap, or alternatively that great fame will be attached to my name surpassing that of thousands of other people much better mentally endowed ... and so I close in the hope that in this sense favourable stars will watch over the success of my labour.[54]

Schreber's labour of writing (re)produces, in textual form, the somatic hallucinations of his delusional state. His *Memoirs* are memories, hysterical re-memberings of his desire to appropriate the place of the mother. Read in this manner, psychosis describes a masculine desire to foreclose the potent mother. While this may be at odds with existing psychoanalytic accounts, it is an attempt to explain the obsessive desire to give birth to the self in both somatic and textual form. In this writing we witness a psychotic desire to create the self. The foreclosed maternal body returns here as hallucination to disturb the authority of paternal law. Such hallucinations became readily encoded in the liminal texts of our culture, in poetry, myth and madness. More importantly, though, they exist as pretexts for the inscription of the masculine imaginary. As such, they mark the limits not only of art and madness, but perhaps more significantly of philosophy itself. The psychotic text of the masculine imaginary literally embodies its maternal pre-text in the figure of the foreclosed and repudiated mother. I have already indicated that Schreber's psychosis can be read alongside other philosophical texts. More specifically we can read his psychotic hallucinations as extreme inscriptions of a similar desire that structures the work of both Plato and Althusser. I think that it is important that we do this, for to isolate Schreber as an insane psychotic is to fail to recognise the fraternal phantasies linking him to his respected philosophical counterparts.

Before concluding our discussion of Schreber I would like to return to Lacan's dismissal of Macalpine and Hunter's reading. Lacan's fundamental complaint can be understood in the following way. He argues that Macalpine (and Hunter) fail to interpret Schreber's phantasy in *symbolic* terms. That is, they resist placing Schreber's phantasies *inside* the symbolic structure of the Oedipal complex. Macalpine and Hunter create a "non-Oedipal" phantasy in which the procreative function is effectively severed from symbolic or paternal law. In effect they refer to Schreber *outside* of any possible symbolic (Oedipal) meaning.[55] I want to suggest that Macalpine and Hunter's reading does not act as a displacement of the symbolic (Oedipal) structure, but rather as an elaboration of it, i.e. their reading helps us to ascertain the imaginary function of the Oedipal structure, a discussion effectively foreclosed by both Freud and Lacan. This entails rethinking the spatial organisation of symbolic and imaginary realms. Lacan's dismissal can indeed be understood in spatial terms. We could say that the symbolic realm remains the space *inside* which all meaning can be articulated. (We could parallel this with a certain philosophy which sees rationality as the space of all possible meaning.) The symbolic is, then, the inside, the privileged space of meaning and voice. Are we then suggesting that phantasies (of self-generation, self-birth) lie *outside* this domain? I think not. I think that the phantasies Macalpine and Hunter read from Schreber's text are ones that, although not symbolic as such, find their expression in that domain. That is to say that Schreber's phantasies are articulated in a space that disrupts the symbolic without displacing it. Whether Schreber's phantasies be, in Lacan's own terms, associated with either the imaginary or the real, they actively inhabit the symbolic, acting something like an internal rather than external limit. The spaces of the imaginary or the real are not spaces *outside* or beyond the symbolic; they are its structuring possibility. This raises some important questions for writing, as it suggests that what we have been calling the masculine imaginary is by no means outside of symbolic language, but rather that which inhabits it. And the abject is in fact an example of this. As we shall see, the abject is a refusal of any simple logic ordered by the opposition inside/out.

The abject: writing (and) the maternal body

Our discussion of psychosis inevitably raises the question of writing. In Schreber's case writing stands in for the act of giving birth; the text is the progeny of his (reproductive) endeavour. But how are we to understand the relation between the two? What does this tell us about masculine desire and the imaginary it conceives? In this final section I shall seek some answers by looking briefly at Julia Kristeva's concept of the *abject*, i.e. the pre-objectal relation with the maternal body. It seems to me that I can make use of what Kristeva has to say about the abject to further my own investigation of the silencing processes that deny woman her voice. While this is arguably not Kristeva's major focus, I consider it to be a legitimate use of her work. Abjection allows us to continue to think about psychosis in terms other than psychoanalytically defined *abnormal* psychic states. It allows us to think about psychosis as the structuring possibility of writing and thus as a *normal* state. As we shall see, the abject text is not the product of a deranged psychosis, but rather the literary production of so-called normal masculine psychosis.

Kristeva argues that writing mobilises the incestuous link to the pre-Oedipal maternal body. While the subject assumes an authority in language and identifies with paternal law, *he* nonetheless retains his psychotic link with the mother's body. (Here we recall Roland Barthes who muses that the writer is someone who plays with his mother's body.)[56] The ambivalent state experienced in relation to the archaic maternal body (the desire to return to and flee from it) culminates in a (masculine) fear and loathing for that body. For Kristeva, this fear is essentially a fear of the mother's generative power. "It is this power, a dreaded one, that patrilineal filiation has the burden of subduing."[57] In an attempt to deny this power the masculine subject takes the place of the mother, giving birth, as it were, to himself. She writes "There are men, enthralled by archaic mothers, who dream of being women or some unapproachable master ... others, classic hystericals, search for that impossible maternal fusion and are exalted in their frustration."[58] Kristeva describes the mystic (evoking the figures of Saint Augustine, Saint Bernard and Meister Eckhart) as the one who takes the maternal upon himself. This fusion with the maternal provides the place from which the mystic erects his love of God. (Certainly Schreber falls within this category.) Kristeva argues that in doing this the mystic resembles his literary brother who shares a similar psychotic identification with the mother. "Rare and 'literary' if always rather oriental, not to say tragic, are the mystics' contemporary counterparts: think of Henry Miller's claim to be pregnant or Artaud's imagining himself to be like 'his girls', or 'his mother'."[59] This psychotic identification with the mother is clearly encoded in what Kristeva identifies as the abject literature of writers such as Dostoevsky, Proust, Joyce and Céline. These are writers of liminal and transgressive texts, who measure themselves against the mother's body and in so doing inscribe an incestuous sexuality. "Know the mother, first take her place, go beyond her."[60]

Kristeva describes poetry as a transgression of paternal law. She argues that the poet enacts his psychotic identification with the maternal, whose body then returns in his writing as rhythm. This threatens the symbolic function of language; "the unsettled and questionable subject of poetic language (for whom the word is never uniquely sign) maintains itself at the cost of reactivating this repressed instinctual, maternal element".[61] She speaks of Dostoevsky who "by symbolizing the abject" delivers himself "of that ruthless maternal burden"; of Proust whose writing is replete with the "erotic, sexual, and desiring mainspring of abjection"; of Joyce whose writing exposes "the maternal body, in its most un-signifiable, un-symbolizable aspect";[62] of Mallarmé who gives birth to his literary creations; of Artaud who claims "I am my father, my mother, my son, and me."[63] Kristeva unearths a similar exploration of Oedipal space in Céline's work, arguing that his writing enacts an obsessive desire to return to the question of birth, fascinated as it is by the maternal body.[64] The obsession with birth that haunts Céline's later work finds early expression in his doctoral thesis. Kristeva tells us that the thesis is concerned with the Hungarian doctor, Ignaz Semmelweis, whose investigation of puerperal fever (the contaminating infection of childbirth) gives birth to a new era of obstetric hygiene. She suggests that Céline is caught between a psychotic identification with the dangerous mother and the self-styled obstetrician, and that he attempts to resolve this by giving birth to himself, signing his labour with his *grand*mother's first name.[65]

While Kristeva's discussion of abjection centres on these liminal and transgressive texts, we can say that all texts structured by the masculine imaginary reveal something of their abject debt. In this sense writing is the attempt to symbolise the abject space. The abject can be understood as what threatens the masculine writer with a suffocating return to the archaic maternal body. But (paternal/symbolic) language intervenes to prevent his total annihilation. In naming the abject, the writer attempts to distance himself from the all-powerful mother. Writing paradoxically enables the writer to take the mother's place while at the same time preserving the distance that stops him from dissolving into her.[66] This suggests that the abject occupies an unstable site somewhere between the structures of repression, denial and foreclosure. In order to appreciate this *ambivalent* positioning of the abject we need to think about writing as a process that simultaneously mobilises the structures that I have, up until this point, isolated and defined as repression, denial and foreclosure.

Kristeva's abject provides us with another way of thinking about the silent place occupied by woman. Plato's mute matrix, Althusser's self-engendering structures and Schreber's psychotic text each assign the maternal to the unspoken realm by speaking it for themselves. The abject alerts us to the fact that writing bears an unspeakable debt to this realm and that it is structured by a psychotic masculine imaginary. Kristeva's discussion of the abject explains how the silence of the maternal body is transformed by/or into writing. Abject literature provides an example of a productive silence, i.e. it is an example of how silence can be spoken as text. Now Kristeva's concern here is not really with silence, certainly not in the sense that I have been discussing it. Indeed Kristeva does not really, in this context, take silence to be a problem at all. Her concern is, rather, with writing, and a very specific form of writing at that. This point is far from insignificant for it is fundamentally linked to my insistence that silence is sexually marked. The productive transformation that the abject enacts is essentially dependent on a (masculine) appropriation of the maternal body as a pre-productive site. While the abject provides a possible way out of the impasse of silence, it ironically reinforces it by being the writing of a particular group, i.e. the writing of a privileged masculine avant-garde. Rather than acting as a resolution of the problem of silence, the abject is more thoroughly a continuation of it. (I shall return to this issue later in the book.)

To conclude, then, the following rather difficult questions remain. Is all writing necessarily a silencing of the maternal? And if so, what does this suggest about women's writing? If the desire to write is structured by the masculine imaginary, i.e. the desire for masculine self-generation, then what does this mean for women's relation to the symbolic? Do women enact a violent foreclosure of the maternal when they write? Can we think of writing only in terms of masculinity? And if so, doesn't this ultimately assign women to the place of silence? I shall suspend these questions momentarily, in order to pursue them more thoroughly in Part II.

4

PHILOSOPHY AND SILENCE

The Différend

> "Language" has no exterior because it is not in space. But it can say
> space. It can say the body. It can say that the body "says" something,
> that silence speaks.[1]

In this chapter I shall continue to explore the question of silence by looking at
the work of the French philosopher Jean-François Lyotard. I intend to use his
observations in order to open further the terrain of our inquiry. After discussing what I believe to be the most relevant aspects of his work for our purposes,
I shall go on to articulate some hesitations that I nonetheless have; hesitations
that arise when reading his work in conjunction with the work of Luce Irigaray.

Jean-François Lyotard: *The Différend*

In *The Différend: Phrases in Dispute* Lyotard argues that the *différend* marks a
wrong which results in silence; he speaks of this as the violence of silencing.[2]
It is "a damage [*dommage*] accompanied by the loss of the means to prove the
damage" (p. 5). This discussion is situated in the larger ethical context of his
investigation of philosophy. In this book he develops an ethical agenda for the
philosopher, an agenda that makes it imperative that the philosopher not only
identify the domain of radical silence associated with (and marked by) the
différend, but more importantly seek to find new idioms, new ways of saying,
this silence. He argues that this enables philosophy to provide itself with a way
out of its contemporary (political) impasse by retrieving its ethical vocation.[3]
Lyotard urges philosophy to broaden what has become a rather narrow concern with speculating on its own foundations, by retrieving this pre-modern
ethical vocation.

The *Différend* is, amongst other things, an observation about judgement. It
raises difficult political questions about who judges, whose authority is presupposed in such judgements, in fact it questions the applicability of universal criteria of judgement. In this book Lyotard distinguishes between a *différend*
and a litigation. For him a *différend* involves a conflict that is impossible to
resolve in any fair way because of the absence of a rule of judgement appropriate to both sides or parties. He argues that: "A wrong results from the fact that
the rules of the genre of discourse by which one judges are not those of the

68

judged genre or genres of discourse" and that "a universal rule of judgement between heterogeneous genres is lacking in general" (p. xi). Lyotard suggests that it is impossible to speak of the wrong that ensues from this lack. To illustrate this point he offers the following double-bind:

> Either you are the victim of a wrong, or you are not. If you are not, you are deceived (or lying) in testifying that you are. If you are, since you can bear witness to this wrong, it is not a wrong, and you are deceived (or lying) in testifying that you are the victim of a wrong.
>
> (p. 5)[4]

For Lyotard there is an important difference between a *plaintiff*, one with the means to prove damage "by means of well-formed phrases and of procedures for establishing the existence of their referent" (p. 8) and a *victim*, one with no such means to prove damage.

> I would like to call a differend [*différend*] the case where the plaintiff is divested of the means to argue and becomes for that reason a victim ... A case of differend between two parties takes place when the "regulation" of the conflict that opposes them is done in the idiom of one of the parties while the wrong suffered by the other is not signified in that idiom.
>
> (p. 9)

The victim attests to the genuine violence associated with the *différend* because s/he is reduced to silence by the word (or law) of the other. The victim has no admissible evidence as s/he does not speak in the language or logic of the other's discourse. For Lyotard, the *différend* is signalled by an inability to speak.

> To be able not to speak is not the same as not to be able to speak. The latter is a deprivation, the former a negation. If [victims] do not speak, is it because they cannot speak, or because they avail themselves of the possibility of not speaking that is given them by the ability to speak?
>
> (p. 10)

Throughout his work Lyotard explores the question that he raises here, whether not speaking is a form of the ability to speak. This question has considerable relevance for my discussion of woman's voice in philosophy so I shall return to it in due course. For the moment, though, I would like to investigate the ways Lyotard's work is tied up with the question of genre. To do this I shall need to say something about his philosophy of phrases.[5]

Lyotard's philosophy of phrases can perhaps best be understood in terms of genre and generic conditions. For him genre comprises the rules of linkage, the linking of heterogeneous phrases. While it is impossible to translate between two distinct phrase regimens, he argues that it is possible to link disparate phrase regimens, usually in terms dictated by a given genre.[6] Genres function to reduce the contingent nature of linking. They do so by providing rules for appropriate or possible linkages.

> A phrase, even the most ordinary one, is constituted according to a set of rules (its regimen). There are a number of phrase regimens: reasoning, knowing, describing, recounting, questioning, showing, ordering, etc. Phrases from heterogeneous regimens cannot be translated from one into the other. They can be linked one onto the other in accordance with an end fixed by a genre of discourse.
>
> (p. xii)

Now Lyotard's task, in *The Différend*, is to bear witness to *différends* that arise from a clash of genres. This, he argues, is, or at least should be, the task of philosophy.[7] The question of linkage is central to this task for it determines what phrases can possibly be said together. The generic rules governing these linkages are discrete and Lyotard argues that a *différend* exists between any two genres. Geoffrey Bennington contends that the most common form of *différend* between genres that Lyotard addresses involves the imposition of the rules of the cognitive genre, and that Lyotard's focus on the "illegitimate extension of the cognitive genre" can be traced back to Kant's distinction between *concept* and *Idea of reason*, where the *Idea of reason* is subsumed beneath the weight of conceptual reality.[8] Conflicts that can be rewritten in terms of either the cognitive or conceptual genre thus become litigations, while those which can not remain *différends*.

Lyotard argues that while linkage between phrases is necessary, any particular linkage is not. Bennington reads Lyotard as saying that genres *seduce* phrases. This seduction is necessary in that each genre provides rival linkages, and in so doing raises the ethical questions of judgement and justice.[9] The notion of seduction goes hand in hand with that of competition. Genres compete amongst themselves for linkages, and this competition ensures that every new linkage will result in a *différend*. The *différend* is thus an intrinsic feature of linguistic functioning.

Certain phrases *permit* following phrases, and reject others.[10] The question of linkage is necessarily, then, the question of the *différend*, for without adequate linkages there will at times be a radical silence in the place of an ability to speak injury or wrong. Our task or obligation is then to find new idioms which register the impossibility of certain linkages so that we can confront the ethical imperative of the *différend*. That which remains silent, and, to paraphrase the Wittgenstein of the *Tractatus*, that which cannot be spoken and is passed over in silence must be voiced.[11] For Lyotard, in as much as there is something unable to be phrased, there *is* something, and this is feeling.

> Insofar as it is unable to be phrased in the common idioms, it is already phrased, as feeling. The avowal has been made. The vigil for an occurrence, the anxiety and the joy of an unknown idiom, has begun. To link is not a duty, which "we" can be relieved of or make good upon. "We" cannot do otherwise.
>
> (p. 80)

Lyotard talks about the necessity of putting as yet unspeakable phrases into language, and in this he includes the negative phrase of silence. He describes the *différend* as an instability in language, a site where potential phrases can and must be spoken. Feeling is constitutive of this instability.

> The *différend* is the unstable state and instant of language wherein something which must be able to be put into phrases cannot yet be. This state includes silence, which is a negative phrase, but it also calls upon phrases which are in principle possible. This state is signalled by what one ordinarily calls a feeling ... *A lot of searching must be done to find new rules for forming and linking phrases that are able to express the différend disclosed by the feeling, unless one wants this différend to be smothered right away in a litigation and for the alarm sounded by the feeling to have been useless.* What is at stake in a literature, in a philosophy, in a politics perhaps is to bear witness to *différends* by finding idioms for them.
>
> (p. 13 emphasis added)

The question of linkage is the question of what will or can come next (the question of what follows or the uptake). For Lyotard this is fundamentally a political question. And indeed for him the political is the question of linkage, it is the question of (possible) phrasing. This philosophy of phrasing is also a question of the "social" because for phrasing to occur a potentially conflictual social context of addresser, addressee, referent and meaning is presupposed. So Lyotard's problem, given the conflict inherent between these phrase worlds, and the absence of what he calls "a universal genre of discourse" (p. xii) capable of regulating them, is the political problem of imagining new possibilities, new linkages that make it possible for the silence of the *différend* to be heard. For Lyotard, silence indicates a *différend*. It indicates the suffering of phrases that remain as yet unphrased.[12] He reminds us that attempts to speak new phrases do not fall between the stark alternatives of sense and non-sense, but rather that they embrace feeling within the domain of knowing. Silence and sentiment are both indicators of the *différend*.[13]

Lyotard urges us to hear the silence of the *différend*, to voice this silence in a now impossible idiom. "One's responsibility before thought", he writes, "consists in detecting *différends* and in finding the (impossible) idiom for phrasing them."[14] Lyotard's "responsibility before thought" sets out the task of the critical philosopher. Critical philosophy is first and foremost the art of marking the silences and exteriority that inhabit language. It is the impossible (and paradoxical) art of signifying what is not spoken.[15] In this the work of the critical philosopher embraces the realm of art;[16] moves toward an avant-garde that constitutes itself by and within the question "What is thinking?" Lyotard uses the question "What is thinking?" to distinguish the philosopher from the intellectual whose responsibility, he argues, lies with the people.[17] He is keen to parallel the situation of the philosopher more closely with that of the avant-garde artist.

> A postmodern artist or writer is in the situation of a philosopher: the text he writes, the work he produces are not in principle governed by preestablished rules, and they cannot be judged according to a deter-mining judgement, by applying familiar categories to the text or to the work.[18]

Lyotard's work provides us with a sophisticated and intricate elaboration of what silence is. It allows us to broaden the parameters of our inquiry into questions of speaking and voice by raising the possibility of new idioms, new spaces in which *women* might speak. While Lyotard's project is certainly not focused on the issue of woman's voice in philosophy I would want to argue that it nonetheless opens up conceptual spaces in which this question can be addressed. In the following section I shall explore the possibility of using Lyotard's work in this way.

Figuring woman: the idiom of sexual difference?

In Bill Readings' book on Lyotard he writes:

> The question for this book is not what to say *about* Lyotard, then, but what to say *after* Lyotard. What phrase to link to Lyotard? ... Rather than an account, Lyotard demands from us a *performance*, a *work* ... After Lyotard, it will not be a question of applying Lyotard.[19]

I think this is a good way to introduce the rest of this chapter because, given what Lyotard has to say about linking, it is important to imagine new ways to link on to his philosophy of phrases. It seems to me that one way we might go about this is to link the question of gender, specifically the question of sexual difference and the *différend*, on to Lyotard's discussion of genre. To my mind this move avoids merely "applying" Lyotard because it demonstrates, as we shall see, a silence enacted by Lyotard's own work.

The question of silence can be used to raise the difficult issue of a feminine *différend*. When asked in an interview whether he thinks there is a feminine *différend*, Lyotard has the following to say. Georges Van Den Abbeele begins "Is there a specifically feminine *différend*, an unlitigatable 'injustice' done to women? In what ways might your work be of interest to (or at odds with) feminism?"[20] Lyotard's response circles the question (an unsettling trajectory, somewhat in the manner of the guerrilla raids he elsewhere champions).[21] He begins by pointing out that "not all oppressions signal *différends*", for oppression can involve litigation, and *différends* need not "give rise to oppression". (The fact that not all oppressions are *différends* is an important one, and I shall return to it later.) Lyotard follows (links) this with a question as to whether the feminine idiom is "untranslatable into the masculine idiom to the same extent that the tragic idiom does not translate into the elegiac nor the mathematic into the epic nor the speculative into the cognitive?" Now the question Lyotard is posing here is whether the masculine and feminine represent different genres. He goes on to suggest that it is this question that motivates a great deal of Freud's work. Freud, he argues, attempts "to delineate a feminine idiom irreducible to the masculine".[22] For Freud the feminine does in fact constitute a genre of its own. And yet, at the same time, he indicates the bisexuality of men and women, implying a continuity between them rather than a sharp generic division.

Lyotard's brief discussion of Freud is an attempt to convey the incoherence of the question Van Den Abbeele has posed. By mobilising Freud in this manner, Lyotard is able to make the distinction between the signifiers *feminine* and *women*. Van Den Abbeele elides the signifiers femininity and women (with feminism), suggesting that one term can substitute unproblematically for the other. Lyotard refuses this gesture. He goes on to say that bisexuality allows for the modes of both masculinity and femininity, i.e. that prior to an interdiction forbidding this particular musical score, masculinity and femininity exist as possibilities for both men and women. He concludes by suggesting that it is in between these modes, of masculinity and femininity, that incommensurability (a *différend*) exists, not between the entities man and woman. It would seem that femininity is a genre, though woman is not. Lyotard demonstrates this point with his final comment: "after reflecting upon it for a moment, I can count many texts relative to the question man/woman from *Discourse, figure* up to a text on Valerio Adami, 'On dirait qu'une ligne ...' (1983), which is *my most feminine text*, I believe."[23]

On his own account Lyotard's *feminine* text would seem to demonstrate the bisexuality of man and woman (or at the very least, of man). Now what are we to make of all this? Can we really use Lyotard's work on silence, the *différend*, to pursue the question of woman's silence in philosophy? At this stage, it would seem that Lyotard's discussion provides a way of thinking about femininity as a *différend*, though not of women. I am not certain if we are to think of femininity as either another term for the *différend*, or that which is silenced

as a result of the *différend*. In one of his earlier pieces, a work written well
before *The Différend*, I think that perhaps Lyotard does provide us with a way
of thinking about woman's silence in philosophy in terms of a potential *différend*.
This piece, "One of the Things at Stake in Women's Struggles", is not about
the *différend*. Here Lyotard makes no reference, major or minor, to it. And yet
it arguably provides the premiss for what he will later introduce as the *différend*.
Here he argues that what is at stake in women's struggles is nothing less than
the destruction of metalanguages. He depicts philosophy as a masculine metalanguage which silences the voices and bodies of women (pp. 118–19). For
Lyotard the masculine metalanguage of philosophy is problematic in that it is
a language that both constitutes femininity and sits in judgement on (by
ignoring) that femininity. It is the supreme court allowing no rival idiom to
speak against its wrongs.

> The language spoken there claims to *constitute* society in its entirety
> … Inasmuch as this discourse concerns femininity (it happens that
> femininity is forgotten), femininity is already constituted, or remains
> to be constituted, as one part of the *corpus sociandum* or even as its
> symbol: passivity.
>
> (p. 119)

Lyotard comes close, here, to articulating something like Le Doeuff's beliefs
about femininity as (at least partially) constituted by a masculine reason. He
goes on to speak of the relation, we might think of this in terms of the masculine imaginary, between political phallocracy and philosophical metalanguage.

> The complicity between political phallocracy and philosophical meta-
> language is made [at the border between empirical women and the
> transcendental order of philosophy that gives her meaning]: the ac-
> tivity men reserve for themselves arbitrarily as *fact* is posited legally
> as the *right* to decide meaning. The social groups of distributors, that
> is, citizens, becomes confused with the principle that there is some-
> thing like distributive reason, matter upon which this reason is in-
> scribed or written, and that there is a distinction between matter and
> reason.
>
> (p. 119)

Perhaps this "right to decide meaning" signals a *différend* wherein women are
reduced, by distributive reason, to the silence of matter. We could argue that
there is no idiom, recognised by philosophical metalanguage, in which women
may speak. As a consequence they may suffer by becoming the foundation of
the social/political body without being recognized as legitimately part of it.
The masculine imaginary imposes meaning (by edict?) onto women's bodies
and denies them any (possible) meanings of their own.

74

However, before judging whether the oppression registered here does signal a *différend* I should like to look at another piece by Lyotard where he analyses philosophy as a genre. In "Analysing Speculative Discourse as Language-Game" Lyotard positions Hegel's speculative discourse as an object-language in order to comment on it.[24] He begins by suggesting that his own analysis is guided by an *interference* between Hegel's discourse (which states what speculative language ought to be), and his own attempts to determine its generic rules (p. 265). This piece belongs to a time before *The Différend*, a time that seems to be ordered by Lyotard's desire to do two (related) things: to analyse philosophy's attempts to establish its own foundations, and to define philosophy's generic conditions, i.e. to speak about philosophy (speculative discourse) as a genre. Having first defined its generic status, Lyotard will later, in *The Différend*, go on to talk about what an alternative philosophical genre, modelled on ethics rather than metaphysics, should do, i.e. the ethical imperative of identifying *différends*.

So, what is it that Lyotard has to say about the genre of philosophy (speculative discourse)? He asks what the rules of speculative discourse amount to. "What prescriptions must the statements of this discourse or a sequence of such statements obey in order to be speculative statements?" (p. 267). He suggests that in Hegel we find that a constitutive rule of speculation entails the safeguarding of equivocalities: "a natural language is in Hegel's eyes the more inhabited by 'a speculative spirit' the more terms it has the significations of which are opposed" (p. 269). By equivocality he means something like the ability to derive meanings from discourse which appear to be in opposition to what that discourse seems to mean. Lyotard talks about the group of rules of equivocality which are "marked at once by the precession and recession of meaning" (p. 266). These include both the duplicity of meanings and their unification. Speculative discourse is structured by this equivocality. Speculative discourse is also a discourse on discourses, a specific attempt to say the truth. Philosophy thus establishes itself, constitutes itself, according to specific generic rules. It develops a metalanguage which speaks about its object-languages in such a way as to position itself as the discourse on discourse, the truth on truth. There are three rules that Lyotard identifies in Hegel's *Logic* which support this metalinguistic pretension. These include: the rule of equivocality, the rule of immanent derivation and the rule of expression (p. 271).

If we read Lyotard's comments about the generic rules governing philosophy along with his earlier statements from "One of the Things at Stake in Women's Struggles", we can see that he provides us with an analysis of how philosophy (whether it be as speculative discourse or metalanguage)[25] locates itself on the terrain of discursive authority or transcendent truth. It is a discourse that obeys certain generic rules and one, he reminds us, that "is already the language of masculinity."[26] Philosophy is the genre of truth, or more specifically, the genre of masculine truth. It is a metalanguage that works in complicity with political phallocracy.

Again, what are we to make of this? Do the generic rules governing philosophy as a masculine discourse signal a *différend* in relation to either femininity or women? I think that in Lyotard's own terms we can argue that femininity suffers a radical silence in relation to metalanguage because it lies beyond this genre of masculine privilege. Either it constitutes a genre of its own and therefore cannot be translated by philosophy, or else it counts as non-discursive, i.e. it does not speak as such. Lyotard offers us ways of positioning "femininity" as that which philosophy silences. This is not so clearly the case, however, when it comes to "women". Arguing, with Lyotard, that women are silenced in this way is more difficult. Nonetheless this is what I intend to do.

In the early piece, "One of the Things at Stake in Women's Struggles", it sounds, if one reads backwards from *The Différend*, as if women (not just femininity) do in fact suffer the pain of radical silence. Here Lyotard speaks of "woman", of "women", and even of "empirical women". And yet, by the time we come to the "Interview", we find a Lyotard who is hesitant to speak on anything other than femininity, and especially, it must be noted, the femininity of the (bisexual) male writer. Keeping this in mind I want to return to *The Différend*, to Lyotard's description of the victim's dilemma, the paradoxical logic that makes it impossible for the victim to be heard. A lengthy quote, resonating with passages I have previously quoted from Irigaray and Woolf, captures the victim's (impossible) trial.[27]

> It is in the nature of a victim not to be able to prove that one has been done a wrong. A plaintiff is someone who has incurred damages and who disposes of the means to prove it. One becomes a victim if one loses these means. One loses them, for example, if the author of the damages turns out directly or indirectly to be one's judge. The latter has the authority to reject one's testimony as false or the ability to impede its publication. But this is only a particular case. In general, the plaintiff becomes a victim when no presentation is possible of the wrong he or she says he or she has suffered. Reciprocally, *the "perfect crime" does not consist in killing the victim or the witnesses (that adds new crimes to the first one and aggravates the difficulty of effacing everything), but rather in obtaining the silence of the witnesses, the deafness of the judges, and the inconsistency (insanity) of the testimony.* You neutralize the addressor, the addressee and the sense of the testimony; then everything is as if there were no referent (no damages). If there is nobody to adduce the proof, nobody to admit it, and/or if the argument which upholds it is judged to be absurd, then the plaintiff is dismissed, the wrong he or she complains of cannot be attested. He or she becomes a victim. If he or she persists in invoking this wrong as if it existed, the others (addressor, addressee, expert commentator on the testimony) will easily be able to make him or her pass for mad.
>
> (p. 8 emphasis added)

76

In this passage Lyotard alerts us to the ways that silence may be imposed. We are not primarily concerned here with overt strategies that actually kill off or exclude women. We are more concerned with those that silence in less obvious ways. There are still two questions that remain to be addressed. Firstly, are we to conclude that women suffer a silence we can name a *différend*? What is at stake in calling women's silence a *différend*? And secondly, what is it that Lyotard is doing when he shifts terrain away from a discussion of women toward a discussion of femininity? What is it that his feminine texts signify?

Let us begin with the first of these questions. Is the silence that women suffer in relation to philosophy, the silence that we have been investigating throughout this book, the kind of radical silence that Lyotard argues is marked by a *différend*? As we have seen, to suggest this is also to suggest that women and women's discourse constitute a genre separate from the masculine genre of philosophy because the *différend* is essentially a question about the relationship of genres. If we think back to our discussion in chapter one, we could say that Le Doeuff and Irigaray have different answers to this question. I should preface this by saying that neither Le Doeuff nor Irigaray work with the same definition of genre as Lyotard or, for that matter, each other, so it is impossible to simply compare them on this point. Le Doeuff's discussion of philosophy as a corporation allows us, however, momentarily to shift Lyotard's preoccupation with genre sideways. She argues that far from constituting a separate realm, women actually exist *within* rationality. Her political project amounts to loosening the corporate rules of rationality so as to allow women (and others) to speak from, rather than merely be, that place. Now Le Doeuff is working with a sociological rather than generic definition of philosophy here; nonetheless I think that the hegemony of reason that she criticises can be thought of in terms of a series of generic conditions that restrict women (and others) from speaking. I want to argue, however, that Le Doeuff is talking about *modifying* the genre (or genres) of rational discourse so as to allow women to be heard. This implies that women's discourse (whatever that might be) does not constitute a genre separate and distinct from philosophy. Certainly it is silenced within this realm, but not to the point of marking the kind of radical silence that, in Lyotard's terms, constitutes a *différend*.

Luce Irigaray: genre and sexual difference

Luce Irigaray's work suggests that women's speech (not just femininity) constitutes a kind distinct from philosophy.[28] She argues that the (generic) rules governing philosophy are unity, sameness, oneness. This privileging of unity over and against plurality closes off philosophy, and phallocentric discourse in general, from the possibility of other genres, ones that would open language to the heterogeneity of meaning and sense. Irigaray talks about the violence women suffer when their bodies are unable to speak other than in a masculine discourse that brutally censors their pleasure and desire. She speaks of the crises women suffer in relation to this mute desire and argues that because of this women are exiled in a language that is not their own.

Although Irigaray's work cannot be defined by Lyotard's project of marking *différends* I think that there are points at which their various concerns converge. I want to explore these by looking at what Irigaray has to say about genre and sexual difference. Throughout the 1970s and 1980s Irigaray has been preoccupied by an ethical concern with sexual difference. Like Lyotard she stresses the ethical requirements and responsibilities of the philosopher, adding that we are obliged to think the question of sexual difference as the ethical question of our time.

> Sexual difference is one of the important questions of our age, if not in fact the burning issue. According to Heidegger, each age is preoccupied with one thing, and one alone. Sexual difference is probably that issue in our own age which could be our salvation on an intellectual level.[29]

Both Irigaray and Lyotard agree that the philosopher is obliged to question the silence imposed by a certain philosophical rationality. Both argue that it is the philosopher's task, not only to question and identify this silence, but more importantly, to find new idioms in which this silence may be spoken. Irigaray's ethical concerns diverge from Lyotard's, however, in their insistence on the question of sexual specificity. She is concerned to show that the question of silence cannot be thought in isolation from the question of sexual difference. For her, ethical obligation is the marking of this difference.

We need to ask what it means when Irigaray speaks of women as a genre for *genre* here does not have the same meaning as it does for Lyotard. For Irigaray genre is an "index and mark of *subjectivity*", tied up with the "ethical responsibility of the speaker".[30] Irigaray's discussion of genre is positioned within her larger concern with what she calls the sexuate dimension of discourse, i.e. the ways in which the masculine sex subordinates the other (women, the feminine, the world) through syntactic laws of dominance. She is concerned to show that the generation of language is not a neutral affair, but is rather sexuate. "Man gives his *genre* to the universe, just as he wants to give his name to his children and his property. Anything which seems valuable to him must belong to his *genre*. The feminine is a secondary mark, always subordinated to the principal genre."[31] When Irigaray says that there are two genres she means that there are two sexual kinds. Men and women constitute a primary and irreducible division, i.e. they are separate and distinct. Genre is, for Irigaray, fundamentally a sexuate category obliging us to think of sexual difference in ethical terms. She argues that by remaining indifferent to the sexuate dimension of discourse we perpetuate a logic and rationality that silences by domination.

The human race is divided into *two genres* which ensure its production and reproduction. Trying to suppress sexual difference is to invite a genocide more radical than any destruction that has ever existed in History. What is important, on the other hand, is defining the values of belonging to a sex-specific *genre*. What is indispensable is elaborating a culture of the sexual which does not yet exist, whilst respecting both *genres*.[32]

Irigaray's notion of genre is based on the use of this term to denote a set of concerns that ranges from the inscription of subjectivity in/by grammatical gender to the division of human society into two kinds. Clearly she is working with a very different understanding of genre than Lyotard. It is fair to say that notwithstanding the use of the term "genre" in her work, Irigaray's concerns do not lie with genre in the sense of "discursive kind".[33] This means that her work does not directly address Lyotard's problematic. There is no simple sense in which we can translate from one to the other. There is a fundamental incommensurability between their terms and yet Irigaray's insistence on sexual difference potentially opens Lyotard's work on genre to what it silences, women. Lyotard's discussion of philosophy as a genre provides us with an invaluable way of thinking about our ethical duties in relation to what is silenced, and yet it works to silence, in an unconscious way, the very sexual difference that Irigaray demands we address. We could say that in obliging us to think the question of sexual difference she responds to Lyotard's insistence on genre with an equal insistence on gender. I think that it is imperative that we make these two questions occupy the same space, for the point of their convergence is, I believe, the conceptual terrain of women's silence.

It seems to me that this raises the rather complex question of how we might begin to articulate the projects that Lyotard and Irigaray are each involved with. We could argue, going back to Van Den Abbeele's question to Lyotard regarding a specifically feminine *différend*, that he attempts to position sexual difference *within* the scope of Lyotard's problematic. By introducing Irigaray's discussion of genre and sexual difference I am strategically attempting to reverse this move. I am exploring the possibility of situating Lyotard's *différend* within the scope of the general problematic of sexual difference. Whether this move is legitimate is indeed a strategic question for any feminist "use" of Lyotard's work. And indeed the question of use is itself contentious here. Does "use" here imply something other than simply applying? (I refer back to Readings' call for a performative relation to Lyotard's work.) I think that Irigaray's work on the sexuate dimension of language shows how it does.

Irigaray attempts to uncover the sexual dynamics at work in the utterance [*énonciation*], i.e. she interprets its sexuation in order to change it. This desire to change the sexuate dimension of discourse is premised on the belief that the rules governing discursive structure privilege a monosexual economy. One sex (men, masculinity) is privileged as a principal mark or "genre". The other sex (women, femininity) remains mute, a secondary mark subordinate to this principal.[34] The privileged position of men within this structure is evidenced in their tendency to assume the "I" in discourse, what Margaret Whitford refers to as "the closed universe of the first-person pronoun";[35] the position of self-affirmation and foundation that tends to silence that other sex, women. Their reluctance to assume the "I" marks women as other, forcing them to appeal to an interlocutor for linguistic validation. According to Irigaray, women more readily address themselves to a "you", to a linguistically determined subject that confers upon them their (secondary) existence.

Irigaray proposes an upheaval of this sexuate relation, one that would permit women to enter discourse as a "genre", distinct and separate from men. Only then, she argues, would we begin to think through the possibilities of sexual difference. At present "we have no positive and ethical values that allow two sexes of the same generation to form a creative, and not simply procreative, human couple".[36] The dominance of men over women means that we have no positive and ethical values that affirm women and femininity in socially just ways. Women remain silenced in a discourse that permits nothing of their sexual specificity to be said. "Equality between men and women cannot be achieved unless we *think of genre as sexuate [sexué]* and write the rights and duties of each sex, insofar as they are *different*, into social rights and duties."[37]

Irigaray's call for an ethics of sexual difference involves two related approaches, each important for establishing "different norms of life"; firstly, as we have already seen, the analysis and interpretation of discursive structures, and secondly, the creation of new writing styles. Her analysis obliges us to transform the speaking position of the subject in language. She suggests that in order to establish this we must refuse the phallocentric gesture of a self-founding (metaphysical) I. "The transformation of the autobiographical *I* into another cultural *I* seems to be necessary if we are to establish a new ethics of sexual difference."[38] Irigaray urges us to expand our linguistic possibilities. For her part this entails a new style (or idiom?) that refuses the existing structures of either narrative or commentary. Of her *Ethique de la différence sexuelle*, for example, she writes that

> There is no basic narrative and no possible commentaries by others, in the sense of an exhaustive deciphering of the text. What is said in this book is conveyed by a double style: a style of amorous relations, a style of thought, exposition, writing. Consciously or unconsciously, the two are connected; on the one hand, there is a more immediately corporeal and affective side and, on the other, a more socially elaborated side.[39]

Irigaray's call for new styles, new idioms, is a call for a new language which necessarily involves the creation of what she calls a sexuate culture, a culture in which men and women are acknowledged as sexually different "genres". Her attempts to find new styles in which to inscribe this difference inaugurates a similarly new way of reading, one that allows for the censured realms of perception, feeling and love.[40] This erotics of reading and writing ushers in a new era of philosophical investigation, new possibilities, and styles that seek to speak the hitherto silenced realms of woman's sexual being. In this her project shares with Lyotard a committed vision of the philosopher ethically engaged in creating new idioms in which to voice the silence of the *différend*.

I think that Irigaray does understand women's silence as a radical silence, and that given this it is plausible to suggest that her work is motivated by the ethical gesture of marking what Lyotard specifically refers to as *différends*. My case for reading Irigaray's discussion of women in philosophy as a contribution to our understanding of the *différend* is strengthened by the emphasis she places throughout her work on sentiment and feeling. It seems to me that Irigaray's project is very much concerned with identifying and attempting to provide new idioms for the *différends* marked by these feelings.

Women and silence: différend

I want to suggest that Le Doeuff and Irigaray have the following relationship to Lyotard's *différend*. Because they both position women as central or foundational to philosophy, they both imply that women are insiders (if indeed mute) to its domain. Indeed they are its domain. However, having established this Irigaray goes on to argue that women are radically silenced as domain, as place and possibility of philosophy. She recognises that women mark the silent, non-discursive space upon which the masculine genre erects its own governing body. From this place it rules, governs and judges in accordance with its own desire. So women's speech needs to be invented as a genre. In Le Doeuff's case the argument follows a different logic. Having established woman's status as internal enemy, she goes on to argue that generically speaking women occupy the same terrain, that they are inside, rather than alien to, the genres of rationality. Indeed there are prohibitions and difficulties that arise when women attempt to speak, but in accordance with the governing rules of rationality these prohibitions must be addressed for they actually constitute transgressions of rational discourse. There is no *différend* in Le Doeuff's account because reason stands as a legitimate judge in this dispute. There is of course a litigation, perhaps even a case for an exacerbated litigation, but certainly not a *différend*.[41]

In Le Doeuff's account we could say that it is unproductive to name woman's silence a *différend* because she conceives of no tribunal, other than reason, equal to the task of settling any such dispute. To speak outside the genre of reason is not to speak at all, at least not philosophically. For Irigaray, the situation is different. If we are to think about her project in Lyotard's terms we could say that in her account the consequences of naming woman's silence a *différend* would amount to the ethical gesture of identifying a wrong. By marking the radical silence of women's suffering as a *différend* the way is opened for new linkages, new idioms to express the suffering of sentiment. For Irigaray rationality is a masculine genre, a phallocentric genre that has imposed its laws and judgement upon the bodies of women.

Perhaps the question comes down to this. If we believe that philosophy is generically defined (and confined) by the privileged logic of rationality, then women have the option either to accept this and attempt to speak within the rules and conventions governing this genre (i.e. in masculine discourse) or else to speak elsewhere, to speak in genres less hostile to their sex. If philosophy is more than this, and I have a great stake in believing it to be so, then women must find ways of opening it out to other logics, other possible ways of inscribing desire. Lyotard reminds us that philosophy should be more than a discourse in search of its own foundations, that it is obliged to be involved in the marking of *différends* and the searching for new linkages and idioms to speak those *différends*.

In saying this Lyotard offers an alternative way of thinking about the status of philosophy. In chapter one I outlined a kind of impasse between Irigaray and Le Doeuff concerning philosophy's privilege. Le Doeuff attempts to deflate philosophy's claims, arguing that we need to resist a hegemonic form of rationality in favour of philosophical work that abandons its desire for a self-foundational totality. Irigaray, on the other hand, tends to accept the privileged position philosophy accords itself, depicting it as the discourse on discourse. Lyotard's discussion of the ethical priority of philosophy offers us a way beyond this impasse by simultaneously accepting and dismantling philosophy's privileged position. He argues that while we cannot stop metaphysics from assuming its inflated position (given its generic construction as "prima philosophia") by simply wishing it, that we can make it face its obligations given this position. The special status of philosophy carries with it equally special obligations. In *The Différend* he suggests that this special obligation necessitates philosophy turning toward ethics as its defining genre.

Lyotard's call to phrasing is an injunction urging philosophy to identify the *différend*. Philosophy is a critical activity, and in this it goes beyond the generic constraints of rationality narrowly defined. It is a critical activity that bears with it the weight of judgement. As philosophers we must seek out the *différend*, judge what is and is not a *différend* if we are "to save the honour of thinking".[42] But if Lyotard's work is about the injustice of judgement, then how are we to judge in a manner that remains just? Geoffrey Bennington, taking his cue from Lyotard, poses the question this way: "But what happens when the judgement that judgement is what we must do is *itself* up for judgement?"[43] How, then, are we to judge Lyotard's judgement that philosophy is obliged to judge? How are we to understand and appreciate the ethical imperative associated with the *différend*?

In order to avoid the closure that might accompany any immediate response to this question, I shall instead conclude with a brief look at the second of our questions, the significance of the shift from *women* to *femininity* and Lyotard's "feminine" texts. I have argued that Lyotard provides us with a way of thinking about femininity as an incommensurable genre in relation to masculinity. His discussion of bisexuality as the suffering or injured party carries on from this to suggest that men and women have the potential to speak both genres, but that this potential is silenced by the injustice of "an interdiction … passed forbidding the latter from assuming their virility, and the former from fulfilling their femininity."[44] So there does seem to be the possibility of a feminine *différend* when masculinity speaks, not just as one genre amongst many, but as the genre of privilege. But there does not seem to be any place for women's silence to register as a *différend*. I am worried about the silencing of women's silence here in favour of a feminine silence, for, as Lyotard himself goes on to show, it is all too easy for femininity to be severed from any connection (linguistic or otherwise) from women. All too quickly it becomes bisexuality that suffers, not women. And this bisexuality, again all too quickly, becomes the province of male writers. Lyotard alerts us to this when he speaks of the need for alternative strategies, i.e. for new idioms such as "theory-fiction" to counter the masculine imperialism of theory: "let us propose this as a kind of theory-fiction. Let us set to work forging fictions rather than hypotheses and theories; *this would be the best way for the speaker to become 'feminine'* "(emphasis added).[45] Does this (Deleuzean) *becoming feminine* announce the possibility of new idioms in which women may speak? Or does it signal yet another appropriation, another *différend*, wherein women remain spoken for? I suspect that Lyotard's *feminine texts* say it all.[46]

Nonetheless I think that Lyotard's *différend* is a useful way of thinking about the silencing of women in philosophy. In the preceding chapters of this book I have argued that women do suffer from something we might now call a *différend*, in that they suffer the pain of silence at the hands of philosophical discourse. More specifically, we can say that there is an injustice, a wrong, inflicted on women by philosophy, a wrong that women do not have the means to speak without becoming embroiled in logical contradiction. Women suffer as mute victims of a discourse that establishes itself at their expense, at the expense of their bodies and their voices. It wrongs them by appropriating their bodies as the silent foundation of their enterprise, by speaking from and for them. Do women have the means to speak this suffering?

Up to this point I have concentrated on identifying the means by which women have been silenced by philosophy. In this I have largely constructed woman as the passive object of silence, the mute body dominated by the masculine imaginary in order to develop a kind of *psychoanalysis of the silenced body*, a symptomatic reading of woman as she erupts in masculine discourse. While I believe that this is an important gesture, indeed a necessary one, I am nonetheless a little uneasy with remaining on such terrain, for this is very much the terrain of the silencer, not the silenced. Lyotard's *différend* has been helpful in that it has given us another way to look at silence, one that re-positions our focus back on philosophical terrain. His ethical imperative allows us to raise the question of silence as a question for philosophy. His recommendation that we invent new idioms shares something with Irigaray's call for a more sensuous and ethical speech, even though it does not recognise the importance of sexual specificity in this account. While this account of silence is clearly of strategic importance for our investigation of woman's voice in philosophy, it is not in itself enough. We need to move beyond this in order to raise the possibility of a more complex notion of silence, perhaps one that speaks. In the next chapter I intend to do just this by shifting away from the silencing gesture of the masculine imaginary, toward something else. I shall introduce Julia Kristeva's work on unquiet silence because I believe it provides us with a way of thinking about silence as something more than the opposite of speech. In this sense *silence* operates here as a bridge, a passage, or hinge (perhaps we could say a new linkage) between at least two kinds of silence. It indicates the possibility of thinking about what silence itself covers over. This operative silence as passage allows us to shift terrain back and forth between reading the silenced body through psychosis and the obligation to speak that silence. Silence comes, in this sense, from the dynamic between these two terrains. In speaking this we engender an alternative linkage making new idioms possible.

5

UNQUIET SILENCE

Kristeva reading Marx with Freud

I rather wish to look at the difference between the types of signifying production prior to the product (value): oriental philosophies have attempted to tackle this from the point of view of work prior to communication.[1]

It is arguably possible to take up the challenge Lyotard offers us, that of finding new idioms in which to speak silence, without questioning the dichotomy of language/silence as such. In this chapter I shall look at the way Julia Kristeva deals with this question by introducing her work on non-productive language. Because Kristeva's discussion is situated in the context of her synthesis of Marx and Freud, I shall begin by looking at the debates that surround Marx's work on production. This serves a number of purposes as it also allows me to draw some links between the productive logic of patriarchal society and masculine phantasies of self-birth. I shall therefore be arguing two (related) things: firstly, that this productive mentality serves to silence the maternal in quite specific ways, and secondly, that Kristeva's discussion of non-productive language practice offers us an alternative to the language/silence opposition, one that makes it necessary to reconsider what silence is.

Reading Marx: production and (masculine) self-production

Labour is man's coming-to-be for himself ... the self-creation and self-objectification [of man].[2]

Some of our most fundamental contemporary ideas about production and labour have been influenced by the work of Karl Marx. Indeed it is difficult to think about productive labour without returning to his ideas. Marx's philosophy links productivity with the attributes of masculinity and virility. I shall investigate these connections in order to illuminate the masculine phantasy of self-genesis that I have discussed in the earlier chapters.

There is a considerable body of Marx's work devoted to the glorification of production (or labour) as a transformative activity. In the *Grundrisse* he writes that: "All production is appropriation of nature on the part of an individual within and through a specific form of society."[3] Indeed production is Marx's theoretical point of departure. In *The German Ideology*, written with Frederick Engels, he argues that: "The first historical act is thus the production of material life itself."[4] Marx refers to the active relationship that develops between the individual (in society) and the external world as *productive life*. He writes that: "It is life creating life."[5] For Marx labour involves man's active self-genesis. It is:

> a process in which both man and nature participate, and in which man of his own accord starts, regulates, and controls the material reactions between himself and nature. He opposes himself to nature as one of her own forces, setting in motion arms and legs, head and hands, the natural forces of his body, in order to appropriate nature's productions in a form adapted to his wants. By thus acting on the external world and changing it, he at the same time changes his own nature.[6]

Labour plays a privileged role in Marx's philosophy because it mediates between man and nature. He speaks of the productive relation that alters both man and his external world as a process that involves man actively fashioning himself, as a self-creation. Man defines himself in his struggle with nature. For Marx history is nothing other than "the creation of man by human labor, and the emergence of nature for man", which gives him "the evident and irrefutable proof of his self-creation, of his own origins."[7] Man sees himself in the products of his labour, he recognises himself in them.[8] But this recognition involves struggle; a struggle from which man emerges as powerful and manipulative.[9]

The productive orientation in Marx's work foregrounds a virile productivity that identifies itself against a passive receptivity.[10] This conceptual elision between productivity and virility forces us to confront the problematic side of man's transformative activity. Productive labour is necessarily implicated in the dominating impulse which transforms and appropriates nature (as external other) in the form of products. It subordinates both nature and the body to the superiority of a creative consciousness, and in so doing enables the *cogito* to pursue what we may call its reign of terror.[11] Here the *cogito* divorces itself from the world of extended matter. It establishes a distance from nature (the external world), setting itself against what it then depicts as a hostile and alien exteriority. By attempting to conquer the irrationality of what remains external, the *cogito* proceeds to domesticate and dominate what escapes it.[12] Man's self-recognition is closely tied to this activity. Indeed we could say that it is dependent upon it. This self-recognition is also tied up, in Marx's philosophy, with the phantasy of self-genesis. There are numerous allusions to birth in Marx's work. We can read these as inscriptions of a masculine imaginary, using Le Doeuff's arguments about philosophy and its metaphors as our guide.

Marx: the language of birth

Linda Nicholson provides us with a useful discussion of the various meanings of production in Marx's texts along with a feminist analysis of their consequences for women's labour.[13] She suggests that a certain ambiguity pervades Marx's use of the term *production*, that he moves from a broad to a narrow definition of the term.

> In effect, Marx has eliminated from his theoretical focus all activities basic to human survival which fall outside of a capitalist "economy". Those activities he has eliminated include not only those identified by feminists as "reproductive" (childcare, nursing) but also those concerned with social organization, i.e. those regulating kinship relations or in modern societies those we would classify as "political".
>
> (p. 18)

She goes on to say that production can refer, broadly, to activities that have consequences, or, more narrowly, to activities resulting in objects, or, more specifically still, to activities resulting in commodities, i.e. objects that can be bought and sold. Marx is rarely specific about his own use of the term. However Nicholson argues that Marx more readily relies on narrow definitions of production, ones concerned with the making of food and objects. As a consequence this eliminates historical considerations of changes in the structure and organisation of childbearing and rearing (p. 24).

If we look to Marx's texts we find that he describes productive life as an active relationship with nature; a form of mastery in which man fashions both himself and the world around him.[14] He writes: "Labour is *man's coming-to-be for himself* within *externalization* or as externalized man ... [that is] the self creation, and self-objectification [of man]."[15] And further: "The *whole of what is called world history* is nothing but the creation of man by human labour, and the emergence of nature for man; he therefore has the evident and irrefutable proof of his *self-creation*, of his own origins."[16] Marx seems to be arguing here that in the process of giving birth to himself, man also gives birth to history. For Marx history is this process of man's birth through labour. Marx appropriates the language of birth in order to give meaning to man's obsessive desire to re-create himself. He speaks of new forms of production emerging from the "womb of bourgeois society"; of men as "producers of their own conceptions"; of force as "the midwife of every old society pregnant with new one."[17] He states repeatedly that men give birth to themselves in the process of history. They are, at one and the same time, "the authors and actors of their history."[18] The assumption is that in making his history, man makes himself.[19] Through productive labour man gives birth to himself, to history and to culture. In the first instance he reproduces himself biologically or physiologically, while in the second he reproduces himself culturally, giving birth to what he calls his second nature. It is through history that man realises this second birth and fashions his second nature.

Erich Fromm argues that Marx's understanding of second nature is tied to man's productive orientation. This involves man experiencing himself as the embodiment of creativity. By giving birth to his second nature man repeatedly gives birth to himself. Fromm writes: "While it is true that man's productiveness can create material things, works of art, and systems of thought, by far the most important object of productiveness is man himself."[20] Of course it is significant that man gives birth to himself (as object), but Fromm goes on to argue that man's intellectual or cultural birth is the true test of his productivity.

> Birth is only one particular step in a continuum which begins with conception and ends with death. All that is between these two poles is a process of giving birth to one's potentialities ... It requires productive activity to give life to the emotional and intellectual potentialities of man, to give birth to his self.[21]

Fromm's discussion of this Marxian world view forecloses the maternal body in order to emphasise second nature. He argues that birth is "only one particular step", and that physical growth "proceeds by itself" (ibid.). He evacuates the role of the maternal body in both birth and nurturance. This foreclosure is notable throughout Fromm's book and is perhaps best captured in its title, *Man For Himself*.

Marx's discussion of productive man is situated within his wider theory of the genesis of social relations. He argues that historically advanced societies emerge from the womb of their predecessors: "higher relations of production never appear before the material conditions of their existence have *matured in the womb* of the old society itself."[22] Capitalist society is the most developed and complex historic organisation of production, and Marx argues that it contains within itself "the structure and the relations of production of all the vanished social formations."[23] He adds that it constitutes the last antagonistic form of social relations, and that a new social formation will emerge from it: "the productive forces developing in *the womb of bourgeois society* create the material conditions for the solution of that antagonism."[24] Marx's appropriation of the reproductive metaphor is instructive, because it goes hand in hand with a world view that positions *man* as the centre of all things. In Marx's philosophy it is social intercourse between men that spawns new productive (social) relations. These relations are both public and cultural. From these, culture goes on to produce itself. Social formations give birth to themselves in a series of spiralling replications. Like Althusser's self-generating structures, this is a world that generates itself without reference to women or their bodies.

The self-generating man of Marx's world is often depicted in a rather hostile relation with nature. He writes that man "opposes himself to nature", that he "appropriates nature's productions in a form adapted to his wants."[25] Nature is the externalised other that must be acted upon, objectified. Marx's discussion of the relation between man and nature is complex. Even so I think that we can discern a recurring theme that suggests that man's productive role is tied with his ability to subdue nature. We must not over-look the significance of this gesture because it is relevant to our ongoing discussion of silencing. I want to argue that the desire to subdue nature links Marx's productive man with the masculine desire to silence the maternal body. Both desires are locked into an imaginary that appropriates the other in order to produce from its place. Marx's productive man brings these together. He is very much preoccupied with rivalling the reproductive capa-bilities of both woman and nature, and does this by acting on the external world in an intentional and productive way.

Baudrillard reading Marx

Jean Baudrillard is concerned with this productive mentality dominating Marx's thought. In his early work he criticises Marx for succumbing to the very logic Marx himself is attempting to subvert.[26] I have two reasons for wanting to discuss Baudrillard's concerns now: firstly, because he provides us with a con-troversial analysis of Marx's reliance on productive logic, and secondly, be-cause, although he does so, he remains himself somewhat caught within the very logic he is criticising. I shall begin by outlining Baudrillard's major criti-cisms of Marx's philosophy.

Baudrillard begins by saying that the spectre of production haunts all revo-lutionary thought and that we find it lurking beneath Marx's critique of the capitalist mode of production.[27] He refers to this as a contagion and elsewhere as a contamination.[28] Baudrillard is critical of the way Marx's metaphysics of production depicts the concept of labour as central to man's identity: "in this Marxism assists the cunning of capital. It convinces men that they are alien-ated by the sale of their labour power, thus censoring the much more radical hypothesis that they might be alienated as labour power".[29] According to Baudrillard Marx's philosophy fails to question the fundamental assumption of man's productive nature, and in this it shares common ground with ration-alist thought. While Marx may have shattered the fiction of *homo economicus*, the naturalisation of the market and its forms, he fails to challenge the more fundamental illusion of man as producer. Baudrillard writes: "Isn't this a simi-lar fiction ... a simulation model bound to code all human material and every contingency of desire and exchange in terms of value, finality, and produc-tion?"[30] In this sense production acts as a mirror reflecting the light of politi-cal economy upon the as yet unformed subject. Baudrillard plays with Lacan's notion here of the mirror stage arguing that man comes to consciousness through this (self)reflective operation. The mirror of production reflects the ideal of a productive ego.

> Everywhere man has learned to reflect on himself, to assume himself, to *posit himself* according to this scheme of production which is assigned to him as the ultimate dimension of value and meaning ... through this scheme of production, this *mirror* of production, the human species comes to consciousness [*la prise de conscience*] in the *imaginary*.[31]

Baudrillard contends that it is impossible for the subject to perceive itself outside the limits of a productive consciousness because it is caught within this infinite regress of mirroring. He argues that it is increasingly difficult to think outside the logic of production let alone to grasp that "the concept of production is itself produced."[32] Indeed he suggests that the whole conceptual edifice of historical materialism, production, productive forces, mode of production and infrastructure, are in fact historical products; "they are only the metalanguage of a Western culture (Marxist to be sure) that speaks from the height of its abstraction."[33] He states repeatedly that Marx raises the concepts of production and labour to the status of universal and unquestioned postulates, and argues that this ideological gesture superimposes the system of political economy over the entirety of history thus rendering production determinant. "It generalises the economic mode of rationality over the entire expanse of human history, as the generic mode of human becoming."[34] For Baudrillard the consequences are grave. By universalising productive logic Marx's philosophy involves itself in a conceptual imperialism that mimics bourgeois (or metaphysical) thought.[35] The elevation of production and labour to central categories of intelligibility inaugurates what Baudrillard refers to as the religion of meaning. It is no coincidence, he argues, that this process occurs at roughly the same time that Marxism establishes itself as scientific and objective truth. Engels' and Althusser's scientific canonisation of concepts, for example, confuses the realm of interpretation with that of repressive simulation. "They set themselves up as expressing an 'objective reality'. They become signs: signifiers of a 'real' signified ... This scientific and universalist discourse (code) immediately becomes imperialistic."[36]

For Baudrillard this religion of meaning exalts labour as a categorical imperative, thereby placing Marxism squarely within the idealist sanctification of labour. He argues that "labour loses its negativity and is raised to an absolute value."[37] Play is subsumed beneath a ruthless and productive mentality and is relegated to a place outside the rationality of political economy. Nature is unleashed as a productive power, thereby providing man with the (instrumental) means to identify himself as labour power. In the process both man and nature become subservient to the dominating rationality of productive logic. Nature becomes "the concept of a dominated essence ... Everything that invokes Nature invokes the domination of Nature."[38]

Baudrillard's work is highly critical of the Promethean vision that projects a future state of freedom brought about by the conscious and intentional domination of nature. He argues that this vision remains wholly within the logic of production because it sustains the separation between the all-powerful *cogito* and its external world. Baudrillard warns that it is imperative to move beyond this logic. He speaks of the necessity, however difficult, to think outside the restrictions of production, i.e. the endless self-reflections imposed by Western metaphysics. He argues that in the final instance the only truly revolutionary perspectives are those that shatter the false unity imposed by the mirror of production. In this sense revolutionary or subversive strategies are those "directed against the axiomatic of productive rationality itself."[39] Baudrillard concludes that Marx's work fails to sustain the radical nature of its own critique. By granting analytical primacy to production, it supports the Western tradition of rationality that manifests itself in a dominating imposition of human will. This productive rationality turns Marxism into "the dialectical apotheosis of political economy."[40] As a result Marxism practises what in theory it aims to demolish.

While Baudrillard's reading is useful for widening the parameters of our discussion of Marx's productive bias, I think that ultimately it fails to take on the ambivalence in Marx's work and thus reduces it to an unproblematic statement or utterance. Ironically, Baudrillard's reading of Marx repeats what it criticises in Marx, i.e. it reads Marx through the mirror of production. Baudrillard can read Marx only as a theorist who is wholly consumed by production. Everything is subsumed beneath the conceptual imperialism of production. This seems to be the case when Baudrillard overlooks a point in which Marx appears to be distancing himself from a straightforward sanctification of labour. He cites the following passage from Marx without commenting upon its disruptive potential. "In fact, the realm of freedom actually begins only where labour which is determined by necessity and mundane considerations ceases; thus in the very nature of things it lies beyond the sphere of actual material production."[41] I think that we can read against this tendency in Baudrillard to simplify and homogenise Marx, by identifying the moments when Marx's texts seem to exceed their own productive bias. Julia Kristeva attempts to do just this, and I suggest that by using her reading of Marx as a starting point we can read Marx in a much more (or less?) "productive" way.

Kristeva reading Marx

Kristeva's reading of Marx is instructive because it focuses on the question of production without reducing it to value. Her reading of what we might call Marx Beyond Marx contrasts sharply with Baudrillard's. Although both are critical of the dominating logic of productivity, it is Kristeva who finds passages in Marx's work gesturing beyond this. She argues that Marx's work foreshadows the possibility of theorising production without reference to the product. In this sense the *spectre* of Marx's philosophy exceeds this productive logic. There are clearly passages that valorise the link between labour and value within Marx's texts, and Kristeva's analysis makes no attempt to repress these. For instance, when Marx examines the laws of capital and exchange, Kristeva concedes that his analysis of production is positioned as determinant, and that it attains the status of value. She argues that while he distinguishes between use value and exchange value, Marx limits himself to a study of the latter. "Marxist analysis rests on *exchange value*, that is, on the circulating *product* of work that enters the capitalist system as value."[42] From the perspective of social consumption or communication work "*represents* nothing outside the value in which it is crystallized, and as such leads to a valorization of productive life."[43]

Yet Kristeva insists that Marx's texts provide an alternative understanding, one beyond considerations of value and circulation. While Marx fails to pursue this "other scene", she argues that his work offers signposts directing the attentive reader beyond productive logic. For example, he writes that "Quite apart from its usefulness, all productivity is ultimately an expenditure of human force."[44] In passages such as this Kristeva reads a productivity that "means nothing", one that "marks and transforms while remaining prior to all circular 'speech' " or communication. She argues that this suggests a powerful and shattering relation between the body and loss. "There, on a scene where work does not yet *represent* any value or *mean* anything, our concern is with the relation of a *body* to expenditure."[45] In these words we can hear the echo of Georges Bataille's voice, for Kristeva's concern with excess, expenditure and loss is heavily influenced by his work on non-productive expenditure.

This glimpse of production as an expenditure involves a process in which work and labour circulate beyond a system of exchange.[46] It is an undecidable production. Kristeva develops this alternative production by bringing together ideas from both Marx and Freud. Here she attempts to bridge the dual economies of social and psychic production, connecting the body to both work and expenditure (or play). She argues that when Marx offers the glimpse of an alternative consideration of work, one where production occurs without reference to value, he anticipates Freud's radical discovery of work prior to meaning. It is Freud who first fully appreciates work that is anterior to meaning. He calls this the *dream-work*, a process that Kristeva describes as a "playful permutation which provides the model for production".[47] Kristeva uses Freud's understanding of the dream-work to read a connection between the body and expenditure in Marx's work, and from this she develops her own concept of production. Before going on to say more about what this involves, though, I want to look at what Kristeva gleans from Freud's discussion of the dream-work.

The dream-work

The dream-work radically subverts communicative speech.[48] It transforms language beyond the circulation and exchange of meaning.[49] The dominant effect of the dream-work is this transformation: it acts upon the dream-thoughts, the residues of daily activity and bodily processes, without creating something new from these. While the dream is the *work* that it carries out, it cannot be understood as the creative product of a logical process. The dream-work is a production without product, a pre-productive chain that does not accumulate value. Indeed Freud himself notes that the dream-work diverges sharply from the productive rationality of conscious thought.

> The dream-work is not more careless, more irrational, more incomplete than waking thought; it is completely different from it qualitatively and for that reason not immediately comparable with it. It does not think, calculate or judge in any way at all; it restricts itself to giving things in a new form … Little attention is paid to the logical relations between thoughts.[50]

The dream-work operates on the dream thoughts without producing meaningful structures or logical relations; it relies on (linguistic) ambiguity to transform and rearrange in non-logical ways.[51]

Freud argues that conscious, rational thought is governed by the secondary processes. These involve an imposition of rigid, logical structures which are both calculating and judgemental. The secondary processes are linked to the ego's desire for mastery and control of both its inner and outer worlds. They involve themselves with the pursuit of clarity and meaningful precision. These are at odds with the processes responsible for structuring the dream-work, the primary processes. The primary processes involve a free flowing of psychic energy that contrasts sharply with the controlled circuits of the secondary processes. They are more concerned with the attainment of pleasure than the attainment of logical, well structured thought. The primary processes are both pre-rational and pre-productive, and are governed by the undisciplined play of unconscious desire. Here we enter the "other scene" of production.

In the dream-work the major mechanisms of transformation include the unconscious processes of condensation and displacement. Each of these involves a sliding or movement of meaning. In condensation multiple meanings converge, resulting in the superimposition of signifiers. This process "joins together in an abbreviated and highly compressed form selected elements from the dream-thoughts, and more remote memories with which they have some feature in common. It treats affinity as the basis for an absolute identification."[52] The mechanism of displacement involves a transference of high psychical intensity from one dream element to another. It involves a kind of veering off that invests a seemingly insignificant element with great significance. Freud writes that in displacement:

> a psychical force is operating which on the one hand strips the elements which have a high psychical value of their intensity, and on the other hand, *by means of overdetermination*, creates from elements

of low psychical value new values, which afterwards find their way into the dream-content.[53]

The mechanisms of condensation and displacement resemble the peculiar processes of poetic language: both practise a sliding of meaning by substituting or superimposing signifiers. Jacques Lacan draws these parallels, arguing that Freud's primary processes of condensation and displacement are akin to the linguistic devices of metaphor and metonymy.[54] While condensation and displacement are the major mechanisms of the dream-work, it is worth noting that Freud identifies an additional function. This process involves the imposition of coherence upon the absurdity of the dream. Freud calls this secondary revision and argues that it is a mechanism that emulates conscious thought. Secondary revision attempts to domesticate the meaningless eruptions of unconscious desire, although it is not always successful. Freud argues that "its purpose is evidently to get rid of the disconnectedness and unintelligibility produced by the dream-activity and replace it by a new 'meaning'."[55] However, this new meaning no longer coincides with the meaning of the dream-thoughts. Secondary revision rivals the logic of conscious thought by demanding systematicity. It is involved in the production of meaningful and coherent structures that organise rational thought. "There is an intellectual function," Freud writes:

> which demands unity, connection and intelligibility from any material, whether of perception or thought, that comes within its grasp; and if, as a result of special circumstances, it is unable to establish a true connection, it does not hesitate to fabricate a false one.[56]

While Lacan reads Freud's dream-work as a series of linguistic processes, it is worth noting that Lyotard resists this now familiar "displacement". Lyotard insists on the spatiality of the dream-work. He speaks of the dream as a text *worked over*, transformed, modified by desire, desire here understood as a force literally crumpling the text.[57] Against Lacan, Lyotard stresses that the dream is not a discourse primarily because the dream-work is different from the operations of speech (p. 30). He describes the spatial operations of the dream-work in the following way. Condensation (*Verdichtung*) must be understood as a physical process which involves reduction of the space occupied by one or more of the dream objects (p. 23). The spatial work of condensation transforms words into things, and in so doing, transgresses the rules of discourse. Displacement (*Verschiebung*), the preparatory step to condensation, is a process involving a "gesticulatory, visual scope"; it works on both "the readable and the visible" elements (p. 23). These spatial, topographical, inscriptions are also evident in secondary revision (*sekundare Bearbeitung*), which involves a "flattening out of the relief by using the humps and hollows, the peaks and valleys, to produce writing" (p. 49). For Lyotard, secondary revision is "the selective power directing these upheavals to deposit their products in a readable manner" (pp. 49–

50). Lyotard's topographical reading of Freud stresses that the transformations of the dream-work must be understood as dismissive of discourse. They involve the force of desire acting upon an intelligible text, not in order to disguise it, but more importantly to forestall it (p. 51).[58]

Silent production?

Now Kristeva uses Freud's theory of the dream-work as an analogy for her discussion of non-productive language. Here work is released from the rigour of meaningful exchange to allow for a process beyond the calculating confines of value and circulation. By theorising non-productive language in this ana-logical way, Kristeva makes it possible for us to link her discussion of produc-tion with our discussion of silence. In fact in her discussion of the critical practice of semiotics she uses the expression "silent production" for non-pro-ductive language: "this *concept* of a 'work' that 'means nothing', and of a silent production that marks and transforms while remaining prior to all circular 'speech', to communication, exchange or meaning."[59] Kristeva's term *silent production* is a little confusing here, because she is really talking about a non-productive language that is anything but silent in the strict sense. I think that she uses this term in a deconstructive manner to displace the dichotomy be-tween language and silence. With this in mind we need no longer simply oppose silence to speech, but think, instead, of an unquiet silence, one that inhabits and disrupts sound.[60]

In Kristeva's work on the semiotic resonance that inhabits poetry there is further evidence of this unquiet silence in non-productive language. For ex-ample, in "The Ethics of Linguistics" she discusses what constitutes the unique nature of Roman Jakobson's contribution to linguistics arguing that he "comes away suspecting that the signifying process is not limited to the language system, but that there are also speech, discourse, and, within them, a causality other than linguistic: a heterogeneous, destructive causality."[61] I take Kristeva to mean here that Jakobson *hears* the "heterogeneous" and "destructive" ele-ments that inhabit the poetic voice. I take her to mean that these elements speak. I think that we can read her description of Jakobson here as another instance of her concern with the relation between an unquiet silence and non-productive language practice:

> It is quite an experience to listen to Harvard University's recording of Roman Jakobson's 1967 lecture, "Russian Poetry of my Genera-tion" – he gave a reading of Mayakovsky and Khlebnikov, imitating their voices, with the lively, rhythmic accents, thrust out throat and fully militant tone of the first; and the softly whispered words, sustained swishing and whistling sounds, vocalizations of the dis-integrating voyage toward the mother constituted by the "trans-mental" ("zaum") language of the second.[62]

She goes on to identify the hidden recesses, "the silent causality and ethics" that Jakobson's listening reveals in this poetry, the vocalisation of language, the rhythm that evades the censoring structure of the symbolic register (p. 30). By doing so she reclaims silence as a voluptuous patina that accompanies voice. Here silence escapes the rigidity of a logic that can conceive of it only as the absence of sound. In demonstrating this Kristeva brings together two important critiques of language. She develops a double disruption of the critique of the sign which draws on the work of both Derrida and Jakobson. She calls on Derrida's *trace* as the displacement of the concept of the sign, and uses Jakobson's reading to disturb his own belief in the unity of the sign.[63] She points out to us that the way Jakobson uses his voice demonstrates that there is no simple or necessary one-to-one correlation between signifier and signified because we can hear evidence of an asignifying sound without a signified.[64] Kristeva draws these two quite different threads together in a novel way to theorise the unquiet silence of non-productive language.[65] The result is that she moves us away finally from any pure concept of silence. The complex terrain of Kristeva's non-productive poetic language practice explodes silence as a concept in opposition to speech. In effect her work makes silence in this sense an inoperative concept.

This non-productive poetic context in which Kristeva situates her discussion of Marx is useful for thinking about the question of the subject. If we return to our earlier discussion we shall recall that his notion of the subject is one dominated by a desire for mastery and control. Marx's subject is a self-made, productive man who is governed by what Freud would call the secondary processes of rationality and logical thought. However, Kristeva's reading of Marx alters this view somewhat. She identifies fleeting glimpses of another possibility in Marx's work. Her non-productive language practice suggests a subject that is not reduced to the self-making activity of conscious rationality but, rather, one that is crossed by the libidinal energy of the primary processes. This is a "poetic subject" structured by the eruptive and playful mechanisms of the unconscious primary processes.[66]

As we shall see in the following chapters, Kristeva theorises a kind of poetic non-productive writing. She argues that this writing shatters the illusion of the subject's mastery and self-control and that it calls into question the rigidity of conscious, rational thought. This type of writing is at odds with the cumulative logic of production and as such shares an uneasy relation with communicative discourse. Kristeva speaks at length about the problems of trying to speak of a production that is not communicative:

> It is virtually impossible to comprehend such a semiotics when it poses the problem of a production that is not that of communication but which at the same time is constituted through communication … I rather wish to look at the difference between the *types* of signifying production prior to the product (value): oriental philoso-

phies have attempted to tackle this from the point of view of work prior to communication.[67]

For Kristeva the writing that inscribes this work prior to communication is one that oscillates between sense and non-sense.[68] It posits a subject that cannot be reduced to conscious intent. From this perspective production is theorised as a process, as a disruption of meaning and identity, unsettling communicative exchange. This production-prior-to-the-product involves an expenditure, a loss of value. It is a pre-communicative production which returns to language as rhythm, gesture, musicality; it involves a relation between the body and expenditure. I have already indicated that Kristeva's focus on expenditure and excess is very much indebted to Georges Bataille, who urges us to acknowledge a non-productive expenditure. Bataille argues that poetry is synonymous with expenditure because it expresses an extreme state of loss. For him it signifies "in the most precise way, creation by means of loss." Bataille uses the term *sovereignty* to denote a kind of general economy of writing that is at odds with the restricted economy of work and value. Sovereignty orients itself toward destruction. It dissolves the value of meaning and truth.[69]

Symbolic exchange

Kristeva's discussion of the unquiet silence that structures non-productive language practice is very much a discussion of writing. She privileges the process of writing over the category of literature and unsettles the opposition of speech and writing (a move not dissimilar to her displacement of the silence/language couple).[70] She does this in the context of her discussion of writing as a production. As we have seen, Kristeva theorises this notion of production by identifying tensions in Marx's work, by rewriting his ideas about production in order to identify a kind of writing that is silently non-productive. Baudrillard disagrees with Kristeva that Marx can be read this way, arguing that Marx is fundamentally concerned with production that is aimed at useful ends, i.e. with the finality of value. He takes Kristeva to task for reading an excessive element into Marx's discussion of labour and suggests that the passage from Marx, that Kristeva cites, is in no sense a celebration of expenditure. This passage is interesting, so I shall quote it here in its entirety.

> The use values, coat, linen, etc., i.e., the bodies of commodities, are combinations of two elements – matter and labor ... We see, then, that labor is not the only source of material wealth, of use-values produced by labor ... *labor is its father and the earth its mother* ... Productive activity, if we leave out of sight its special form, viz., the useful character of the labor, is nothing but the expenditure of human labor-power.[71]

Baudrillard chides Kristeva, arguing that she attributes to Marx a philosophy of embodiment, excess and expenditure: "She would have him read Bataille before he wrote – but also forget him when it is convenient. If there was one thing Marx did not think about, it was discharge, waste, sacrifice, prodigality, play, and symbolism."[72] He admonishes her for raising labour to the status of a revolutionary concept when, as he believes, it is well and truly time to submit Marx's productive logic to a radical critique in order to expose the ideological nature of its construction. He writes:

> The quotations from Marx to which Kristeva refers do not at all carry the meaning she gives them ... The "discharge" of human power Marx speaks of is not a discharge with a pure waste, a symbolic discharge in Bataille's sense (pulsating, libidinal): it is still an economic, productive, finalized discharge precisely because, in its mating with the other, it begets a productive force called the earth (or matter).
>
> (p. 43)

In spite of his inability to fathom an excessive moment in Marx's writing, Baudrillard follows Kristeva in that he also champions a kind of silently productive writing. He calls this *symbolic exchange*.[73] This involves a process of exchange beyond production, a writing that aims at the destruction of accumulated (stable) meaning. Symbolic exchange is a deliberate strategy of anti-production, and is more concerned with the loss and sacrifice of meaning than its accumulation. For Baudrillard it involves:

> the uninterrupted cycle of giving and receiving, which, in primitive exchange, includes the consumption of the "surplus" and deliberate anti-production whenever accumulation (the thing not exchanged, taken and not returned, earned and not wasted, produced and not destroyed), risks breaking the reciprocity and begins to generate power.[74]

Baudrillard argues that in order to practise symbolic exchange it is important to theorise the destruction of value and meaning. He suggests that certain art practices, such as (poetic) writing are involved in doing just this.[75] So while Kristeva and Baudrillard disagree about Marx's stance on production, they both end up theorising what I am calling non-productive practices.

Jean-François Lyotard's call for a conception of both work and language beyond value is pertinent for our discussion here, for Lyotard appears to touch upon the pre-productive practices designated by Baudrillard's symbolic exchange and Kristeva's silent production.[76] But he is himself uneasy about Baudrillard's critical position *vis-à-vis* Marx. He argues that Baudrillard's work remains trapped within the very system it attempts to escape. He suggests that Baudrillard's notion of symbolic exchange operates *inside* the (productive) system of critique or theory which Marx himself establishes. This, of course, parallels Baudrillard's critique of Marx. In *Libidinal Economy* Lyotard admonishes Baudrillard (along with Deleuze and Guattari) for producing another (critique or) theory of Marx's theory. He suggests that Baudrillard succumbs to the lure of Marx's rational thought by answering it in the rational language of theory: "Now this problematic of symbolic exchange, don't go thinking that it is a phantasy foreign to the desire named Marx, it is one of its principal formations." And further:

> This perfectly simple trap consists in *answering the demand of van-quished theory*, and this demand is: "put something in my place". Now the important thing is the place, not the content of the theory. It is the place of theory which must be beaten. And that can only be done by displacement and flight.[77]

Lyotard is concerned that the productive rationality of theory must not (and indeed cannot) be countered with theory itself. And this is what he believes Baudrillard attempts. Baudrillard's symbolic exchange remains a theoretical/critical production, a productivity which needs to be shattered by the displacing movement of what Lyotard calls a *libidinal economy* or *politics*. Here he summons desire as the energetic force of displacement and disruption. So it is a libidinal expenditure, not a symbolic exchange that Lyotard champions against productive rationality.[78] Now this is interesting because it suggests that something of Kristeva's unquiet silence may in fact inhabit Lyotard's work after all. While I began this chapter by suggesting that Lyotard's *différend*, for all its value, keeps in place the silence/speech dichotomy, I suspect that the rather radical departure he takes in his writing on libidinal economy goes some distance toward unsettling this.

In concluding this chapter I shall return to Kristeva in order to say that the way we can now talk about silence in philosophy is thoroughly altered because of her work. In effect Kristeva moves us away from a silence/language opposition toward an understanding of the rather more complex relation between the logos and its other. We can use her work not to pit silence against this logos, but rather to think of silence as a metaphor for the otherness that inhabits the logos, an otherness that is anything but quiet. Indeed her theory of non-productive language practices points us toward this unquiet silence. In the following chapters I shall explore the consequences of this displacement for the ways in which we can theorise the subject. Kristeva's poetic subject, as we shall see, is a subject structured by the eruptive and playful mechanisms of the unconscious primary processes. These processes bring back to language silent bodily traces or asignifying sounds that are the condition of language.

Part II

SPEAKING SILENCE

6

KRISTEVA
Naming the problem

Throughout this book I have been attempting to demonstrate the complexity of silence. I have discussed some of the possible ways that we may conceptualise silence, through exclusion, denial, repression and foreclosure, and have gone on to argue that it need not be theorised in opposition to language. In my discussion of Lyotard's work on the *différend* I have argued that a radical concept of silence can in fact help us to uncover what remains unheard, if not unspoken. Following this I have adapted Kristeva's work on non-productive language practice to show how she displaces the dichotomy of language/silence. Her work on the semiotic dimension that inhabits language complicates any simple understanding of silence. In this chapter I shall continue to explore the complex non-oppositional relations between silence and speech. I shall do so by referring, once again, to Kristeva's work. I have chosen this time to focus on her various discussions of the links between language, subjectivity and the maternal. It seems important to do this because it allows me to orient questions of voice back toward the terrain of the maternal body. Kristeva uses the emblem of the maternal in various ways, and I am keen to engage with the debates that question whether these can be mobilised for feminist explorations of speaking.

Before going on to Kristeva's work, however, I wish briefly to recall a thing or two about speaking. A simplistic analysis of the relation between men and women (whether in philosophy or elsewhere) is that men speak and women remain silent. Importantly this implies that women's silence is in opposition to men's speech. I have attempted to show why I find analyses such as these inadequate and yet I am wondering whether something like this in fact supports the psychoanalytic distinction between the imaginary and the symbolic. The conceptual framework that collapses the imaginary with the maternal and the symbolic with the paternal often goes unchallenged. I am concerned that it both rests on, and in its turn reinforces, a "men speak, women don't" way of thinking. In this light I am interested to find out how Kristeva theorises the relation between the imaginary and the symbolic and what associations she makes between this and questions of sexual difference. So I am concerned to ask two related questions: whether, in her work, the maternal occupies a speaking place, and what consequences, if any, the answer to this question has for women. It seems to me that these questions need to be considered within the context of Kristeva's psychoanalytic preoccupations. Her work on subjectivity, language and the maternal is influenced, though not wholly determined, by the theories of both Freud and Lacan. Any discussion of silence and speech in her work needs, then, to be read with this in mind. In what follows I shall chart the sites where the maternal emerges in Kristeva's thought – the poetic subject, bodily crisis and the avant-garde text. I shall mark these sites and ask what functions they perform, what their psychoanalytic context conveys, and what we might gain from this for feminist scholarship.

The poetic subject and negativity

Kristeva's work on the poetic subject is one response to the set of problems raised by the productive subject. The solution she proposes is centred around her exploration of transgressive practices that she simply calls "poetic". Her belief that the poetic disrupts the logical operations of subjectivity stems primarily from her concern with the textual practices of the avant-garde. The historical specificity of Kristeva's work in this area is significant because she formulates her notions of subjectivity and agency during a time in France when the literary avant-garde occupied a privileged position with a generation of intellectuals. Roland Barthes, Phillipe Sollers and others associated with the journal *Tel Quel* represent her immediate intellectual context. The questions they ask and the concerns they raise serve as a critical backdrop to Kristeva's own theoretical pursuits. This focus on the avant-garde is evident throughout her work; indeed it is impossible to disentangle the complexity of her arguments from reference to it. We need to be aware of this, for any feminist considerations of Kristeva's work needs to engage with it.

Kristeva's theory of the speaking subject is fundamentally informed by both psychoanalytic and linguistic preoccupations. In her work she introduces us to the symbolic function constituting the speaking subject. She is concerned to show how, through this symbolic function, the speaking subject attempts (unsuccessfully) to reassure itself of its stable and fixed identity. This (productive) subject attempts to impose a singular meaning or order upon its disorder. Kristeva's critique of the productive subject prepares the way for a discussion of the poetic subject. This poetic subject can be understood in relation to our previous discussion of non-productive language practice in that it displaces the productive bias of the self-generating, masculine subject.

Kristeva presents her poetic subject as one crossed by the disruptive forces of negativity. She borrows this term (*Negativität*) from Hegel, and goes on to radicalise it. For her negativity is a process that liquefies and dissolves the rational attempt to define and stabilise thought and language through concepts.[1] Kristeva is critical of idealist representations of negativity and offers the terms *expenditure* or *rejection* as possible alternatives, nonetheless adding:

"The sole function of our use of the term *negativity* is to designate the process that exceeds the signifying subject, binding him to the laws of objective struggles in nature and society" (p. 119).

Negativity cannot be understood without referring to the kind of subject it constitutes. For Kristeva this is the subject in process (*le sujet en procès*), the divided or pluralised subject which occupies multiple and mobile sites. The subject in process is an intersection or crossroads, an impossible unity caught between the symbolic function and negativity.[2] This speaking subject is at odds with classical conceptions of the unified transcendental ego. It is crossed by the two modalities of significance, which are for Kristeva the semiotic (*le sémiotique*) and the symbolic (*le symbolique*). The symbolic is the "inevitable attitude of meaning" identified with consciousness and the transcendental ego. It is the modality of truth and meaning. The symbolic, coinciding with Lacan's mirror stage, is implicated in the acquisition of language. It encompasses the domain of law, order and name. The semiotic is the negativity heterogeneous to meaning and signification. Nonetheless it erupts within the symbolic, being "always in sight of it or in either a negative or surplus relationship to it."[3] The semiotic is the pre-Oedipal, pre-linguistic modality. It becomes important for our purposes here because it enjoys a privileged relation to the maternal body. It is the domain of rhythm, intonation and gesture. For Kristeva the semiotic is the rhythmic space analogous only to vocal or kinetic rhythm. It is pre-thetic and thus prior to signification. This vocal and gestural organisation connects the body to its world, and in so doing opens the subject to the "other scene of pre-symbolic functions."[4]

Kristeva argues that the poetic subject is constituted by the dialectic between the semiotic and the symbolic modalities.[5] Signifying practice (*signifiance*) is constituted by and within this play between the semiotic and symbolic. Kristeva's understanding of signifying practice emphasises process and play rather than a fixed meaning. This is a kind of negativity, a division, that questions unity. It is a process that dissolves and deconstitutes the subject's cohesion. It is a force heterogeneous to rational logic.

Kristeva's work on negativity is strongly influenced by Freud's discussion of the role played by negation in the production of meaning. We could say that she takes Hegel's notion of negativity and radicalises it with Freud's psychoanalytic orientation. Freud explores the action of judgement (affirmation and negation) in relation to the twin drive functions of introjection and expulsion. In respect of this he states: "The polarity of judgment appears to correspond to the opposition of the two groups of instincts which we have supposed to exist. Affirmation – as a substitute for uniting – belongs to Eros; negation – the successor to expulsion – belongs to the instinct of destruction."[6] The process of expulsion is the essential moment of symbolic function for Freud. Expulsion, activated by the drives, re-orients the "signifying body back to biological a-significance".[7] In the process it ruptures unity and meaning. It works against the unifying nature of the pleasure principle (affirmation, introjection) and thus embodies a dis-ordering process. This is how Kristeva interprets Freud's work on expulsion and negation in terms of a disruptive negativity. She locates this disruption with the semiotic, and labels this space the maternal *chora*. Elsewhere she will refer to this disruption as rejection.

So Freud uses the category of expulsion to trace the movement that Kristeva now calls negativity. He does so in order to chart the production and arrangement of the instinctual drives, thereby mapping the relation between the psychic and the somatic. This particularly interests Kristeva who writes: "Rejection, which is the signifying process' powerful mechanism, is heterogeneous, since it is, from a Freudian standpoint, *instinctual*, which means that it constitutes an articulation [*charnière*] between the 'psychical' and the 'somatic'."[8] For Kristeva this emphasises the embodied nature of the social process of signifying practice. This means that negativity (or rejection) is a somatic process which is both heterogeneous to and constitutive of the symbolic. In spatial terms this suggests that the semiotic (the locus of negativity) inhabits the symbolic (or language) rather than being positioned outside or prior to it. From this internal position it introduces the non-productive elements of rhythm, vocalic timbre and laughter.

Kristeva opposes "scientific" writing to "poetic" writing. Scientific discourse is constituted by the symbolic, i.e. by the rational repression of the drives, which attempt to reduce, as far as possible, any trace of the semiotic. The poetic text, on the other hand, is one of the privileged sites of the semiotic, one that is demonstrably unsettled by the negativity of the semiotic *chora*. This poetic negativity offers glimpses of the heterogeneity of the drives which erupt within the language of the semiotic body. The poetic subject that embodies this text or writing is one crossed by the negativity of the semiotic. It is not reduced to the rational terrain of the (productive) symbolic. Kristeva contends that there is a semiotic disposition (*dispositif*) at work in any text, poetic or scientific. What she means by this is that any text will be constituted by both the semiotic and the symbolic. The disposition is the mechanism that determines the play between these modalities. Traces of the semiotic exist within all texts, even those such as theory or philosophy which attempt to disavow its eruptions. The disposition of such texts works to minimise though certainly not erase these unsettling textual elements. Poetry, on the other hand, will privilege and highlight the semiotic to the point of sometimes erasing any discernible symbolic framework. However, while unsettling the unity of symbolic rational discourse, poetic language nonetheless retains its thetic function allowing it to move as "an undecidable process between sense and nonsense."[9] Now the important thing to understand, in relation to this discussion, is that Kristeva's work on the poetic subject and negativity occupies the site of the maternal. Her discussion of the semiotic and the *chora* position the maternal as the locus of a heterogeneous and disruptive negativity. To this point her references to this maternal are somewhat minimal, perhaps even a little oblique. Nonetheless they gesture toward a concern that Kristeva will go on to elaborate.

The body in crisis

To understand Kristeva's notion of subjectivity we need also to understand her ideas about bodily crisis because for her the body is constitutive of the subject. Her poetic subject embodies a kind of lived contradiction, literally an unliveable state of crisis. The sensuous nature of this crisis forces us to rethink our entire philosophical tradition because it displaces the illusion of the stable productive subject we have already explored. While challenges to this productive subject have often occurred hand in hand with a denial of agency, such as in the case of some structuralist accounts,[10] I think that Kristeva's challenge offers us a way beyond this impasse. Her poetic subject in crisis offers us the rudiments of an agency poised between the practices of body, society and text.

At first glance the poetic subject seems to be a loose assemblage of disparate parts, a subject without centre. Not, perhaps, an ideal locus of action or change. But it is the contradictory state of this poetic subject that propels it toward continually new configurations with the symbolic order. It is the very lack of centre that constitutes its driving force. We might think of this state of crisis or contradiction in terms of its instability. As we have seen, Kristeva refers to this state as a kind of process, a subject in process. This process positions the subject in a transgressive relation with the symbolic, thus subject and society collide and re-collide in an endless play of movement. This state of crisis she refers to can be understood in linguistic terms, as a kind of dialectical play between the somatic and the symbolic. It is important to note that Kristeva does not attempt to position the body, at any stage, as anterior to its symbolic signification. She displaces those accounts attempting to revive a romantic organicism, a body prior to signification and meaning. At the same time she refuses to reduce subjectivity to a purely conscious, non-sensuous domain. The poetic subject is constituted (and de-constituted) by the powerful force of negativity. It is this negativity that propels the subject, in process, toward its transgressive relation with the symbolic order. It is this negativity that positions and re-positions it in ever changing constellations with the symbolic. Kristeva's speaking subject experiences a reversal or confrontation in its perpetual movement with and against the symbolic.[11] She wants to remind us of the active and constitutive role of the signifying process. While the productive subject tends to posit its self as an isolated, unitary self, an autonomous self, Kristeva's poetic subject is immediately constituted by the intersubjective play of social dialogue.[12] Her "I" is not an all-knowing, all-powerful "I". It is not the illusory "I" of productive logic, the stable site of all meaning and sense. It is not the solitary "I". Kristeva rejects the ideological notion of a subject positioned at and as the centre of meaning, the individual who projects a wilful and intentional subjectivity. She insists that this illusory coherence and control shuts off any awareness of the negativity suffusing the subject, the contradictory and chaotic movement positioning it in collision with the social, symbolic order.

By positioning the subject as the site of conflictual process and change Kristeva shows that it does not "take place as such", but is rather a kind of practice.[13] The subject in process has a special relation to the problem of intention. Kristeva does not conceptualise it as *possessing* intention but rather as occupying the site of intention; this site is understood here as an agency without a specific intentionality, that is "an agency without a telos",[14] an agency devoid of wilful control. This agency is the outcome of the subject's bodily crisis. Whether the subject is aware of this crisis, or not, it is nonetheless constituted by its process. The productive subject cannot escape the negativity of the semiotic. Its attempts to posit itself as whole in the face of this heterogeneity are literally meaningless. Subject unity is continually shattered by an unliveable, bodily contradiction returning from the repressed semiotic. The symbolic is continually engaged in struggle with the disruptive energy of this semiotic. Evidence of this struggle, Kristeva assures us, is encoded in certain textual practices. This means that the somatic crisis of the poetic subject can be read in what she calls limit or borderline texts. She insists that these texts encode the crises and contradictions of the subject in process. They embody the material conditions that are unliveable for this subject and because of this are marginal to social meanings and formations. They encode the negativity of the drives, the conflictual and disturbing energy of the semiotic function. The body is the locus of this expenditure or rejection, this heterogeneous movement of the drives. As such it is constituted as a signifying body, the site of practice "where an always absent subject is produced."[15] The borderline text inscribes the negativity of this signifying body, rather than subsuming it under consciousness.[16]

The negativity involved in this process can again be understood in psychoanalytic terms.[17] Kristeva positions this crisis between the contradictory drives of life and death, of ego and sexuality. She rewrites the Freudian topology to emphasise opposition and conflict. She gives psychoanalysis back to us as a theory of embodied contradiction and struggle. This is a struggle at once somatic and social. Ariel Kay Salleh, a reader who is particularly sensitive to the affirmative potential of Kristeva's practice, argues that in crisis, "the body returns to a state of *difference*, heavy, wandering, dissociated" a state of anguish "which gives up to a new productive unity, reaffirms the subject as active *signification in process*."[18] Salleh stresses that contradiction throws up the (continual) process of change. I take her to mean that Kristeva's crisis is one that permits a range of new signifying practices, a range of new subjective processes. Here we have the basis for a rejection of a static and totalising account of the productive, masculine subject. The crisis invoked by semiotic negativity re-orients the subject in process toward ever changing relations or configurations with the symbolic order. It severs existing bonds between the subject and society, thus exposing everyday appearance and reality as an ideological façade.

The subject in process resulting from this crisis will therefore correspond to a new reality (*un nouveau réel*), which is, for Kristeva, "the most intense moment of rupture and renewal."[19] Subject and society are thus entwined in a spiral choreography of contradiction and change.[20] For Kristeva it is the signifying body that articulates the play or movement between the subject and the symbolic. It is the body which inscribes the material contradiction between these domains. She writes: "For what you take to be a shattering of language is really a shattering of the body."[21] Because of the complex interplay between the body and its social context Kristeva points out that the drive functions, rejection or negativity, must be understood within the context of constraining historical relations. What she means by this is that, while the drives are potentially disruptive, they may become invested within existing social structures. When this occurs the symbolic order binds them, thus diffusing their negativity. This ideological binding of drives to the order and dictates of symbolic demand serves as the basis for our strong (and often passionate or erotic) identification with the institutions of family, work and religion. However, if the subject no longer recognises itself within these institutions, i.e. if the subject fails to cathect its libidinal energies on to these structures, then the potential exists for radical social upheaval. The newly activated subject in process that emerges from this upheaval collides with the existing social (symbolic) order head on.[22]

Kristeva conceptualises this upheaval in terms of radical change. This represents the utopian moment of her thought, the desire to tie bodily crisis to a general societal crisis that ultimately restructures social relations as we know them. She contends that the material contradiction lived by the body in this state propels it into ever changing configurations with the social order. This state of crisis positions the subject at the margins of society, and in so doing unmasks the ideological façade of the dominant symbolic order. New constellations between body, history, language and politics emerge in response to the sensuous crisis of this unliveable state. Salleh shares this optimism, suggesting that if the subject in question already occupies a conflictual site in the symbolic order there will be an intensification of this upheaval.[23] Although Salleh herself does not explicitly ask this, we may pause to consider what this crisis would mean for women who already occupy a conflictual site in the symbolic order. I think that it is important to raise this question here as, to this point, Kristeva's discussion of bodily crisis makes no reference to a sexed subject. We are left to presume that the sex of this embodied subject experiencing a somatic state of disintegration is perhaps either unimportant or unquestionably male. Kristeva's silence on this point is symptomatic of a larger problem with her work on subjectivity. It serves to cover over the question of sexual difference. Kristeva's way of thinking about subjectivity has to be understood in terms of the psychoanalytic theory of drive function which is itself arguably a theory that ignores questions of sexual difference. While Freud's work provides us with a sophisticated articulation of the links between *the* body and psychic representations of it, he too fails to register the question of sexual difference as one that is relevant to this discussion. Reading Freud with Kristeva at this point we can describe *the* body as the site of sensuous practice, *the* place upon which the constraints, restrictions and contradictions of the symbolic come to be inscribed. But *whose* body is this?

The work of Jacques Lacan provides another context in which to situate Kristeva's discussion of subjectivity. However, I want to qualify this by emphasising that Kristeva provides us with a more thoroughly corporeal account. In psychoanalytic terms the body is an ensemble of disarticulated parts. Its imaginary wholeness, integrity or unity, is constituted through the complex process of certain ideological formations. In this respect psychoanalysis offers a materialist theory of subjectivity. It charts the subject's identity in and through the material or sensuous processes of signification. Lacan's work is exemplary in this regard. He charts the movement of the subject (*imago*) from disarticulation to articulation, emphasising the aggressive character of this (developmental?) synthesising progress. Lacan argues that the subject gains an illusory sense of identity or cohesion, but that this is undercut by the reality of fragmenting and aggressive libidinal forces (or drives) that cross the body leaving behind a disintegrating sense of self experienced in conjunction with the desired wholeness. Lacan's mirror stage marks the moment when the emerging subject first experiences itself as a unified totality. He tells us that it is only at this stage that we can even begin to speak of a *self* as prior to this the subject exists as a fragmented body, a body literally in bits and pieces (*le corps morcelé*):

> The *mirror stage* is a drama whose internal thrust is precipitated from insufficiency to anticipation – and which manufactures for the subject, caught up in the lure of spatial identification, the succession of phantasies that extends from a fragmented body-image to a form of its totality that I shall call orthopaedic – and, lastly to the assumption of the armour of an alienating identity, which will mark with its rigid structure the subject's entire development.[24]

This "alienating identity" is the embodied experience of a dialectical play between integrity and dissolution. As far as psychoanalysis is concerned it is the limit of consciousness. It displaces the ego as presumed master of a unified and totalised subject. Lacan goes on to argue that it is the process of *méconnaissance* (misrecognition) that structures the ego. The ego literally misrecognises itself at the mirror stage.[25] The aggressivity that Lacan elsewhere speaks of is an experience of corporeal dislocation. It is an experience of the fragmented body bursting forth in images of castration, mutilation and dismemberment.[26] He informs us that the fragmented body "appears in the form of disjointed limbs, or of those organs represented in exoscopy, growing wings and taking up arms for intestinal persecutions".[27]

The mirror stage inaugurates the separation between the pre-linguistic imaginary and the linguistic symbolic.[28] It is the source of aggressivity because, as Fredric Jameson notes, it marks "a fundamental gap between the subject and its own self or *imago* which can never be bridged."[29] After the mirror stage the ego will nonetheless seek mastery (albeit illusory) in its quest for an imaginary wholeness and unity. Because this mastery is structured by a denial of bodily fragmentation it necessarily results in the formation of a subject alienated from itself. This self can only assume its integrity or identity by separating from and repressing the mobility of the drives, the "constant flux of instinctual energy across its body."[30] Kristeva insists that we re-activate the negativity that resides within this repression. She demands that we "break out of our interpersonal and intersocial experience if we are to gain access to what is repressed in the social mechanism: the generating of significance."[31] Communicative language (of the symbolic order) is constituted by the repression of negativity. Kristeva believes that we need to reactivate this repression by rupturing it with the semiotic motility of poetic language. This motility stems directly from the body, the semiotic body.[32]

We must remember that for Kristeva this semiotic or polylogical body (let us think of them together at this stage) is not an identity, it is a process. It is the site of instinctual (drive) energy. Kristeva insists that "significance is indeed inherent in [this] ... body."[33] Her subject in process is "a body that is pulverised, dismembered, and refashioned according to the polylogue's bursts of instinctual drive-rhythm."[34] This semiotic/polylogical body shatters the logical coherence of symbolic thought and language. It reorients the subject in process toward a conflictual relation with existing social structures.[35] The polylogical body disrupts the clarity of consciousness. It carries semiotic motility and reaffirms the subject as the site of radical contradiction. Because it exists momentarily in a pre-linguistic state the polylogical body incorporates a pain that cannot be articulated as such. "The instant the attack begins, there is a loss of self and of knowledge, the pain of schism, a brush with death, and the absence of meaning."[36] However this subject in process reforms and in so doing goes on to embody an active signification. Returning to Salleh we find her explaining that this momentary experience of dislocation and pain "becomes a phenomenological laser; it fractures appearance and the false, commonsense consciousness that rests on it," allowing the subject to "glimpse essential relations at work behind the ideological façade."[37] To recognise this is therefore to affirm the radical subjectivity of pain, its potential to reorder and relocate the subject in relation to the symbolic order. This kind of pain resists communicative language. Elaine Scarry describes it as "an immediate reversion to a state anterior to language, to the sounds and cries a human being makes before language is learned."[38] The pain of this crisis reorders the body, preparing it for another subjectivity, another discourse.

While it remains captive to the symbolic order the body is disarticulated, unvoiced. This alienation in language is reinforced by the dominating violence of rationality. It enslaves the body, mutilates it. Indeed Theodor W. Adorno describes the infliction of violence upon the body, in the form of an instrumental rationality, as the condition of modernity.[39] Against this rationality Kristeva stresses the inseparability of body and meaning. She argues for a close and intimate articulation between body and text, suggesting that bodily crisis or desire can rupture the symbolic through the discursive field. The corporeal crisis of Kristeva's subject in process transforms the social order by shattering repression and returning it back to the system as text. This means that the radical crisis of subjectivity is valorised as the site of both new significations and social structures.[40] Textual practice is thus understood to be a transgressive practice: "the text's function is therefore to lift the repression that weighs heavily on this moment of struggle, one that particularly threatens or dissolves the bond between subject and society, but simultaneously creates the conditions for its renewal."[41]

Kristeva's text embodies contradiction (negativity) and is propelled by its own internal struggle. It is the site of a radical subversion of meaning, a practice dissolving the coherence of subject-identity. This dissolution makes it possible for the repressed semiotic to emerge in the symbolic order. For Kristeva writing (or textual practice) is a risky reinscription of desire and negativity which reveals the multiple contradictions at work within society at any given time.[42] Certain ideologies will seek to repress these contradictions, and will therefore consider this kind of writing with either suspicion or contempt. The subject of this textual practice is constantly formed and reformed in its encounters with social contradiction. This subject in process is literally a social mis-fit unable to recognise itself in the various social institutions that demand its allegiance. It is no longer a sutured element of the social totality. It disrupts the monological façade of the social contract, threatening it with the eruption of multiple and discordant voices. In capitalist society this will mean that voices hitherto unheard will break forth exposing the mythology of democratic and just social relations.

Kristeva's notion of practice is indebted to Mao whose work emphasises the indispensably sensuous nature of contradiction. He writes: "the standpoint of practice is the primary and basic standpoint, in the dialectical-materialist theory of knowledge", and that "all genuine knowledge originates in direct [bodily] experience."[43] Kristeva uses Mao's foregrounding of direct and personal experience to affirm the subversive potential of the subject in crisis, the subject of the "highest contradiction". She argues that this crisis "dissolves the subject's compactness and self-presence", that it "de-centres and suspends the subject", constructing it as "a passageway, a non-place". The pulverised subject that emerges from this is set "against natural structures and social relations", so that it "collides with them, rejects them, and is de-posited by them."[44]

Kristeva explains that there are two types of text that may emerge from this crisis, and she labels these "experience" and "practice". The experience text, while it does inscribe the forces of contradiction, nonetheless diffuses this negativity by investing it in what she calls "a strictly individual, naturalist, or esoteric representation". By doing so it reduces contradiction to "the presence of the ego". The practice text, on the other hand, maintains the threat of this contradiction as "an indispensable precondition for the dimension of practice through a signifying formation".[45] This binds it to social practice and thus maintains its unsettling potential. While a text may embody traces of contra-diction and negativity Kristeva points out that its subversive power may be compromised by a solipsistic investment of negativity in an ego-centred prac-tice. Such a text will be readily co-optable by the existing symbolic system of circulation and exchange. The practice text, however, will work to displace the individualistic and atomistic subject of this system.

Kristeva believes the risky text is very much concerned with shattering the monological coherence of the social narrative. She argues that the poetic, abject or practice text dissolves the illusion of a singular voice. It refuses a stable and singular identity and allows for multiple and discordant voices to erupt within them. These are the voices of the silenced, the repressed. The polylogical text that emerges from this practice thus inscribes the heterogene-ity repressed by the social contract, it literally gives voice to those that remain unvoiced within it. In this sense the term polylogue refers to a project of pluralising the logos, making space for multiple logics within the symbolic. We can compare this to Derrida's *trace* or *différance* where the emphasis seems to lie more on undoing the logos. Kristeva's use of this term is significant; it is not strictly a synonym for the semiotic, though it certainly does touch up against it. It is a term that marks a debt in her work to Mikhail Bakhtin's concept of the *dialogic*, a plural dialogue that disrupts the symbolic with plurality, heterogeneity and contradiction.[46] Kristeva's polylogue brings us back to the body as the site of practice. Because it incorporates the pain of (social and symbolic) contradiction the polylogical body partakes of the sub-ject's unsettling process, one that "splinters and refashions our language, our body, and our time."[47] In Kristeva's polylogue we are returned to the sensuous element of social and linguistic crisis. Her work provides us with an explora-tion of the intricacies of the body/text relation, one that is framed by an appreciation of the heterogeneous force of negativity. Kristeva's subject in process offers us a way of rethinking subjectivity that begins with the silenced body in crisis and in pain. However it is problematic to the extent that it overlooks questions of sexual difference. The maternal body operates here as a subtext barely surfacing to the level of critical thought. Nonetheless in Kristeva's discussion of the semiotic motility that crosses the polylogical body we can discern traces of a submerged maternal.

Poetic language as revolution: reading the avant-garde

Earlier in this chapter I suggested that Kristeva's writing on the poetic subject needs to be situated in the context of her discussion of avant-garde textual practice. I also indicated that, in her work, the avant-garde text occupies another site of the maternal. I want to turn to this discussion now, because it helps us to understand what Kristeva means when she refers to limit, border-line or risky texts. This discussion will, of necessity, involve an analysis of what Kristeva sees as the revolutionary potential of poetic language, for this is how she understands the radical gesture the avant-garde makes.

Kristeva attempts an ambitious analysis, in her terms *semanalysis*, of poetic discourse. She is interested in signifying processes which inhabit an unstable position within language. Semanalysis, her materialist theory of signification, focuses largely upon the texts of the literary avant-garde, what she calls *limit texts*. She argues that such texts attempt, and have always attempted, to in-crease what can be signified. Semanalysis breaks from semiology and the study of the sign-system in order to concentrate upon the signifying process. Be-cause it is structured by psychoanalytic concerns it charts, unlike semiology, the release and articulation of the drives, those restrained by, yet not reducible to, the language system.[48] What follows from this is a discussion of poetic language as a revolutionary, fragmentary force capable of unsettling and dis-placing the (assumed) identity of the speaking subject. Semanalysis sets itself the task of analysing the crises poetic language provokes in the related spheres of signification and subjectivity. Kristeva insists that while poetic language shares in the communicative (symbolic) function of signification, it is crucial that we recognise that its symbolic involvement does not thoroughly define and circumscribe it.[49]

Kristeva argues that the limit texts of the avant-garde defy the productive logics of narrative and self-presence, thus challenging the illusion of a shared social reality premised on a singular truth. She argues that avant-garde texts exist in tension with the dominant (linguistic) law, and that because of this they are well placed to work against, even dissolve, its political tyranny. Her analysis of avant-garde practices since the late nineteenth century focuses on their ability to explode the categories of identity and conceptual thought. By shattering unity these limit texts produce rhythm, tone and silence and in so doing reorganise a new economy of bodily drives. This permits a reintroduc-tion of the semiotic. In the process it provides access to the repressed (or foreclosed) space that Kristeva designates as the maternal. By lifting this re-pression the limit text reinvests the symbolic with a corporeal language, a language with links to the silenced maternal body. It exceeds the logic of rational symbolic thought by voicing this silence. Kristeva uses Mallarmé's metaphorical relation between body and word to exemplify her claim that the avant-garde reinscribe this disruption.[50] She uses Céline's writing to exemplify the fracturing of narrative unity,[51] and Pound's and Mayakovsky's work to exemplify a writing that inscribes the uncertainty of both meaning and sub-jectivity.[52]

Because it is anterior to symbolic function the textual practice of the avant-garde is fraught with the dangers of a marginal existence. The borderline (poetic) subject lives an impossible contradiction between sense and nonsense and thus embodies an active form of madness. In poetic language the tension between madness and sociality has become text. This madness erupts as laughter indicating an aggressive negativity toward unity and law. Lautréamont, another of Kristeva's limit writers, celebrates this laughter which introduces an impossible state of aggressivity and violence.[53] Of this laughter, Kristeva herself writes: "The laughter of the one who produces that laughter is thus always painful, forced, black."[54] Kristeva believes that the kind of text crossed by this laughter provides a significant challenge to the existing order. However, because it is a real risk to the subject, the force of its negativity should not be underestimated. This repression, erupting as laughter, madness or even psychotic discourse, positions the subject on contradictory terrain, and is "one of the most daring explorations the subject can allow himself, one that delves into his constitutive process."[55]

Poetic language simultaneously affirms and negates symbolic function. It contests the symbolic order by freeing "the subject from certain linguistic (psychic, social) networks."[56] Because it re-introduces negativity within language, the poetic marks the return of what the symbolic order has repressed. Kristeva is adamant that this repressed space is in fact the maternal *chora*. For her the chora is the maternal locus of the poetic subject. It is the site that constantly subverts the stability and coherence of the symbolic. It appears to be at odds with the paternal authority of the symbolic. According to Kristeva the semiotic chora is "no more than the place where the subject is both generated and negated", it is the (maternal) locus of the process of negativity. Negativity can be understood here as the instinctual drive charges which are heterogeneous to meaning.

Elizabeth Grosz notes that Kristeva borrows the term *chora* from Plato's *Timaeus*.[57] Kristeva's description of the *chora* summons the rather ambigious "space" that it occupies in Plato's work:

Plato emphasizes that the receptacle, which is also called space vis-à-vis reason, is necessary – but not divine since it is unstable, uncertain, ever changing and becoming ... Is the receptacle a "thing" or a mode of language? Plato's hesitation between the two gives the receptacle an even more uncertain status. It is one of the elements that antedate not only the *universe* but also *names* and even *syllables* ... The Platonic space or receptacle is a mother and wet nurse.[58]

Grosz contends that Kristeva's maternal *chora*, far from representing a feminine space of the mother, is in actuality a phallic fantasy, a masculine construction. She goes on to argue that the *chora* is the pre-imaginary locus of the drives. Grosz writes: "'She' is thus the consequence of a *masculine* fantasy of maternity, rather than women's lived experience of maternity" (*ibid.*). The issue that Grosz raises here is an important one. It forces us to question the implications of Kristeva's maternal in the light of some very real feminist concerns. We need to ask whether this transgressive maternal space can be useful for any feminist analysis given that, according to Grosz, it ultimately rests upon, and stands in for, a phallic paternal phantasy. We need to ask whether this space has anything to do with women and their voices.

Poetic language and the maternal body

To this point Kristeva's work has provided us with an alternative set of questions for thinking about subjectivity. Her focus on the negativity of avant-garde writing allows us to theorise a poetic subject, one that is very much constructed by unstable somatic processes. Her subject is an embodied subject that is constituted by the motility of semiotic drive forces. This is all very well and good, but we are left wondering what all this can possibly mean for women. In the first section of this book I argued that the productive subject silences woman's (maternal) body by setting itself in her place. Are we to trust Kristeva's poetic subject to avoid this gesture? I am inclined to think that, in many respects, it does not. Because Kristeva positions her work in a tradition that is wholly preoccupied with questions of men's (avant-garde) writing we are left with little in the way of a direct discussion of women's role in this transgressive practice. To add to this it seems problematical to theorise an embodied subject, as Kristeva does, without reference to its sexual specificity. At first glance, then, Kristeva's response to the crisis of subjectivity seems somewhat lacking from a feminist perspective. It may well be that Freudian psychoanalysis and the avant-garde are dangerous contexts in which to situate questions of women's silence. This is one way to pose the difficulty that Kristeva's work offers from a feminist perspective. Another is to consider the question of what the "maternal" actually signifies in psychoanalytic discourse. What work is the maternal meant to do here? What does it represent, and in so doing what does it fail to represent? In order to address this question I shall follow Kristeva's discussion toward the place she designates as the maternal.

If we shift our focus away from her broad concern with the avant-garde toward her discussion of the maternal body we are more likely to approach the question of woman's silence. Kristeva has some useful things to say about the maternal body and, although these are bound up with her discussion of the avant-garde, we can at least attempt to tease them from their rather masculine context. With Roland Barthes, Kristeva is acutely aware of the writer's dependence on the maternal as the source of filial transgression.[59] For her the maternal semiotic is an excess that is ordered and disordered by this *maternal* body. Confronting the poetic means also confronting this "archaic authority, on the nether side of the proper Name."[60] The relation between the mother's body and the child begins as a pre-linguistic one. It is prior to significance and meaning. Because it is structured by the primary processes its logic is that of gesture and sound, of rhythm and intonation. Language, in the form of grammar and syntax, are effects of the secondary processes and are thus not

116

introduced until a (partial) separation occurs from the mother's body. Entry into the (paternal) symbolic, Lacan's mirror stage, will occur by repressing the maternal. However the maternal will remain an ordering principle, mediating the play or *dispositif* between semiotic and symbolic modalities.

Poetic language recalls the repressed maternal because it is marginal to signification. It disrupts the veneer of stability within what is typically designated in Lacanian psychoanalytic theory as the paternal symbolic realm. According to Kristeva: "the unsettled and questionable subject of poetic language (for whom the word is never uniquely sign) maintains itself at the cost of reactivating this repressed instinctual, maternal element."[61] The poetic is a kind of metaphorical relation with the mother's body and because of its incestuous overtones Kristeva marks it as transgressive of both social and linguistic order.[62] The poetic destabilises the order of linguistic certainty by flaunting the prohibition with the maternal body. This involves a return to a place before identity, "the near side of syntactic articulation, a pleasure of merging with a rediscovered, hypostatized maternal body."[63] By dissolving the thetic function of the linguistic code the poetic engages in an "archaic outcry", an annihilation of "all communities, either destroying them or identifying with the moment of their subversion."[64] For Kristeva the pleasure of this transgression is precisely the pleasure *of* the mother's body. "To rediscover the intonations, scansions, and jubilant rhythms preceding the signifiers position as language's position is to discover the voiced breath that fastens us to an undifferentiated mother."[65]

This pleasurable, incestuous relation Kristeva is describing is the model she provides us with for understanding the mother's mediating role between the artist and his work. She tells us that the avant-garde artist gains access to his "translibidinal jouissance" by returning to the archaic place of the mother. The artist (poet) appropriates the maternal, speaks it for himself, in order to defy the laws of the (paternal) symbolic domain. "At the intersection of sign and rhythm, of representation and light, of the symbolic and the semiotic, the artist speaks from a place where she is not, where she knows not. He delineates what, in her, is a body rejoicing [*jouissant*]."[66] We cannot pass over the fact that Kristeva *identifies* the artist here as male. She herself claims that there are different consequences, for men and women, associated with this practice of inscribing the maternal body. We have already seen that she focuses on male artists who flaunt paternal order. She argues that we seldom find evidence of the maternal semiotic in texts written by women. Kristeva foregrounds the pre-Oedipal attachment of the male child to the maternal body. She contends that it this early relationship the adult male artist will recall in his work. By accessing this pre-thetic, pre-symbolic state the artist obtains a critical position that will align his work with the powerful negativity of the drives. He will employ the rhythmic and gestural quality of the primary processes in order to shatter the coherence of his paternal domain.

In the process the artist will encounter the phallic mother, the maternal body in its all-powerful guise prior to castration.[67] This is significant because in *normal* Oedipal terms the (boy) child will break his dependence on the mother's body at the discovery of (her) castration. This separation from her body, at the mirror stage, coincides with the acquisition of language and the formation of the symbolic function. Kristeva writes: "This is a decisive moment fraught with consequences: the subject, finding his identity in the symbolic, *separates* from his fusion with the mother, *confines* his jouissance to the genital, and transfers semiotic motility onto the symbolic order."[68] Accordingly, dependence on the mother will be transformed into an identification with the (paternal) symbolic. This represents, for Kristeva, "the first social censorship."[69] The acquisition of language during this stage buffers the body from the motility of the drive function precisely by fixing it as a stable site.

However, the artist's return to the pre-symbolic maternal undoes the repression enforced by the paternal order. It allows him to access the prohibited space of maternal jouissance, thereby threatening society (civility) with an incestuous mother tongue. Poetic language is thus evidence of a castration that has failed in its task of repression.[70] It has failed to insinuate the subject entirely into the law of paternal authority. Nonetheless the threat of castration has been registered and we know this because the artist is able to signify. If castration had been foreclosed, as in the case of psychosis, for example, the subject would be left in a pre-symbolic state. "The subject must be firmly posited by castration so that drive attacks against the thetic will not give way to fantasy or to psychosis but will instead lead to a 'second-degree thetic'."[71] Kristeva is suggesting here that the poetic does not refuse the thetic function of language but that it replaces it. This will distinguish it from mere nonsense.[72] This also distinguishes the poetic from fetishism, which substitutes an object for symbolic functioning. While the poetic and fetishism occupy similar terrain, they cannot be reduced to one another.[73]

In her discussion of the poetic inscription of the maternal body by the male artist it is interesting to note that Kristeva employs a language of appropriation, of possession, one of speaking *for*. For example, of Giovanni Bellini, she writes: "A kind of incest is then committed, a kind of possession of the mother, which provides motherhood, that mute border, with a language."[74] The mother, reduced to an imaginary maternal body, is spoken for by the male artist/son. She herself never speaks. This great debt to motherhood, owed by Western art, is never repaid by recognising her right to speak for herself. This appropriation effectively silences the mother whose body has been (poetically) plundered. The pain of this artistically imposed silence is seldom spoken or registered. In the light of this we need to ask what it means for women to risk this inscription of the maternal body. Is it possible that women could inscribe the pre-symbolic relation with the mother without eliding her voice? Can we imagine new idioms that defy the paternal prohibition of the mother without speaking for her? Before taking up these questions in the following chapter let us stay with Kristeva a moment to clarify some of her ideas about women's writing.

Women do experience their incestuous relation with the mother in a different fashion. To a certain extent the daughter can identify with the mother's body. Kristeva argues that because they do not repress the maternal as strongly as boys do, it is in fact easier for them to access the semiotic. While not all little boys will be Oedipalised into identifying with the paternal order (artists for her are exceptions) fewer still little girls will be able to do so, and thus will remain more proximate to the mother. Kristeva writes: "It is also possible that women have some very special characteristics (psychoanalytic in nature) which, if you will, propels them towards a semiotic type of representation in their paintings" enticing them toward the "games one can play with colour, form, and distortion."[75] However this appears to contradict her observation that we seldom find evidence of a semiotic bodily writing in work written by women. What she seems to be saying is that though women do occupy a privileged relation *vis-à-vis* the semiotic they seldom risk speaking from that place as the stakes of doing so for them are so high. Kristeva's discussion of the suicides of Virginia Woolf, Sylvia Plath and Maria (Marina) Tsvetaieva sheds some light on what she means by this:

> For a woman, the call of the mother is not only a call from beyond time, or beyond the socio-political battle. With family and history at an impasse, this call troubles the Word: It generates hallucinations, voices, "madness". After the superego, the ego founders and sinks. It is a fragile envelope, incapable of staving off the irruption of this conflict, of this love which had bound the little girl to her mother, and which then, like black lava, had lain in wait for her all along the path of her desperate attempts to identify with the symbolic paternal order. Once the moorings of the word, the ego, the superego, begin to slip, life itself cannot hang on: death quietly moves in. Suicide without a cause ... I think of Virginia Woolf, who sank wordlessly into the river, ... Haunted by voices, waves, lights, in love with colours – blue, green ... Or ... Maria Tsvetaieva, fleeing the war, hanged herself: the most rhythmic of Russian poets ... Or Sylvia Plath, who took refuge in lights, rhythms and sounds: a refuge that already announces ... her silent departure from life.[76]

Because there are no objective ties mooring women's lives securely to the stability and privilege of the paternal order they are at great risk when they flout the little security they do possess. The few who do, Woolf, Plath, Tsvetaieva and the like, demonstrate the dangers inherent in reactivating the maternal bond.

When it comes to contemporary women writers, especially those in France, Kristeva is less than enthusiastic about their work. She seems to find it difficult to think of this writing as anything other than derivative of truly transgressive masculine texts.[77] For example she is critical of those writers who, in her eyes, adopt the stylistic affectations of the Joycean text. Such works are, she argues, merely pseudo-transgressions: "the pseudo-transgression evident in a certain modern 'erotic' and parodic literature ... seeing itself as 'libertine' and 'relativising', operate according to a principle of *law anticipating its own transgression*."[78] A more explicit criticism of women's writing (*écriture féminine*) is evident in her dismissal of the naively sentimental: "the aesthetic quality of productions by women, most of which ... are a reiteration of a more or less euphoric or depressed romanticism and always an explosion of an ego lacking narcissistic gratification."[79]

While this is perhaps disappointing it is important to note that Kristeva believes that there has only ever been a handful who have managed to inscribe the shattering negativity of the semiotic. And while she remains hesitant to celebrate women's writing as having done so she nonetheless affirms the fact that women are now attempting to write:

> Although these writings in the wake of the experiments of Mallarmé and Joyce, have not brought about stylistic, that is, specifically literary innovation, they *do* demonstrate in an important way, women's attempt to articulate their own body-to-body discourse with the mother.[80]

Elsewhere she writes: "no matter how dubious the results of these recent productions by women, the symptom is there – women are writing, and the air is heavy with expectation: What will they write that is new?"[81] She adds:

> What we want to know at this time, is whether the women of today who become more and more involved in culture will just pick up on the already established tradition of avant-garde i.e. Artaud, Joyce ... or maybe discover other forms of avant-garde. The question remains an open one.

And more than a little patronisingly:

> What we need to do is help women to understand that these modern breaks with tradition and the development of new forms of discourse are harmonious with the women's cause. By participation in this activity of subversion (which exists on a linguistic, family, and social level) and in the growth of new epistemes they will be able to see this as well.[82]

Curiously, Kristeva goes on to speak of a bisexuality in writing (reminding us of Lyotard) arguing that, once again, women today have a somewhat privileged access to its bodily rhythm. She speaks of an oscillation or play between the semiotic and symbolic modalities, a bisexual exploration of mastery and its denial. "All speaking subjects have within themselves a certain bisexuality which is precisely the possibility to explore all the sources of signification, that which posits a meaning as well as that which multiplies, pulverizes, and finally revives it."[83] Kristeva insists that women oscillate between these gestures in order to avoid being trapped within the marginal realm of the purely transgressive. She writes: "if one assigns to women that phase alone, this in fact amounts to maintaining women in a position of inferiority, and, in any case, of marginality, to reserving for them the place of the childish, of the unsayable, or of the hysteric."[84] She urges us think and write in both modes:

> One must try not to deny these two aspects of linguistic communication, the mastering aspect and the aspect which is more of the body and of the impulses, but to try, in every situation and for every woman, to find a proper articulation of these two elements.[85]

Woman as negativity

Although Kristeva's work offers a radical critique of the productive subject I think that it is more than a little disconcerting that we find her concentrating on the way men (male avant-garde writers) manage to displace this ideological topos. To be fair, her work attempts to shatter our commonsense and philosophical assumptions about identity, and sexual identity is certainly not immune from this attack. Kristeva offers us ways of thinking beyond strict masculine and feminine distinctions and yet this remains troubling when in the process the empirical subjects of (maternal) silencing – women – seem to be left out in the cold. Kristeva's focus on the limit texts of the masculine avant-garde needs to be questioned. We need to consider carefully the political and philosophical implications of privileging this male revolt. If we ignore or marginalise the important work that women are doing, simply dismissing it as derivative, we are surely making it much more difficult for their voices to be heard, thereby colluding in keeping them quiet.

Having said this I would like to point out that Kristeva's position on this question is by no means straightforward or fixed. She appears to move between a privileging of certain male texts and a firm conviction that women occupy the truly radical site. Indeed she positions *woman* as the locus of negativity.

> The avant-garde has always had ties to the underground. Only today, it is a woman who makes this connection. This is important. Because in social, sexual, and symbolic experiences, being a woman has always provided a means to another end, to becoming something else; a subject-in-the-making, a subject on trial.[86]

Kristeva urges woman to assume a negative function, to reject existing structures, in order to place her "on the side of the explosion of social codes: with
revolutionary moments."[87] What remains unclear, though, is the relation
Kristeva envisages between the category of woman and the experiences of
women. There seems little attempt in her work to clarify this uncertainty.
Indeed one could argue that Kristeva's work positions itself precisely at this
imprecise or ambiguous place, this contradictory terrain. Because her challenge to the stasis of identity acts as a framework for her discussion of sexual
identity, it is not surprising to find that the categories of woman and women
remain in (unmediated) tension throughout her work. So while at times she
will speak of women, at others she will deny the very category as a hopelessly
romantic, outmoded identity or essence. The following passages illustrate
this ambivalence: "And sexual difference, women: isn't that another form of
dissidence?"[88] "The belief that 'one is a woman' is as absurd and obscurantist
as the belief that 'one is a man' ... woman cannot be."[89]

Kristeva's ambiguity on this matter refuses an "either–or" logic, a rationality
that would, in her own terms, rob her work of negativity. It is perhaps because
of this that her work remains frustrating to a certain feminist political agenda.
She resists the impulse in rational (or identitarian) thought toward coherence
and against contradiction. This makes it difficult to pin her own thought
down, to appropriate it for certain political gain. By both positing and displacing the category of woman (in good Lacanian fashion) Kristeva defies a
logic which tolerates no uncertainty, no dissension, no contradiction.

Kristeva announces that even though women are estranged from language,
she is now awaiting *their* attempts to write themselves into it. "[W]omen are
writing, and the air is heavy with expectation: What will *they* write that is
new?"[90] Women's "language" occupies the repressed negativity of the symbolic. It reinvests this with a libidinal economy of drives, voicing what would
otherwise remain a suffering body. "In women's writing, language seems to be
seen from a foreign land; is it seen from the point of view of an asymbolic,
spastic body?"[91] Women's writing articulates a repressed maternal language
and because of this threatens the structure of the (paternal) social contract. It
literally reincorporates what the symbolic can least tolerate, the relation with
the mother's body. In the process, it unleashes a powerful and disturbing
heterogeneity: "A piece of music whose so-called oriental civility is suddenly
interrupted by acts of violence, murders, bloodbaths: isn't that what 'women's
discourse' would be?"[92] However, while Kristeva is enthusiastic about the idea
of women's writing, she seems less than enthusiastic about what actual women
write. I have already suggested that she declares much contemporary women's
writing derivative and that she distances herself from those who merely adopt
(or mimic) the stylistic innovation of the Joycean text.[93] Given this we need to
return and ask once again what it means for Kristeva to privilege the textual
processes of the male avant-garde.

Perhaps one way of answering this question, or at least of attempting to answer it, is to look at what Kristeva has to say about the links between women, maternity and the symbolic. She begins by arguing that women occupy the site of numerous tensions, that perhaps they are this site. In one sense they are bound to the dictates of the (paternal) symbolic because they play a decisive role in reproducing it; thus "a woman takes social constraints even more seriously."[94] Are they then, she asks, "the last guarantee of sociality?"[95] However, women are only ambiguously poised in the symbolic. Their relation to child-bearing does not only act to secure them on this terrain, it also serves, para-doxically, to sever them from it. Kristeva argues that we see this at those special moments when the symbolic breaks down. She writes:

> a woman has nothing to laugh about when the symbolic order col-lapses. She can enjoy it if, identifying with the mother's vaginated body, she imagines herself thus to be the sublime repressed which returns in the fissures of the order. She can also easily die of it ... if, without successful maternal identification, the symbolic paternal order were her only tie to life.[96]

Kristeva is suggesting here that women risk a great deal more than men in writing. If they are not successfully identified with the repressed maternal body, then they literally have nothing to cling to in times of symbolic rup-ture, and this is exactly what poetry entails. Men, however, can play with the repressed maternal body, signifying its negativity, while remaining more se-curely anchored in the stability of their own paternal symbolic privilege. This is not to say that the male avant-garde risk nothing in writing, certainly not. But rather that what they risk is perhaps literally not of the same order as those women who write. Could this be why, in certain societies, we find such work being carried out more often by men? We need to ask ourselves whether this is true, and even if it is, whether it always need be so. I am not certain that Kristeva is helpful on this point.

Kristeva is clear, though, that in pregnancy women experience negativity. For her it is a process at once facilitating and destroying, it is an impossible state between support and dissolution of the symbolic order. She contends that in pregnancy women embody a split identity simultaneously plural and one. It is "an institutionalised form of psychosis ... an identity that splits, turns in on itself and changes without becoming other."[97] Kristeva is sug-gesting that, given the negativity of pregnancy, women risk (symbolic) death if they dare to step *outside* the confines of symbolic law. They are encour-aged, then, to confine themselves to the (re)productive function of mater-nity, thus ensuring the father's symbolic continuity. Nonetheless, while she recognises the strictures placed upon women, in this regard, she is adamant that when women do attempt to subvert symbolic law that they do so from a privileged place, the place of the "spasmodic force" linking them to the mother's body.[98] It seems, then, that women's relations to the symbolic are necessarily mediated by their access to what we have already spoken of as the pre-verbal semiotic.[99]

The question of women's relation to negativity remains, I believe, one of the most important issues to be addressed in any assessment of Kristeva's work. While she insists that women (sometimes woman) occupy a privileged site in this regard, she seems to undercut this by focusing almost exclusively on the poetic texts of the male avant-garde. It is thus not surprising to find the ambiguity of her own position(s) echoed by the contradictory readings her work inspires. Some admonish Kristeva for resorting to an implicit essentialism by identifying negativity with "actual women", while others reject her phallocentric gesture of consistently identifying the borderline or poetic subject as male. Drucilla Cornell and Adam Thurschwell, for example, criticise Kristeva for attempting to impose determinate content on negativity.[100] The kind of essentialism they hint at is openly criticised by Ann Rosalind Jones.[101] In a different vein Juliet MacCannell challenges Kristeva for ignoring women and always designating "devotees of the abject" as men.[102] It is worth asking why certain commentators reduce Kristeva's work to a problematic essentialism while others admonish her for doing exactly the opposite.[103] Perhaps we need to ask what is at stake in each reading, what is repressed by the desire to reduce Kristeva's work to a series of non-conflictual assertions.

In an article that attempts to read Kristeva against existing feminist interpretations Ewa Ziarek suggests that we can identify two familiar sides to the Kristeva debate. She argues that the intense discussion surrounding her work centres on the question of the maternal and its role in discourse.[104] Ziarek identifies the two sides of this debate with, on the one hand, theorists such as Moi, Gallop, Burke, Jacobus and Suleiman who focus on the subversive aspects of Kristeva's work and Silverman, Jones, Rose, Kuykendall, Grosz and Butler, on the other, who argue that Kristeva's transgressions rely on a conception of the maternal that ultimately silences the feminine in the symbolic. Given the play inherent in Kristeva's textual practice it is not difficult to understand how these seemingly opposed readings can co-exist. We might think of this in terms of the way Kristeva's own writing shifts between semiotic and symbolic modalities. Kelly Oliver suggests that Kristeva privileges both, though at different times and in different places, thus making it impossible to tie her work to a singular reading. According to Oliver, "Kristeva's own oscillation on the priority of the semiotic or the symbolic can be read as a mirror of the dialectical oscillation between semiotic and symbolic that she describes."[105] What one-sided readings of Kristeva miss is the importance she herself places upon keeping ambiguity alive in her work. Kristeva's texts refuse the simple binary logic that would settle the matter for all time. Her semanalysis frustrates the rationalist mentality. By simultaneously advocating maternal dissidence and criticising female romanticism she challenges us to shake the bonds of rigid, conformist thought. She refuses the self-evidence of woman's identity.[106]

Even though much of her work focuses on the "maternal" as the privileged locus of negativity, Kristeva refuses to give determinate content to what it signifies. Alice Jardine contends that Kristeva "has consistently rejected the notion that women should either valorize or negate this feminine whose function in Western culture is still changing with the evolution of our modernity."[107] Jardine insists that Kristeva refuses to speak *for* women and thus avoids a closure of meaning. For her Kristeva plays "the discourse of power/ truth off against itself ... by placing a violent new thought where the old thought falters" thus "creating a new fiction".[108] While Jardine is right to emphasise the political difference that this ambiguity performs, I remain nonetheless a little uneasy about the almost total eclipse of women from Kristeva's work. It is still not clear to me that Kristeva's maternal is a category that has much to do with women. While I am willing to accept that she resists determining this site for sound philosophical reasons, I am nonetheless troubled by the fact that the maternal remains a site spoken for and by the symbolic, and that these both remain gendered in apparently uncontested ways. The maternal can be accessed in order to disrupt paternal sense, but I fear that, once again, this access is primarily the prerogative of male dissidents. If we accept that she relies quite heavily on Lacan's separation of imaginary and symbolic, then Kristeva metaphorically reproduces the maternal as a place that is spoken rather than one that speaks.

Perhaps there is another way to approach this problem. We could say that Kristeva's work raises difficulties for a feminist analysis because it relies uncritically upon a psychoanalytic inscription of the maternal, quite specifically a Lacanian inscription. What I mean by this is that the maternal operates in Lacanian psychoanalysis as a metaphor. For Lacan, the maternal is a way of not raising the question of the "real" mother. By shifting psychoanalytic theory into the domain of language Lacan enacts a curious elision of the "real" mother that we find (albeit with difficulty) in Freud's own texts. Freud's position, arguably a realist account in comparison with Lacan's more nominalist one, provides some possibility to speak about mothers, about women. The fact that he seldom bothers to do so is symptomatic in itself, and says much about the general tendency of psychoanalysis to silence the mother. The problem with Kristeva's maternal is that it operates as a metaphor for transgression, and as such, has little if anything to do with actual mothers. The literal mother who can be discerned with difficulty in Freud's text is largely absent from Kristeva's account. Her Lacanian focus on the linguistic dimension of the maternal ends up severing it from any strategic relation with women, so that by the time she uses it to theorise the work of the avant-garde it offers little for feminist analysis. A contrast is offered by Irigaray's work on the maternal which operates in a radically different manner. She begins with Lacan and returns to Freud and in the process manages to inscribe the mother in psychoanalytic discourse. She creates a space where the maternal can be played against and with the mother. In so doing she displaces the nominalist tendency in Lacan and Kristeva by refusing to isolate language as a practice different from all others. For Irigaray the maternal is both metaphor and mother, and she insists on retaining the slide between them. There is a certain irreverence in Irigaray's gesture. By inserting the mother into psychoanalytic discourse she reproduces the scandal of a generation of earlier theorists such as Melanie Klein. There are some important things that can be said about this and I intend to do so in the following chapter, but for the moment I shall stay with Kristeva.

Kristeva's work on the maternal and language does open new conceptual terrain. It does challenge many of the somatophobic tendencies underpinning existing theories of the subject. Nonetheless it does not clearly and unambiguously use this as a political base for challenging the masculine pretensions of the speaking subject. However, I have already indicated we are perhaps misguided in asking it to do so. An example of the problem is Ziarek's work which attempts to salvage Kristeva for a feminist reading. Ziarek is concerned to show how Kristeva challenges the distinctions between the discursive and the pre-discursive, that is between speaking and its absence. She argues that for Kristeva the maternal is not a pre-discursive position, but a heterogeneous one. Ziarek suggests that this claim is tied up with Kristeva's desire to formulate a new linguistics (semanalysis) that "indicates both the limitations of structuralist linguistics and the need to rethink the process of signification."[109] Kristeva's semanalysis moves from language as a sign system to language as a signifying process. In doing so it charts the structuring and de-structuring processes of every signifying practice. Ziarek claims that Kristeva's focus on the multiplicity of signifying practices means that the symbolic paternal realm is no longer conceived as the exclusive realm of signification. The semiotic maternal *chora* also signifies. But how does it do this? Ziarek argues that we need to understand Kristeva's signifying process as a dialectical play involving three moments: (i) a pre-symbolic choric rhythm of accumulation and dissolution, (ii) a thetic stage transforming the semiotic into the symbolic, (iii) and a post-symbolic poetic pseudo-moment. While the second movement is usually held to be the exclusive domain of meaning, Ziarek argues that Kristeva draws our attention to the other two in order to posit the semiotic as a signifying realm (pp. 95–6).

In arguing this Ziarek is trying to do a number of things. She is attempting to dispel the notion that the symbolic is the only site of signification. She contends that the semiotic *chora* is the site of the mother and she goes on, by association, to link these together to suggest that the mother speaks. For her the semiotic maternal body is not beyond either language or signification. It is heterogeneous to the symbolic.

> The fact that the semiotic never becomes a part of the symbolic, that it never enters the nexus of the signs but instead disrupts their order, does not mean that it is not linguistic. On the contrary, for Kristeva the semiotic is perhaps the most important linguistic force.
>
> (p. 98)

The semiotic maternal is not part of the symbolic and yet it is not "outside" it. The fact that it is heterogeneous to the symbolic does not mean that it does not speak. I think that Ziarek's focus on the linguistic nature of the semiotic is important. She reminds us that Kristeva is at her best when she refuses the simple opposition between silence and speech. For her the semiotic is a kind of unquiet silence, a silence that speaks. I remain unconvinced, however, that Kristeva's semiotic maternal has anything to do with women. Ziarek fails to show that the semiotic, the maternal or the *chora* work as anything other than metaphorical terms. Indeed she argues that the semiotic is in fact a "theoretical fiction."[110] This is not to suggest that metaphor or "theoretical fiction" remain inferior to "truth" or "empirical reality", far from it. It is rather to suggest that in Kristeva's work they seem to preclude reference to women.

Ziarek attempts to stamp the semiotic as the place of women by appending a discussion of Kristeva's work on pregnancy. Now I think that Kristeva's work here is useful because it does inscribe women into her theoretical account. In fact I look at this work in the following chapter. However, I am not convinced that this discussion can unproblematically be linked with Kristeva's work on the semiotic maternal *chora*. There is no necessary relation between her metaphorical discussion of the maternal and her theoretical discussion of mothers. Ziarek makes this link, but I think she manages to do so only by labouring the point.

I feel somewhat ambivalent about evaluating Ziarek's arguments. On the one hand she does alert us to the necessary ambiguity in Kristeva's work, but I am left wondering whether, in the process, Ziarek has constructed a phallic mother of her own. Curiously she alerts us to the anxieties that lead us to symbolise the mother in coherent or phallic terms when she writes:

> Since semiotic discontinuity is so much more threatening to the mastery of the subject and the stability of social codes when it is associated with the mother, maternal lucidity is constantly erased and subordinated to the demand for the presence of the maternal body as a form of embodiment and a warranty of symbolic coherence.
>
> (p. 104)

Is Ziarek's reading of Kristeva an attempt to do just this? Is it "subordinated to the demand for the presence of the maternal body as a form of embodiment and a warranty of symbolic coherence"? Is she demanding that Kristeva's work fulfil all feminist needs, create coherence, answer all questions and install women in the place of the speaking subject? She quotes Kristeva saying:

> On the other hand, we immediately deny it; we say there can be no escape, for mamma is there, she *embodies* this phenomenon; she warrants that *everything* is, and that it is representable ... Because if, on

127

the contrary, there were no one on this threshold, if the mother were not, that is if she were not phallic, then every speaker would be led to conceive of its Being in relation to some void, a nothingness asymmetrically opposed to this Being, a permanent threat against, first, its mastery, and ultimately, its stability.[111]

Is it too threatening for feminists to imagine that the mother is not phallic? I ask this question in relation to Kristeva's work because it seems that it is all too easy to adopt a position either "for" or "against" Kristeva. Ziarek is right when she implies that discussions of Kristeva are structured by this kind of oppositional mentality. Perhaps this signifies a kind of transferential reading; we either adopt or reject Kristeva, and in the process miss the actual importance that her work represents. I think that all too often our readings of Kristeva are circumscribed by our transferential desire for her as phallic mother,[112] our desire that she provide us with not just the questions but also the answers. If this process remains unanalysed then Kristeva's work ceases to be the site of critical inquiry and Kristeva herself becomes the proper Name that is to be either accepted or rejected. When this happens the questions that her critical research opens for us risk becoming obscured. By constructing Kristeva as the phallic mother we expect *her* to do too much, to answer decisively the questions that her own theory marks as ambiguous. Furthermore, ironically, we silence feminist inquiry by assuming that there is no more to be said. I am concerned that Ziarek's reading tends to this outcome by constructing Kristeva, the proper Name, as the replete body of feminist theory, the body that fulfils all need and all demand. By reinstating Kristeva as authorial voice, Ziarek fails to respond to the feminist alternative of inscribing multiple voices. In order to counter the problems inherent in focusing exclusively on Kristeva, then, I shall finish this chapter with a discussion of possible responses to certain aspects of her work that have been addressed here.

Beyond the proper name

It is fair to say that there is much in Kristeva's work on the avant-garde that today appears a little dated. From a feminist perspective it offers little in the way of a sustained discussion of women and mothers primarily because its discourse is overdetermined by orthodox psychoanalytic inscriptions of the maternal. This inscription, as I have already argued in this chapter, encodes the maternal as a metaphor and in so doing represses any discussion of the mother. To challenge this silence we need to think about transgressive writing in very different ways. We need to look at women's writing, to investigate the ways the maternal surfaces there as an emblem of women's defiance or perhaps even indifference to patriarchal stability/meaning. We can take our cue from Kristeva's work on the maternal but we must re-situate this within a larger concern for women's work. Susan Suleiman's critical work on the avant-garde does just this.[113] She raises a series of complex questions around the coupling of women and avant-garde practice. Like Kristeva, she is concerned to chart the radical difference that avant-garde practice makes. And yet, unlike Kristeva, she is preoccupied with demonstrating the silence this practice imposes on the bodies of women. She breaks this silence by doing a number of related things. She demonstrates how essential the maternal body is to the masculine imaginary that generates the avant-garde. She reclaims the work of women who were both centrally and peripherally involved in avant-garde circles, women whose names have been silenced by overbearing masculine portrayals. Perhaps more importantly, though, she asks difficult questions about the links between writing and maternity. She manages to avoid the opposition between not just women and writers, but also mothers and writers. She goes well beyond Kristeva's concerns by investigating the mother *as* writer rather than as the place of writing. Suleiman's contribution to our understanding of the avant-garde is considerable and yet I suspect she would herself acknowledge that her questions are possible because of Kristeva's work. As problematic as they are, Kristeva's concerns have opened a space for women to begin to reconceptualise our philosophical, artistic and literary traditions. Taking my cue from Suleiman I want to reconsider our concerns with the poetic subject and writing in the light of women's work. I intend to do this by revisiting Kristeva's preoccupation with bodily crisis and pain, this time asking what it means for women to experience pain. I hope to show that we can reclaim the silence that accompanies bodily crisis as a speaking silence and in this way begin the process of lifting the repression on the mother.

The body in a state of crisis is the mute and insensate object at which language is targeted; it is *subject-to* an ordering rationality. It is fair to suggest that while Kristeva, Freud and others speak of *the* body in unsexed terms, the silence it incorporates is very much a silence we can recognise in terms of women's experience. In the following passage Francis Barker suggests that the body outside language, the silent body, is the body of woman:

> if the new regime in inaugurating itself deploys a pattern of speech and silence, a semiosis, in which the discoursing I is held to be constitutive, then it is clear that the designated woman is positioned extraneously to the constitutive centre where the male voice speaks. The woman is allotted to the place of the body outside discourse, and therefore also outside the pertinent domain of legitimate subjecthood.[114]

While in the early chapters of this book we have seen that one does not need to be located *outside* a given domain to be effectively silenced, I nonetheless believe that Barker's point is an important one because it alerts us to the sexual specificity of silence. Kristeva's discussion of symbolic and semiotic modes must be understood in terms of the ideological and philosophical positioning of women, their bodies and voices. Women are silenced because they are radically alienated from the discourses constructing their bodies.[115] Woman's disarticulated body remains both unspeakable and unspoken in the symbolic domain. It is the site of a contradictory and unliveable state; a body in crisis. Woman may attempt to articulate her desire. If she does it might propel her toward new discursive constructions, new signifying practices that shatter the law and order of symbolic prohibition. Otherwise she might remain silent, embodying her pain mutely as the suffering hysteric.

The hysteric incorporates the pain of contradiction in the "theatre of the body". The symptoms of crisis are metaphorically inscribed or written on to that body. However we must say *metaphorically* here because these symptoms only constitute a language by analogy. Catherine Clément argues that "the hysteric does *not* write, does *not* produce, does nothing – nothing other than make things circulate without inscribing them."[116] She writes that the hysteric is "A witch in reverse, turned back within herself, she has put all her eroticizing into internal pain" (p. 39). Hélène Cixous, in an exchange with Clément, challenges this view of the hysteric without words. She argues that while hysterics (like Freud's Dora) are deprived of a direct speech, they nonetheless make their disruption known, burst the family structure to pieces, with a "force capable of demolishing those structures" (p. 154). Cixous acknowledges that the hysteric occupies shaky ground and that her crises can both disturb and conserve the existing order, yet she wants to draw our attention to the radical difference that the hysteric can make:

> I imagine hysteria as distributing itself along a scale of the possible intensity of disturbance … There are structures characteristic of hysteria that are not neuroses, that work with very strong capacities of identification with the other, that are scouring, that make mirrors fly, that put disturbing images back into circulation.
>
> (p. 155)

Clément rejects Cixous' attempt to reclaim the hysteric, arguing that this dissension does not explode anything because it is not in the order of a symbolic act.[117] The hysteric is silent, she has no voice or language within the symbolic order. Nonetheless she is still important for the continuation of that order. The symbolic circulates, but without inscribing her voice within it. The lack of productivity typical of hysterical silence contrasts sharply with Kristeva's notion of abjection. If we recall Kristeva's discussion of the texts of Céline and others, in chapter three, we can see that the subject of abjection remains, as Kristeva herself puts it, "eminently productive of culture."[118] The abject subject rejects and reconstitutes himself through his textual practice in language. Kristeva is quite clear, the hysteric does not symbolise her pain: "the hysteric spasm will never find a proper symbolic, will at best be enacted as a moment inherent in the rejection in the processes of the ruptures, of the rhythmic breaks."[119] It would seem that the hysteric provides the model of suffering and pain that the abject subject or poet will then proceed to symbolise: "The hysterical woman, as woman, as the other, heterogeneous to the 'poet', represents what poetic discourse brings about but what man is not ... which he experiences only in a text."[120] Are we to suppose, then, that woman's hysterical body remains the pre-text for the production of the masculine poetic text?[121] If this is so, then I would argue that woman's hysterical body occupies the same terrain as the maternal. At least this would be the case in Kristeva's work.

I am more than a little troubled by the position assigned to the hysteric. While hysteria is not exclusively a position occupied by women, it is quite clear from Kristeva's discussion that it is the place of femininity.[122] Femininity, in this scheme, is the place of silence. What we seem to have here is a division between a productive abject (or poetic) and an unproductive hysteric. However we can attempt to rewrite the asignificance of the hysteric, and in the process undo her silence by recognising her voice. We could argue, along with others, that the hysteric "speaks" through her bodily symptoms in a manner more forceful and shattering than any abject text. The fact that the symbolic can tolerate the abject may suggest that it provides a recognised place for those marginalised and disaffected males.

In Lacanian terms the hysteric is defined by her denial of the phallus. She is the "something which says 'no' to phallic enjoyment."[123] For Lacan this effectively places her *outside* the symbolic realm of language and speech. I think, though, that we can question the external position he assigns her.[124] Irigaray has done just this. Her discussion of hysteria allows us to think of the hysteric in *uncertain* terms. By this I mean that Irigaray provides us with a way of thinking about hysteria, not just as a state *outside* or *anterior* to language, but one that also *inhabits* it.[125] Irigaray reconsiders the conventional wisdom that defines the hysteric as one who suffers silently in bodily pain. She contends that a certain symbolic refusal can be read in the gestures of this pain, a radical refusal which signifies as such. In order to emphasise this point she draws our attention to the asymmetrical discussions of schizophrenia and hysteria:

> In certain circles, certain forms of madness, especially schizophrenia, are at the moment valorized because of the movement they bear. But I have never heard the word "hysteria" being used in a valorising way in these progressive circles. Yet there is a revolutionary potential in hysteria. Even in her paralysis, the hysteric exhibits a potential for gestures and desires ... A movement of revolt and refusal, a desire for/of the living mother who would be more than a reproductive body in the pay of the polis, a living, loving woman. It is because they want neither to see nor hear that movement that they so despise the hysteric.[126]

While Irigaray's discussion has to be read within its historical specificity, i.e. the valorisation of the schizophrenic state as a radical refusal,[127] it opens up alternative ways of thinking about hysteria. The re-valorisation she proposes is not enough, but I want to argue that Irigaray demonstrates that by assigning hysteria, like maternity, to an external position (i.e. *out*side the symbolic), patriarchal society conveniently chooses to read its symptoms as silence. It decides that nothing *intelligible* is spoken, in fact that nothing is spoken. For Irigaray, the hysteric's bodily symptoms are a language, though not one that can be readily translated into masculine terms.[128]

We could suggest that the hysteric's "speech" is the sign of a kind of *différend*. If we think back to our discussion of Lyotard in chapter four we can argue that the hysteric's symptoms signal an alarm that some violence or wrong is being committed and that there is an absence of a symbolic language in which to speak these. Irigaray's discussion of bodily suffering can, in this sense, be read with Lyotard's insistence that we find new idioms in which to speak the violence of this suffering. Irigaray writes:

> It is not certain that we even have the right to madness. Or in any case to a certain type of madness to which one accedes only through language [*langage*]. How can we define the madness in which women are placed? You often need something of language [*du langage*], some delusion [*délire*], to signal that you are living in madness. Women do not in fact suffer much from delusions. If they could, it would protect them. They suffer in their bodies. An absolutely immense bodily suffering.[129]

This "immense bodily suffering" is a language, though not one we can readily decipher. It suffers for want of being heard. It is not outside. It is very much inside our cultural practices. According to Irigaray, it is the unacknowledged basis of these practices. So rather than remaining anterior to symbolic structuration, woman's desire, and the pain of its disarticulation, should be theorised as threatening that masculine order. While this desire is not identical to the semiotic, it nonetheless touches up against it. Even though Kristeva's semiotic is marked as a maternal space there is no direct or necessary connection with women. The semiotic is a disruptive space within the symbolic that can be accessed by poets, writers and artists. The semiotic is not a speaking position for Kristeva. It is the necessary condition for speaking, but not a speaking position in and of itself. Irigaray's work on hysteria avoids the problems of Kristeva's semiotic by re-conceptualising the silent space of hysterical pain as a speaking position, one that must be listened to and acknowledged. She affirms the radical voice of women from this place. Irigaray emphasises the affirmative potential of bodily crisis, and inserts women as the active site of signification. From this perspective the sensuous contradiction of the hysteric is read as an emblem of social transgression, one that silently produces new significations. She insists that we:

> Turn everything upside down, inside out, back to front. *Rack it with radical convulsions*, carry back, reimport, those crises that her "body" suffers in her impotence to say what disturbs her. Insist also and deliberately upon those *blanks* in discourse which recall the places of her exclusion and which, by their *silent plasticity*, ensure the cohesion, the articulation, the coherent expansion of established forms. Reinscribe them hither and thither *as divergencies*.[130]

For her, woman's desire challenges existing social structures by shattering the alleged coherence of masculine discourse. Irigaray is not content to have woman remain mutely positioned beyond the signifying practices of the symbolic as the blanks in discourse. She contends that by voicing her desire woman actively organises and gives meaning to an otherwise silenced body. For a woman to experience subjectivity she must first experience her body. In this regard Kaja Silverman writes that woman's subjectivity "begins with the body, a body which is quite literally written."[131] Silverman argues that while the body pre-exists discourse it gains meaning and identity only through those discursive formations or practices which organise it. There exists, according to Silverman, an anaclitic relation between "real" and discursive bodies. By this she means that the body is supported materially by the various discourses shaping it. Given this, Silverman goes on to argue that in order for woman to subvert the territorialisation of her body she needs to speak against the meanings that currently exist. The silencing and territorialising of woman's body "will never read otherwise until the female subject alters her relation to discourse – until she succeeds not only in exercising power, but exercising it differently."[132] Silverman's call to alter our relation to discourse reminds us to look at what women are doing in order to symbolise their difference. It is a reminder, as well, to think of this difference in terms of multiple voices rather than through the phallic security of the proper Name.

7

COLLECTING MOTHERS

Women at the Symposium

> When feminists call for a new representation of femininity, they seem
> to identify maternity with this idealized misapprehension; and femi-
> nism, because it rejects this image and its abuses, sidesteps the real
> experience that this fantasy obscures. As a result, maternity is repudi-
> ated or denied by some avant-garde feminists, while its traditional
> representations are wittingly or unwittingly accepted by the "broad
> mass" of women and men.
>
> (Julia Kristeva, "Stabat Mater")

In the previous chapter I argued that Kristeva reduces the maternal to a metaphorical term and that, as a consequence, she silences any discussion of the
mother. In this chapter I shall return to this question simply by asking whether
it is either possible or desirable to speak of the *real* mother. As a way of proceeding with this question I have chosen to gather together a number of
women whose work on the mother enables us to hear the differences that
women's writing makes. This is a Symposium where, contra Plato, women are
present and speak. As such it begins a philosophy amongst women, rather
than one about them. It is a philosophy that allows us to think of women in
philosophical dialogue with one another. Taking my cue from Irigaray, this
other Symposium refuses the Platonic gesture that constructs the masculine
realm of philosophical discussion as the only place of philosophy. I offer, in
place of this, the voices of women speaking amongst themselves.

Irigaray's reading of Diotima's speech moves the terrain of philosophical
reflection toward a community of women. She makes Diotima *speak* by demonstrating the radical implications of her dialectical intermediaries.[1] Andrea
Nye enters this dialogue by suggesting that Irigaray "sabotages" Diotima's
voice by reducing it to a "marginal skirmish" mounted against an authorita-
tive Platonic text.[2] She goes on to say that Irigaray is wrong to reduce Diotima
to a "co-opted feminine marginality" because in actuality Diotima is the "hidden host" of the *Symposium*. Nye reinstates Diotima to what she sees as her
rightful place in the Platonic canon, arguing that because of this "any woman
enters into the discussion of love with perfect right" (p. 77). I think that Nye's
point here is a version of the *woman as internal support of philosophy* argument
that we addressed in the first chapter of this book. Given this, I am not so sure

that I would agree with her reading of Irigaray's reading. As we have seen, Irigaray is aware of the paradoxical positioning of woman in relation to philosophy. Nonetheless, what I find interesting about Nye's text is not so much that it is right or wrong, but that it contributes to an ongoing philosophy amongst women. Indeed I certainly endorse her belief that women enter the philosophical domain with perfect right.

Exploring the maternal metaphor

As a preliminary to assembling my own Symposium I shall ask some questions about both the maternal and metaphor by beginning with Hélène Cixous' claim that the mother is a metaphor.[3] What can she possibly mean by this? There are various ways that we can think about metaphor; it exceeds denotation; it is a surplus of meaning, a vehicle propelling meaning beyond its limits. According to Jacques Lacan, metaphor crosses the bar of repression facilitating the poetic to emerge from "common-sense" meaning. He speaks of the "creative spark of the metaphor" flashing "between two signifiers one of which has taken the place of the other ... a continuous stream, a dazzling issue".[4] The mother as a metaphor facilitates the undoing of paternal repression. In this sense the mother carries or transports meaning beyond sense. She permits the unrepresentable to emerge from the patriarchal restrictions of representation. She is a transgression of the patriarchal sense of self and law, marginal to its truth and rationality. The mother encoded as the feminine, exists in opposition to the stability of the father's universe.[5] She is movement, flux and undecidability. Here the maternal acts as a metaphor for tension, ambivalence and ambiguity. More specifically the maternal body, the mother's body, comes to occupy the site of this tension. We can see this in the writing of many women who adopt the mother, or the mother's body, as an emblem of defiance. They use the maternal to express emblematically the tensions women experience in their lives.

There are potential problems associated with the maternal metaphor. It may silence woman by reducing her to a productive body, subsuming her sexuality beneath the exigencies of birth. This maternal image is, to paraphrase Domna Stanton, the concrete agent of patriarchy's reproduction,[6] or the accomplice of reproduction, according to Cixous.[7] Woman's desire dissolves before this image of the productive mother. Her sexuality is repressed, along with her voice and breath. Her pleasure becomes tied to a virile productivity. For Luce Irigaray, "the idea has been introduced in women's imagination that their pleasure lies in 'producing' children: which amounts to bending them to the values of production, even before they have had an occasion to examine their pleasure."[8] Irigaray argues that patriarchal (or phallocentric) society privileges the values associated with productivity. These are the values of making which seek visible proof of its action. The child, the visible object of maternal production, is celebrated as the product of woman's labour under patriarchy. This productive mentality elides feminine sexuality with maternity, and is thus "a privileging of the maternal over the feminine. Of a phallic maternal, at that."[9] This phallic mimicry constructs woman as the virgin mother. The mother who scarcely knows her own desire; the de-sexualised mother of masculine mythology. Her sexuality simply does not exist beyond her reproductive potential.[10] In patriarchal terms the feminine should be either woman or mother, never both. Here it is the *woman-mother* that represents the greatest threat. While the virgin mother abounds, the woman-mother is exiled to the margins of society. For Cixous, "if there's one thing that's been repressed here's just the place to find it: in the taboo of the pregnant *woman*."[11]

Patriarchal systems of representation repress the (carnal) knowledge that the mother's body is a sexual one. What these systems seem to find difficulty with is that the mother's body, as Susan Suleiman points out, "is *also* that of a woman".[12] In the light of this, Christianity gives us the domesticated image of the Virgin Mary, the mother devoid of sexual desire. Mary literally embodies the fate of the virgin mother, existing only in relation to her perfect product, Christ. According to Adrienne Rich, "The divisions of labour and allocations of power in patriarchy demand not merely a suffering Mother, but one divested of sexuality: The Virgin Mary, *virgo intacta*, perfectly chaste."[13] Mary lives the impossible dilemma of femininity under patriarchy. She is appropriated as a vessel for divine productivity, and is represented as both virtuous and asexual. The contradictory logics of production and (sexual) reproduction are contained within her mute and silenced body. Mary has no sexuality and her only proof of physicality lies in the iconic representations of her milk and tears, symbols beyond language. The Virgin has no language in which to voice her own desire, a desire which Christianity, in any case, resolutely denies. According to Marina Warner, "it is this very cult of the Virgin's 'femininity', expressed by her sweetness, submissiveness, and passivity that permits her to survive, a goddess in a patriarchal society."[14] The idealisation of the asexual yet productive Virgin counters the threat of aggressive sexuality embodied in Eve. Christianity balances its ambivalence toward women, its contempt and idealisation, in the figures of Mary and Eve. The message here seems to be that woman is sanctioned only in her role as passive and silenced mother. Her desire is wholly contained within her maternal role and serves only the glory of devout and sacred reproduction.[15]

If women's resistance to patriarchal authority is focused on the mother's body it is arguable that this resistance will remain within a productive logic. Women (and others) may choose to speak from the place of the mother, in a contempt for the father's law, perhaps, though, patriarchal foundations can be threatened more radically from some other site. In this light Barbara Johnson argues that today (as always?) it is those *marginalised* men who are considered to speak most convincingly from the mother's body. She goes on to consider the possibility of women refusing to mimic these masculine mothers: "Were women to take over the critique of the paternal position, they might not remain content with the maternal role."[16] Domna Stanton is another who argues that both the maternal and metaphor remain locked within a paternal logic. She suggests that the metaphorical trope and the image of a productive maternity both reinforce phallocentric notions of self-presence and identity. Citing Derrida and Heidegger for support, she argues that metaphor serves an ontological function, one which posits a hidden essence.[17] In this logic woman is defined in terms of her essential maternity. Her identity is fixed to a static and theological conception of maternal presence. Stanton is suggesting that the image of the all-defining mother and, indeed, the rhetorical strategy of metaphor itself, are questionable tactics to adopt if women are to refuse the phallocentric imposition of a fixed and immutable identity. If women are to define themselves in terms other than patriarchal logic, then the appropria-tion of an onto-theological maternal metaphor may be at odds with their task.[18] Stanton's discussion draws upon Jacques Derrida's work which is criti-cal of the psychoanalytic understanding of metaphor elaborated by Lacan. Derrida claims that Lacan's discussion of metaphor reinforces a metaphysics of presence. Stanton uses Derrida's work to warn against the emergence of a theology of the mother, stressing that "the maternal, which is metaphorized as total being to substantiate a notion that can combat the paternal, represents only one aspect of potential female difference."[19]

Perhaps the mother's body is, in the end, no resistance to the father at all. Replacing paternal authority with an archaic maternal authority may ulti-mately amount to the same thing. The mother may exist only within the masculine imaginary, and thus offer no resistance to it. As far as Mary Daly is concerned, the image of the phallic mother represents a real threat to feminist struggle. She remains "boxed into the father's house of mirrors, merely re-sponding to the images projected/reflected by the Possessors".[20] When femi-nists theorise women only in these terms, as mother and bearer of a productive body, they risk falling into a similarly patriarchal trap: "Thus it is a pitfall simply to reverse 'penis envy' into 'womb envy', for such theories trick women into fixating upon the womb, female genitalia, and breasts as our ultimately most valuable endowments."[21] Daly exposes the phallocentrism behind the desire to fetishise the mother's body. She calls for a celebration of *woman* to replace the cult of the *mother*, and in so doing rejects the maternal metaphor as an emblem of feminist struggle. She claims that while man's envy of woman relates to the entirety of female creative energy, it becomes narrowly focused upon her reproductive ability.

Rich nonetheless alerts us to the problem of rejecting, out of hand, woman's maternal role.[22] While it is imperative that we question the status of our own arguments and assumptions, it is equally important that we keep sight of our initial concerns. The critique of the maternal metaphor is indispensable to contemporary feminist thought, though we must realise that in some respects it partakes of the logic to which it is opposed. We could argue that to some extent this critique reproduces the patriarchal foreclosure of the mother, that it silences the voice of the maternal body, demanding that woman voice her desire beyond its realm. In the light of this I think that it is important to focus on how the mother acts as both guarantor *and* disruption of man's sociality because any attempt to simply legislate against woman's maternity would amount to yet another repression of this radical ambivalence.

Mother's white ink: Hélène Cixous

Cixous is critical of the new form of repression or prohibition evident in certain feminist denunciations of maternity.[23] She writes, "Rather than depriving woman of a fascinating time in the life of her body just to guard against procreation's being recuperated, let's de-mater-paternalize. Let's defetishize."[24] Her texts are littered with references to the mother and her body, and for this reason they are a good place to pursue our discussion of the maternal. Cixous takes the necessary risk of employing the maternal metaphor in her work, arguing that it is only through the mother's body that women come to writing. For her the mother's body is the privileged metaphor of literary production; a production linked to excess and sexuality which breaks the narrow confines of patriarchal meaning and sense.

The pre-Oedipal terrain of the mother's body is the privileged site of the mother–daughter bond. For Cixous, the daughter learns her pre-verbal language here, her mother tongue. The mother's discourse is a language of voice and body, a maternal song. Cixous celebrates voice as a pre-symbolic fusion of body and breath, a continuum that refuses the division and separation of the father's speech.[25] "The Voice sings from a time before law, before the symbolic took one's breath away and reappropriated it into language under its authority of separation."[26] The mother's text re-establishes this link between writing and voice.[27] Cixous' writing enacts the breathless rhythm of the mother's song; the excessive movement of meaning and sense.[28] For her writing is a rhythm, a movement that defies the stability of definition and meaning. It is a song that involves the body in a breathless expenditure of self. Cixous' poetics encode this sense of movement, a gesture that returns again and again to the mother's body.[29] Her writing performs an elision of body, text and song in a style that captures the rhythmic movement of sexual encounter. Here woman comes to language in a breathless song of desire:

> Text: my body – shot through with streams of song … what touches you, the equivoice that affects you, fills your breast with an urge to come to language and launches your force; the rhythm that laughs you; the intimate recipient who makes all metaphors possible and desirable; body (body? bodies?), no more describable than god, the soul, or the Other; that part of you that leaves a space between yourself and urges you to inscribe in language your woman's style.[30]

Cixous' rhythmic texts defy the rigid grammatical divisions that impose an order on language. Her work shows how speech that has become disconnected from the body is a speech devoid of the body's gestures and breath. She seeks to undo this repression by resuscitating the censored body in writing. The mother, she argues, has a memory of such writing. Through the labour of child/self birth, the mother regains her censored body and breath. Her special relation to breathing allows the mother to write her body, to inscribe it in, what Cixous terms, her "mother's milk". The breast acts as a privileged topos of female expression: "a woman is never far from 'mother' ... There is always within her at least a little of that good mother's milk. She writes in white ink." And further: "Voice: milk that could go on forever. Found again. The last mother/bitter-lost. Eternity: is voice mixed with milk."[31]

The desire to write is linked continually with the desire to give birth. Cixous argues that language and writing find their own expression in pregnancy, which is experienced as a series of rhythms and exchanges. It is a metamorphosis that blurs the distinction between self and other, between writer and text. Pregnancy is experienced as a contradictory terrain, "where pleasure and reality embrace".[32] It is "the irreplaceable experience of those moments of stress, of the body's crises, of that work that goes on peacefully for a long time only to burst out in that surpassing movement, that time of childbirth".[33] Like the desire to write, the desire to give birth is "a desire to live self from within, a desire for the swollen belly, for language, for blood".[34] Both writing and birth are depicted as continuous processes, as metaphors for bringing forth and delivering.[35] Here body and text are conceived as sensuously linked to something other than an origin or source. The undecidability of mother and child, is mirrored in the fusion of body and text. "How", Cixous asks, "could the woman, who has experienced the not-me within me, not have a particular relationship to the written?"[36] Once again, the maternal body is the emblem of a fluid and mutable identity. Once again the maternal body pre-figures the fluid and mutable text.

Cixous' texts rewrite the Oedipal narrative of psychoanalytic theory toward both the mother and life. They reorient psychoanalysis toward the woman by focusing upon writing from and toward women. To this end, they redress the silence of a mute and mutilated mother whose repressed body serves as the unacknowledged support of patriarchal law:

> It is by writing, from and toward women, and by taking up the challenge of speech which has been governed by the phallus, that women will confirm women in a place other than that which is reserved in and by the symbolic, that is, in a place other than silence.[37]

Cixous' discourse of presence, of the body and voice, is a strategy aimed at dislodging the dominance and orthodoxy of a language that encodes absence and death. Where the mother, the self and the body are absent from patriarchal discourse they are conspicuously present in the maternal text. Cixous' writing inscribes this discourse of presence in order to shatter the disembodied logic of patriarchal philosophy. Presence, for her, is a splitting, an indistinct identity that has nothing to do with the subject's death.[38]

For Cixous there is indeed everything yet to be written by women. However, the question remains: how are we to write in a language that has so effectively silenced our voices? She claims that women are to begin simply *by* writing, and by doing so we will refuse to be the *dark continent* for a masculine imaginary which too readily designates this shadiness as evil. By reclaiming breath and word women will shatter the symbolic radiance of both father and son. While the Oedipal narrative reigns, women will remain confined to our traditionally passive role in the mother–son relation, a functional site reproducing the goods for a masculine economy of exchange, trapped, as Irigaray puts it, "in a single function – mothering."[39] Cixous urges us to write against this masculine narrative, to write toward the place of the mother as both body and breath.

While Cixous calls women to writing through the mother's body in an attempt to bypass the Oedipal relation with the son, there is a sense in which her own work fails to do this. There is arguably an uncritical adoption of the maternal metaphor in her work, one that reinforces rather traditional depictions of the mother. By focusing metaphorically on the mother's breast as the site of woman's (self)expression Cixous re-presents to us a maternal whose terrain is historically, socially and sexually overdetermined in rather masculine ways. To focus on the breast rather than the breasts is already to de-eroticise the mother's body reducing it to the site of nurturance.[40] It is a way of ensuring that the mother remains a mother only in relation to birth and suckling. There is something decidedly Oedipal lurking behind Cixous' celebratory manifesto of the mother.[41] Her simple yet lyrical assertion that women must write themselves with the mother's white ink reduces both woman and mother to stereotypically eroticised sites. There is something of a romantic polemicising that pervades Cixous' writing, an unreflective gaze that threatens to return us to a fairly traditional cult of the mother.

We need to do more than merely reproduce the mother as breast. We need an inscription of the maternal that does at least two things; one that actually refers to women as mothers (contra Kristeva) and one that theorises the terrain of the mother's body in less reductive terms (contra Cixous). We need to re-chart the maternal as a terrain of body *and* word. Irigaray's work arguably does both. In her writing we witness a metonymic displacement from the mother's breast toward the ambiguous terrain of the labia. The uncertain "lips" of Irigaray's poetic texts evoke a mother whose sexuality is always tied to speech, rather than the invisible (non-signifying?) ink of the breast. Before moving on to discuss Irigaray's work, though, we shall pause a while in order to look for the mother in the texts of Klein, Kristeva, Young and Rich. In doing so we shall resume our search for the *real* mother over and against her metaphorical inscriptions.

Writing the mother: Melanie Klein

Any discussion of the mother in psychoanalytic terms must necessarily engage with the work of Melanie Klein for it is she who most insistently returns to what we have provisionally termed the *real* mother in analytic theory and practice. While Freud manages mostly to avoid the question of the mother and Lacan erases her almost entirely behind the linguistic operation of metaphor, Klein insists that we think through the mother's body. According to Hanna Segal there are three distinct phases in Klein's work.[42] The first (around 1932) where Klein lays the foundations for child analysis, developing and perfecting her revolutionary "play technique". This is also the period where she begins to trace the Oedipus complex and super-ego to its early origins.[43] The second phase (1934–40) sees Klein formulating her concepts of the *depressive position* and the manic defence mechanisms.[44] The third phase (1946–57) is dominated by Klein's path-breaking work on the *paranoid-schizoid position*, the earliest developmental stage of pre-Oedipal psychic life.[45] From 1934 on, Klein begins the theoretical and clinical work necessary to develop her original psychoanalytic interventions. During this time she formulates her ideas on the "positions", and it is this work that marks her difference from Freud.[46] Now what are these positions and how do they operate? The paranoid-schizoid position is Klein's reworking of Freud's death instinct. She argues that this position, typically ranging from 3 to 4 months, is characterised by the child's relationship with part objects and its lack of awareness of whole "persons". In this position the ego splits in order to project its death instinct onto the external object, the breast. As a consequence the breast is experienced as bad and threatening to the remaining ego. Fear returns to the ego in the form of persecution from this threatening breast. Alongside this phantasy relation with the bad breast there co-exists a relation with the ideal breast, the projected libido that constructs the good breast as that which will endlessly satisfy the ego's preservative instincts. What occurs, then, is that part of the death instinct is projected out toward the bad and persecuting breast while part is retained and converted into aggressive impulses which attack this breast. Likewise, part of the libido is split off and projected out toward the loving and ideal breast while part is retained in order to establish a libidinal relationship with it.

Segal emphasises that we can understand this complex process of object relations in Klein's work only in relation to the *real* mother. For example, she writes: "The phantasy of the ideal object merges with, and is confirmed by, gratifying experiences of love and feeding by the real external mother" (p. 26). The same holds true for the *depressive position*, which starts from roughly the second half of the child's first year, and is distinguished from the paranoid-schizoid position by its awareness of the mother as a whole person. The child

relates himself more and more, not only to the mother's breast, hands, face, eyes, as separate objects, but to herself as a whole person, who can be at times good, at times bad, present or absent, and who can be both loved and hated.

(p. 68)

The depressive position first appears during the oral stage and it is marked by the child's development of a whole or unified ego, one that is not so distinctly split between its good and bad components. It is characterised as depressive because it is a time when the child feels its dependence on the mother who is independent and able to go away. During this time the child experiences guilt and mourning for the mother (object) it has lost or destroyed. Segal writes:

At the height of his ambivalence he is exposed to depressive despair. He remembers that he has loved, and indeed still loves his mother, but feels that he has devoured or destroyed her so that she is no longer available in the external world.

(p. 70)

While there is much debate as to how far Klein's work represents a departure from Freudian orthodoxy,[47] it is fair to say that with her focus on the positions we gain something new in psychoanalytic theory, a discourse on and of the mother. Klein's work shifts Freud's Oedipal focus back toward the earliest months of life, back toward the sensuous body-to-body relation with the mother, particularly the mother's breast. This represents a revolutionary moment in psychoanalytic theory, one that was in its time radical enough to split the British Psycho-Analytical Society in two.[48]

Klein's re-evaluation of the Oedipal complex demonstrates her theoretical shift toward the mother. She argues that Freud's work on the super-ego in the genital stages needs to be understood as a final stage of a much longer and more complex development reaching right back to the earliest months of life. These earlier stages are characterised by what Klein calls *object relationships*; they involve anxieties, defences, part object relations and whole object relations.[49] Simply put, Klein is suggesting that the child constructs a complex internal world initially in relation to the breast, and then later to the mother as a whole. The anxieties produced by these object relations are largely the result of phantasy, and they can and do have implications for how later Oedipal formations are played out.

Klein's discussion of the child's oral sadistic phase sheds some light on what she means by these object relations. She suggests that during this phase there is a parallel structure of love and destruction operating in the child's psychic relation with the part object, i.e. the mother's breast. On the one hand the child experiences the breast as "a bad persecuting internal breast", the destructive object that the child has incorporated into its own internal world. Segal notes that for Klein, this represents the "earliest root of the persecuting and sadistic aspect of the super-ego."[50] On the other hand, the child's experiences of love and gratification lead toward an introjection of a good or ideal loving breast which becomes the root of the ego-ideal aspect of the super-ego.[51] Eventually this part relationship with the breast is extended toward the mother's entire body. This whole relationship with the mother is characterised by a similar ambivalence. The movement from the breast to the mother's body will entail a flood of libidinal desire as well as an excess of destructive impulses prompted by the frustration and envy experienced in relation to the "bad" breast.[52]

Klein's genius is to focus on the bodily relation (both psychic and actual) with the mother. Her emphasis on the pre-Oedipal phase makes it possible to concentrate on the period of time when the mother's body dominates the child's phantasy world. Klein demonstrates the link between the child's relation with the mother's body and the development of symbol formation by showing how anxiety displaces the child's focus from that body to the external world.

> Thus through symbolization his interest in his mother's body begins to extend to the whole world around him. A certain amount of anxiety is a necessary spur to this development. If the anxiety is excessive, however, the whole process of symbol-formation comes to a stop.[53]

Klein manages to capture something that Freud does not, the overwhelming importance of the mother in the period before paternal authority intervenes with Oedipus. She introduces us not only to the phantasy mother, the ambivalent body that is, for the child, both loving and destructive, but also to the "real" mother. She explains that the "real" mother often reassures the anxious child who is terrified by the destructive mother or breast that it has internalised. The "real" mother also figures in relation to the child's own destructive phantasies. According to Segal "There is also a wish to make restitution and reparation to the real mother in real intercourse for damage done in phantasy" (p. 7). Klein believes that the anxieties produced from the part or whole object relations forces the child into a relation with the real or actual mother. As a consequence, Freud's Oedipal complex must be understood in relation to this maternal pre-history. Klein remains an insistent yet often unheard voice in the male-dominated institution of psychoanalysis. Her work on the mother's body, though historically derided by many of her male colleagues, brings to psychoanalytic theory a radical new dimension.

Given Klein's insistence on the mother it seems odd to me that she remains a somewhat symptomatic silence in the work of contemporary writers such as Cixous and Irigaray. What might this silence be symptomatic of? I think that Cixous' *white ink* bears some kind of maternal lineage with Klein's (ideal) breast and that Irigaray's work on reclaiming (or reparations toward?) the mother is Kleinian in its inspiration. Why, then, their silence? What does it mean for these daughters to silence their theoretical mother? This could be symptomatic of the fact that there is no Symposium operating between these women other than at the level of my text. The real question of silence operating here is perhaps not so much the repression of one individual text, but silence at the level of women speaking amongst themselves within the tradition of philosophy. In order to create an ongoing Symposium we need to do further work to draw out these connections between Klein and her philosophical "daughters".

At the time when Irigaray entered psychoanalytic discourse, Lacan's maternal metaphor held sway over French readings of Freud. In the previous chapter I hinted that Irigaray's contribution is to bring back the repressed and silenced mother, to speak the mother's body. Her play between the literal and metaphorical counters the nominalist tendencies of both Kristeva and Lacan. Her work entails a careful choreography between the kind of gesture Klein makes and the more linguistic preoccupations of French psychoanalysis. Given this I think that it is somewhat problematic that Irigaray focuses her psychoanalytic discussions around Freud and Lacan. A critical discussion or dialogue with Klein's work would certainly be a strategic contribution to (psychoanalytic) discourse amongst women. It would also constitute an attempt, on her part, to enter into philosophical dialogue with another woman. Given Irigaray's own views on the importance of a genealogy of women I find the absence of this dialogue more than a little disappointing. If Irigaray can *speak* with Diotima why can she not speak with Klein?

Mothers and the art of birth: Julia Kristeva

I have already indicated my concern about the metaphorical status of the maternal in Kristeva's work. I have argued that by avoiding reference to mothers her maternal *chora* serves to silence women in the place of theory. What I now want to say is that although her work is at times disconcerting from a feminist perspective it is, nonetheless, an extraordinarily fertile site of inquiry. By reading Kristeva I have managed to develop a series of questions around the maternal body and writing. As I continue to explore these questions I find, perhaps not surprisingly, that the status of Kristeva's work changes for me. My relation to her work on the maternal becomes more ambivalent as I proceed. I would even risk saying that her work becomes for me a kind of maternal text, one that oscillates between phallic and maternal mother. In the previous chapter I warned against constructing Kristeva too readily as the phallic mother, the theoretical text replete with all meaning and sense. Now I shall introduce a Kristeva that counters this phantasy, a Kristeva that might be thought of as maternal mother, one who speaks of the mother's body, the mother's desire and the mother's love.

While it is true that Kristeva's discussion of the transgressive maternal *chora* is not obviously a discussion about women it is not true to say that she ignores the question of the mother altogether. The mother's body, especially in pregnancy, is valorised in her work as the site of a disruptive refusal of paternal/

Oedipal logic. Even though her discussion shifts toward this body as once again a metaphor of transgression, it nonetheless speaks of the mother. There is a slide between the maternal and the mother that is largely absent from Kristeva's work on the *chora*.

Kristeva adopts the maternal body as an emblem or metaphor of the subject's ambivalent positioning. Maternity is for her the privileged realm of the subject's ambiguous stance between the sensuous pre-Oedipal bonds of maternal attachment and the disciplined separation of Oedipal (or symbolic) detachment. The mother's body is the lived terrain of this contradiction, serving as both source of a disruptive semiotic and as pre-condition for the productive symbolic. She reproduces the father's symbolic order while simultaneously destroying it with her pre-symbolic links to the disruptive realm of (unrestrained) libidinal drives. Kelly Oliver points out that, for Kristeva, the subjective processes of negation and identification are operating within the maternal prior to the subject's entry into the symbolic. She contends that: "This has tremendous consequences for psychoanalysis," because "In traditional Freudian and Lacanian psychoanalysis it is the paternal function that initiates the negation and identification that finally propels the infant into both language and subjectivity."[54] As a consequence, Kristeva's work threatens the primacy accorded to the paternal function. "Like the logic of negation, the logic of identification is already operating on the level of the semiotic body prior to the child's entrance into the Symbolic order" (p. 4).[55]

The struggle between identity and non-identity played out on this maternal terrain emphasises the significance of the body in questions of subjectivity. Again Oliver argues that this insistence on the body marks Kristeva's difference from structuralism in general and Lacan in particular. She shows how Kristeva herself fights against Lacan's "castration" of Freud by bringing back the drives.[56] All this suggests that the slippage between an active (phallic) mastery and a fluid (maternal) identity is necessarily experienced as a bodily struggle. It is an ongoing process that will never be fixed. We have already seen that for Kristeva the stable identity of humanist philosophy is an illusion. Subjectivity is a process, a movement that constantly transgresses the limits of identity. Remember that she speaks of the subject-in-process, rather than the stable subject; the subject caught between the primary processes of the body (the terrain Kristeva designates as the semiotic) and the secondary processes of signification (the symbolic). A subject that moves between identity and its splitting apart. Kristeva contends that the maternal is implicated in this catastrophe of identity.[57] The divided subject of modernity finds its most eloquent expression in the mother; "a woman or mother is a conflict – the incarnation of the split of the complete subject, a passion".[58] The maternal body constitutes a fold (*pli*) between the natural and the cultural, between the semiotic and the symbolic, between identity and its erasure. With pregnancy this fold becomes an explosive site, turning identity (culture and the symbolic) in on itself.[59] The catastrophe of the maternal body saves the mother from merely becoming the productive machine of symbolic reproduction. It effects an explosion of identity that places the mother on the other side of paternal law. Here Kristeva "prefigures" the Oedipal set up of Freudian psychoanalysis in her emphasis on the maternal function. According to Oliver this newly figured triangle includes "the narcissistic subject (the child), the abject mother (the mother's body), and the imaginary father (the mother's love)." She suggests that these terms correspond to "the mother's breast (maternal body), the mother's sex (birth), and the mother's womb (conception)."[60]

The maternal body shifts between the static terrain of identity (where the subject is positioned as master of an intentional and conscious agency) and the shifting ground of identity's dissolution. While pregnancy is a fundamental challenge to identity,[61] it is nonetheless accompanied by a fantasy of totality, a belief in the all-powerful phallic mother who is master of her (self)birth. The illusion of this totality is disrupted however by the embodied knowledge of the subject's division.[62] Pregnancy is the terrain of splitting that rehearses the mother's exile from the father's law. It is the separation of her sensuous and desiring body from the authority of his word.

We have already discussed the tendency in Kristeva's work to reduce the maternal body to a pre-symbolic experience of "self" that is later symbolised by the male artist. Given this, it is worth commenting on the different ways that Klein and Kristeva approach the question of the mother. Klein is primarily concerned with the child's phantasised and actual relation with the maternal figure, while Kristeva concentrates on the mother's relation with the foreign body of her pregnancy. For Kristeva, the mother's experience serves as the model, extreme though it is, for the (male) subject's radically split self.

While the mother's body is silenced by serving as the unacknowledged emblem of a divided self, it is also silenced by the discourses (such as science, Christian theology and Freudian psychoanalysis) that attempt to account for maternity. Kristeva explores these and argues that scientific language employs an objective discourse that evacuates subjective experience, focusing on the mother as merely the receptacle of the maternal function. In the language of Christian theology, the subject of maternity becomes enshrined as the sacred vessel of divinity associated with the cult of the Virgin.[63] The later expression of this divine maternity will culminate in the association of motherhood with the socially reproductive and conservative virtues of love, self-effacement and self-sacrifice. In the theoretical language of Freudian psychoanalysis she suggests that we find maternity described in terms of the daughter's repressed desire to bear her own father's child. Like the canonical discourse of Christian theology, Freud's discourse represents maternity in a wholly patriarchal context. The mother's desire exists only in so far as it is related to the father of the Oedipal text. Here the maternal body is robbed of its ambiguity and defined solely in its socially conservative reproductive sense. In the discourses of Western science, Christian theology and psychoanalytic theory, the reproduction of existing (patriarchal) society is made possible through a mother who is either evacuated or fashioned to the prevailing desire of masculinity.

However Kristeva argues that the mother's desire exceeds this paternal causality. And this is where her work again becomes interesting for our purposes because it brings the mother back into theoretical focus. She contends that motherhood is associated as well with the pre-Oedipal, maternal desire. She speaks of this as the homosexual-maternal facet of motherhood, one that disrupts the heterosexual-paternal orientation of the mother within symbolic relations. "The homosexual-maternal facet is a whirl of words, a complete absence of meaning and seeing; it is a feeling, displacement, rhythm, sound, flashes and fantasised clinging to the maternal body as a screen against the plunge."[64] This aspect of motherhood is repressed by Freud as it dislodges the authority of Oedipal dynamics. It speaks of a space elsewhere to the Oedipal drama, celebrating the woman-to-woman relations that Freud has largely ignored.

> Such an excursion to the limits of primal regression can be phantasmatically experienced as the reunion of a woman-mother with the body of *her* mother ... By giving birth, the woman enters into contact with her mother; she becomes, she is her own mother; they are the same continuity differentiating itself. She thus actualizes the homosexual facet of motherhood, through which a woman is simultaneously closer to her instinctual memory, more open to her own psychosis, and consequently, more negatory of the social, symbolic bond.[65]

Though Kristeva is not explicit on this point I would suggest that this homosexual facet of motherhood situates the woman in an entirely different position from the man when she takes the place of the mother. In chapter three I argued that masculine psychosis involved a murderous appropriation of the mother's role. The psychosis that Kristeva evokes here might arguably be understood as anything but murderous. It is, in effect, a sensuous re-attachment to the maternal body achieved at the cost of negating the father's law. The repression of mother–daughter love is lifted in a flagrant denial of paternal authority. If there is a murder committed, it is the unholy execution (and denial) of the father's phallic law. Kristeva's homosexual-maternal facet of motherhood resists the paternal representation of motherhood in patriarchal discourses. She argues that against this maternal facet patriarchy erects the mother as a phallic mother, a living likeness of the masculine subject who is (the imagined) master of his own house. This phallic mother is a ruthless master of her own interiority, the self-conscious subject in control of the processes of maternity and birth. Kristeva distinguishes the *mother* from the *genetrix*. These would seem to correspond roughly to her identification of maternal and paternal mothers. The genetrix is ordered by the paternal function and is thus associated with his law. The genetrix reproduces the father's obsession with production, meaning and sense. It is implicated in the reproductive chain of value and exchange.[66] While the genetrix is reduced to generation, the giving of both birth and meaning to the father's law, the mother stands outside this, refusing to produce in the father's name.[67] The mother's desire is thus meaningless from the father's perspective. It transgresses his need to acquire, to appropriate and to have. It goes beyond the procreative function that he historically subordinates to his name.

We find evidence of this maternal germination in what Kristeva terms the genotext. Like the semiotic, the *genotext* undermines the structure, sense and significance of the symbolic or paternal text (the *phenotext*). It resists the production of meaning that accompanies the paternal function. While the phenotext articulates the secondary processes of signification, the genotext inscribes the primary process of the body dominated by rhythm, gesture and intonation. The genotext inscribes the semiotic maternal rhythms that disrupt the logic of grammar and nomination. It is writing that involves the instinctual motility of the body; the libidinal drives that escape the discipline of productive law. This semiotic inscription is prior to (paternal) signification. It links the text to the mother's jubilant body: "To rediscover the intonations, scansions, and jubilant rhythms preceding the signifier's position as language's position is to discover the voiced breath that fastens us to an undifferentiated mother."[68]

In her exploration of mother love in "Héréthique de l'amour" Kristeva reproduces the play between semiotic and symbolic modalities. She constructs a maternal text that follows the association of writing with both the body and love, and positions it as a marginal inter-text to the "main" text. In this piece of writing the linearity, coherence and meaning of the paternal text is spatially and logically disrupted by the semiotic eruption of the maternal inter-text.[69] The authority of the paternal text is put into question by the rhythmic play of the maternal inter-text. Body, rhythm and writing are entwined in a poetic inscription of the maternal body/text. "What is love, for a woman, the same thing as writing ... WORD FLESH. From one to the other, externally, fragmented visions, metaphors of the invisible ... a submerged, transverbal correspondence of bodies."[70] This work inscribes the contradictions of the maternal body and seeks to give voice to the repressed (mother) tongue of maternity. It disrupts the civility of symbolic (paternal) law, and attempts to redress the foreclosure of the mother by celebrating her body/text.[71] Kristeva urges us to explore maternity for its wealth of repressed material. Various analyses of the maternal function can be found throughout the entire corpus of her work. Indeed the maternal serves to organise her major theoretical preoccupations, whether these be literary, philosophical, psychoanalytic or linguistic. We could say that the maternal functions in a rather semiotic way in her work in that it both orders and at times disorders the sharp precision of her prose.[72]

Kristeva contends that the language of women's love for one another,[73] hidden within the mother–daughter bond, must be spoken in order to disorder the patriarchal representations of love that deny this intimacy:

> For more than a century now, our culture has faced the urgent need to reformulate its representations of love and hate, inherited from Plato's *Symposium*, the troubadours, and Our Lady, in order to deal with the relationship of one woman to another.[74]

However, she argues elsewhere that this intimacy between mother and daughter must ultimately be mediated by the paternal symbolic. She writes:

> Is it not true that [for] a woman … to have access to the symbolic-thetic level, which requires castration and object, she must tear herself from the daughter–mother symbiosis, renounce the undifferentiated community of women and recognize the father at the same time as the symbolic?[75]

This forces us to think about the relationship between maternal and paternal tongues. How are we to characterise the nature of the ambivalent bond spoken between women? Kristeva posits a maternal economy working in parallel with paternal or symbolic language. Are we to characterise these economies in spatial terms? Is the maternal outside the symbolic, or part of it? These questions take us back to the concerns of our opening chapter, and I shall return to them in the conclusion of this book.

Toward a feminist poetics: writing (and) the mother's body

Kristeva's focus on woman's pregnant body has influenced the work of Iris Marion Young. In Young's writing we find a commitment to inscribing the subjectivity of pregnancy. Hers is a phenomenological account centred on and in the mother. She begins by repeating Kristeva's claim that there is little literature, scientific or otherwise, "concerned with the subject, the mother as the site of her proceedings."[76] She confirms Kristeva's account of the split subjectivity of the pregnant woman and goes on to say that the pregnant woman is split between self and other, between her own body and the memory of her mother's, and finally between an experience of self that moves between past and future.[77] Young's account of the "lived pregnant body" is an elaboration and critique of existential phenomenological accounts such as Maurice Merleau-Ponty's. It is an attempt to write in and through the experience of being pregnant, one that we could perhaps characterise as more "personal" than Kristeva's theoretical discussion of splitting. Young's writing, while touching up against these theoretical concerns, provides a style that is fully sensuous so I quote from it at length here:

As my pregnancy begins, I experience it as a change in my body; I become different from what I have been. My nipples become red-dened and tender; my belly swells into a pear. I feel this elastic around my waist, itching, this round, hard middle replacing the doughy belly with which I still identify. Then I feel a little tickle, a little gurgle in my belly. It is my feeling, my insides, and it feels somewhat like a gas bubble, but it is not; it is different, in another place, belonging to another, another that is nevertheless my body.

(pp. 162–3)

The birthing process entails the most extreme suspension of the bodily distinction between inner and outer. As the months and weeks progress, increasingly I feel my insides, strained and pressed, and increasingly feel the movement of a body inside me. Through pain and blood and water this inside thing emerges between my legs, for a short while both inside and outside me. Later I look with wonder at my mushy middle and at my child, amazed that this yowling, flailing thing, so completely different from me, was there inside, part of me.

(p. 163)

There is an attempt to reach the sexual and desirous nature of the mother's pregnant body in Young's writing. She is concerned to chart the possible meanings supporting the cultural desexualisation of pregnancy, suggesting that, in an affirmative sense, this may liberate the woman from the "sexually objectifying gaze that alienates and instrumentalizes her when in her non-pregnant state" (pp. 166–7). This has the potential to release her from the "leer of sexual objectification", making it possible to experience a kind of self-love that is not typical in our present societal relations.

The pregnant woman's relation to her body can be an innocent nar-cissism. As I undress in the morning and evening, I gaze in the mir-ror for long minutes, without stealth or vanity. I do not appraise myself, ask whether I look good enough for others, but like a child take pleasure in discovering new things in my body. I turn to the side and stroke the taut flesh that protrudes under my breasts.

(p. 166)

The sensual subjectivity that Young inscribes in her discussion of pregnancy makes it possible to locate the mother in theoretical discourse. Her text avoids silencing the mother behind a screen of metaphors designed largely to release her from any subjective or speaking position. Young's phenomenological ac-count provides us with a mother's discourse.

A mother's discourse would also be a good way to describe the work of

Adrienne Rich. The tensions inherent in motherhood form the basis of her highly influential book, *Of Woman Born*. Rich's study analyses the contradiction between the images of a potential maternity and the sharp reality of its daily practice. She examines the contrary meanings of motherhood in contemporary Western societies, arguing that the potential experience of a woman to her body and children are at odds with the patriarchal expression of that experience. The institution of motherhood, she claims, works against woman's reproductive potential. This is most obvious in woman's relation to her silenced body. "In the most fundamental and bewildering of contradictions, it has alienated women from our bodies by incarcerating us in them."[78] Rich's study explores the content of women's contradictory experience, and in the process enacts its own contradiction. The impossibility of writing a scholarly book on motherhood results in a poetic mingling of textual forms. On the one hand Rich constructs a scholarly text, a careful analysis of research and critique. Opposed to this is a poetic text, a literary inscription of Rich's maternal experience found in diary entries or work parenthetically marginalised from the text. The themes of attachment and detachment are played out in both the form and content of Rich's work, resulting in an ambivalent text that wavers chiastically between the paternal and the maternal, between philosophy and literature, between reflection and experience. So, like the maternal body, Rich's text inhabits a contradictory terrain. Woven amongst the threads of linear argument are moments of rhythmic intensity which reinforce the undecidable nature of mothering: "My children cause me the most exquisite suffering of which I have any experience. It is the suffering of ambivalence: the murderous alternation between bitter resentment and raw-edged nerves, and blissful gratification and tenderness." And later: "(the unconscious of the young mother – where does it entrust its messages, when dream-sleep is denied her for years?)".[79] In the second passage (an afterthought, carefully marginalised from the surrounding text) Rich associates her poetic text with the unconscious, that which consciousness represses in its relentless search for meaning and truth. Rich's text, then, stands in metaphorically for the maternal body, a complex weave of order and disorder, of play and display.[80]

The ambivalence of the maternal body is further explored by Rich through the twin poles of power and vulnerability. She examines the ways in which patriarchy has been unable to situate woman's body, how it has defied a stable representation. Woman's body remains an enigma for men, an undecidable space that lacks a coherent identity.

> The woman's body, with its potential for gestating, bringing forth and nourishing new life, has been through the ages a field of contradictions: a space invested with power, and an acute vulnerability; a numinous figure and the incarnation of evil; a hoard of ambivalences.[81]

These competing images of woman's body within patriarchal ideology are paralleled by the contradictory images of her body as both pure and impure. Patriarchal mythology (in its many guises of literature, dream-symbolism, and philosophy) constructs woman's body as "impure, corrupt, the site of discharges, bleedings, dangerous to masculinity, a source of moral and physical contamination", while at the same time representing (phantasising) the mother's body as "beneficent, sacred, pure, asexual, [and] nourishing".[82] Here the age-old contradiction of the asexual mother is opposed to the sexual woman; one nourishing, the other a threat.

We can read Rich's text as autobiography,[83] i.e. her attempt to chronicle the contradictions and tensions of her own birth through the twin processes of mothering and writing. In her work she makes overt references to self-birth and gestation:

I knew I was fighting for my life through, and against, and with the lives of my children, though very little else was clear to me. I had been trying to give birth to myself; and in some grim, dim way I was determined to use even pregnancy and parturition in that process.

I cannot imagine having written this book without the presence in my life of my mother, who offers a continuing example of transformation and rebirth.

I wanted to give birth, at twenty-five, to my unborn self, the self that our father-centred family had suppressed in me, someone independent, actively willing, original – those possibilities I had felt in myself in flashes as a young student and writer, and from which, during pregnancy, I was to close myself off. If I wanted to give birth to myself as a male, it was because males seemed to inherit these qualities by the right of gender.[84]

Read as autobiography Rich's text offers an insight into the complexity of women's writing. As mother, daughter and honorary male, Rich explores the multiple identities of women in relation to birth and writing. The impossibilities of writing as a woman are painfully inscribed in her fight for an independence and identity which, in our society, is too often still encoded as male. In her account pregnancy is both consonant with, and distinct from, the writing process. The maternal body is once again the site of an extraordinary struggle.

A daughter's discourse about the mother is evident in Luce Irigaray's work. Irigaray celebrates the body-to-body relation of women in her poetic writing. She rejects the phallocentric gesture that relegates femininity to an unspoken position in discourse, arguing that the psychoanalytic insistence on Oedipus effectively censors the girl's relation to her mother:

she has, imposed on her, a language, fantasms, a desire which does not "belong" to her and which establishes a break with her auto-eroticism. The kind of *schizo* which every woman experiences, in our socio-cultural system, only leaves her with nothing more than somatisations, corporal pains, mutism, or mimetism with which to express herself: saying and doing "like men".[85]

For Irigaray women literally embody the crisis of a silence symbolically imposed. Women's return from this state of exile is dependent upon their exploring this bodily crisis in writing. Irigaray insists that we chart the excesses and ambiguities that surround the prohibition distancing us from our mothers' bodies. In doing so we shall shatter the exclusive privilege of the male poet's incestuous mother-tongue. Her own work begins the preliminaries toward a possible exchange:

> Haven't you let yourself be touched by me? Haven't I held your face between my hands? Haven't I learned your body? Living its fullness. Feeling the place of its passage – and of the passage between you and me. Making from your gaze an airy substance to inhabit me and shelter me from our resemblance. From your/my mouth, an unending horizon. In you/me and out of you/me, clothed or not, because of our sex. In proportion to our skin. Neither too large nor too small. Neither wide open nor sutured. Not rent, but slightly parted.[86]

Irigaray's texts evoke the excesses of language, the pluralities and multiplicities of meaning that are repressed by the pursuit of singular and rational truth. Her work performs a kind of delirium that inscribes multiple voices in an operatic cacophony of sound. "Hers are contradictory words, somewhat mad from the standpoint of reason."[87] From this perspective a congealed and stable meaning gives way to the fluidity (or negativity?) of speech. "You remain in flux, never congeal or solidifying. What will make that current flow into words? It is multiple, devoid of causes, meanings, simple qualities."[88]

Irigaray's celebration of plurality is the basis for her bodily poetics (*poétique du corps*). In later work she celebrates the visionary role of the poet/lover, who literally embodies the sonorous vibrations of a language excessive to meaning. Her poet/lover risks all by refusing the stability of dwelling or abode in order to enter a boundless openness:

> And so, those who renounce their own will go towards one another. Calling on one another beneath all saying [*dire*] already said, all words already uttered, all speech [*parole*] already exchanged, all rhythms already hammered out. They draw one another into the mystery of a word [*verbe*] seeking to be made flesh. Trusting inordinately in that which makes the body and the flesh of all diction: air, breath, song.

Giving, receiving themselves/one another in the as yet unfelt/beyond reason [*l'encore insensé*]. So as to be reborn of it, invested with the telling [*dire*] of a forgotten inspiration. Buried beneath all logic. Surplus to any existing language [*langage*].[89]

Through her writing Irigaray attempts to exceed masculine representations of woman's sexuality. Her seductive elision of body and text links woman to an ambiguous textual process: "Her sexuality, always at least double, goes even further: it is *plural*. Is this the way culture is seeking to characterize itself now? Is this the way texts write themselves/are written now?"[90]

While the practice of writing *about* women's bodies has long been seen as a transgressive one, I think that what Irigaray is proposing here is something quite different. Her writing *from* and *by* women challenges the monopoly of an incestuous poetic masculinity that has always spoken *for* them. Irigaray's poetic excesses unsettle even the most uncivil of sons, those marginal men who flaunt paternal authority from the safety of the maternal apron.[91] In this she departs significantly from Kristeva's work. Her *poétique du corps* exceeds avant-garde textual practice by conjuring a radical sexuality. Here she plays with an understanding of the body somewhere between textual and referential sites.[92] By inscribing a plural sexuality Irigaray creates new possibilities for women's sexual experience, ones that exceed existing phallocentric accounts. This textual *poïesis* brings new "bodies" into play. We might think of her poetics as an undecidable practice that slips back and forth between "real" and discursive bodies, an a-topos that refuses to be fixed in either terrain. This strategy of slippage (*glissement*) confounds the certainty of a (masculine) logic that would seek to identify woman once and for all. Could this slippage be close to what Derrida calls "a strategy without finality", a play that is not bound by mastery, domination or truth?[93] Derrida also speaks of a sliding and with it a twist: "A certain strategic twist must be imprinted upon language; and this strategic twist, with a violent sliding, furtive movement must inflect the old corpus in order to relate its syntax and its lexicon to major silence."[94]

The sliding Derrida has in mind here is a poetic one that forces language to confront the silence that inhabits it. Irigaray's *poétique du corps* performs this "strategic twist", this "violent sliding", this "furtive movement", by confounding the stability of language. Her textual *poïesis* has this impulsional quality; it moves back and forth between the indeterminable sites of sexuality and text. Her play on the "lips" performs this slippage (one that locates itself between anatomical reference and modernist text).[95] Irigaray's more recent work on the space of "*l'intervalle*" also performs this slippage. Carolyn Burke tells us that, in her insistence on *l'intervalle*, Irigaray:

abandons the definitions and distinctions of conventional discourse
to explore those intermediary rhythms and spaces in the human passions (such as admiration of the other, the caress, and the moment of

the nuptials) where a regenerating sense of mutuality can still be found.[96]

The ambiguous and slippery terrain of woman's sexuality that Irigaray writes, at once metaphorical and not, is powerfully poetic in its excess of language and word:

> Between our lips, yours and mine, several voices, several ways of speaking resound endlessly, back and forth. One is never separable from the other. You/I: we are always several at once. And how could one dominate the other? impose her voice, her tone, her meaning? One can not be distinguished from the other; which does not mean that they are indistinct.[97]

Irigaray writes the mother into discourse via the daughter. She shows us how writing from and toward the mother's body exceeds a simple imitation of masculine texts. She inscribes the mother's body as sexual and desiring and perhaps most poignantly as one with language. By shifting her focus away from the maternal breast, as privileged topos of female sexuality, toward the ambiguous lips, Irigaray forces us to confront the possibility of a speaking mother who offers us words.

From body to voice: labial logic

I hope that by gathering together the voices of various women we have been able to hear something that we do not usually hear when we read their work in isolation. It seems to me that we can resist the temptation toward constructing our own phallic theoretical mothers by situating individual works within the context of a maternal genealogy. I suggest that Klein's work serves as just this kind of context. Klein provides us with a discussion of the mother as pivotal to the acquisition of language. The possibility of symbolisation, for the child, is inseparable from the separation or movement away from the mother's body. How successfully we negotiate this movement is what interests Klein. I suggest that what we need to be interested in, as feminists and philosophers, is how successful we have been in separating from the theoretical body of Klein's work. Only by separating from her can we actually recognise her in order to bring her into the "canon". I suspect that neither Irigaray nor Cixous have adequately separated from her body of theory and that this prevents them from entering into theoretical dialogue with her. While Klein remains a silent part of them they are precluded from entering into theoretical dialogue with her. We need to acknowledge rather than to silence Klein. By doing so we can begin to ask serious questions about the role of her work in feminist theory. I am not fully convinced that this has been the case, particularly in psychoanalytic circles where Freud and Lacan retain central stage. I am suggesting that we are in danger of silencing Klein if we fail to think through the maternal genealogy that ties our theoretical and conceptual problems to her earlier work.

Melanie Klein's work, though it stays pretty close to the breast, does signal a movement from the mother's body to a speech of sorts. Her own theoretical movement between the phantasised and *real* mother in the child's psychic life provides us with an intriguing account of the incorporation and expulsion of the mother's body as a fundamental basis for the child's acquisition of language and symbolisation. Recall that Klein links the internal psychic processes of phantasy and unconscious anxiety with the development of symbol-formation. These internal processes, focused as they are on the mother's body, propel the child out toward the world. The child's interests and anxieties with the mother's breast, and then later her entire body, become displaced through symbolisation to the world around it. Klein emphasises the pivotal role of the mother, here, by adding that if, for whatever reason, the child's anxiety is excessive, the entire process of symbol-formation will cease. Klein provides us with a way of thinking language through the mother's body, one that starts with the breast and continues on through to the symbolic realm. In effect she theorises the mother's body as the necessary condition of language. It is perhaps fair to say, though, that her focus really remains the child. And this is, I would suggest, one of the major problems of those accounts positing a *real* mother. Klein positions her saga on the child's terrain, arguably reinforcing the mother's body as the necessary and yet silent space of the *child's* symbolic articulation. It is the child who acquires symbolisation not the incorporated and expelled mother/breast. Of course, we could argue that this is a problem if we can only think of the child as a boy, because the mother–daughter bond destabilises the identity and distinction of mother and child. Klein's account arguably retains this distinction or separation between mother and child, an opposition that is later problematised in Irigaray's mother–daughter bond where the mother and child are no longer clearly opposites.

Hélène Cixous positions her call to women around the mother's breast, adopting it as an emblem of patriarchal defiance. There is a movement of sorts from the mother's breast to writing, in that Cixous exhorts women to "express themselves" in their mother's white ink. While I have criticised her for romanticising the figure of the mother and focusing unreflectively on the breast as the archetypal topos of femininity, I suppose that in fairness we could say that Cixous' breast is at least a writing one. In contrast to Klein's breast, it provides women with a site of self-expression, of language. While Klein's breast provides the child with its drama of anxiety and phantasy necessary to propel it out into the world of symbolisation, Cixous' breast is theorised as the place of the mother writing.

The ambiguity of Kristeva's work on the mother/maternal makes it difficult to summarise, nonetheless we must ask whether we can discern a movement

156

from the mother's body to writing in her account. I have already indicated that I do not believe this to be so in her work on the maternal, but what of her work on the mother? The mother who comes to us in Kristeva's discussion of pregnancy is not a writing or speaking one. She is the model of a split and divided identity, a catastrophe that threatens the illusory coherence of the paternal order. She does not write. She does not speak. We can speak and write this mother's body for her in genotextual, semiotic or poetic forms, but there is no evidence, in Kristeva's work, that *she* can do this for herself. Kristeva's work remains located on the terrain of the child, poet or artist as speaking subject, not on that of the mother.

Iris Marion Young's work is interesting in this regard, for although there is no movement theorised from the mother's body to writing in her account, it is significant that she writes *as* mother. Her work *performs* this movement rather than theoretically pre-supposing or accounting for it. (Perhaps the same can be said of Kristeva's performance in "Stabat Mater".) She provides us with a sensuous account of her own body, a text that shifts registers from phenomenological description to the pleasures of a mother's private thought. This kind of performance is also evident in Adrienne Rich's work where the everyday reality of her motherhood finds its way into both the analytic and poetic structures of her text. Rich goes beyond Young's rather earnest account, though, by presenting her work on motherhood in a more self-consciously autobiographical form, one that draws out the affinities between the processes of writing (on motherhood) and giving birth to herself. For Rich the experiences of the mother's body provide a pre-text or con-text for the act of writing. For her it is the mother who writes.

These kinds of mother's discourses have something in common with Luce Irigaray's work, in that each attempts to write the mother into the symbolic realm. Irigaray, however, is more explicit in her concern to theorise the movement from the mother's body to language. Positioning herself as daughter she self-consciously moves from the topos of masculine phantasy – the breast – around the mother's body, a metonymic movement from the breast to the lips. In doing so Irigaray displaces the traditional metaphor of mother as nourishment with the disruptive figure of an ambiguous labial sexuality that speaks the complex relationality of mother and girl-child. Irigaray's bi-labial trope is important because it deconstructs the oppositional nature of the self–other relation. It is deconstructive because it shifts "language" away from an oppositional logic of reference versus metaphor toward something much closer to the play of *différance*. It displaces the problematic of "the Other" by "speaking to the same". The singularity of the labia is always *double*, never one. This labial logic confounds oppositional thinking. It displaces oppositions such as inside and outside, self and other, reference and metaphor. What this means for our purposes is that Irigaray's work disrupts the entire terrain of our earlier discussion. Questions of exclusion (of inside/outside, of speaking/not speaking, of silence/speech) lapse with the labial logic that now focuses on *how* to speak.

This deconstructive gesture summons an ambiguous space that is no longer concerned with the theoretical or spatial organisation dominated by *the* symbolic. Irigaray shifts us away from a concern with the symbolic, a concern that readily opposes representation to non-representation, symbolic to semiotic (Kristeva), denotation to metaphor (Lacan), in the manner of more orthodox psychoanalytic linguistic accounts. Her labial logic is not about the symbolic, it is, rather, about difference. While others, such as Kristeva and Lacan, remain covertly concerned with language as a system of representation, Irigaray moves against this by offering us lips that are different, lips that are not one but two in one. The difference Irigaray makes is thus a speaking difference, a labial difference grounded in non-identity. What this implies for women's speech is that we need no longer organise our discussions around the conceptual oppositions of silence and speech. Rather we need to focus on the conditions of possibility of that speech. Irigaray's labial logic enables us to do this by situating the play of difference ambiguously somewhere between the mothers' and daughters' lips. And I contend that this makes a world of difference to simply repeating the same.

8

MOTHERS AND DAUGHTERS
Speaking

For more than a century now, our culture has faced the urgent need to reformulate its representations of love and hate, inherited from Plato's *Symposium*, the troubadours, and Our Lady, in order to deal with the relationship of one woman to another. Here again, maternity points the way to a possible solution: a woman rarely, I do not say never, experiences passion – love or hate – for another woman, without at some point taking the place of her own mother – without becoming a mother herself and, even more importantly, without undergoing the lengthy process of learning to differentiate herself from her daughter, her simulacrum, whose presence she is forced to confront.

(Julia Kristeva, "Stabat Mater")

In the previous chapter I gathered together, in the manner of a Symposium, writing by women on the mother. I did so in order to raise the possibility of talking about the *real* mother over and against her metaphorical inscription. What emerged from that discussion was a set of problems arising from various attempts to theorise this *real* mother. The problems of these accounts tend toward the following: either they subsume the mother beneath a theoretical concern with the child, or they sustain an oppositional division between mother and child. However, Irigaray's work offers us a different way of thinking through these questions, one that refuses to position mother and daughter in oppositional terms. It is this complex relationality of the mother and daughter that provides the focus for this final chapter.

Mothers and daughters writing

Susan Suleiman explains that for Freud the real Oedipal drama unfolds between the father and the son and that the mother functions only incidentally as mediator between them.[1] However, feminist work seeks to theorise how the mother's sexual body threatens this Oedipal scenario. From this perspective the mother is no longer content to remain the body upon which the father and son will stage their deathly battle; the mother proceeds to voice a desire of her own. In such accounts the mother is the subject, rather than the object, of critical inquiry. This is significant, because the mother's arrival as subject does more than revise Freud's theory; it displaces the Oedipal saga. This involves writing a philosophy *from* the mother, not one *about* her. A philosophy of birth explores the repressed mother of patriarchal love and foregrounds the relations between women, especially the mother–daughter bond.

As we have seen with Klein, in psychoanalytic theory since Freud the mother has been partially regained with an emphasis on the pre-Oedipal phase. Here the child's relation to the maternal body is analysed as a legitimate concern. The pre-Oedipal marks the period prior to the child's inscription into both language and culture. It is the maternal phase that pre-dates entry into paternal law and authority. Often, it is described as a pre-verbal or pre-linguistic phase, a time when bodily drives and sensuous attachment to the maternal body are not yet disciplined by the father's social demands. We have seen how Object-relations theory posits the primacy of this pre-Oedipal phase.[2] It attempts to explain the processes whereby the infant gradually becomes an individuated identity, a self. The role of the mother's body is central to such an understanding, and is therefore privileged in this scheme. The individuation-separation process constituting the subject or self is analysed in relation to the mother. Feminists working in psychoanalytic theory have adapted the insights of Object-relations in their attempt to give priority to the repressed mother of the Oedipal narrative.[3] Much of this work focuses on the continuity of the self and other in the mother–infant relation, the space prior to individuation, where identity is perceived as a continuous rather than separate construction. It focuses, too, on the neglected story of the mother-daughter bond.

This stress on the pre-Oedipal mother–daughter bond finds parallel expression in literature and literary criticism.[4] Here feminists explore the hidden representations of mothers and daughters arguing that, as Marianne Hirsch puts it, they constitute "the hidden subtext of many texts".[5] The close bond of mother and daughter is often enacted in the various strategies of a text. The relationship between characters, between the author and her characters, between the author and the reader are all encoded as textual strategies which aim to deconstruct the logic of patriarchal discourse. The sharp distinction between autonomous and distant characters is replaced with a writing that stresses affiliation, interrelation and community. According to Hirsch, this involves a strong emphasis on the relational nature of the mother–daughter bond.[6]

The pre-verbal bond between the mother and daughter is reawakened in much women's literature when the daughter gives birth herself. In this act she recaptures the intense attachment to her own mother's body, an embodied memory that exists prior to, and beyond, language. For Adrienne Rich, this is a subversive memory, one that exceeds the civility of the father's law: "Mothers and daughters have always exchanged with each other – beyond the verbally transmitted lore of female survival – a knowledge that is subliminal, subversive, preverbal: the knowledge flowing between two alike bodies".[7] The undecidability of woman's identity is played out in this mother–

daughter bond. Daughters become mothers, and mothers remember themselves as daughters in a process that blurs the stability of distinction. When
a woman gives birth she does so to a child, yet in another sense also to her
self. A popular theme of feminist literature explores women's attempts to
give birth to themselves. We might argue that unlike the phantasies of patriarchal mothering (where men violently repress or foreclose the image of the
mother in order to master themselves), women's stories of self-birth involve
an attempt to recapture the sensuous experience of their own mother's body
within themselves.

A number of contemporary women writers entwine the themes of creativity, birth and myth. Rachel Du Plessis, Adrienne Rich, Muriel Rukeyser,
Margaret Atwood and Hélène Cixous are amongst those who do so. In each
case a phantasy of self-birth is invoked in order to convey woman's awaken-
ing. Alicia Ostriker points out that in Rachel Du Plessis' poem-sequence
"Eurydice" woman withdraws within herself becoming "a self-generating
plant and finally, amid an efflorescence of organic images, her own mother,
giving birth to the girlchild who is herself – or, since the sequence can be
read as an allegory of female creativity, the poem."[8] In *Surfacing* Margaret
Atwood explores a woman's quest for her own rebirth. Haunted by the memory
of her dead mother, she goes in search of herself.[9] Susan Gubar describes the
journey:

> she must become her own mother. When she solves the mystery of
> her own identity, she emerges to give birth to a divine child as in the
> old myth and to a new and more integrated self ... she is clearly in
> the process of bearing herself anew.[10]

Hélène Cixous carries the theme of rebirth throughout her work. She argues that the body is censored at the same time as breath and speech are
denied. This lifeless body is consequently reborn through the labour of
heavy breathing, an act which is synonymous with both speech and writing. For Cixous woman returns to herself through writing, and emerges
with her body intact. She explores the maternal imagery of breathing and
labour, and as Susan Suleiman points out, her writing enacts the breathless
act of birth itself.

> The primary voice who speaks in the text and who says "I" fantasizes
> several violent scenes of birth, both by herself and by another – per-
> haps her own – mother. She herself harbours a number of mothers
> within her, and eventually gives birth to a young woman who is per-
> haps another version of herself. She also gives birth to this text, which
> is "delivered" from her body. Throughout there is a tremendous ver-
> bal energy and a kind of breathlessness ... as if everything were being
> written in a single breath.[11]

Phil Powrie uses the metaphor of the *womb-room* to trace the twin themes of independence and rebirth in the texts of the recent French women writers Chantal Chawaf, Marie Cardinal and Annie Leclerc. Powrie argues that in their attempts at (textual) rebirth they employ the womb-room metaphor "to radically and increasingly dis/organize paternal fictions" (p. 197) and contends that in these texts "the womb-room is less a trope for confinement and monstrosity, and more a sign of independence and locus of transformation, usually linked with writing, a necessary extension to the prison-house of patriarchal language" (p. 198).[12]

This sketch of the literary evidence suggests that women's explorations of birth involve a merger with the maternal body rather than an appropriation, denial or foreclosure of it. Indeed, Luce Irigaray argues something like this when she suggests that there is no symmetry between masculine and feminine gestures toward the maternal origin. She writes:

> if you are a boy, you will want … [to] get inside the mother who is the place of origin, in order to re-establish continuity with it and to see and know what happens there … If you are born a girl, the question is quite other. The girl will herself be the place where the origin is repeated, re-produced and reproduced.[13]

With Irigaray's argument in mind we can suggest that a woman will experience the continuity between herself and her mother in her literary mythologies of self-birth. Her identification with the maternal body will not be equivalent to (or repeat) the psychotic foreclosure typical of masculine desire. It will not of necessity be a phantasy of origins, or a ruthless act of mastery. It seems to me that women attempt to bridge the chasm between themselves and their mothers in writing, a chasm that patriarchal society has such a stake in maintaining. In knowing and gaining pleasure from (as) the mother, women are able to locate and identify themselves in what Irigaray calls a (repressed) genealogy of women.[14] It is in and through writing that they seek to speak *with* rather than *for* the mother. However, having said this I think that it is equally valid to argue that a woman's desire to give birth to herself (either in an embodied sense in parturition, or in a textual sense in literature) speaks of the ambivalence of the mother–daughter bond. Like the maternal body itself, the mother–daughter relation is an experience of contradiction: of love and hate, of mutuality and estrangement, of anger and desire, of unity and separation.[15] In women's writing we can see the co-existence of these seemingly contradictory expressions. The mother–daughter bond, with its rich (pre)history of tensions, offers an alternative to the one-sided story of patriarchal relations. It provides an intense and often harrowing model of continuity in the face of a detached and autonomous self.[16] This continuity, however, is not to be understood in terms of an undifferentiated fusion where both mother and daughter disappear.[17]

Reproduction and repetition

Let us take up again the question of repeated origins. Irigaray characterises the boy's relation to the mother as a return. She suggests that he attempts to repeat the place of his origin through this return. In contrast to this the girl will be the site of this repetition, the place of its reproduction. The sexual asymmetry is of interest here. If we return to Kristeva we can rehearse this question of repetition and reproduction in a quite different manner. Recall that she considers much women's writing derivative, arguing that at best it *imitates* the texts of the male avant-garde contributing little to the corpus of modernist work. I want to suggest that when Kristeva indirectly (silently) accuses Cixous and others of imitating Joyce,[18] she is distinguishing between productive and reproductive texts, opposing these in terms of creativity and repetition. She is implying that women's writing rarely exceeds this repetitive form, that it *merely* reproduces or imitates more powerful (original) avant-garde transgressions. In doing so Kristeva appears to accept associations between repetition, reproduction and femininity. Let me demonstrate why I think this is so.

Repetition has been thought in the West in broadly two (antagonistic) positions. We might characterise these, for our purposes here, as *repetition-as-same* and *repetition-as-difference*. Gilles Deleuze associates the first with Plato and the second with Nietzsche, suggesting that these models have come to serve as imagined alternatives. Platonic repetition involves a mimetic fidelity to an (imagined) reality or truth, a correspondence which seeks to faithfully copy a master without changing its essential nature. Nietzschean repetition, on the other hand, is the subversion of this principle. Sameness is disavowed in favour of difference and repetition takes on the form of a doubling or ghostly structure which produces phantasms rather than faithful copies. In *Logique du sens* Deleuze writes:

> It is a question of two readings of the world in the sense that one asks us to think of difference on the basis of pre-established similitude or identity, while the other invites us on the contrary to think of similitude and even identity as the product of a fundamental disparity.[19]

These variations on repetition parallel Plato's own distinction between good and bad mimesis and thus the tension between the two forms is inscribed at the birth of Western thought.[20] Mimesis, like repetition, will be thought as both similitude/identity (Aristotle) and difference/play (Adorno).[21] What is interesting for our purposes is that the similitude and identity associated with repetition-as-same is constantly evoked in relation to reproduction and the maternal body. The subversive play of repetition-as-difference is somehow distanced from the archaic stability of woman as nature. In the work of Sigmund Freud, Simone de Beauvoir and Gilles Deleuze we find significant examples of the uncanny return of the mother. Each in quite different ways

locates the maternal as somehow bound to the structure (or process) of repetition. This insistent coupling of maternity and repetition warrants critical
appraisal for it constructs an ideological topos in which the mother is sen-
tenced to silence.

In a rather lengthy passage from *Beyond the Pleasure Principle* Freud provides us with a fascinating discussion of the links between reading, repetition
and reproduction.

> At first the analysing physician could do no more than discover the
> unconscious material that was concealed from the patient, put it to-
> gether, and, at the right moment, communicate it to him. Psycho-
> analysis was then first and foremost an art of interpreting. Since this
> did not solve the therapeutic problem, a further aim quickly came in
> view: to oblige the patient to confirm the analyst's construction from
> his own memory. In that endeavour the chief emphasis lay upon the
> patient's resistances: the art consisted now in uncovering these as
> quickly as possible, in pointing them out to the patient and in in-
> ducing him by human influence – this was where suggestion operat-
> ing as "transference" played its part – to abandon his resistances.
>
> But it became ever clearer that the aim which had been set up – the
> aim that what was unconscious should become conscious – is not
> completely attainable by that method. The patient cannot remember
> the whole of what is repressed in him, and what he cannot remember
> may be precisely the essential part of it ... He is obliged to *repeat* the
> repressed material as a contemporary experience instead of, as the
> physician would prefer to see, *remembering* it as something belonging
> to the past. These reproductions, which emerge with such unwished-
> for exactitude, always have as their subject some portion of infantile
> sexual life – of the Oedipus complex, that is, and its derivatives; and
> they are invariably acted out in the sphere of the transference, of the
> patient's relation to the physician ... It has been the physician's en-
> deavour to keep this transference neurosis within the narrowest lim-
> its to force as much as possible into the channel of memory and to
> allow as little as possible to emerge as *repetition*.[22]

Freud speaks here of the compulsion to repeat, and characterises psychoanalysis first and foremost as a reading, "an art of interpreting", an "uncover-
ing" of the repressed material of the unconscious text. This developmental
account of the stages of psychoanalysis provides us with a narrative that traces
the relations between reading, resistance, repression, repetition and remembering. While there is much that can be made of this rich ensemble, it is
worth emphasising the apparent opposition Freud draws between repetition
and *remembrance*.[23] Repetition appears to occupy the site of an eternal dynamic that *reproduces* the same, while remembrance occurs when the patient

or analysand *produces* a difference that frees *him* from his repressions.[24] Repetition as reproduction is thus the embodiment of circularity, stasis and sameness, while remembrance as production involves movement, difference and change. Freud tells us that the compulsion to repeat is a "manifestation of the power of the repressed"; it is "a perpetual recurrence of the same thing", compelling the analysand to "a repetition of the same experiences" (pp. 14, 16). It is "the re-experiencing of something identical" (p. 30).

It is significant that Freud's elaboration of the repetition compulsion is made possible because of an earlier discussion of the (boy) child's instinctual renunciation of the mother. Freud's "*fort-da*" provides the bridge that translates between his discussions of repetition-as-same and the maternal body which, incidentally, provides the impetus for repression in the first instance. The mother surfaces here in an uncanny fashion. She is the familiar thing "that has undergone repression and then emerged from it".[25] She is what "ought to have been kept concealed but which has nevertheless come to light."[26] She is what reproduces the same and is thus opposed to the productive difference of *re*membrance. The process of reading (of psychoanalysis) is thus a process gesturing beyond the repetitious cycle of reproduction. It is a process that brings the mother's body to light only to transcend it. It is a passage beyond the immobilising force of her body. It is a lifting of the repressions and resistances that in effect construct that body. Freud bequeaths to us a theory and practice that situates the mother's body in the static realm of the same. It is a world arguably beyond time, movement and change.

This elision of reproduction with repetition-as-same is also evident in Simone de Beauvoir's *Second Sex*, where it is clearly contrasted with production figured by repetition-as-difference. In a chapter entitled "The Nomad" reproduction is constructed as static, feminine nature in opposition to production as active, masculine culture. Beauvoir writes:

> The woman who gave birth … did not know the pride of creation; she felt herself the plaything of obscure forces, and the painful ordeal of childbirth seemed a useless or even troublesome accident. But in any case giving birth and suckling are not *activities*, they are natural functions; no project is involved; and that is why woman found in them no reason for a lofty affirmation of her existence – she submitted passively to her biological fate. The domestic labours that fell to her lot because they were reconcilable with the cares of maternity imprisoned her in repetition and immanence; they were *repeated from day to day in an identical form*, which was perpetuated almost without change from century to century; *they produced nothing new*.
>
> … but this creation results only in *repeating the same* Life in more individuals. But man assures the repetition of Life while transcending Life through Existence; by this transcendence he creates values that deprive *pure repetition* of all value … the human male also

remodels the face of the earth, he creates new instruments, he invents, he shapes the future.

[Woman's] *misfortune* is to have been biologically destined for the *repetition* of Life, when even in her own view Life does not carry within itself its reasons for being, reasons that are more important than the life itself... but in maternity woman remained closely bound to her body, like an animal ... It is male activity that in creating values has made of existence itself a value; this activity has prevailed over the confused forces of life; it has subdued Nature and Woman.[27]

Here the passivity of reproduction is contrasted with the activity of production in what is effectively a damning denial of woman's creative potential. Ironically, Beauvoir shows no sensitivity to the socially mediated and constructed values apportioned to human behaviour among the mythical "nomads". She writes: "the bondage of reproduction was a terrible handicap in the struggle against a hostile world. Pregnancy, childbirth, and menstruation reduced their capacity for *work* and made them at times wholly dependent upon the men for protection and food" (p. 94 emphasis added). While there is an apparent division, then, between the immanence of repetitive reproduction and the transcendence of active production, Beauvoir's text enacts a curious displacement that momentarily depicts woman exceeding her *natural* role.

For she, too, is an existent, she feels the urge to surpass, and her project is not *mere repetition* but transcendence towards a different future – in her heart of hearts she finds confirmation of the masculine pretensions. She joins the men in the festivals that celebrate the successes and the victories of the males.

(p. 96 emphasis added)

Woman is complicitous in man's denigration of *her* natural realm, for she, too, strives beyond the restrictions and immanence of her maternal curse. "Her misfortune is to have been biologically destined for the repetition of Life" (p. 96). In Beauvoir's depiction of nomadic life the mother's biological body is distinct and separate from the cultural realm of transcendence. Cultural activities such as reading exceed the natural flows of biological rhythm, and yet are strangely dependent upon them. The mother's body continues to serve as the material support for the reproduction of culture and society.

Deleuze's science of itineration brings us once again to the nomad, and yet this is no simple repetition of Beauvoir's claims. For Deleuze the nomad provides an itinerary that refuses the sedentary iteration of reproduction. Here repetition is revealed as an ambivalent process encompassing both stasis and similarity as well as mobility and difference. But while repetition is accorded this undecidable status, reproduction remains curiously caught within the bonds of similarity, territorialisation and permanence. Reproduction, as we shall see, is accorded the status of the same. Deleuze uncovers the paradoxical processes of the repetitive gesture, and brings our attention to the productive difference of its movement. He suggests that while repetition might be thought within the parameters of similarity, that it necessarily exceeds this. Repetition, when thought through Deleuze's nomadic science, produces difference. This ambulatory model is repeatedly counterposed to reproduction in Deleuze's scheme. The trajectory of Deleuze's nomad is always away from the reproductive realm of fixity and sedentary life.

Deleuze traces his eccentric science of the nomad back to the atomic physics of Democritus and Lucretius, and the geometry of Archimedes. He suggests that an alternative to the royal or imperial sciences has always existed, though has been, and continues to be, repressed by the demands of this State science. He distinguishes between the procedures of knowledge in the following manner:

> one consists in reproducing, the other in following. The first has to do with reproduction, iteration and reiteration; the other, having to do with itineration, is the sum of the itinerant, ambulant sciences ... following is not at all the same thing as reproducing, and one never follows in order to reproduce ... Reproducing implies the permanence of a fixed point of **view** that is external to what is reproduced: watching the flow from the bank. But following is something different from the ideal of reproduction ... with the [reproductive] model, one is constantly reterritorializing around a point of view, on a domain, according to a set of constant relations; but with the ambulant model, the process of deterritorialization constitutes and extends the territory itself.[28]

The ambulant or itinerant sciences of the nomad are always prevented from being completely internalised within the reproductive sciences; "they inhabit that 'more' that exceeds the space of reproduction" (p. 39). Itineration involves thought as a proceeding or a process rather than as a product. Its space is that of the intermezzo, the relay or trajectory between (sedentary) points. This relay provides us with a metaphor for reading. The nomadic process is a reading that is set up against the sedentary activity of theory. Reading is the trajectory that refuses the customary function of sedentary thought, which is for Deleuze the "royal" science. Reading effaces and displaces the topos of theory, throwing its sedentary space into disarray. It refuses the enclosure, the striation of theoretical space. It is an intermezzo incalculable from the perspective of a theoretical score. The repetitive structure of Deleuze's reading is an itineration that refuses the iteration (or re-iteration) of repetition-as-same.[29] Most importantly it exceeds the territorialisation of the (enclosed) reproductive sphere. Following Deleuze, then, we might repeat that reading exceeds theory.

In order to discuss the kind of repetition that promotes difference are we led beyond the sedentary spaces and uterine enclosures of *reproduction* toward the excessive phallic trajectories of de-territorialised *productions*? In this nomadic enterprise, might we characterise reading as an active masculine relay between passive feminine theoretical sites? Is it a trajectory that points beyond feminine space? Is the active production of repetition-as-difference to be firmly pitted against the passive reproduction of repetition-as-same? Reading Deleuze in the context of the overdetermined coupling of reproduction and inertia (Beauvoir and Freud) I was initially tempted to think so. And yet there is nothing to suggest that Deleuze constructs his ambulatory science in terms of any sexual determination. Deleuze's references to reproduction do not reproduce-as-same the conceptual associations with femininity. Reproduction is not obviously a sexually marked space in Deleuze's work. We can re-trace (without re-producing) Deleuze's itinerary and suggest that his critique of the imperial or royal sciences, through the figure of the nomad, is really a critique of the sedentary thought inherent in conceptual formulations of transcendence and immanence. Deleuze is critical of the stasis implied in the vertical opposition transcendence/immanence. Against models such as Beauvoir's that perpetuate this he posits an alternative space, a horizontal space that privileges nomadic movement over and against the fixed point. He is critical of the kind of model that Beauvoir proposes, one that urges us to *ex/(s)ist*, to go beyond the seat of being, to transcend. Deleuze's nomad is infinitely more interesting than Beauvoir's because it literally moves away from the theoretical model of transcendence and immanence with its conceptual associations with masculinity and femininity respectively. His horizontal plane suggests the possibility of thinking movement and gender differently. In this light it is possible to argue that Deleuze offers us a way to reclaim nomadic woman from Beauvoir. Her work on the nomad remains effectively an anthropological gesture that positions women's oppression in the context of patriarchal prehistoric research and ethnography. It does not, however, unsettle this. It does not challenge the status of the masculine claim to transcendence. Deleuze, on the other hand, offers us a picture of the nomad as movement away from this thought.

What, then, can we say about the nomad? We know that it operates outside the terrain of stasis and sedentary position, but can we claim its itinerant wanderings for women? We know that Deleuze privileges his nomadic line of flight as a kind of becoming feminine. Are we to assume, then, that the nomad operates a simple reversal of the usual logic assigning femininity to stasis and masculinity to movement? Perhaps so, and yet it could be that the nomad deconstructs sexual identifications altogether. If this is the case it will be difficult to claim the nomad as any kind of specifically feminine movement. There is another possibility, the nomad may remain without any sexual identity in Deleuze's work. If it does then the nomad can be appropriated (occupied?), reconceptualising nomadic woman as an emblem of resistance to the stasis of patriarchal thought.[30]

Having suggested that we can read Deleuze in this way I nonetheless remain a little concerned about the manner in which he opposes the operations of movement and occupation. In his work occupation can be thought only in the negative terms of colonisation, that is in opposition to movement and change. But what if we were to think of occupation beyond the colonising gesture? Elizabeth Grosz raises exactly this possibility. She thinks the question of feminist occupation in a way that I find particularly useful. In her discussion of Julia Kristeva, Luce Irigaray and Michèle Le Doeuff, she points toward the necessity of claiming conceptual terrain in a manner that refuses colonisation while enabling women to gain a site from which to work, write and speak. She argues that their work:

> seems less a form of colonisation than the search for a place in which to live, to inhabit, to cultivate, to produce in ways undreamed of before. This occupation is not a proprietorial seizure but more a stake in and commitment to kinds of intellectual struggle and productivity feminists today recognise is necessary in the transvaluation of existing knowledges.[31]

This suggestion provides women with strategies which may be limited by Deleuze's nomadic enterprise. For Grosz, occupation is not a term opposed to difference and change. On the contrary, it is one that seeks to promote these. I can see no reason why women cannot occupy both Deleuze's and Grosz's positions at one and the same time. We need to be nomadic in our resistance to masculine power; we need to disrupt the imperial heights of a transcendental thought, and yet, at the same time, we need a place from which to speak.

To return, however repetitiously, to the mother, we might ask what all this implies for the question or questions which bind writing to her body. Kristeva's claim that writing by women is largely derivative reduces this work to the status of repetitive text. Her analysis is somewhat problematic here because, as I have shown, it relies on an uncritical elision of the terms reproduction, repetition and sameness. By reading women's writing in this way Kristeva arguably reinforces an Oedipal scenario where women are reduced to the status of daughters who faithfully desire to reproduce their father's words. The best that women can hope to do is to imitate the gestures of the fathers who precede them. In this respect Kristeva's analysis reveals its debt to (repeats or rehearses) Freud's own beliefs about femininity. Recall that the father of psychoanalysis, Freud, posits three paths that women's psychic development might take. A woman might *deny* her femininity, such as in the case of frigidity, she might *accept* it and thus become a properly feminine woman, or she might *reject* it by imitating (mimicking, repeating) masculinity. I think that ultimately Kristeva leaves us little opportunity to imagine women beyond this drama of daughters who desire to repeat their fathers. From this perspective writing by women is constantly reduced to the dictates of a certain masculine Imaginary.[32]

I think that the problem of repetition in Kristeva's analysis becomes more obvious when we place it beside Irigaray's work on mothers and daughters. Irigaray indirectly poses the question of whether daughters repeat their mothers. While she warns that patriarchal culture places the two within a deadly immediacy where the daughter becomes the image of her lifeless mother, she gestures beyond this by providing us with a celebration of an ambiguous labial sexuality. Here repetition opens out toward difference. The repetitive Oedipal relation of father and daughter is left behind for the difference the mother and daughter make. We might think of this in terms of relations between women in philosophy. At the beginning of this book I discussed the work of Michèle Le Doeuff in relation to her "dialogue" with Simone de Beauvoir. I think that we can, with Irigaray, celebrate the difference that such dialogues between women make.

Mother-daughter poetics: Luce Irigaray

Irigaray's attempts to symbolise the mother centre around her focus on the mother–daughter relation. She celebrates the voicing of desire between this pair, inscribing the complex and ambivalent nature of this bond which remains largely unrepresented in mythological, philosophical and literary traditions. She contends that while the mother has been recognised in terms of her attachment to her son, and the daughter has been portrayed largely in relation to her father, the story of mother–daughter love exists as the repressed text of patriarchal culture. Irigaray writes: "In our societies, the mother/daughter, daughter/mother relationship constitutes a highly explosive nucleus. Thinking it, and changing it, is equivalent to shaking the foundations of the patriarchal order."[33] Irigaray seeks to write the intracies of mother–daughter love, a love that exists prior to the paternal restrictions of Oedipal law.

The confusion of identities in the mother-daughter bond is a recurring theme of Irigaray's work. The daughter experiences the mother as both oppressive and liberating. The mother is at once the space of her confinement and of her release. Irigaray captures this ambivalence in two of her texts. In "And the One Doesn't Stir without the Other" the mother is experienced as a suffocating entity that threatens to engulf the daughter with her all-consuming desire. "When Our Lips Speak Together" evokes a space of love between mother and daughter beyond this confinement.[34] The texts play with the metaphors of mobility and immobility as a way of capturing the fused and often confused identities of the two.

"And the One Doesn't Stir without the Other" laments the oppressive nature of maternal love. It is an exploration of the daughter's immobility in the face of a devouring phallic mother. Irigaray recreates the daughter's confinement in her multiple references to paralysis and dependency. The daughter's dependency is maintained through the mother's obsessive desire to fill her(self), to immobilise her(self) with food.[35] The relationship between food and immobility is expressed in the mother's milk. In contrast to Cixous' white ink, Irigaray's use of this trope denotes paralysis. The mother transfers her own passivity to her daughter through this icy medium:

> With your milk, Mother, I swallowed ice. And here I am now, my insides frozen. And I walk with even more difficulty than you do, and I move even less. You flowed into me, and that hot liquid became poison, paralyzing me.[36]

The mother disappears behind her function as nourisher. She becomes the icy milk that immobilises her daughter, reducing them both to oblivion. This all-consuming desire replaces other possibilities that the mother and daughter might experience.[37] The intimacy of attachment between mother and daughter is exchanged for a suffocating confusion of identity when the mother plays the phallic role of the productive body. Her sexless identity is experienced by the daughter as a threat to her own sense of self. The daughter incorporates the rigid, lifeless body of the phallic mother, learning to repress her own desire. Her sexuality becomes immobilised; "Trapped in a single function – mothering".[38]

Irigaray claims that mother and daughter exist within a deadly immediacy. Because their relation is not symbolised, has no symbolic language to accompany its gestures, they "remain and move in an immediacy without any transitional, transactional object."[39] There is a "distanceless proximity" between mother and daughter, one that cannot be spoken as such.[40] Within this space the daughter feels abandoned. She lives in a state of *déréliction* that allows her no independence or (symbolic) home of her own. Here she fails to recognise the mother as woman. As a consequence she will incorporate the mother, take her body in, in a vain attempt to produce a protective outer skin of her own. In doing so she consumes the mother, leaving no trace of woman behind. Irigaray writes:

> The daughter-woman tries to re-wrap herself in the desiring flesh of the other, clothes herself in it again and again, heedless of her own birth and of her own retouching. She makes for herself protective gestures, without knowing from whence she obtains what shelters her, helps her.[41]

All this occurs, Irigaray claims, because of the lack of a *sensible-transcendental*; a female transcendental that would provide the mother and daughter with a measure outside themselves. According to Irigaray:

> the struggle for superiority between two sames persists in the absence of the discovery and valorization of a sensible-transcendental – a female transcendental against which each woman can measure herself

rather than progressing only by taking the place of the mother, the other woman or the man.[42]

A (divine) space is necessary for the daughter to appreciate her mother as a woman, as a sexually desiring woman. In positing this space Irigaray is also voicing the daughter's fear of identifying too closely with the mute and silent mother of patriarchal law.[43] The daughter refuses a bond that would mean her own eclipse, her own death as a desiring subject. This kind of fusion with the mother is experienced as a confusion, an immobilising state that reduces the daughter to her mother's static image. The daughter resists this, pleading with the mother to keep her distance. Irigaray contends that Freud's depiction of woman as castrated leads to a deadly merger or non-differentiation between mother and daughter. In this scheme there is no symbolic representation of the generational difference between them.[44]

When Freud discusses the little girl's recognition of her (and her mother's) castration, he is remarkably close, according to Irigaray, to his ideas on melancholia. Margaret Whitford infers that we can better understand the deadly immediacy of the mother-daughter bond by following Irigaray's parallel. She writes:

> Irigaray insists that the impossibility of mourning arises from the fact that the girl child cannot grasp consciously what it is that has been lost, so she cannot mourn it … Freud states that in melancholia, the work of mourning is hindered by the (unconscious) ambivalence, both love and hate, which the person feels for the lost object.[45]

The consequence of this melancholic state is an ambivalence toward the devalorised mother. An ambivalence that remains unspoken, unsymbolised. Irigaray resists this state of affairs by asking the mother to be present for the daughter:

> Put yourself less in me, and let me look at you. I'd like to see you while you nurse me; not lose my/your eyes when I open my mouth for you; have you stay near me while I drink you. I'd like you to remain outside, too. Keep yourself/me outside, too. Don't engulf yourself or me in what flows from you into me. I would like both of us to be present. So that one doesn't disappear in the other, or the other in the one.[46]

The elision of I/you mirrors the undecidability of mother and daughter, gesturing beyond a simple eclipse of identity. The immobilising fear of the daughter gradually thaws, and she calls to the mother. "I would like us to play together at being the same and different. You/I exchanging selves endlessly and each staying herself."[47] The possibility of a fusion between mother and daughter that would not reproduce their immobility is momentarily glimpsed. "Haven't you let yourself be touched by me? Haven't I held your face between my hands? Haven't I learned your body?"[48] And yet this remains an impossible dream, a utopian text that is all too quickly reabsorbed into its patriarchal context: "But we have never, never spoken to each other. And such an abyss now separates us that I never leave you whole, for I am always held back in your womb. Shrouded in shadow. Captives of our confinement."[49] The promise of mobility gives way to the re-establishment of paralysis. The sensuous bond of mother and daughter is once again reduced to the lifeless representation of the mirror image: "Each of us lacks her own image; her own face, the animation of her own body is missing. And one mourns the other. My paralysis signifying your abduction in the mirror."[50] The text concludes with a powerful coupling of movement with life. Here the daughter voices her desire to break the endless repetitions that reproduce her (still) birth as the mother's death:

> And the one doesn't stir without the other. But we do not move together. When the one of us comes into the world, the other goes underground. When the one carries life, the other dies. And what I wanted from you, Mother, was this: that in giving me life, you still remain alive.[51]

This immobilised desire of mother and daughter is at odds with the fluidity celebrated in "When Our Lips Speak Together". Here the rigid phallic mother is replaced with what we might call a maternal mother. The allusions to stasis and solidity give way to images of fluid movement and flux. Indefinite voices merging mother with daughter (or lover) replace the daughter's voice that, in the first text, speaks in the mother's absent place.[52] Identity is experienced as a fusion of self with other, rather than a confusion or eclipse. Different ones become *indifferent*.

> Between our lips, yours and mine, several voices, several ways of speaking resound endlessly, back and forth. One is never separable from the other. You/I: we are always several at once. And how could one dominate the other? impose her voice, her tone, her meaning? One cannot be distinguished from the other; which does not mean that they are indistinct.[53]

The associations of orality with food and nourishment are displaced in favour of the mouth as an eroticised site. Language replaces food as the link between mother and daughter. Through language the two express their love for one another; "let's try to take back some part of our mouth to speak with … I love you: our two lips cannot separate to let *just* one word pass … You? I? that's still saying too much. Dividing too sharply between us: all".[54] The

173

language of separation and division is exchanged for one that would allow the fusion of these two indifferent ones to be voiced.

The distinction of mother and daughter is refused as this separates, too violently, the bond between them. The love of one woman for another is exiled when their fluid identities congeal into phallocentric essence: "You/I become two, then, for their pleasure. But thus divided in two, one outside, the other inside, you no longer embrace yourself, or me."[55] The indifferent ones of Irigaray's text call for a language that speaks the body's gestures. Such a language would thaw the immobility and paralysis of the mother-daughter relation under patriarchy: "If we don't invent a language, if we don't find our body's language, it will have too few gestures to accompany our story ... we will remain paralyzed. Deprived of *our movements*. Rigid, whereas we are made for endless change."[56] Movement and flux remain the focus of this relationship, where (self) identity is experienced as an ongoing process. "How can I speak to you? You remain in a flux, never congealing or solidifying." This fluid expression of identity strives to reproduce itself in language; "What will make that current flow into words?" All of this, Irigaray reminds us, "remains very strange to anyone claiming to stand on solid ground".[57]

The fluidity of identity merges with the fluidity of both the body and language, forming an indistinct relation between the three. "Speak, all the same. Between us, 'hardness' isn't necessary. We know the contours of our bodies well enough to love fluidity."[58] This is a logic that refuses the disembodied self of patriarchal thought. It is an inscription of identity as a sensuous and ongoing process: "And what I love in you, in myself, in us no longer takes place: the birth that is never accomplished, the body never created once and for all, the form never definitively completed, the face always still to be formed."[59]

The sensuous play between the two texts we have discussed so far is carried through into a later piece by Irigaray. In *Le Corps-à-corps avec la mère* she practises an embodied prose, an erotic writing that refuses the paralysis of the mother-daughter bond under patriarchy.[60] In this text the physicality of the body-to-body relation between mother and daughter replaces the stark intellectualism of theory between father and son. Irigaray also imagines a more erotic play between mother and daughter in "The Limits of the Transference".[61] Here she writes: "Woman must ceaselessly measure herself against her beginning and her sexuate determination, beget anew the maternal within her, give birth within herself to mother and daughter in a never-completed progression."[62] An amorous language becomes the basis for Irigaray's later works where an eroticism between female bodies merges into the preliminaries toward a sexual encounter between bodies both female and male.[63] This is an erotic language beyond the rigour of phallic thought.[64]

Throughout her work Irigaray refuses to be drawn into a religion of the mother. She rejects the onto-theological premises of a philosophy that would install the mother, as essence, in the father's place. The mother is not a fixed identity. She is rather a space, a feminine one to be sure, wherein women can explore the myriad contradictions of their bodies, speech and thought. She is a space that re-establishes the pre-Oedipal libidinal bonds that the father's law has forced her to relinquish. When the daughter forgoes the security of the sexless phallic mother, and the mother risks her identity in favour of desire, it is only then that they are able to act and speak as women in a drama that unfolds in this space. I think that ultimately her focus on movement and speech is a decisive move away from the more romanticised mother/breast of Cixous' work. It enacts a displacement of the Oedipal structure that works to silence the mother. I also think that whereas Cixous proposes the mother as a romantic solution and hence closure to the question of woman's silence, Irigaray offers us the mother as the question or problem to be explored. Perhaps another way of putting this is to suggest that the differences here between answers and questions corresponds to the generic differences between the manifesto and philosophy. I would suggest that Irigaray's work remains philosophical by keeping the question of the mother open and alive. It problematises the mother in ways that force us to reflect critically on the status of the mother in and for feminist philosophical thought. The "real mother" that arguably emerges is not a solution for feminist inquiry, but rather a set of questions in its own right. We need to articulate these questions, to ask what the "real mother" means in terms of our ability to theorise maternity. We need to ask if mothers are the only ones capable of doing this work authentically. Indeed we need to ask if authenticity is a suitable term in relation to the experience of motherhood. In thinking through these questions we inevitably raise the more difficult question of man's relationship to the authentic experience of maternity and its theoretical expression.

In November 1980 Louis Althusser murdered his wife Hélène Rythmann. The dead body of Hélène Rythmann has served, in this book, as an emblem of woman's silenced body. It is a body that does not speak. It is a body that is spoken of only in relation to a male philosopher. To remain with the body of Hélène Rythmann is to remain with the problems elaborated in the first section of this book. It is to remain, problematically, on the terrain of silence where woman is consistently theorised as victim, ghost, corpse. I have chosen to move from this terrain, from the corpse, the dead woman's body, toward the corpus of women's writing, the body of women's work on the mother. In these last two chapters I have assembled the women whose writing on the mother has helped to focus our discussion on something other than silence. My gesture here has fallen somewhere between Irigaray and Plato in that it has gathered together women in the manner of either a *Symposium* or a *Genealogy of Women*. This has been a different kind of Symposium to be sure. It has been one that celebrates women's voices, not one that relegates them to the back rooms where they simply cannot be heard. The voices at this gathering have offered us differing ways into the question or questions of the mother.

CONCLUSION
Speaking with(in) the symbolic

> Women's language is not ... a transgressive language, a language-against, which refers to the weight of a norm. Nor is it a language of panic (although it may be the panic of language), nor an avant-garde language. It is a free language, supremely indifferent, which is displaced from one genre to another, an extra territorial language whose frontiers do not need to be crossed so much as displaced.
>
> (Françoise Collin, "Polyglo(u)ssons")[1]

The space of women's writing is still undetermined. Is it outside the symbolic or part of it? Where do women speak from? In the 1990s it may seem inappropriate to conclude a book by suggesting that women's voices are silenced when all around us we hear evidence to the contrary. In many significant respects the situation has changed since the 1970s for some women. Today we hear certain women speak within the symbolic domain of the public forum. The relatively successful, though admittedly always precarious, institutionalisation of feminist concerns in Women's Studies programmes means that paradoxically we can now access a significant body of published work on questions of women's silence. Indeed this book attests to this fact. So where does this leave us? Leaving to one side the decidedly complex issue of just how precarious these advances are, I shall suggest that we risk silencing the substantial gains that this body of work represents if we go on simply to assume that our task is complete, that there is nothing left to be said on the matter. Let us return, then, to the question at hand: what can we say about the space of women's writing? I suspect that the complex spatial metaphor that emerged at the beginning of this book helps us to imagine where this writing lies. It is neither simply *inside* nor *outside* the symbolic domain. The ambiguity that is symbolised in writing between mother and daughter, the undecidable difference between the two, mirrors the disruption of our sense of space in such a way as to re-figure relations between inside and out. With Françoise Collin we could say that the space of women's writing is *extra territorial*, that it exceeds placement, if placement is to be thought through traditional or canonical classifications. There is arguably an elastic dimension to this writing, one that resists the planar geometrical or spatial organisation of inside and out. This elasticity might usefully be thought through a topological model, one that problematises any simple spatial opposition. Topological tropes, such as the rubber sheet, allow us to rearticulate spatial relations in ways that preclude the reinstatement of an oppositional logic.

Throughout this book I have argued that the relation between women's writing and the masculine symbolic is infinitely more elastic than we are led to believe. I have said that this relation cannot be contained within a spatial model that positions it as outside to a privileged inner domain. Nonetheless we still find these models holding sway. A simple representation of inside and outside spaces in language appears to underpin psychoanalytic presuppositions. The symbolic is usually perceived as the privileged space of representation, as the *inside* of language. It is the realm of signification. One can make no sense *outside* it. It is instructive to turn to Lacan at this point for his discussion of the symbolic is crucial for our understanding of feminist resistances to the law of paternal authority. Lacan chides feminists, and others, for repressing the significance of the symbolic which he designates the paternal order. He argues that an overarching focus on the maternal (mother–child) relationship fails to grasp the "truth" of the symbolic, i.e. the truth of castration. Lacan contends that this focus on the maternal goes hand in hand with a denial (or oversight) of Freud's great discoveries regarding castration. He writes:

> A notion of emotional deprivation linking disturbances of development directly to the real inadequacies of mothering has been overlaid with a dialectic of fantasies which takes the maternal body as its imaginary field ... What is unquestionably involved here is a conceptual foregrounding of the sexuality of the woman, which brings to our attention a remarkable oversight.[2]

Although Lacan directs his comments here primarily to an earlier generation of psychoanalysts, Melanie Klein in particular, we can read his admonishing tone as a critique of contemporary psychoanalytic theorists who have resumed (or exhumed) this imaginary field of the maternal body.[3] By focusing on the maternal these theorists have, according to Lacan, lost sight of the fact that we can only make sense of the mother–child bond in relation to the paternal third term, that is in relation to the symbolic.[4] Lacan attempts to undo this repression by reinscribing desire into the discussion of sexuality. He claims that with the advent of desire we return to the symbolic as the place of paternal law that Freud first imagined it to be. The prolonged discussion of desire throughout his work is really, therefore, a return to the father.[5]

In her introduction to Lacan's work on feminine sexuality, Jacqueline Rose provides a succinct account of this return.[6] She shows how Lacan insists that the mother–child relation be severed by the father's symbolic intervention:

> In Lacan's account, the phallus stands for that moment of rupture. It refers mother and child to the dimension of the symbolic which is

figured by the father's place ... The phallus therefore ... breaks the two term relation and initiates the order of exchange.[7]

Rose goes to some length to point out that the father functions here metaphorically. His is the place Lacan will call the *paternal metaphor*. This metaphor refers to the symbolic place of law and order, beyond the imaginary relation between mother and child. The paternal metaphor will sever the child from its sensuous (imaginary) maternal beginnings and Lacan will argue that there is no return to this place.[8] For him there is "no pre-discursive reality ... no place prior to the law which is available and can be retrieved ... there is no feminine outside language."[9] In fact we could say that there is no mother.

Lacan's theoretical perspective would seem to preclude any possibility of writing the repressed bond between mother and daughter because it remains *outside* the linguistic order. Or does it? Maggie Berg suggests, following Irigaray, that Lacan's scheme excludes women by positioning them *inside* a system from which they cannot escape:

> What we have is a prediscursive state construed within discourse as identification with the mother; a nature–culture opposition is created in a system that purports to deny it ... Lacan now makes women's exclusion [as Irigaray puts it] "*internal* to an order from which nothing escapes."[10]

We seem to have an unusual, though not unfamiliar, temporal and spatial organisation operating in Lacan's work: the pre-Oedipal maternal imaginary is depicted as chronologically and spatially prior to or outside the Oedipal symbolic. The maternal body is the unmediated origin outside symbolisation that cannot be spoken without relegating women exterior to language, society and history.[11] This exterior, though, turns out to be internal to the symbolic.

So what does it mean to say, as Lacan does, that the symbolic has an outside? And what are the implications of this when we consider that this *outside* is repeatedly symbolised as a *feminine* space? Does this all amount to relegating relations between women, especially the relation between mother and daughter, to an unspeakable realm? We need to resist this logic by finding elastic spaces where such relations can and do symbolise.[12] Julia Kristeva's work on the symbolic manages to avoid some of the problems associated with Lacan's formulation. Kelly Oliver suggests that we can isolate two definitions of the symbolic in Kristeva's work, and that her symbolic differs from Lacan's in that it hovers between these two possible meanings. According to Kristeva the Symbolic is the place of signification that contains both semiotic and symbolic modes. It is thus simultaneously the place that orders and disorders language, meaning and sense.[13] Kristeva's semiotic, much more radically conceived than Lacan's imaginary, displaces a simple oppositional logic that would have it placed beyond symbolisation. It is at once within and beyond the order of signification; not simply outside it. Oliver reminds us that, for Kristeva, the Symbolic is not only the order of law but also the order of resistances to this law.[14] Bearing in mind Oliver's distinction between symbolic and Symbolic, Kristeva's revolution might be thought in terms of her reconceptualisation of Symbolic space. As a result it offers us alternative ways to imagine the delicate balance between paternal law and maternal indifference.[15] This delicate balance is elastic; it contrasts with the fiction of the paternal order that retains an image of itself as a privileged and stable inner domain.

Luce Irigaray also manages to displace the spatial logic of Lacan's symbolic. While she is often criticised for saying that women are excluded from the symbolic, it is really more the case that she sees women excluded from Lacan's symbolic.[16] Irigaray's project is one of extending the realm of possible significations.[17] She is concerned that we make or invent spaces in which to symbolise relations between women, especially the mother–daughter bond. She suggests that systems, such as Lacan's, are blind to their own phallocentric assumptions for they repress the representations that women might forge amongst themselves. By doing so they appropriate the symbolic for themselves, placing women on the nether-side of language. Women remain silenced in this system, not by placing them outside the symbolic, but rather by positioning their silent (maternal) bodies as the very possibility of that system. "Woman as womb," Irigaray writes, "the unconscious womb of man's language" who "cannot in any way order themselves within and through a language that would be on some basis their own."[18]

Margaret Whitford observes that while her Lacanian detractors accuse Irigaray of constructing a feminine specificity at the level of the drives, Irigaray is in fact focusing on feminine specificity as it is silenced by symbolic representation.[19] This is born out in Irigaray's fear that the bond between mother and daughter, because it has not been represented symbolically, predisposes women to a kind of psychosis,[20] though one that barely resembles the psychotic state of the man. Irigaray writes:

> [Woman] borrows signifiers but cannot make her mark, or re-mark upon them. Which all surely keeps her deficient, empty, lacking, in a way that could be labelled "psychotic": a *latent* but not actual psychosis, for want of a practical signifying system.[21]

Women are thus outsiders in the symbolic as it is conceived by Lacan and others. They are not *naturally* predisposed to this exteriority. They are *socially* positioned as outsiders within a discursive system that constructs its own politically motivated spatial and logical arrangements between in and out. This system prohibits women from representing (imagining, conceiving of) their relations to one another. The solution to this silencing lies in the production of a new symbolic based on difference. For Irigaray this entails, amongst other things, a notion of a feminine divine, a sensible transcendental that would serve to loosen the deadly immediacy between mother and daughter. Along with this she theorises the need for a maternal genealogy, a symbolic representation of the generational differences between women that would make it possible for the daughter to experience her mother as woman.[22] This newly organised symbolic would ultimately rest upon the representation of sexual difference.

Irigarary insists that women enter symbolism in a different way to men. Against the linear, analogous and objectifying gesture of the boy's *fort-da*[23] she posits a gesture more consonant *with* the mother than *against* her:

> In the absence of her mother, a girl's gestures are not the same. She does not play with a string and reel symbolizing her mother, for her mother's sex is the same as hers and the mother cannot have the objective status of a reel. The mother's identity as a subject is the same as hers.[24]

Irigaray is suggesting that boys symbolise the anxiety of the mother's absence quite early in their linguistic patterns, and that as a result their entry into the symbolic universe does not follow the same path as that of the girl. Because girls can find their mothers in the morphology of their own bodies, their early linguistic utterances will not repeat this masculine anxiety and its accompanying desire for mastery. This has enormous implications for the way women enter the symbolic register and how they fare once there.[25] Irigaray suggests:

> If she speaks, it is mostly in a playful way, without giving special importance to syllabic or phonemic oppositions. It may be bisyllabic, or like a litany, and rather singsong, modulated tonally. This language corresponds to a rhythm and also to a melody. Sometimes it takes the form of tender or angry words addressed to the doll, sometimes it takes the form of silence.[26]

This difference in speech, in symbolisation, is intimately bound with the girl's bodily gestures. Irigaray tells us that girls enter language by producing spaces, rhythms, dances and song. The sensuous bond between like bodies – mother and daughter – will be performed or symbolised without recourse to substitution or objectification.[27] The symbolic difference that Irigaray describes might be a useful way of thinking about women's writing. Perhaps the bodily rhythms and gestures that she alludes to can be seen as emblems of women's sexually specific spatial relation to a symbolic that is infinitely more elastic than Lacan and others imagine it to be.[28]

The topological shift toward this elastic positionality has structured (or destructured) my exploration of the maternal body. Throughout this book I have sought to problematise the spatial arrangements and agreements that have characterised our historical beliefs about the maternal in relation to the privileged domain of philosophy. By articulating the opposition language/silence with the opposition inside/outside I have demonstrated that alternative logics can be imagined. The complex relationality that emerges from the disruption of these binaries has proved to be invaluable for appreciating other ways of characterising the mother–child relation. Here the oppositional duality of mother and child is displaced in favour of an ambiguous space that refuses mother and child as either separate or fused. Work by women, notably Luce Irigaray, on the mother–daughter bond demonstrates this radical displacement. It performs a serious displacement of traditional Western constructions of the mother as the silent term in relation to the son.

It would seem that the maternal can never be articulated in any radical manner until the mother–daughter relation is addressed. Another way of saying this is to suggest that it is not simply the maternal that is silenced but more insidiously the mother–daughter bond. To say as much is to admit that, in a sense, this book is really about a false problem. I began by arguing that women are silenced because they are mothers. It is perhaps more correct to say, though, that women are silenced because they are considered to be mothers *only* of sons. When theorised as mothers of daughters, women always speak.[29] Indeed, it is this point that marks a difference between much of the work of Kristeva and Irigaray. It is to Irigaray's credit that she offers us a more serious displacement of the Freudian/Lacanian paradigm, the paradigm that establishes quite ruthlessly the reign of the Oedipal son. The mother–daughter relation unsettles the Oedipal eclipse of the dutiful mother beneath the all-consuming concerns of the son. When women are theorised as mothers of daughters there is much to be said. In our early discussion of Michèle Le Doeuff I made reference to the import of her *dialogue* with her philosophical *mother* Simone de Beauvoir. I wish to think of this work partly as a generational dialogue between mother and daughter, in order to repeat that the mother–daughter relation has always provided women a terrain from which to speak. But of course we must remember that it is not the only place for women to speak. Women have always spoken to one another in various places and in various ways, and indeed this is what any Symposium seeks to encourage. By providing an elastic space in which women continue to speak with each other the Symposium ensures that this terrain of dialogue resists closure. At the Symposium we are never *simply* mothers to daughters or daughters to mothers, but women amongst ourselves.

NOTES

In the quotations throughout the book, all emphases not described as "added" are in the original text.

INTRODUCTION

1 See my "Reproduction: Feminist Footnote to Marxist Text?", *Arena* 77, 1986, pp. 155–66.

1 SPEAKING SILENCE: WOMAN'S VOICE IN PHILOSPHY

1 An early version of the argument presented in this chapter appears in my "Silence and Reason: Woman's Voice in Philosophy", *Australasian Journal of Philosophy* 71(4) 1993, pp. 400–24.
2 Michèle Le Doeuff, "Women and Philosophy", trans. D. Pope, *Radical Philosophy* 17 (Summer) 1977, p. 7.
3 Having said this I shall resist the tendency to pit these two positions in dialectical debate. I think Le Doeuff's own work provides a rationale for avoiding this. She writes:

> Perhaps, having been asked to speak about feminism in French philosophy, should I have surveyed the various strands of feminist philosophy and proposed a discussion of them. But this would have started a sort of internal debate, debate supposedly taking place in a determinate field – and certainly creating the closure of that field.
>
> (p. 54)

See: "Ants and Women, or Philosophy without Borders" in *Contemporary French Philosophy*, A. Phillips Griffiths ed. (Cambridge: Cambridge University Press, 1987, pp. 41–54).
4 See Genevieve Lloyd and Elizabeth Spelman for similar arguments: Genevieve Lloyd, *The Man of Reason: "Male" and "Female" in Western Philosophy* (London: Methuen, 1984, p. 37); Elizabeth V. Spelman, *Inessential Woman: Problems of Exclusion in Feminist Thought* (London: The Women's Press, 1988, p. ix).
5 Elizabeth Grosz, *Jacques Lacan: A Feminist Introduction* (Sydney: Allen and Unwin, 1990).
6 Margaret Whitford provides an invaluable analysis of Irigaray's work on exclusion in philosophy. See: *Luce Irigaray: Philosophy in the Feminine* (London: Routledge, 1991, pp. 99–191).
7 Indeed Irigaray contends that the entire edifice of Western culture is erected on this silencing. She argues that matricide is the founding instance of a patriarchal imaginary, and cites Clytemnestra as a mythical inscription of this. See: "The Bodily Encounter with

the Mother", trans. David Macey, in *The Irigaray Reader*, Margaret Whitford ed. (Oxford: Basil Blackwell, 1991, pp. 34–46). See also: Luce Irigaray, "Women, the Sacred and Money", trans. Diana Knight and Margaret Whitford, *Paragraph* 8 (October) 1986, pp. 6–18.

8 Luce Irigaray, *Speculum of the Other Woman*, trans. Gillian C. Gill (Ithaca, NY: Cornell University Press, 1985).

9 Cf. *The Symposium* (176e) where Plato positions woman (in the figure of the flute girl) in opposition to voice, speech and conversation.

10 In the *Cratylus* Plato writes: "*Gyne* (woman) I suspect to be the same word as *gone* (birth): *thely* (female) appears to be partly derived from *thele* (the teat), because the teat is like rain, and makes things flourish (*tethelenai*)" (414a).

11 I think there is a resonance here with Julia Kristeva's notion of the semiotic *chora* as that which orders/disorders symbolic language, i.e. the structural possibility of speech, the maternal body as the site or *dispositif* of language. For her the maternal body (*chora*) is the ordering principle or logic of language, the (silent) place and possibility of the subject having no subjectivity of its own. It seems to me that what is different about these accounts is that Kristeva celebrates this silence while Irigaray attempts to articulate it as voice, as subjectivity. A discussion of Kristeva's *chora* can be found in chapter six.

12 Phil Powrie charts some contemporary attempts to reappropriate the metaphor of the womb by such recent French women writers as Marie Cardinal, Annie Leclerc and Chantal Chawaf. Powrie writes: "[here] the womb-room is less a trope for confinement and monstrosity, and more a sign of independence and locus of transformation, usually linked with writing, a necessary extension to the prison-house of patriarchal language" (p. 198). See: Phil Powrie, "A Womb of One's Own: The Metaphor of the Womb-room as a Reading-effect in Texts by Contemporary French Women Writers", *Paragraph* 12(3) 1989, pp. 197–213.

13 Not only is woman the matrix for reproducing man, but also her body is the (immobilised) substance from which he constructs his "house of language". See Irigaray's discussion in *L'Oubli de l'air chez Martin Heidegger* (Paris: Minuit, 1983). See also: Margaret Whitford's discussion in *The Irigaray Reader, op. cit.*, pp. 163–4.

14 Irigaray, "Volume-Fluidity" in *Speculum, op. cit.*, pp. 227–40. Reprinted as "Volume without Contours", trans. David Macey in *The Irigaray Reader, op. cit.*, pp. 53–67. See Whitford's useful discussion of this in her introduction, pp. 27–9.

15 *Timaeus* 51a–b (cited in *Speculum* p. 307).

16 Cf. Jacques Derrida on Plato's depiction of Socrates as midwife. See also his discussion of Plato on "place" as matrix, mother and nurse. *Dissemination*, trans. Barbara Johnson (Chicago: University of Chicago Press, 1981, pp. 154, 160).

17 Just before this Plato has written: "Consider then what *deliverance* from their bonds and the curing of their ignorance would be if something like this **naturally** happened to them. Whenever one of them was freed, had to stand up suddenly, turn his head, walk and look up towards the light, doing all that would give him pain" (515c emphasis added).

18 Raoul Mortley, *French Philosophers in Conversation* (London: Routledge, 1991, p. 82).

19 Michèle Le Doeuff, *The Philosophical Imaginary*, trans. Colin Gordon (Stanford, CA: Stanford University Press, 1989, p. vii).

20 Le Doeuff provides a wonderful discussion of how her own concerns *deviate* from the contemporary male philosophers in France, in "Ants and Women, or Philosophy without Borders", *op. cit.*

21 Meaghan Morris's discussion would suggest that Gordon has overlooked the possible ways in which Le Doeuff might (at least provisionally) be positioned as postmodern, and yet she is hesitant to reduce Le Doeuff's work to this. See: Meaghan Morris, "Operative Reasoning: Reading Michèle Le Doeuff" in *The Pirate's Fiancée: Feminism/Reading/ Postmodernism* (London: Verso, 1988, p. 4).

22 Elizabeth Grosz puts it this way: "Philosophical self-reflection ... abrogates the right to

(sole) self-critical understanding. Its capacity to constitute itself as a metaphilosophy depends on its ability to accept this thinking-in-images as only an aberration capable of elimination". Elizabeth Grosz, *Sexual Subversions: Three French Feminists* (Sydney: Allen and Unwin, 1989, p. 188).

23 Cf. Alfred Jost's "Le Développement sexuel prénatal" in *Le Fait féminin* (Paris: Fayard, 1978).

24 Le Doeuff, "Women and Philosophy", *op. cit.*, pp. 2–11.

25 For Le Doeuff: "The danger of amateurism and the particular position it implies is still there, the only difference being that our female predecessors were condemned to it, while we are merely exposed to it" (p. 108).

26 Barry Smith alerts us to the cultural context of the commentary, i.e. the different place accorded to commentary in differing cultures, and argues that commentary has never occupied the significant space in the Anglo-Saxon philosophical tradition that it has in the German or French traditions. It might be important to think about this cultural bias against commentary in the Anglo tradition if we are to think through the relationships between women and the discipline of philosophy in these differing cultural contexts, i.e. is the role of faithful commentator one in fact available to women working within the Anglo tradition? See: Barry Smith, "Textual Difference", *American Philosophical Quarterly* 28(1) 1991, pp. 1–12.

27 It is interesting to note the spatial metaphors Gallop uses in her discussion of feminism as a practice of infidelity. She writes:

> Infidelity then is a feminist practice of undermining the Name-of-the-Father. The unfaithful reading strays from the author, the authorized, produces that which does not hold as a reproduction, as a representation. Infidelity is not outside the system of marriage, the symbolic, patriarchy, but hollows it out, ruins it, from within. Unlike such infidelity, a new system, a feminist system, one constant, faithful to the tenets and dogmas of feminism would be but another Name-of-the-Father, feminism as a position and a possession.
>
> Jane Gallop, *Feminism and Psychoanalysis: The Daughter's Seduction*
> (London: Macmillan, 1982, p. 48).

28 In *Hipparchia's Choice* Le Doeuff writes: "we can admit that an element of non-knowledge unavoidably inhabits any undertaking, including a philosophical one. Instead of always pushing questions as far as they will go, it is sometimes permissible to leave them halfway. Rather than trying to prove everything, we can allow beliefs, opinions and experiences to express themselves as such" (p. 8). *Hipparchia's Choice: An Essay Concerning Women, Philosophy, Etc.*, trans. Trista Selous (Oxford: Basil Blackwell, 1991. Also pp. 56, 115).

29 See Morris's comments on the relation between Le Doeuff's essay writing and the "feminine" writing she distances herself from. Morris, *op. cit.*, p. 4.

30 In *Hipparchia's Choice* Le Doeuff writes: "this recognition of the always incomplete and limited character of philosophical effort has advantages, if only that of the hope of finding a new way of thinking philosophically, a way which, unlike so many others, would not be hegemonic. Once we stop trying radically to justify a project from its roots to its ultimate effects, part-objects abound" (p. 8).

31 Morris, *op. cit.*, pp. 99, 100.

32 Le Doeuff, *Hipparchia's Choice*, *op. cit.* See also pp. 56, 115.

33 Cf. Michèle Le Doeuff, "Operative Philosophy: Simone de Beauvoir and Existentialism", *Ideology and Consciousness* 6, Autumn 1979, pp. 47–57 *Hipparchia's Choice*, *op. cit.*, pp. 55–133.

34 Le Doeuff, cf. "Ants and Women, or Philosophy without Borders", *op. cit.*

NOTES

2 PHILOSOPHY: READING DENIAL

1 When Plato speaks of *turning* here, it has been suggested that he is in fact comparing the process that the soul undergoes to the process of scene changing at the theatre. While this movement is not unequivocally a somatic property, it is nonetheless an obviously physical one, that may arguably rest upon a somatic analogy itself.

2 There is another sense in which bodily fluids and the eye might be linked. We could argue that Plato's discussion of sprouting wings is a good example of the sexual perversion of *scopophilia*. Freud suggests that scopophilia entails a perverse pleasure that bypasses the genitals. The eyes become an erotogenic zone, substituting the pleasure of sexual union with the pleasure of looking. The key to understanding the perversions is that they are a substitute for genital union, so that in them certain areas of the body will behave in a manner similar to the genitals. See: Sigmund Freud, "Three Essays on the Theory of Sexuality: No. 1 The Sexual Aberrations"(1905), pp. 135–72 (esp. p. 169) in *The Standard Edition of the Complete Psychological Works* Vol. VII, (James Strachey ed.) (London: Hogarth Press, 1953). Returning to the previous passages from the *Phaedrus* we can suggest that the act of looking takes on a significantly sexual (genital?) function. Looking elicits a "shudder" that runs through the lover, "an unusual fever and perspiration". Having received this stimulation "through his eyes", the lover "grows warm, and through the perspiration that ensues, he irrigates the sprouting of his wing." The unfurling of his wings involves a swelling of the stump, "from the root upward", an experience we might equate with (male) genital erection. Plato himself gains a perverse pleasure by displacing erection from the physical to the "spiritual" body, i.e. he hallucinates a tumescent soul in the figure of the swollen stump of the wings. So Plato's scopophilic perversion is Freudian in the following ways. Firstly, it focuses on the eyes as an initial and significant site of sexual pleasure. Sexual pleasure in Plato is first and foremost the pleasure of looking. Secondly, it displaces this libidinal cathexis of the eyes to other areas of the body; it eroticises what we might call (along with Merleau-Ponty) the *imaginary body*. It is not the genitals that become erect but the imaginary wing stumps. We could say that this involves a hysterical displacement on Plato's part. And finally, it replaces the pleasure of "normal" *physical* sexual union with other "perverse" pleasures, in this instance the pleasure of looking, and the pleasure of *spiritual* union.

3 See Luce Irigaray's attempt to reclaim Diotima's notion of love as an intermediary between opposites: "Sorcerer Love: A Reading of Plato's *Symposium*, Diotima's Speech", trans. Eleanor H. Kuykendall in *Revaluing French Feminism: Critical Essays on Difference, Agency, and Culture*, Nancy Fraser and Sandra Bartky eds. (Bloomington: Indiana University Press, 1992, pp. 64–76). For further discussion of Irigaray's reading see the following papers from the same volume: Andrea Nye, "The Hidden Host: Irigaray and Diotima at Plato's *Symposium*", pp. 77–93; Diana J. Fuss, " 'Essentially Speaking': Luce Irigaray's Language of Essence", pp. 94–112.

4 For a discussion of the links between philosophical discourse and Greek (sexual) practices involved in the ethical formation of the (male) self see: Michel Foucault, *The Use of Pleasure: The History of Sexuality Volume 2*, trans. R. Hurley (New York: Random House, 1985).

5 Louis Althusser, "From *Capital* to Marx's Philosophy" in *Reading Capital*, Louis Althusser and Etienne Balibar, trans. Ben Brewster (London: Verso, 1979, pp. 13–78).

6 For an excellent discussion of Lacan's exemplary reading lesson see: Shoshana Felman, "Renewing the Practice of Reading, or Freud's Unprecedented Lesson" in *Jacques Lacan and the Adventure of Insight: Psychoanalysis in Contemporary Culture* (Cambridge, MA: Harvard University Press, 1987, p. 20).

7 And further: "If there are no innocent readings, that is because every reading merely reflects in its lessons and rules the real culprit: the conception of knowledge underlying the object of knowledge which makes knowledge what it is" (p. 34).

185

8 In his discussion of the innocence/guilt of the reader J. Hillis Miller claims the following:

> Any repetitive structure of the "uncanny" sort, whether in real life or in words, tends to generate an irrational sense of guilt in the one who experiences it ... I am guilty if I reveal what ought to have been kept secret. I am guilty if I refuse the demand it makes on me to "get in", to penetrate all the way to the bottom of the mystery.

See: J. Hillis Miller, *Fiction and Repetition: Seven English Novels* (Oxford: Basil Blackwell, 1982, pp. 69, 70). Luce Irigaray has something pertinent to say in this regard. I shall simply repeat her here:

> Must we kill then? That's not the goal. Uncovering murders doesn't necessarily mean killing, but suspending hidden crime, aggression and sacrifice. This would force a rebalancing of the group, of groups and of individuals. To tell the other that he is a criminal, often involuntary, doesn't mean imposing any sanction on him other than that of becoming conscious of himself and of permitting the other to become so as well. Of course this will modify the economy of consciousness [*conscience*].
>
> Luce Irigaray, "Women, the Sacred and Money", trans.
> Diana Knight and Margaret Whitford, *Paragraph* 8
> (October) 1986, p. 16.

9 Monique Plaza, "Ideology Against Women", *Feminist Issues* 4(1) 1984, pp. 73–82. Somer Brodribb's discussion of the murder of Hélène Rythmann should be read along with Plaza's article. She provides a wonderful sampling of the various responses to Althusser's crime. Somer Brodribb, *Nothing Mat(t)ers: A Feminist Critique of Postmodernism* (Melbourne: Spinifex Press, 1992, p. 3).

10 Louis Althusser, "Ideology and Ideological State Apparatuses (Notes towards an Investigation) in *Lenin and Philosophy: And Other Essays*, trans. Ben Brewster (New York: Monthly Review Press, 1971, pp. 127–86).

11 Louis Althusser, "Freud and Lacan" in *Lenin and Philosophy, op. cit.*, pp. 189–219.

12 Virginia Woolf, *A Room of One's Own*, Morag Shiach ed. (Oxford: Oxford University Press, 1992, pp. 42–3, 48–9, emphases added).

13 Irigaray, "Women, the Sacred and Money", *op. cit.*, p. 14 (emphasis added).

14 It is worth noting that Irigaray's comparison between women and intellectuals stands in sharp contrast to the antagonistic relation Woolf depicts between her woman and the professor. Woolf's professor occupies the privileged power relation conferred upon him by patriarchal society. He is not only professor, but also proprietor of the paper, Foreign Secretary, Judge; in short "the power and the money and the influence". In Woolf's text it is the person reading the headlines, the person who had that morning been reading in the British Museum, who occupies simultaneously the (marginal) place of both woman and intellectual.

15 Maria-Antonietta Macciocchi, *Deux mille ans de bonheur* (Paris: Grasset, 1983, p. 537) cited in Brodribb, *op. cit.*, p. 3.

16 Brodribb, *op. cit.*, p. 3. This *self*-destruction is more than a little reminiscent of Plato's "black horse of the soul". If we think back to our discussion in the previous chapter we might say that Althusser falls prey to the unruly destruction of unreined desire, an internal force constructing the masculine imaginary as the site of unresolved conflict between self-destruction and self-restraint.

17 Louis Althusser, *"L'Avenir dure longtemps" suivi de "Les Faits": Autobiographies* (Paris: Stock, 1992), cited in John Sturrock, "The Paris Strangler", review of *L'Avenir* in *London Review of Books* 17 December 1992, p. 6.

18 Sturrock, *ibid.*, p. 6.

19 This idea is prompted by Meaghan Morris's discussion of nagging in "Introduction: Feminism, Reading, Postmodernism" in *The Pirate's Fiancée: Feminism/Reading/Postmodernism* (London: Verso, 1988, pp. 15–16). For a discussion of a feminist recuperation of nagging see my "The Aesthetics of Detail" in *Aesthetics After Historicism*, Wayne Hudson ed. (Brisbane: Institute of Modern Art, 1993, pp. 79–91).

20 Catherine MacKinnon risks what some consider to be the unfashionable and tasteless gesture of referring to these abused bodies of women. It seems to me that gestures such as these provide feminism with its real political difference in an era when "risking the referential" is synonymous with finding oneself well and truly out in the cold. In this instance MacKinnon's work provides a strategy for fighting (rather than reinforcing) the silence imposed upon already mute bodies. See: Catherine A. MacKinnon, "Does Sexuality Have a History?" *Michigan Quarterly Review* XXXL (1) 1991, pp. 1–11. Somer Brodribb's work provides another instance of such risk. Her feminist critique of postmodernism attacks the silencing of women and their bodies by contemporary masculine thought. See: Brodribb, *op. cit.*

3 READING PSYCHOANALYSIS: PSYCHOTIC TEXTS/MATERNAL PRE-TEXTS

1 Jerre Collins, Ray Green, Mary Lydon, Mark Sachner and Eleanor Honig Skoller, "Questioning the Unconscious: The Dora Archive" in *Dora's Case: Freud, Hysteria, Feminism*, Charles Bernheimer and Claire Kahane eds (London: Virago, 1985, p. 251).

2 Teresa de Lauretis, *Alice Doesn't: Feminism, Semiotics, Cinema* (London: Macmillan, 1984, p. 156).

3 Sigmund Freud, *Beyond the Pleasure Principle* (1920), trans. J. Strachey (London: W.W. Norton, 1961, p. 9).

4 For a discussion of the psychoanalytic fear and loathing of the mother see: Monique Plaza, "The Mother/The Same: The Hatred of the Mother in Psychoanalysis", *Feminist Issues* 2(1) 1982, pp. 75–99. Madelon Sprengnether provides a detailed analysis and discussion of Freud's ambivalence toward the mother in *The Spectral Mother: Freud, Feminism, and Psychoanalysis* (Ithaca, NY: Cornell University Press, 1990).

5 Julia Kristeva, "Stabat Mater", trans. Arthur Goldhammer in *The Female Body in Western Culture: Contemporary Perspectives*, Susan Rubin Suleiman ed. (Cambridge, MA: Harvard University Press, 1986, p. 112). This denial of the mother is evident in Freud's case history of Dora. Here there exists a structural parallel between his dismissal of Dora's mother and the eclipse of the mother in his Oedipal theory. See: Jerre Collins *et al., op. cit.*, pp. 243–53.

6 Louis Althusser, "Freud and Lacan" in *Lenin and Philosophy: And Other Essays*, trans. Ben Brewster (New York: Monthly Review Press, 1971, p. 217).

7 Bice Benvenuto and Roger Kennedy, "Psychosis" in *The Works of Jacques Lacan: An Introduction* (London: Free Association Books, 1986, pp. 143–4).

8 Sigmund Freud, "Neurosis and Psychosis" (1924) in *The Standard Edition of the Complete Psychological Works of Sigmund Freud*, Vol. XIX, trans. James Strachey (London: Hogarth Press, 1961, p. 149).

9 *Ibid.*, p. 187.

10 Jacques Lacan, "On a Question Preliminary to any Possible Treatment of Psychosis" in *Ecrits: A Selection*, trans. Alan Sheridan (New York: W.W. Norton, 1977, pp. 188–9).

11 *Ibid.*, pp. 191–2.

12 Julia Kristeva, *Revolution in Poetic Language*, trans. Margaret Waller (New York: Columbia University Press, 1984, p. 47).

13 Sigmund Freud, "From the History of an Infantile Neurosis" (1918 [1914]) in *Three Case Studies* (New York: Collier, 1963, p. 270).

14 Freud, *Standard Edition*, Vol. XVII, p. 85.

15 Benvenuto and Kennedy, *op. cit.*, pp. 151f. The story of Lacan's translation of this term is quite fascinating. In his foreword to Elisabeth Roudinesco's epic history of psychoanalysis in France, Jeffrey Mehlman informs us that Roudinesco reclaims one of psychoanalysis's own repressed moments in the figure of Edouard Pichon. She alerts us to Pichon's influence on Lacan. By translating Freud's *Verwerfung* with Pichon's *forclusion* Lacan effectively revives that part of psychoanalysis that had been repressed by the ascendancy of Marie Bonaparte and Rudolph Loewenstein in France. See: Jeffrey Mehlman's foreword to Elisabeth Roudinesco, *Jacques Lacan and Co: A History of Psychoanalysis in France, 1925–1985*, trans. Jeffrey Mehlman (Chicago: University of Chicago Press, 1990, pp. xi–xvi).

16 Serge Leclaire, "A propos de l'episode psychotique que presenta l'homme-aux-loups" 1957, p. 96.

17 François Roustang, *Dire Mastery: Discipleship from Freud to Lacan*, trans. Ned Lukacher (Baltimore, MD: Johns Hopkins University Press, 1982, p. 135).

18 Lacan, *op. cit.*, p. 193.

19 *Ibid.*, p. 215.

20 Translator's note, *ibid.*, p. x (emphasis added).

21 This opposition between repression and foreclosure is further elaborated in Elizabeth Grosz's discussion of fetishism and psychosis. She explains that fetishism involves a *displacement* of the maternal phallus, while psychosis involves a *hallucination* of it. Elizabeth Grosz, *Sexual Subversions: Three French Feminists* (Sydney: Allen and Unwin, 1989, p. 58).

22 Julia Kristeva, *Powers of Horror: An Essay on Abjection*, trans. Leon S. Roudiez (New York: Columbia University Press, 1982, p. 64).

23 Freud, 'Loss of Reality', *op. cit.*, p. 187.

24 *Ibid.*, p. 183.

25 Martin Thom, "Verneinung, Verwerfung, Ausstossung: A Problem in the Interpretation of Freud" in *The Talking Cure: Essays in Psychoanalysis and Language*, Colin MacCabe ed. (New York: St Martin's Press, 1981, p. 179).

26 Cf. Benvenuto and Kennedy, *op. cit.*, p. 142.

27 Freud, *Beyond the Pleasure Principle, op. cit.*, pp. 8–9.

28 *Ibid.*, p. 9.

29 *Ibid.*, p. 10.

30 Rosi Braidotti stresses the relation between the *fort-da* game and the symbolic form of theory. She argues that all theorisation must be *thought* in terms of the maternal body. See: "Desidero Ergo Sum: The Improbable Tête-à-Tête between Philosophy and Psychoanalysis" in *Patterns of Dissonance: A Study of Women in Contemporary Philosophy*, trans. Elizabeth Guild (Oxford: Polity Press, 1991, p. 31).

31 Freud, *Beyond the Pleasure Principle, op. cit.*, p. 10 (emphasis added).

32 Martin Thom, "The Unconscious Structured as a Language" in MacCabe, *op. cit.*, p. 33.

33 Freud, *Beyond the Pleasure Principle, op. cit.*, n. 1, p. 10.

34 Luce Irigaray, "The Gesture in Psychoanalysis" in *Between Feminism and Psychoanalysis*, Teresa Brennan ed. (London: Routledge, 1989, p. 132).

35 Elizabeth Grosz provides an interesting discussion of psychosis, masculine self-engenderment and body-space in "Lived Spatiality: Insect Space/Virtual Sex", *Agenda: Contemporary Art Magazine* 26/27 1992–3, pp. 5–8.

36 Lacan, *op. cit.*, n. 10, p. 222 (emphasis added).

37 Ida Macalpine and Richard A. Hunter, "Observations on the Psychoanalytic Theory of Psychosis", *British Journal of Medical Psychology* 27 1954, pp. 175–6.

38 Daniel Paul Schreber, *Memoirs of My Nervous Illness*, trans. and ed. Ida Macalpine and Richard A. Hunter (London: W.M. Dawson and Sons, 1955, p. 407).

39 *Ibid.*, pp. 381–4. They conclude: "It is noteworthy that cases of pregnancy fantasies *[sic]* quoted in the literature had somatic symptoms predominantly; however, they are not

accorded any significance and are therefore scattered at random through the case histories"
(p. 385).

40 Cf. Grafton Elliot Smith, *The Evolution of the Dragon* (Manchester: Manchester University
Press, 1919, p. 211).

41 Schreber, *op. cit.*, p. 72.

42 *Ibid.*, pp. 73–4.

43 *Ibid.*, n. 1, pp. 42–3.

44 *Ibid.*, p. 25. "If such confusion about sex identity is termed homosexuality then of course
schizophrenic 'homosexuality' is of a different order, and should be clearly differentiated
from passive homosexual wishes towards members of the same sex, as is implied in Freud's
use of the term."

45 *Ibid.*, p. 132.

46 *Ibid.*, p. 148.

47 *Ibid.*, p. 205.

48 *Ibid.*, p. 99.

49 *Ibid.*, p. 395.

50 *Ibid.*, pp. 402–3.

51 Sigmund Freud, "Psycho-analytic Notes upon an Autobiographical Account of a Case of
Paranoia (Dementia Paranoides)" (1911) in *Standard Edition* Vol. XII.

52 Schreber, *op. cit.*, p. 402.

53 Irigaray, *op. cit.*, p. 137. Irigaray claims that Freud's Schreber (paranoiac) and Dora (virgin
woman) form a "strange couple", one that is symptomatic of the fact that we have no
symbol of sexual difference or fecundity between man and woman.

54 Schreber, *op. cit.*, pp. 214, 215. In their critique of another of Freud's case studies, Macalpine
and Hunter note the importance of the book, in this case Diary, as the medium through
which the psychotic gives birth to himself. See: Macalpine and Hunter, *op. cit.*

55 John Muller and William Richardson reinforce the severity of this crime. See: *Lacan and
Language: A Reader's Guide to Ecrits* (New York: International Universities Press, 1982,
p. 206). For their discussion of Macalpine and Hunter see pp. 205f. They go on to parallel
Macalpine and Hunter's crime with Jung's formulation of the Other (p. 209).

56 Roland Barthes, *The Pleasure of the Text*, trans. R. Miller (New York: Hill and Wang, 1975).

57 Julia Kristeva, *Powers of Horror: An Essay on Abjection*, trans. Leon S. Roudiez (New York:
Columbia University Press, 1982, p. 77).

58 Julia Kristeva, "The Novel as Polylogue" in *Desire in Language: A Semiotic Approach to
Literature and Art*, trans. Thomas Gora, Alice Jardine and Leon S. Roudiez (New York:
Columbia University Press, 1980, p. 166).

59 Julia Kristeva, "Stabat Mater", trans. Arthur Goldhammer in *The Female Body in Western
Culture: Contemporary Perspectives*, Susan Rubin Suleiman ed. (Cambridge, MA: Harvard
University Press, 1986, p. 100). Also in *Tales of Love*, trans. Leon S. Roudiez (New York:
Columbia University Press, 1987, pp. 234–63).

60 Kristeva, "The Novel as Polylogue", *op. cit.*, p. 191.

61 Julia Kristeva, "From One Identity to an Other" in *Desire in Language, op. cit.*, p. 136.

62 Kristeva, *Powers of Horror, op. cit.*, p. 20.

63 Kristeva, "From One Identity to an Other", *op. cit.*, p. 139.

64 Kristeva, *Powers of Horror, op. cit.*, p. 155.

65 *Ibid.*, p. 174. Elsewhere Kristeva discusses Lautréamont's self-engendering via his use of
two signatures. See: *Revolution in Poetic Language*, trans. Margaret Waller (New York:
Columbia University Press, 1984, p. 220–1).

66 The abject traces a psychotic link to the physicality of the archaic maternal body. The
intolerable maternal debt that emerges when the child's body is violently separated from
the mother is later encoded in a psychotic discourse which attempts to replace the mother,
to be the mother. From this perspective writing displaces the violence of this separation
onto the realm of signification. Like the sacred, writing helps to save the subject from his

fear of "sinking irretrievably [back] into the mother"(*Powers of Horror, op. cit.*, p. 64). It is a symbolic (paternal) appropriation of the abject (maternal) space; both an identification with and distancing from it. For a discussion of this point see: Elizabeth Grosz, "The Body of Signification" in *Abjection, Melancholia and Love: The Work of Julia Kristeva*, John Fletcher and Andrew Benjamin eds. (London: Routledge, 1990, pp. 80–103) and *Sexual Subversions: Three French Feminists* (Sydney: Allen and Unwin, 1989, p. 78).

4 PHILOSOPHY AND SILENCE: *THE DIFFÉREND*

1 Jean-François Lyotard, "Interview" with Georges Van Den Abbeele, *Diacritics* 14(3) 1984, p. 17.
2 Jean-François Lyotard, *The Différend: Phrases in Dispute*, trans. Georges Van Den Abbeele (Minneapolis: University of Minnesota Press, 1988).
3 We might think of this impasse in terms of various debates around "the end of philosophy"; cf. Kenneth Baynes, James Bohman and Thomas McCarthy eds. *After Philosophy: End or Transformation?* (Cambridge, MA: The MIT Press, 1987).
4 Lyotard illustrates this dilemma by reference to Faurisson's argument concerning the "alleged" existence of Nazi gas chambers. Faurrisson's argument is as follows: "in order for a place to be identified as a gas chamber, the only eyewitness I will accept would be a victim of this gas chamber; now, according to my opponent, there is no victim that is not dead; otherwise, this gas chamber would not be what he or she claims it to be. There is, therefore, no gas chamber" (pp. 3–4).
5 Cf. David Carroll, "Rephrasing the Political with Kant and Lyotard: From Aesthetic to Political Judgments", *Diacritics* 14(3) 1984, pp. 74–88 where he argues that Lyotard's major contribution lies in his recasting of the political in terms of a "philosophy of phrases" (p. 75).
6 Lyotard, *The Différend, op. cit.*, p. 128.
7 Geoffrey Bennington argues that while there is a substantial shift in Lyotard's work over time, there are nonetheless some tasks he views as fundamental to philosophy. Even a book as contentious as *Libidinal Economy* would evidence this. Geoffrey Bennington, *Lyotard: Writing the Event* (Manchester: Manchester University Press, 1988, p. 46). See: Jean-François Lyotard, *Libidinal Economy*, trans. Iain Hamilton Grant (Bloomington: Indiana University Press, 1993).
8 Bennington, *op. cit.*, pp. 145, 146.
9 *Ibid.*, pp. 134–5.
10 *The Différend, op. cit.*, p. 80. For example, Hegel's *Science of Logic* circumscribes the linkages for modern dialectics. Or more pointedly, modern logic circumscribes the rules for the theory genre, i.e. "consistency, completeness, decidability of the system of axioms, and independence of the axioms." See: "Interview", *op. cit.*, p. 19.
11 "What we cannot speak about we must pass over in silence." Ludwig Wittgenstein, *Tractatus Logico-Philosophicus*, trans. D. Pears and B. McGuinness (London: Routledge and Kegan Paul, 1961, p. 7).
12 David Carroll writes, "When the phrasing of injustice is prohibited, it is only the nonphrased, silence that testifies to it and must be listened to." Carroll, *op. cit.*, p. 78.
13 Bennington urges us not to think of sentiment in psychological terms, but rather as a "negative presentation of the indeterminate" (Lyotard's words). Bennington *op. cit.*, p. 148. See also his: " 'Ces petits différends': Lyotard and Horace" in *Judging Lyotard*, Andrew Benjamin ed. (London: Routledge, 1992, p. 156).
14 Lyotard *The Différend, op. cit.*, p. 142.
15 In an earlier work, *Discours, figure*, Lyotard suggests that "what is wanted is to have words *say* the preeminence of the figure, to *signify* the other of signification" (p. 18). He contends that critical philosophy seeks to open language (or discourse) to the transgressive moments, figures, or events, that refuse the rule of meaning. In so doing it leaves open the possibility

of new idioms, new significations shot through with the disruptive energy of the sensible. Jean-François Lyotard, *Discours, figure* (Paris: Klincksieck, 1971), cited in David Carroll, *Paraesthetics: Foucault/Lyotard/Derrida* (New York: Methuen, 1987, p. 31).

16 Meaghan Morris discusses this artistic moment in Lyotard's work and yet is careful to point out that the affinities between art and theory do not become, for Lyotard, the pretext for their total dissolution. See: "Postmodernity and Lyotard's Sublime" in *The Pirate's Fiancée: Feminism/Reading/Postmodernism* (London: Verso, 1988, pp. 213–39). See also: Jean-François Lyotard, "Theory as Art: A Pragmatic Point of View" in *Image and Code*, W. Steiner ed. (Ann Arbor: University of Michigan Press, 1981).

17 Lyotard, "Representation, Presentation, Unpresentable" in *The Inhuman: Reflections on Time*, trans. Geoffrey Bennington and Rachel Bowlby (Cambridge: Polity Press, 1991, p. 128).

18 Jean-François Lyotard, *The Postmodern Condition: A Report on Knowledge*, trans. Geoff Bennington and Brian Massumi, Theory and History of Literature Series, Vol. 10 (Minneapolis: University of Minnesota Press, 1984, p. 81). The relationship between the avant-garde and postmodernism is an interesting one. On this point Meaghan Morris claims that Lyotard appropriates the gestures typically associated with the avant-garde for postmodernism, and that in so doing ensures that we remain within an avant-garde problematic. Morris, *op. cit.*, p. 236.

19 Bill Readings, *Introducing Lyotard: Art and Politics* (London: Routledge, 1991, pp. xxv, xxvi).

20 "Interview", *op. cit.*, p. 20.

21 Jean-François Lyotard, "One of the Things at Stake in Women's Struggles", trans. D.J. Clarke, W. Woodhill and J. Mowitt, reprinted in *The Lyotard Reader*, Andrew Benjamin ed. (Oxford: Basil Blackwell, 1991, pp. 111–21). Originally published in *Sub-Stance* 20 1978, pp. 9–17. Lyotard cautions women that they "should not attack [masculine imperialism] head-on but wage a guerrilla war of skirmishes and raids in a space and time other than those imposed for millennia by the masculine logos" (p. 118). It would seem that he has read his Wittig.

22 "Interview", *op. cit.*, p. 20. (Quotations cited in my text immediately before this one are from the same page.)

23 *Ibid*.

24 Jean-François Lyotard, "Analysing Speculative Discourse as Language-Game", trans. Geoffrey Bennington, in *The Lyotard Reader, op. cit.*, pp. 265–74. Originally published in English in *The Oxford Literary Review* 4(3) 1981, pp. 59–67.

25 Bennington describes Lyotard's views on speculative discourse in the following manner:

> For Lyotard, it is not that speculative discourse is "wrong" in the sense of being incorrect, but in the sense of being unjust. This injustice consists in its assigning of hegemonic status to a particular regime of sentence (the cognitive), which, in formulating the speculative "truth", *quotes* other sentences and in so doing deprives them of their immediate value.
>
> Bennington, *Lyotard: Writing the Event, op. cit.*, p. 136.

26 "One of the Things at Stake in Women's Struggles", *op. cit.*, p. 119.

27 See pp. 43–4. References are to passages taken from the following works: Virginia Woolf, *A Room of One's Own*, Morag Shiach ed. (Oxford: Oxford University Press, 1992, pp. 42–3, 48–9) Luce Irigaray, "Women, the Sacred and Money", trans. Diana Knight and Margaret Whitford, *Paragraph* 8 (October) 1986, p. 14.

28 For Irigaray woman's speech is inseparable from woman's body. In this she is different from Lyotard who, in his work on the *différend*, does not talk about the body as such. However, as we have seen, the body is by no means absent from the *corpus* of Lyotard's work. *Discours, figure* is replete with accounts and criticisms of phenomenological descriptions of the body

(see Carroll, *Paraesthetics*, *op. cit.*); as is "Can Thought Go On Without a Body?", in *The Inhuman, op. cit.*, pp. 8–23.

29 Luce Irigaray, "Sexual Difference" in *The Irigaray Reader*, Margaret Whitford ed. (Oxford: Basil Blackwell, 1991, p. 165).

30 Luce Irigaray, "The Three *Genres*", in *The Irigaray Reader, op. cit.*, p. 140.

31 *Ibid.*, p. 144.

32 Luce Irigaray, "Equal or Different?" in *The Irigaray Reader, op. cit.*, p. 32.

33 Margaret Whitford contends that it is a term that hovers between genre understood as sexual kind and genre as literary or artistic type. She suggests that *genre* has no fixed or determinate sense in Irigaray's work. See Whitford's "Glossary" in *The Irigaray Reader, ibid.*, p. 17. *Genre* is arguably a misleading translation of what Irigaray is trying to convey here, as her concerns are very much more focused on "kind". The French *genre littéraire* or *genre de discours* denote more readily what the English term *genre* conveys.

34 Monique Wittig also discusses these issues in her work. See especially: "The Point of View: Universal or Particular" and "The Mark of Gender" in *The Straight Mind: And Other Essays* (Boston, MA: Beacon Press, 1992, pp. 59–67, 76–89).

35 See: Whitford's introduction to Section II of *The Irigaray Reader, op. cit.*, p. 78.

36 Irigaray."Equal or Different?", *op. cit.*, p. 32.

37 *Ibid.*, p. 33. Irigaray begins to do just this in "How to Define Sexuate Rights?", *The Irigaray Reader*, pp. 204–12, where she presents the preliminaries toward a Bill of Rights for women. She argues that we desperately need to begin with and recognise woman's identity as a genre distinct and separate from men. In "The Necessity for Sexuate Rights", pp. 198–203, she suggests that each genre has sexually specific rights and responsibilities that can be inscribed in the rights of the couple.

> It necessitates the inscription of the rights of every man and woman in civil law. The inscription of the rights of the couple in civil law would have the effect of converting individual morality into a collective ethic, of transforming relations between genres within the family, or its substitute, into rights and duties concerning culture in general.
>
> (p. 202)

Irigaray continues this work in *Je, tu, nous: Toward a Culture of Difference*, trans. Alison Martin (London: Routledge, 1993).

38 Irigaray, "The Three *Genres*", *op. cit.*, p. 147.

39 *Ibid.*, p. 147. Irigaray claims that such style resists the oppositional structure underpinning existing discourse.

40 *Ibid.*, p. 149.

41 This notion of an exacerbated litigation comes from Bennington who chides Lyotard for not classifying or thematising the range of possibility from *différend* through to litigation. Bennington, " 'Ces petits différends' ", *op. cit.*, pp. 152–3. The question arises, can the silence of women in philosophy be best understood in terms of a *différend* or an exacerbated litigation? Bennington insists that the obligation to note *différends* should not involve making every conflict or oppression a *différend*, that we should take care not to equate every silence with a radical silence.

42 Lyotard, *The Différend, op. cit.*, p. xii.

43 Bennington, " 'Ces petits différends' ", *op. cit.*, p. 164.

44 Lyotard, "Interview", *op. cit.*, p. 20.

45 Lyotard, "One of the Things at Stake in Women's Struggles", *op. cit.*, p. 118.

46 Alice Jardine reminds us that we should be wary of the consequences of this *gynesis*, this putting into discourse of the feminine. See: Alice A. Jardine, *Gynesis: Configurations of Woman and Modernity* (Ithaca, NY: Cornell University Press, 1985).

5 UNQUIET SILENCE: KRISTEVA READING MARX WITH FREUD

1 Julia Kristeva, "Semiotics: A Critical Science and/or a Critique of Science", trans. Sean Hand in *The Kristeva Reader*, Toril Moi ed. (New York: Columbia University Press, 1986, p. 85).

2 Karl Marx, *Writings of the Young Marx on Philosophy and Society*, Loyd D. Easton and Kurt H. Guddat eds. (New York: Anchor, 1962, pp. 322, 332).

3 Karl Marx, *Grundrisse: Foundations of the Critique of Political Economy*, trans. M. Nicolaus (New York: Penguin, 1973, p. 87).

4 Karl Marx and Frederick Engels, *The German Ideology* (Moscow: Progress Publishers, 1976, p. 47).

5 Karl Marx, *Economic and Philosophic Manuscripts of 1844*, in *Early Writings*, T.B. Bottomore ed. (London: Lawrence and Wishart, 1959, p. 101).

6 Karl Marx, *Capital* Vol. I. (New York: International Publishers, 1975, pp. 197–8).

7 Marx, *Economic and Philosophical Manuscripts of 1844*, op. cit., p. 139. Elsewhere Marx distances himself from the individualism implicit in *self-creation*. He writes: "it is evident that individuals undoubtedly make one another, physically and mentally, but do not make themselves, either in the nonsense of Saint Bruno, or in the sense of the 'unique', or the 'made' man", *The German Ideology*, op. cit., p. 59.

8 Alexandre Kojève suggests that Hegel anticipates Marx's later emphasis on work, consciousness and self-recognition. See: *Introduction to the Reading of Hegel*, trans. James Nichols (New York: Basic Books, 1969, p. 25). Isaac Balbus distinguishes between Hegel and Marx on this point, arguing that labour represents for Hegel only *one* aspect of the struggle for recognition. See: *Marxism and Domination: A Neo-Hegelian, Feminist, Psychoanalytic Theory of Sexual, Political, and Technological Liberation* (Princeton, NJ: Princeton University Press, 1982, pp. 14–15).

9 In Volume III of *Capital* Marx writes: "Just as the savage must wrestle with Nature to satisfy his wants, to maintain and reproduce life, so must civilized man, and he must do so in all social formations and under all possible modes of production." Karl Marx, *Capital* Vol. III (Moscow: Foreign Languages Publishing House, n.d., pp. 799–800).

10 For an elaboration of this virile productivity in Marxian philosophy see: Erich Fromm, *Marx's Concept of Man* (New York: Frederick Unger, 1966, pp. 29, 30). See also: Jacques Derrida, *Spurs: Nietzsche's Styles*, trans. Barbara Harlow (Chicago: University of Chicago Press, 1979, pp. 77, 79). Alison Jaggar and William McBride argue that Marx and Engels' definition of labour evaluates *productive* (masculine) and *reproductive* (feminine) activity in fundamentally different ontological terms (p. 255). See: " 'Reproduction' as Male Ideology" in *Hypatia Reborn: Essays in Feminist Philosophy*, Azizah Y. Al-Hibri and Margaret A. Simons eds. (Bloomington: Indiana University Press, 1990, pp. 249–69).

11 For a discussion of the way that the *cogito* dominates the objective body see: David Michael Levin, "The Body Politic: Political Economy and the Human Body", *Human Studies* 8(4) 1985, p. 251. Fred Dallmayer refers to the dominating impulse of the rational subject as a *possessive individualism* that installs the *cogito* as a self-controlling, autonomous agency. See: Winfried R. Dallmayer, "Beyond Possessive Individualism" in *Twilight of Subjectivity: Contributions to a Post-Individualist Theory of Politics* (Amherst: University of Massachusetts Press, 1981).

12 For a discussion of this point I refer the reader to the work of Theodor W. Adorno, *Negative Dialectics*, trans. E.B. Ashton (London: Routledge and Kegan Paul, 1973, p. 177). Productive labour is fundamentally linked with activity aimed at imposing a rational will. Indeed it involves a dominating imposition of that will. For Stanley Aronowitz "rationality consists in the subordination of nature to human (i.e. bourgeois) will", with nature being that which is transformed by the labour process. See: *The Crisis in Historical Materialism: Class, Politics and Culture in Marxist Theory* (New York: Praeger, 1981, p. 23). According to William Leiss this will to power involves a concomitant desire for men to dominate each

other (or women?). See: *The Domination of Nature* (New York: George Braziller, 1972, pp. 15–16).

13 Linda Nicholson, "Feminism and Marx: Integrating Kinship with the Economic" in *Feminism As Critique: On the Politics of Gender*, Seyla Benhabib and Drucilla Cornell eds (Minneapolis: University of Minnesota Press, 1986, pp. 16–30).

14 Marx, *Economic and Philosophic Manuscripts, op. cit.*, p. 138.

15 Marx, *Writings of the Young Marx, op. cit.*, pp. 322, 332.

16 Marx, *Economic and Philosophical Manuscripts, op. cit.*, p. 139.

17 Marx cited in Erich Fromm's *Marx's Concept of Man, op. cit.*, pp. 18, 20, 24. Jean-François Lyotard captures the masculine phantasy of a self-generating capital in Marx's use of the term "Mother Earth" (in *Capital* III, VII, xxv) with some irony. He writes: " 'Mother Earth' disappears, Messieurs Father-Capital and Son-Work consider themselves sufficient for the *corpus sociandum* to reproduce itself without recourse to any external force." See: Jean-François Lyotard, "One of the Things at Stake in Women's Struggles", trans. D. J. Clarke, W. Woodhill and J. Mowitt, in *The Lyotard Reader*, Andrew Benjamin ed. (Oxford: Basil Blackwell, 1991, p. 116, n.10, p. 121).

18 Marx cited in Fromm's *Marx's Concept of Man, op. cit.*, p. 13.

19 Mary O'Brien raises a pertinent point in relation to this assumption. She writes: "Underlying the doctrine that man makes history is the undiscussed reality of why he must." See: Mary O'Brien, *The Politics of Reproduction* (London: Routledge and Kegan Paul, 1981, p. 53).

20 Erich Fromm, *Man For Himself: An Enquiry into the Psychology of Ethics* (London: Routledge and Kegan Paul, 1949, p. 91).

21 *Ibid.*

22 Karl Marx, *Preface to a Contribution to a Critique of Political Economy*, cited in Fromm, *Marx's Concept of Man, op. cit.*, p. 18 (emphasis added).

23 Marx, *Grundrisse, op. cit.*, p. 105.

24 Marx cited in Fromm, *Marx's Concept of Man op. cit.*, p. 18 (emphasis added).

25 *Capital* Vol. I, *op. cit.*, pp. 197, 198.

26 Chris McAuliffe provides a useful discussion of the movement of Baudrillard's concerns over time. See: "Jean Baudrillard" in *The Judgement of Paris: Recent French Theory in a Local Context*, Kevin Murray ed. (Sydney: Allen and Unwin, 1992, pp. 97–111).

27 Jean Baudrillard, *The Mirror of Production*, trans. M. Poster (St Louis, MO: Telos Press, 1975, p. 17).

28 *Ibid.*, pp. 18, 22.

29 *Ibid.*, p. 31.

30 *Ibid.*, p. 19.

31 *Ibid.*, p. 19.

32 *Ibid.*, p. 48.

33 *Ibid.*, p. 85.

34 *Ibid.*, p. 33.

35 *Ibid.*, p. 47.

36 *Ibid.*, p. 48.

37 Baudrillard applauds Benjamin, Lafargue and Marcuse for their violent attacks upon this sanctification of labour. He cites: Walter Benjamin, *Poésie et révolution* (Paris: Denoel, 1971); Paul Lafargue, *The Right to Be Lazy*, trans. C. Kerr (Chicago: Kerr, 1917). Herbert Marcuse, *Eros and Civilization* (New York: Vintage, 1962). In his "Theses on the Philosophy of History" Benjamin criticises the vulgar-Marxist conception of labour, but elsewhere notes that Marx was himself suspicious of this theology of labour. See: Walter Benjamin, *Illuminations: Essays and Reflections*, trans. Harry Zohn (New York: Schocken Books, 1969, p. 259).

38 Baudrillard, *op. cit.*, pp. 55, 56, 58.

39 *Ibid.*, p. 152.

40 *Ibid.*, p. 50.

41 Karl Marx, *Capital* Vol. III, *op. cit.*, pp. 799–800. Adorno recognises a powerful aesthetic of non-work at play in Marx's texts. See: *Negative Dialectics*, *op. cit.*, pp. 177–8.

42 Kristeva, "Semiotics", *op. cit.*, pp. 81–2. For Kristeva, Marx's analysis of the system of exchange parallels the contemporary critique of the sign and the circulation of meaning. In fact this work acknowledges its debt to Marx's analysis of money. See: Jacques Derrida, *Of Grammatology*, trans. Gayatri Spivak (Baltimore, MD: Johns Hopkins University Press, 1974, p. 300).

43 Kristeva, *op. cit.*, p. 82.

44 Marx, *Capital* Vol.I, cited in Kristeva, *op. cit.*, p. 82.

45 Kristeva, *op. cit.*, pp. 83, 82.

46 Compare Gallop's discussion of Lacan on "woman" as that which exceeds exchange value, i.e. the *pas-tout* (not-everything) which displaces Freud's notion of woman as castrated: "the use, the enjoyment, the *jouissance*, which exceeds exchange." Jane Gallop, "*Encore*, Encore" in *Feminism and Psychoanalysis: The Daughter's Seduction* (London: Macmillan, 1982, p. 50).

47 Kristeva, *op. cit.*, p. 83.

48 Kristeva provides a useful introduction to Freud's impact on our understanding of language through the dream processes. See: Julia Kristeva, "Psychoanalysis and Language" in *Language: The Unknown: An Initiation into Linguistics*, trans. Anne M. Menke (New York: Columbia University Press, 1989, pp. 265–77).

49 Lyotard takes great care to emphasise the *transformative* nature of the dream-work. He argues that Freud understands the dream-work as activity unrelated to interpretation or transcription. See: Jean-François Lyotard, "The Dream-Work Does Not Think", trans. Mary Lydon in *The Lyotard Reader*, *op. cit.*, pp. 20–1.

50 Sigmund Freud, *The Interpretation of Dreams* (1900), trans. James Strachey (New York: Avon Books, 1965, p. 545).

51 *Ibid.*, p. 348.

52 Kaja Silverman, *The Subject of Semiotics* (Oxford: Oxford University Press, 1983, p. 91).

53 Freud, *op. cit.*, pp. 342–3.

54 Jacques Lacan, "The Subversion of the Subject and the Dialectic of Desire in the Freudian Unconscious" in *Ecrits: A Selection*, trans. Alan Sheridan (New York: W.W. Norton, 1977, p. 298). Lacan's position here is influenced by Roman Jakobson's work on the speech act. See: "Two Aspects of Language and Two Types of Aphasic Disturbances" in R. Jakobson and M. Halle, *Fundamentals of Language* (The Hague: Mouton, 1956, Part II, chs 1–4). For a contemporary discussion of Lacan's treatment of the dream-work see: Slavoj Zizek, "Two Ways to Avoid the Real of Desire" in *Looking Awry: An Introduction to Jacques Lacan through Popular Culture* (Cambridge, MA: The MIT Press, 1991, pp. 48–66, esp. pp. 50–4).

55 Sigmund Freud, *Totem and Taboo*, trans. James Strachey (London: Routledge and Kegan Paul, 1950, p. 95).

56 *Ibid.*

57 Lyotard, "The Dream-Work Does Not Think", *op. cit.*, p. 24.

58 For extended discussions of Lyotard's displacement of Lacan see: Peter Dews, "The Letter and the Line: Discourse and its Other in Lyotard", *Diacritics* 14(3) 1984, pp. 40–9, and Geoffrey Bennington, *Lyotard: Writing the Event* (Manchester: Manchester University Press, 1988, pp. 79–91).

59 Kristeva, "Semiotics", *op. cit.*, p. 83.

60 In a quite different vein George Steiner alerts us to the *vitality* of an unquiet silence. See: "The Retreat from the Word" in *Language and Silence: Essays on Language, Literature, and the Inhuman* (New York: Atheneum, 1974, pp. 12–35). Steiner goes on to speak of the revaluation of silence, in figures as diverse as Wittgenstein, Webern, Cage and Beckett, as "the most original, characteristic acts of the modern spirit" (p. 48). See: "Silence and the Poet" in the same book.

61 Julia Kristeva, "The Ethics of Linguistics" in *Desire in Language: A Semiotic Approach to Literature and Art*, trans. Thomas Gora, Alice Jardine and Leon S. Roudiez (New York: Columbia University Press, 1980, p. 27).

62 *Ibid.*

63 Tilottama Rajan contends that Kristeva inflects Derrida's focus on *différance* (and thus *trace*) toward the body that he neglects, and that by doing so she occupies a site ambiguously between post-structuralism and phenomenology (pp. 220, 221). See: "Trans-Positions of Difference: Kristeva and Poststructuralism" in *Ethics, Politics, and Difference in Julia Kristeva's Writing*, Kelly Oliver ed. (New York: Routledge, 1993, pp. 215–37). In the same volume Suzanne Guerlac argues that Kristeva "revolutionizes" Derrida's *différance* by thinking of it as a bodily practice through Bataille's terms "expenditure, ecstasy, and eroticism" (p. 242). See: Suzanne Guerlac, "Transgression in Theory: Genius and the Subject of *La Révolution du langage poétique*" in Oliver, *op. cit.*, pp. 238–57.

64 Kelly Oliver suggests that Kristeva is interested in demonstrating how poetry disrupts the necessary relation between signifier and signified (pp. 2–3). See: Kelly Oliver, "Introduction: Julia Kristeva's Outlaw Ethics" in *Ethics, Politics, and Difference in Julia Kristeva's Writing*, Oliver, *op. cit.*, pp. 1–22.

65 Rajan suggests that *gesturality* "is a way for Kristeva to posit a 'productivity anterior to the product,' and thus to representation. This productivity (later called the semiotic) marks Kristeva as post-phenomenological in her theorizing of a prelinguistic signifier prior to representation." Rajan, *op. cit.*, p. 220. Rajan insists that even though Kristeva allies her *semiotic* with Derrida's *écriture*, because the two unsettle an illusory unity, she rewrites Derrida's work on the opposition of writing and voice by theorising voice as one of the sites of the semiotic (p. 222).

66 In his discussion of Kristeva's poetic subject Philip Lewis writes:

> The reconstituted poetic subject is not a stable "je" or "ego" which states meanings and thus constructs itself (its self, its identity) within the structure of language; it is a double subject, at once the modality of the linguistic system and of its breakdown or splitting-apart; the poetic subject is a dialectical process in which the structured language of the ego comes into contact with a violent, heterogeneous force which is its ground.
>
> Philip E. Lewis, "Revolutionary Semiotics", *Diacritics* 4(3) 1974, pp. 30–31.

67 Kristeva, "Semiotics", *op. cit.*, p. 85.

68 Kristeva's understanding of writing both influences and is influenced by the work of Roland Barthes. We can discern a similar interest in the oscillation between sense and non-sense in Barthes' account of a writing that "constantly posits meaning, but always in order to evaporate it." See: "The Death of the Author" in *The Rustle of Language*, trans. R. Howard (New York: Hill and Wang, 1986, p. 54). Barthes shifts emphasis away from the concept of *work* toward the practice of the *text*. See: "From Work to Text" in *The Rustle of Language*, pp. 56–64. Also: "Research: The Young", pp. 69–75. Incidentally, Lyotard re-claims the category of *work* as a disruptive (figural) force over and against the semiotic movement that Barthes enacts toward the *text*. See: Jean-François Lyotard, *The Différend: Phrases in Dispute*, trans. Georges Van Den Abbeele (Minneapolis: University of Minnesota Press, 1988, p. 12). Barthes' textual practice is concerned with exploding the singularity of meaning. See: *S/Z*, trans. R. Miller (New York: Hill and Wang, 1974, p. 6).

69 Georges Bataille, "The Notion of Expenditure" in *Visions of Excess: Selected Writings 1927–1939*, trans. and ed. A. Stoekl (Minneapolis: University of Minnesota Press, 1985, p. 120). Jacques Derrida celebrates the "revolutionary" implications of Bataille's sovereign writing, which is, he argues, "revolutionary as concerns a revolution which would only reorganise the world of work and would redistribute values within the space of meaning,

that is to say, still within restricted economy (p. 337 n. 33). Like Kristeva he is concerned to follow the implications of Bataille's entwining of poetry, writing and loss. See: Jacques Derrida, "From Restricted to General Economy: A Hegelianism without Reserve" in *Writing and Difference*, trans. Alan Bass (Chicago: University of Chicago Press, 1978, p. 261).

70 Kristeva, "Semiotics", *op. cit.*, p. 86. This concern with writing over literature in Kristeva's work finds parallel expression in the work of others associated with the group *Tel Quel*. See: Phillipe Sollers, "Programme", *Tel Quel* 31, cited in Kristeva, *ibid.*

71 *Capital* Vol. I, *op. cit.*, pp. 43–4 (emphasis added).

72 Baudrillard, *op. cit.*, p. 42.

73 See: Jean Baudrillard, *Symbolic Exchange and Death* (London: Sage, 1993).

74 Baudrillard, *The Mirror of Production, op. cit.*, p. 143. He writes that in capitalist relations "nothing can be given without being returned, nothing is ever won without something being lost, nothing is ever produced without something being destroyed, nothing is ever spoken without being answered. In short, what haunts the system is the symbolic demand" (p. 147).

75 *Ibid.*, p. 99. Baudrillard speaks of a *demiurgical labour*, one that does not produce value (p. 101).

76 Jean-François Lyotard, *The Différend: Phrases in Dispute, op. cit.*, p. 12.

77 Jean-François Lyotard, *Libidinal Economy*, trans. Iain Hamilton Grant (Bloomington: Indiana University Press, 1993, pp. 127, 129). Originally published as *Economie Libidinale* (Paris: Minuit, 1974).

78 In his discussion of Lyotard, Julian Pefanis notes that the relationship between Lyotard and Baudrillard is significant in that, despite their differences, each writes from a (postmodern) site between theory and fiction. Here he seems to be suggesting that Baudrillard is perhaps not so far from Lyotard after all. See: Julian Pefanis, "Jean-François Lyotard" in *The Judgment of Paris: Recent French Theory in a Local Context*, Murray, *op. cit.*, p. 126.

6 KRISTEVA: NAMING THE PROBLEM

1 Julia Kristeva, *Revolution in Poetic Language*, trans. Margaret Waller (New York: Columbia University Press, 1984, p. 113).

2 *Ibid.*, p. 118.

3 Julia Kristeva, "From One Identity to an Other" in *Desire in Language: A Semiotic Approach to Literature and Art*, trans. Thomas Gora, Alice Jardine and Leon S. Roudiez (New York: Columbia University Press, 1980, p. 133).

4 Kristeva, *Revolution in Poetic Language, op. cit.*, p. 27.

5 Philip E. Lewis, "Revolutionary Semiotics", *Diacritics* 4(3) 1974, p. 31.

6 Sigmund Freud, "Negation" (1925) in *The Standard Edition of the Complete Psychological Works,*, Vol. XIX, James Strachey ed. (London: Hogarth Press, 1961, pp. 238–9).

7 Kristeva, *Revolution in Poetic Language, op. cit.*, p. 160.

8 *Ibid.*, p. 161.

9 Kristeva, "From One Identity to an Other", *op. cit.*, p. 135.

10 David Carroll argues that by simply proscribing the question of the subject much structuralist theory remains committed to the conceptual edifice of the subject. See: *The Subject in Question: The Language of Theory and the Strategies of Fiction* (Chicago: University of Chicago Press, 1982, p. 18). The problems associated with a simple anti-humanist position are also discussed by Joel Whitebook, "Saving the Subject: Modernity and the Problem of the Autonomous Individual", *Telos* 50 (Winter) 1981–2, pp. 79–102.

11 Julia Kristeva, "The Novel as Polylogue", in *Desire in Language, op. cit.*, p. 160.

12 *Ibid.*, p. 164. Here Kristeva is influenced by the important work of Benveniste on the subject of enunciation. See: Emile Benveniste, *Problems in General Linguistics*, trans. M.E. Meek (Coral Gables, FL: University of Miami Press, 1971, p. 223).

13 Kristeva, "The Novel as Polylogue", *op. cit.*, p. 165. This process is captured in Brecht's

pronouncement that "The continuity of the ego is a myth. Man is an atom that perpetually breaks up and forms anew." Bertolt Brecht, *Brecht on Theatre: The Development of an Aesthetic*, J. Willet ed. (London: Methuen, 1964, p. 15). And similarly by Singer, who demands "a concept of subjectivity which might be wrested from the pre-emptive totalizations of teleological narrative will." Alan Singer, "Desire's Desire: Toward an Historical Formalism", *Enclitic* 8(1–2) 1984, p. 62.

14 This is Singer's phrase (*op. cit.*, p. 64). I am using it here to describe the kind of agency Kristeva's work allows us to imagine.
15 Kristeva, *Revolution in Poetic Language, op. cit.*, p. 167.
16 *Ibid.*, p. 184.
17 See Julia Kristeva, "Psychoanalysis and the Polis", trans. Margaret Waller in *The Politics of Interpretation*, W.J.T. Mitchell ed. (Chicago: University of Chicago Press, 1983, pp. 83–98).
18 Ariel Kay Salleh, "On the Dialectics of Signifying Practice", *Thesis Eleven* 5/6 1982, p. 76.
19 Kristeva, *Revolution in Poetic Language, op. cit.*, p. 204.
20 *Ibid.*, p. 205.
21 Kristeva, "The Novel as Polylogue", *op. cit.*, p. 162.
22 Kristeva, *Revolution in Poetic Language, op. cit.*, p. 205.
23 Salleh, *op. cit.*, p. 77.
24 Jacques Lacan, "The Mirror Stage as Formative of the Function of the I as Revealed in Psychoanalytic Experience", *Ecrits: A Selection*, trans. Alan Sheridan (New York: W.W. Norton, 1977, p. 4).
25 Jacques Lacan, "The Subversion of the Subject and the Dialectic of Desire in the Freudian Unconscious", in *Ecrits, op. cit.*, p. 300.
26 See: Jacques Lacan, "Aggressivity in Psychoanalysis", in *Ecrits, op. cit.*, p. 11.
27 Lacan, "The Mirror Stage", *op. cit.*, p. 4. The "growing of wings" makes another look at Plato's *Phaedrus* seem in order. See my discussion in chapter two.
28 Lacan's imaginary *roughly* equates with Kristeva's maternal semiotic, though it should be noted that while Lacan designates this as a conservative space, Kristeva posits it as the site of radical upheaval.
29 Fredric Jameson, "Imaginary and Symbolic in Lacan: Marxism, Psychoanalytic Criticism, and the Problem of the Subject" in *Literature and Psychoanalysis: The Question of Reading Otherwise*, Shoshana Felman ed. (Baltimore, MD: Johns Hopkins University Press, 1982, p. 353).
30 Rosalind Coward and John Ellis, *Language and Materialism: Developments in Semiology and the Theory of the Subject* (London: Routledge and Kegan Paul, 1977, p. 109).
31 Kristeva, *Revolution of Poetic Language, op. cit.*, p. 13.
32 Kristeva, "From One Identity to an Other", *op. cit.*, p. 136.
33 Julia Kristeva, *Powers of Horror: An Essay on Abjection*, trans. Leon S. Roudiez (New York: Columbia University Press, 1982, p. 10).
34 Kristeva, "The Novel as Polylogue", *op. cit.*, p. 186.
35 *Ibid.*, p. 162.
36 *Ibid.* p. 185.
37 Salleh, *op. cit.*, p. 72.
38 Elaine Scarry, *The Body in Pain: The Making and Unmaking of the World* (Oxford: Oxford University Press, 1985, p. 4). Scarry is not referring to Kristeva's notion of the polylogical body here, though I think her comments are nonetheless relevant. Note that she speaks of a "state anterior to language"; I would stress that this does not suggest a state anterior to signification. That is to say, it is a signifying silence.
39 See especially: Theodor W. Adorno and Max Horkheimer, *Dialectic of Enlightenment*, trans. J. Cumming (London: Verso, 1979, pp. 231f). See also my "Reason, Identity and the Body: Reading Adorno with Irigaray" in *Reason and its Other: Rationality in Modern*

German Philosophy and Culture, Dieter Freundlieb and Wayne Hudson eds (Oxford: Berg, 1993, pp. 199–216).

40 For a discussion of the dialogic interaction of text and context see: Nancy Fraser, "On the Political and the Symbolic: Against the Metaphysics of Textuality", *Enclitic* 9(1–2) 1987, pp. 100–14.

41 Kristeva, *Revolution in Poetic Language, op. cit.*, p. 208.

42 Kristeva, "The Novel as Polylogue", *op. cit.*, p. 163.

43 Mao Tse-Tung, "On Practice" in *Four Essays On Philosophy* (Peking: Foreign Language Press, 1968, pp. 4, 8).

44 Kristeva, *Revolution in Poetic Language, op. cit.*, p. 203. All quotations in the text immediately prior to this are from the same page.

45 *Ibid.*, pp. 195–6. All quotations immediately prior to this are from the same pages.

46 Kristeva's *polylogue* has something in common both with Mikhail Bakhtin's *dialogic* and Fredric Jameson's *political unconscious*. In each there is a concern with symbolic heterogeneity and contradiction. Each theorises the disruption of the symbolic by discursive means. Arguably, though, Kristeva's polylogue is more attuned to the sensuous element of this disruption. See: Mikhail Bakhtin, *Problems of Dostoevsky's Poetics*, trans. R.W. Rotsel (Ann Arbor, MI: Ardis, 1973); Fredric Jameson, *The Political Unconscious: Narrative as a Socially Symbolic Act* (Ithaca, NY: Cornell University Press, 1981). Another foregrounding of the discursive construction of contradiction can be found in the work of Ernesto Laclau and Chantal Mouffe, *Hegemony and Socialist Strategy: Towards a Radical Democratic Politics* (London: Verso, 1985, especially ch. 3).

47 Kristeva, *Revolution in Poetic Language, op. cit.*, p. 204.

48 Julia Kristeva, "The System and the Speaking Subject", in *The Tell-Tail Sign: A Survey of Semiotics*, T.A. Sebeok ed. (Lisse, Netherlands: Peter De Ridder Press, 1975, p. 50). For a contemporary discussion of Kristeva's contribution see Kelly Oliver, "Revolutionary Language Rendered Speechless" in *Reading Kristeva: Unraveling the Double-bind* (Bloomington: Indiana University Press, 1993, pp. 91–113).

49 Kristeva, "From One Identity to an Other", *op. cit.*, p. 132.

50 See: Stéphane Mallarmé, "Les Mots anglais" (p. 901), cited in Julia Kristeva, "Phonetics, Phonology and Impusional Bases", trans. Caren Greenberg, *Diacritics* IV, 4(3) 1974, p. 35.

51 According to Kristeva the suffering and horror typical of Céline's work disrupts the traditional narrative form: Kristeva, *Powers of Horror, op. cit.*, p. 141.

52 George Steiner argues that this poetic "crisis" arose from reflecting on the gap between traditional modes of rhetorical and poetic statement and the emerging psychological reality of the later nineteenth century. See: "The Retreat from the Word" in *Language and Silence: Essays on Language, Literature, and the Inhuman* (New York: Atheneum, 1974, pp. 12–35). Elsewhere Steiner writes:

> From Medieval Latin poetry to Mallarmé and Russian Symbolist verse, the motif of the necessary limitations of the human word is a frequent one. It carries with it a crucial intimation of that which lies outside language, of what it is that awaits the poet if he were to transgress the bounds of human discourse.
>
> (p. 39)

Unlike Kristeva, Steiner seems to be operating here with an notion of silence as that which lies *outside* language, not as that which *inhabits* it. See his: "Silence and the Poet" (pp. 36–54) in the same book.

53 Kristeva's other favourite limit writers include Antonin Artaud and William Burroughs.

54 Kristeva, *Revolution in Poetic Language, op. cit.*, p. 224.

55 *Ibid.*, p. 67.

56 Julia Kristeva, cited in Evelyn H. Zepp, "The Criticism of Julia Kristeva: A New Mode of Critical Thought", *Romanic Review* 73(1) 1982, p. 84.

57 Elizabeth Grosz, "Lacan and Feminism" in *Jacques Lacan: A Feminist Introduction* (Sydney: Allen and Unwin, 1990, p. 151).

58 Kristeva, *Revolution in Poetic Language, op. cit.*, pp. 239–40.

59 Roland Barthes, in *The Pleasure of the Text*, writes that "The writer is somebody who plays with the body of his mother". Compare this with Kristeva's comment, in *Desire in Language*: "poetic language would be for its questionable subject in process the equivalent of incest".

60 Kristeva, *Powers of Horror, op. cit.*, p. 75.

61 Kristeva, "From One Identity to an Other", *op. cit.*, p. 136.

62 *Ibid.*, p. 137.

63 Kristeva, "The Novel as Polylogue", *op. cit.*, p. 174.

64 *Ibid.*

65 *Ibid.*, p. 195.

66 Julia Kristeva, "Motherhood According to Giovanni Bellini" in *Desire in Language, op. cit.*, p. 242. See also: "From One Identity to an Other", where Kristeva writes: "the questionable subject in process appropriates to itself this archaic, instinctual, and maternal territory" in *Desire in Language*, p. 136.

67 Kristeva, *Revolution in Poetic Language, op. cit.*, p. 47.

68 *Ibid.*

69 *Ibid.*, p. 48.

70 *Ibid.*, p. 51.

71 *Ibid.*, p. 50.

72 *Ibid.*, p. 62.

73 *Ibid.*, p. 65.

74 Kristeva, "Motherhood According to Bellini", *op. cit.*, p. 249.

75 Julia Kristeva, "China, Women and the Symbolic", Interview with Josette Féral, *SubStance* 13 1976, p. 16.

76 Julia Kristeva, *About Chinese Women*, trans. A. Barrows (London: Marion Boyars, 1977, pp. 39–40). The translation of this passage has been adapted by Séan Hand in *The Kristeva Reader, op. cit.*, pp. 156–7.

77 Judith Butler suggests that poetic writing by women threatens society because it simultaneously breaks the taboos of incest and homosexuality (p. 86). It might be that women's poetry is not only a threat to women, but perhaps more significantly, a threat to patriarchal society itself. If so, Kristeva's tendency to overlook the poetic writing of women might literally serve to "reinforce" this society. See: "The Body Politics of Julia Kristeva" in *Gender Trouble: Feminism and the Subversion of Identity* (New York: Routledge, 1990, pp. 79–93).

78 Julia Kristeva, "Word, Dialogue, and Novel", in *Desire in Language, op. cit.*, p. 71.

79 Julia Kristeva, "Women's Time", trans. Alice Jardine and Harry Blake, *Signs* 7(1) 1981, p. 25.

80 Julia Kristeva, "Postmodernism?", trans. Alice Jardine and Tom Gora (unpublished paper), p. 8.

81 Kristeva, "Women's Time", *op. cit.*, p. 32.

82 Kristeva, "China, Women and the Symbolic", *op. cit.*, p. 17. In "Oscillation Between Power and Denial" we find a rare reference to the work of a contemporary woman writer. Here she comments that the work of Sophie Podolski (*Le Pays ou tout est permis*) exhibits a "certain sensitivity to language, to its phonetic texture, its logical articulation, and throughout this entire written and sketched universe, the ideological, theoretical, political conflicts of our time." See: "Oscillation Between Power and Denial", Interview with Xavière Gauthier, trans. M. A. August in *New French Feminisms: An Anthology*, Elaine Marks and

Isabelle de Courtivron eds. (Cambridge, MA: University of Massachusetts Press, 1980, pp. 165–7).

83 Kristeva, "Oscillation Between Power and Denial", *op. cit.*, p. 165.

84 Cited in Elaine Hoffman Baruch and Perry Meisel, "Two Interviews with Julia Kristeva", *Partisan Review* 51(1) 1984, pp. 122–3.

85 *Ibid.*, p. 123.

86 Kristeva, "Oscillation Between Power and Denial", *op. cit.*, p. 167.

87 *Ibid.*, p. 166.

88 Julia Kristeva, "A New Type of Intellectual: The Dissident" in *The Kristeva Reader*, *op. cit.*, p. 296

89 Julia Kristeva, "Woman Can Never Be Defined", Interview with "Psych et Po", trans. M.A. August in *New French Feminisms, ibid.*, p. 137.

90 Kristeva, "Women's Time", *op. cit.* p. 32 (emphasis added)

91 Kristeva, "Oscillation Between Power and Denial", *op. cit.*, p. 166. And further: "Estranged from language, women are visionaries, dancers who suffer as they speak."

92 Julia Kristeva, "Stabat Mater", trans. Arthur Goldhammer in *The Female Body in Western Culture: Contemporary Perspectives*, Susan Rubin Suleiman ed. (Cambridge, MA: Harvard University Press, 1986, p. 114).

93 See, for example: Kristeva, "Postmodernism?", *op. cit.*, p. 8; "Women's Time", *op. cit.*, p. 32; "China, Women and the Symbolic", *op. cit.*, p. 17.

94 Kristeva, "Woman Can Never Be Defined", *op. cit.*, p. 138.

95 Kristeva, "A New Type of Intellectual: The Dissident", *op. cit.*, p. 296. Domna Stanton argues that Kristeva's work is pervaded by a Freudian phallocentrism in that it privileges the male as artist/dissident. See: Domna Stanton, "Difference on Trial: A Critique of the Maternal Metaphor in Cixous, Irigaray and Kristeva" in *The Poetics of Gender*, Nancy K. Miller ed. (New York: Columbia University Press, 1986, p. 167).

96 Kristeva, *About Chinese Women, op. cit.*, p. 35.

97 Kristeva, "A New Type of Intellectual: The Dissident", *op. cit.*, p. 297. It is interesting to note Kristeva's use of the term psychosis here, given our discussion in chapter three.

98 Kristeva cited in Josette Féral, "Antigone or the Irony of the Tribe", trans. Alice Jardine and Tom Gora, *Diacritics* 8(3) 1978, p. 10.

99 Josette Féral confirms this reading of Kristeva. *Ibid.*

100 Drucilla Cornell and Adam Thurschwell, "Feminism, Negativity, Intersubjectivity" in *Feminism as Critique*, Seyla Benhabib and Drucilla Cornell eds (Minneapolis: University of Minnesota Press, 1987, pp. 143–62).

101 Ann Rosalind Jones, "Julia Kristeva on Femininity: The Limits of a Semiotic Politics", *Feminist Review* 18 1984, pp. 56–74.

102 Juliet Flower MacCannell, "Kristeva's Horror", *Semiotica* 62(3–4) 1986, p. 329.

103 Tina Chanter addresses this question by situating Kristeva's work in the context of Anglo-American reading traditions. She argues that essentialist readings have largely been generated by an undiagnosed fear of the body in certain feminist work. See her: "Kristeva's Politics of Change: Tracking Essentialism with the Help of a Sex/Gender Map", in *Ethics, Politics, and Difference in Julia Kristeva's Writing*, Kelly Oliver ed. (New York: Routledge, 1993, pp. 179–95).

104 Ewa Ziarek, "At the Limits of Discourse: Heterogeneity, Alterity and the Maternal Body in Kristeva's Thought", *Hypatia* 7(2) 1992, pp. 91–108, p. 91. In a later piece Ziarek offers a discussion of the ethical potential of Kristeva's work. Here she argues for a

non-essentialist reading. See her: "Kristeva and Levinas: Mourning, Ethics, and the Feminine" in *Ethics, Politics, and Difference...* Oliver, *op. cit.*, pp. 62–78.

105 Kelly Oliver, "Introduction: Oscillation Strategies" in *Reading Kristeva: Unraveling the Double-bind, op. cit.*, p. 11. See also her: "Kristeva's Imaginary Father and the Crisis in the Paternal Function", *Diacritics* 21(2–3) 1991, pp. 43–63 esp. n. 6, p. 47.

106 Kristeva, "Women's Time", *op. cit.*, p. 33.

107 Alice Jardine, "Opaque Texts and Transparent Contexts: The Political Difference of Julia Kristeva", in *The Poetics of Gender*, Miller, *op. cit.*, p. 110. An abridged version of Jardine's paper has since been published in *Ethics, Politics, and Difference*. Oliver, *op. cit.*, pp. 23–31.

108 Alice Jardine, "Theories of the Feminine: Kristeva", *Enclitic* 4(2) 1980, p. 14. The following articles by Jardine are also useful for thinking about the difference Kristeva's work performs: "Pre-texts for the Transatlantic Feminist", *Yale French Studies* 62 1981, pp. 220–36 and "Introduction to Julia Kristeva's 'Women's Time'", *Signs* 7(1) 1981, pp. 5–12.

109 Ziarek, *op. cit.*, p. 94.

110 Ziarek claims that Kristeva's first moment, the pre-symbolic semiotic, "is only a theoretical presupposition, a theoretical fiction" that retrospectively produces a genealogical description. It is not a description of "a natural psychic development" (p. 96).

111 Kristeva, *Desire in Language, op. cit.*, p. 238, cited in Ziarek, *op. cit.*, p. 104. For another elaboration of the phallic mother in Kristeva's work see: Allison Weir, "Identification with the Divided Mother: Kristeva's Ambivalence" in *Ethics, Politics, and Difference*. Oliver, *op. cit.*, pp. 79–91.

112 Jane Gallop discusses her own transference on to Kristeva as phallic mother. Gallop's concern is also with Kristeva's own attempts to position herself as phallic. She goes on to say that given that the phallus plays its role only when veiled then perhaps "to refuse and deny the phallic position may mean to veil it and be all the more phallic, whereas blatantly, audaciously, vulgarly to assume it may mean to dephallicize." See: "The Phallic Mother: Fraudian Analysis" in *Feminism and Psychoanalysis: The Daughter's Seduction* (London: Macmillan, 1982, p. 120).

113 Susan Rubin Suleiman, *Subversive Intent: Gender, Politics, and the Avant-Garde* (Cambridge, MA: Harvard University Press, 1990). A further discussion of women and surrealism can be found in Renée Riese Hubert's "Gender, Genre, and Partnership: A Study of Valentine Penrose" in *The Other Perspective in Gender and Culture: Rewriting Women and the Symbolic*, Juliet Flower MacCannell ed. (New York: Columbia University Press, 1990, pp. 117–42).

114 Francis Barker, *The Tremulous Private Body: Essays on Subjection* (London: Methuen, 1984, p. 100).

115 Luce Irigaray is amongst the most vocal of those who claim that psychoanalysis participates in this silencing. She argues that it is implicated in the denial of woman's desire. See: Luce Irigaray, "The Power of Discourse and the Subordination of the Feminine" in *This Sex Which Is Not One*, trans. Catherine Porter (Ithaca, NY: Cornell University Press, 1985, p. 77).

116 Catherine Clément, "The Guilty One" in *The Newly Born Woman*, Hélène Cixous and Cathérine Clément, trans. Betsy Wing (Minneapolis: University of Minnesota Press, 1986, p. 37).

117 For an excellent discussion of this exchange see: Jane Gallop, "Keys to Dora" in *Feminism and Psychoanalysis: The Daughter's Seduction* (London: Macmillan, 1982, pp. 132–50).

Reprinted in *In Dora's Case: Freud/Hysteria/Feminism*, Charles Bernheimer and Claire Kahane eds (London: Virago, 1985, pp. 200–20). Gallop suggests that Cixous' decision to publish her own work, *Portrait de Dora*, through the publishing house *des femmes* provides woman with an agency or symbolic that is missing from either Freud's account of Dora or Dora's own account of herself.

118 Kristeva, *Powers of Horror, op. cit.*, p. 45.

119 Julia Kristeva, *Polylogues*, cited in Josette Féral, "Antigone or the Irony of the Tribe", *op. cit.*, p. 12.

120 Kristeva, "The Novel as Polylogue", *op. cit.*, p. 197.

121 Mary Jacobus provides an interesting discussion of the role of the hysteric's body as pre-text for the hysterical narratives generated by psychoanalytic theory. She claims that psychoanalysis is the shadow-image of hysteria, and that "the one constitutes and is constituted by a reading of the other" (p. 199). See: "Anna (Wh)O.'s **Absences**: Readings In Hysteria" in *Reading Woman: Essays in Feminist Criticism* (New York: Columbia University Press, 1986, pp. 197–274).

122 Freud himself believed that both men and women could be hysterics. However for a discussion of hysteria as predominantly a woman's condition see: Dianne Hunter, "Hysteria, Psychoanalysis, Feminism in the Case of Anna O", *Feminist Studies* 9(3) 1983, pp. 465–86, Jennifer L. Pierce, "The Relation between Emotion, Work and Hysteria: A Feminist Reinterpretation of Freud's *Studies on Hysteria*", *Women's Studies* 16 1989, pp. 255–70.

123 Bice Benvenuto and Roger Kennedy, *The Works of Jacques Lacan: An Introduction* (London: Free Association Books, 1986, p. 188).

124 For Lacan the hysteric is very much a woman. His seminar entitled *Encore* addresses the question of feminine pleasure in such a way as to tie it directly with considerations of hysteria. Benvenuto and Kennedy unwittingly make this link when they write: "Lacan asked, can the woman express herself in language without subverting her very essence, which is to disown (*méconnaitre*) the indecent truth of her enjoyment?" (*Ibid.*, p. 195). See Jacques Lacan, *Encore: Le séminaire XX, 1972–3* (Paris: Seuil, 1975).

125 Jacobus argues that the hysteric restores the "original" bodily meaning of words, and that hysterical symptoms serve as traces of this meaning (p. 244). Hysterical language "attempts to recover a lost, literal dimension in language" (*op. cit.*, p. 209). Jacobus finds evidence of this bodily meaning in the following hysterical texts: Charlotte Perkins Gilman's *The Yellow Wallpaper* and George Eliot's *The Lifted Veil*.

126 Luce Irigaray, "Women-Mothers, the Silent Substratum of the Social Order", trans. David Macey in *The Irigaray Reader*, Margaret Whitford ed. (Oxford: Basil Blackwell, 1991, pp. 47–8).

127 I am thinking here of Deleuze and Guattari's *Anti-Oedipus* and, to a lesser extent, Lyotard's *Libidinal Economy*. See: Gilles Deleuze and Félix Guattari, *Anti-Oedipus: Capitalism and Schizophrenia*, trans. Robert Hurley, Mark Seem and Helen R. Lane (New York: Viking Press, 1977). And Jean-François Lyotard, *Libidinal Economy*, trans. Iain Hamilton Grant (Bloomington: Indiana University Press, 1993).

128 Elizabeth Grosz points out that hysteria plays a central role in Irigaray's own subversion of phallocentric modes of thought. She contends that Irigaray imitates/parodies/mimes the position of the hysteric in relation to philosophy: "Irigaray herself is the hysteric insofar as she wants to make woman's body *speak*, be representable, articulate itself". In fact Grosz positions Irigaray as both hysteric and analyst, and in so doing identifies both the radical and conservative moments of hysteria. See: Elizabeth Grosz, *Sexual Subversions: Three French Feminists* (Sydney: Allen and Unwin, 1989, p. 135).

129 Irigaray, "Women-Mothers", *op. cit.*, p. 48.

130 Luce Irigaray, "Any Theory of the 'Subject' Has Always Been Appropriated by the 'Masculine' ", in *Speculum of the Other Woman*, trans. Gillian C. Gill (Ithaca, NY: Cornell University Press, 1985, p. 142).

131 Kaja Silverman, "Histoire d'O: The Story of a Disciplined and Punished Body", *Enclitic* 7(2) 1983, p. 66.

132 *Ibid.*, p. 78.

7 COLLECTING MOTHERS: WOMEN AT THE SYMPOSIUM

1 Luce Irigaray, "Sorcerer Love: A Reading of Plato's *Symposium*, Diotima's Speech", trans. Eleanor H. Kuykendall in *Revaluing French Feminism: Critical Essays on Difference, Agency, and Culture*, Nancy Fraser and Sandra Lee Bartky eds (Bloomington: Indiana University Press, 1992, pp. 64–76).

2 Andrea Nye, "The Hidden Host: Irigaray and Diotima at Plato's Symposium" in Fraser and Bartky, *ibid.*, pp. 77–93. Originally published in *Hypatia* 3(3) 1989.

3 Hélène Cixous, "The Laugh of the Medusa", trans. K. Cohen and P. Cohen, *Signs* 1(4) 1976, p. 881.

4 Jacques Lacan, "The Agency of the Letter in the Unconscious or Reason since Freud" in *Ecrits: A Selection*, trans. Alan Sheridan (New York: W.W. Norton, 1977, p. 157). Lacan argues that this *crossing* is essential for signification to emerge. Metaphor is "the substitution of signifier for signifier" producing poetic signification (p. 164). See also pp. 53, 156, 199–200, 303–4.

5 Alice Jardine analyses how the feminine has consistently been encoded as what exceeds symbolic logic. See: *Gynesis: Configurations of Woman and Modernity* (Ithaca, NY: Cornell University Press, 1985).

6 Domna C. Stanton, "Difference on Trial: A Critique of the Maternal Metaphor in Cixous, Irigaray, and Kristeva" in *The Poetics of Gender*, Nancy K. Miller ed. (New York: Columbia University Press, 1986, p. 160).

7 Hélène Cixous, "Sorties: Out and Out: Attacks/Ways Out/Forays" in *The Newly Born Woman*, trans. Betsy Wing (Minneapolis: University of Minnesota Press, 1986, p. 89).

8 Luce Irigaray, "Women's Exile", trans. C. Venn, *Ideology and Consciousness* 1 (Spring) 1977, p. 66.

9 Luce Irigaray, *This Sex Which Is Not One*, trans. Catherine Porter (Ithaca, NY: Cornell University Press, 1985, p. 30).

10 Irigaray argues that Freud's developmental model of sexuality is tied to the reproductive function, and asks what the implications would be of severing this link. See: "The Power of Discourse and the Subordination of the Feminine" in *This Sex Which Is Not One, op. cit.*, p. 71.

11 Cixous, "The Laugh of the Medusa", *op. cit.*, p. 891. For a discussion of the pregnant *woman* see my "Unsettling Terrain: Mark Davies and the Problem of (Maternal) Space" (unpublished MS). See also Ella Dreyfus, *The Body Pregnant* (Sydney: McPhee-Gribble, 1993).

12 Susan Rubin Suleiman, "Pornography, Transgression, and the Avant-Garde: Bataille's *Story of the Eye*" in Miller, *The Poetics of Gender, op. cit.*, p. 130.

13 Adrienne Rich, *Of Woman Born: Motherhood as Experience and Institution* (London: Virago, 1979, p. 183).

14 Marina Warner provides a detailed and critical analysis of the cult of the Virgin in her brilliant study *Alone of All Her Sex: The Myth and the Cult of the Virgin Mary* (New York: Vintage Books, 1976, p. 191). For a discussion of the semiotic significance of the Virgin's milk and tears see: Julia Kristeva, "Stabat Mater", trans. Arthur Goldhammer in *The Female Body in Western Culture*, Susan Rubin Suleiman ed. (Cambridge, MA: Harvard University Press, 1986, pp. 108–10).

15 This sacred maternity of the Christian tradition finds parallel expression in certain Hindu texts. Once again woman receives legitimation only through her maternal role. Religious symbolism is allocated to woman solely on the basis of her potential to produce sons. Her sexuality, such that it is, finds expression only through motherhood. She is at once fulfilled and restrained through her maternal office. Along with Confucianism, Hinduism elevates woman in her sacred role as suffering mother. Diana Y. Paul provides a brief discussion of motherhood in Hinduism as background to her examination of secular motherhood in Mahāyāna Buddhist texts. See: *Women in Buddhism: Images of the Feminine in Mahāyāna Tradition* (Berkeley, CA: Asian Humanities Press, 1979, ch. 2).

16 Barbara Johnson, "Mallarmé as Mother" in *A World of Difference* (Baltimore, MD: Johns Hopkins University Press, 1987, pp. 141, 142). The all too simple elision of the feminine with maternity risks reducing woman to a preconceived essence, a congealed identity. In her role as mother she risks becoming the origin, the lost terrain that man will ceaselessly seek to recapture. Elizabeth Berg voices her concerns regarding this problematic status in her article "The Third Woman", *Diacritics* 12 1982, p. 18.

17 Stanton, *op. cit.*, p. 161.

18 *Ibid.*, p. 163.

19 *Ibid.*, pp. 174–5. Stanton argues for the substitution of metonymy for metaphor in feminist discourse (p. 175).

20 Mary Daly, *Gyn/Ecology: The Metaethics of Radical Feminism* (Boston, MA: Beacon Press, 1978, p. 47).

21 *Ibid.*, p. 60.

22 Rich, *op. cit.*, p. 40.

23 Ariel (Kay) Salleh is also critical of such denunciations. See: Ariel (Kay) Salleh, "Contribution to the Critique of Political Epistemology", *Thesis Eleven* 8 1984, p. 39.

24 Cixous, "Sorties", *op. cit.*, pp. 89–90.

25 Cixous' discussion of the importance of "poetic thinking", the crossroad of philosophical thought and song, highlights this bodily continuum. See: Hélène Cixous, "Conversations" in *Writing Differences: Readings from the Seminar of Hélène Cixous*, Susan Sellers ed. (Oxford: Open University Press, 1988, pp. 141–54). For an excellent collection of Cixous' work see: *The Hélène Cixous Reader*, Susan Sellers ed. (London: Routledge, 1994).

26 Cixous, "Sorties", *op. cit.*, p. 93.

27 *Ibid.*, p. 92. Cixous asks: "How come this privileged relation with voice? Because no woman piles up as many defenses against instinctual drives as a man does" (p. 93).

28 *Ibid.*, p. 94.

29 Cixous, "The Laugh of the Medusa", *op. cit.*, p. 881.

30 *Ibid.*, p. 882.

31 *Ibid.*, p. 881; Cixous, "Sorties", *op. cit.*, p. 93.

32 Cixous, "The Laugh of the Medusa", p. 891.

33 Cixous, "Sorties", p. 90.

34 Cixous, "The Laugh of the Medusa", p. 891.

35 For a discussion of Cixous on the theme of giving birth in texts by women see: Cixous in Sellers ed., *Writing Differences*, *op. cit.*, p. 151. A further discussion of the birth metaphor in writing by Cixous and others associated with the group "Psych et Po" can be found in Clare Duchen, "French Feminists and Motherhood" in *Feminism in France: From May '68 to Mitterand* (London: Routledge and Kegan Paul, 1986). See also: Diane Griffin Crowder, "Amazons and Mothers? Monique Wittig, Hélène Cixous and Theories of Women's Writing", *Contemporary Literature* 24(2) 1983, pp. 117–44.

36 Cixous, "Sorties", p. 90.

37 Cixous, "The Laugh of the Medusa", p. 881.

38 Cixous, "Sorties", p. 90.

39 Luce Irigaray, "And the One Doesn't Stir Without the Other", trans. H.V. Wenzel, *Signs* 7(1) 1981, p. 66.

40 Jane Gallop alerts our attention to the (sexual) difference between the breast and breasts. See: "The Teacher's Breasts" in *Jane Gallop Seminar Papers*, Jill Julius Matthews ed. (Canberra: Humanities Research Centre, Australian National University, 1994, pp. 1–12). I am inclined to think that in Gallop's terms Cixous' breast remains singular and nurturing.

41 In "My Monster/My Self" Barbara Johnson suggests that the issues of mothering and the woman writer can be explored through the meaning of autobiography. ("My Mother/My Self" in Johnson, *op. cit.*, pp. 144–54). Taking the work of Nancy Friday, Dorothy Dinnerstein and Mary Shelley as her starting point, she investigates the relation between the desire to write and the desire to give birth to oneself. In the case of autobiography, she asks, is one always involved in symbolically killing the mother? Does the desire to give birth to a self, to write one's own story, amount to an inevitable search for identity that culminates in the mother's death (through separation)? These are important questions, for they force us to consider the manner in which women experience their maternal bond through writing. And yet they too remain disturbingly Oedipal in both their formulation and inflection.

42 Segal is one of Klein's most prominent disciples. I am indebted to her lectures for the following discussion of Klein's work. See: Hanna Segal, *Introduction to the Work of Melanie Klein* (London: Hogarth Press, 1982).

43 See: Melanie Klein, *The Psycho-Analysis of Children* (London: Hogarth Press, 1932). Also: "The Importance of Symbol Formation in the Development of the Ego", *International Journal of Psycho-Analysis* 11, 1930. Reprinted in *Love, Guilt and Reparation, and Other Works, 1921–1945* (London: Hogarth Press, 1975, New York: Delacorte Press, 1975, pp. 219–32).

44 See: Melanie Klein, "Contribution to the Psycho-genesis of Manic-Depressive States (1935)" in *Contributions to Psycho-Analysis, 1921–45* (London: Hogarth Press, 1948). Reprinted in *Love, Guilt and Reparation, op. cit.*, pp. 262–89. Also: "Mourning and its Relationship to Manic-Depressive States (1940)" in *Contributions to Psycho-Analysis, op. cit.* Reprinted in *Love, Guilt and Reparation*, pp. 344–69.

45 See: Melanie Klein, "Notes on some Schizoid Mechanisms (1946)", *International Journal of Psycho-Analysis* 27 1946. Also in *Developments in Psycho-Analysis*, Joan Rivière ed. (London: Hogarth Press, 1952). Reprinted in *Envy and Gratitude: And Other Works, 1946–1963* (London: Tavistock, 1957; New York: Delacorte Press, 1975, pp. 1–24). Also: "On Identification" in *New Directions in Psycho-Analysis* with P. Heimann, R. Money-Kyrle, *et al.* (London: Tavistock, 1955). Reprinted in *Envy and Gratitude, op. cit.*, pp. 141–75.

46 Segal, *op. cit.*, pp. 1–2.

47 Although she notes the critical difference that distances Klein from Freud, Teresa Brennan brings our attention to the "striking agreement" in their work over the question of repression. She suggests that comparative discussions of the two often obscure the fact of this convergence. See: Teresa Brennan, "The Original Superego" in *The Interpretation of the Flesh: Freud and Femininity* (London: Routledge, 1992, esp. pp. 190–4).

48 For a detailed discussion of Klein's effect on the British Psycho-Analytical Society see: Phyllis Grosskurth, *Melanie Klein: Her World and Work* (Toronto: McClelland and Stewart, 1986). Should we think of this split in terms of "good" and "bad" societies?

49 Segal, *op. cit.*, p. 4.

50 *Ibid.*

51 *Ibid.*

52 The libidinal desires entail a phantasy of scooping the precious contents of the breasts and devouring them, while the destructive tendencies entail aggressive phantasies of biting, tearing and destroying the insides of the mother's body (*ibid.*, p. 5).

53 Segal, *op. cit.*, p. 5.

54 Kelly Oliver, *Reading Kristeva: Unraveling the Double-bind* (Bloomington: Indiana University Press, 1993, p. 3).

55 See: "The Prodigal Child" and "The Abject Mother" in Oliver, *ibid.*, pp. 18–47, 48–68, for an extended discussion of this point.

56 Kelly Oliver, "Kristeva's Imaginary Father and the Crisis in the Paternal Function", *Diacritics* 21(2–3) 1991, p. 43. A modified version of this paper appears in Oliver's *Reading Kristeva*, *op. cit.*, pp. 69–90. Kristeva argues that Lacan dismisses and forgets the bodily basis of desire; that in his work the body is subsumed beneath an analytical concern and priority with desire. Lacan can conceive of this desire only in terms of its symbolic representation or articulation, not in terms of its basis in bodily drives. Now in Oliver's reading of Kristeva she attempts to reclaim the imaginary father (the prehistoric father–mother conglomerate) as that which makes it possible for the child to move from the mother's abject body to the mother's desire. In so doing she moves us away from the body to the abstract realm of representation (Oliver 1991, *op. cit.*, p. 52). I am a little concerned that in doing so Oliver is rehearsing Lacan's flight from the body.

57 Kristeva, "Stabat Mater", *op. cit.*, p. 100.

58 Julia Kristeva, "A New Type of Intellectual: The Dissident" in *The Kristeva Reader*, Toril Moi ed. (New York: Columbia University Press, 1986, p. 297).

59 Kristeva, "Stabat Mater", *op. cit.*, p. 115.

60 Oliver, "Kristeva's Imaginary Father", *op. cit.*, pp. 57–8.

61 This fundamental challenge to the self in pregnancy finds its way (metaphorically?) from the maternal body to the maternal text. The stable unity of the autonomous ego is put into question by women who write (of) the ambiguity of the self. Maternal themes of fusion/splitting and of unity/division are reinscribed in texts which bear the ambivalence of the mother's body. Carolyn Burke explores the "crisis in consciousness" undertaken by the early modernist poets Mina Loy, Marianne Moore and Laura Riding. She contends that contemporary preoccupations with questions of the subject, such as Kristeva's, are already encoded in the work of these women. Their poetry defies a stable subject, giving rise to a complex play of multiple subject positions. See: Carolyn Burke, "Supposed Persons: Modernist Poetry and the Female Subject", *Feminist Studies* 11(1) 1985, p. 136. Ellen Friedman makes an interesting point about modernist works. She argues that masculine modernist texts typically reveal an Oedipal preoccupation with missing, lost or inaccessible fathers, an occupation that thematises a nostalgia for a past identity (p. 241). She goes on to suggest that this Oedipal structure is inappropriate for understanding what it is that women's works of modernity inscribe. See: Ellen G. Friedman, "Where are the Missing Contents? (Post)Modernism, Gender, and the Canon", *PMLA* 108(2) 1993, pp. 240–52. For a discussion of the problems associated with using an Oedipal structure to read women's reading and writing, Friedman recommends Susan Winnett's "Coming Unstrung: Women, Men, Narrative, and Principles of Pleasure", *PMLA* 105(3) 1990, pp. 505–18.

62 Julia Kristeva, "Women's Time", trans. Alice Jardine and Harry Blake, *Signs* 7(1) 1981, p. 31.

63 Julia Kristeva, "Motherhood According to Giovanni Bellini" in *Desire in Language: A Semiotic Approach to Literature and Art*, trans. Thomas Gora, Alice Jardine and Leon S. Roudiez (New York: Columbia University Press, 1980, p. 237).

64 *Ibid.*, pp. 239–40.

65 *Ibid.*, p. 239. For a critical appraisal of the homosexual-maternal facet as an emergence of psychosis into culture see: Judith Butler, "Subversive Bodily Acts" in *Gender Trouble: Feminism and the Subversion of Identity* (New York: Routledge, 1990, pp. 85–6).

66 Julia Kristeva, "The Novel as Polylogue" in *Desire in Language, op. cit.*, p. 200.

67 Kristeva explores the mechanisms whereby the body is given significance and meaning under patriarchy. The body is literally identified as an object/product of patriarchal nomination. However, the mother resists this imposition of meaning and sense. Julia

Kristeva, *Researches pour une sémanalyse* (Paris: Seuil, 1969, p. 285) cited in Philip E. Lewis, "Revolutionary Semiotics", *Diacritics* 4(3) 1974, p. 30.

68 Kristeva, "The Novel as Polylogue", *op. cit.*, p. 195.

69 Susan Suleiman suggests reading these two texts as "mother" (analytic) and "child" (lyrical). See: "Writing and Motherhood" in *The (M)other Tongue: Essays in Feminist Psychoanalytic Interpretation*, S. Nelson Garner, C. Kahane and M. Sprengnether eds (Ithaca, NY: Cornell University Press, 1985, p. 369).

70 Julia Kristeva, "Héréthique de l'amour", *Tel Quel* 74 (Winter) 1977. Reprinted as "Stabat Mater" in *Histoires d'amour* (Paris: Denoel, 1983). Translated as "Stabat Mater" in *The Female Body in Western Culture*, Suleiman, *op. cit.*, pp. 100, 114.

71 *Ibid.*, pp. 112–13.

72 Oliver suggests that we can trace a journey toward and within the maternal body throughout the entirety of her work. Oliver, *Reading Kristeva, op. cit.*, pp. 5, 70. Other discussions of Kristeva's work on the maternal include: Ewa Ziarek, "At the Limits of Discourse: Tracing the Maternal Body with Kristeva", *Hypatia* 7(2) 1992, pp. 91–108; Elizabeth Grosz, "Julia Kristeva: Abjection, Motherhood and Love" in *Sexual Subversions: Three French Feminists* (Sydney: Allen and Unwin, 1989, pp. 70–99).

73 Kristeva suggests that what the mother most wants is her own mother. This (narcissistic) love between women provides a rudimentary model for "herethics" (*hérétique*). Oliver describes this as "an ethics founded on the relationship between the mother and child during pregnancy and birth, one that sets up one's obligations to the other as obligations to the self and obligations to the species. It is founded on the ambiguity in pregnancy and birth between subject and object positions", Oliver, "Kristeva's Imaginary Father", *op. cit.*, p. 59.

74 Kristeva, "Stabat Mater", *op. cit.*, p. 116.

75 Julia Kristeva, "Place Names" in *Desire in Language, op. cit.*, p. 279.

76 Kristeva, "Motherhood According to Giovanni Bellini", *op. cit.*, p. 237, cited in Iris Marion Young, "Pregnant Embodiment: Subjectivity and Alienation" in *Throwing Like a Girl and Other Essays in Feminist Philosophy and Social Theory* (Bloomington: Indiana University Press, 1990, pp. 160–74), p. 160. In the notes to her text Young identifies two books that do attempt to write the mother as the subject of pregnancy: Ann Lewis, *An Interesting Condition* (Garden City, NY: Doubleday, 1950); Phyllis Chesler, *With Child: A Diary of Motherhood* (New York: Thomas Y. Crowell, 1979).

77 Young, *ibid.*, p. 160.

78 Rich, *Of Woman Born, op. cit.*, p. 13.

79 *Ibid.*, pp. 21, 32.

80 Mary Jacobus argues that Rich's work can be categorised as psychosocial, i.e. a politics of mothering, and opposes this to psychobiological works such as Kristeva's which explore the female body and subject. See: Mary Jacobus, *Reading Woman: Essays in Feminist Criticism* (New York: Columbia University Press, 1986, pp. 144f.). However I do not think that we can sustain this distinction if we read Rich's text in the way that I am proposing.

81 Rich, *op. cit.*, p. 102.

82 *Ibid.*, p. 34.

83 Jane Gallop also chooses to read Rich's text as autobiography. Gallop manages, in her brief discussion, to situate Rich's autobiographical work within the context of her own autobiographical statements. See: Jane Gallop, *Thinking Through the Body* (New York: Columbia University Press, 1988).

84 Rich, *op. cit.*, pp. 29, 19, 193.

85 Irigaray, "Women's Exile", *op. cit.*, p. 75.

86 Irigaray, "And the One Doesn't Stir without the Other", *op. cit.*, p. 66–7.

87 Luce Irigaray, "This Sex Which Is Not One" in *This Sex Which Is Not One, op. cit.*, p. 29.

88 Luce Irigaray, "When Our Lips Speak Together" in *This Sex Which Is Not One, op. cit..*, p. 215.

89 Luce Irigaray, "He Risks Who Risks Life Itself", trans. David Macey in *The Irigaray Reader*, *op. cit.*, pp. 217–18.

90 Irigaray, "This Sex Which Is Not One", *op. cit.*, p. 28.

91 Rosi Braidotti asks whose voices flaunt this paternal authority in the context of her analysis of the relation between philosophy and psychoanalysis. She suggests that a fatherless society creates a climate of loss in which it is the sons who can well and truly be heard. See: "Desidero Ergo Sum: The Improbable Tête-à-Tête between Philosophy and Psychoanalysis" in *Patterns of Dissonance: A Study of Women in Contemporary Philosophy*, trans. Elizabeth Guild (Oxford: Polity Press, 1991, pp. 16–45).

92 Jane Gallop notes the significance of this play, commenting: "For if Irigaray is not just writing a non-phallomorphic text (a rather common modernist practice) but actually constructing a non-phallomorphic sexuality then the gesture of a troubled but nonetheless insistent referentiality is essential." See: "Quand nos lèvres s'écrivent: Irigaray's Body Politic", *Romanic Review* 74(1) 1983, p. 83.

93 Jacques Derrida, "Différance" in *Margins of Philosophy*, trans. Alan Bass (Chicago: University of Chicago Press, 1982, p. 7).

94 Jacques Derrida, "From Restricted to General Economy: A Hegelianism without Reserve", in *Writing and Difference*, trans. Alan Bass (Chicago: University of Chicago Press, 1978, pp. 263–4).

95 Maggie Berg offers an insightful discussion and analysis of Irigaray's play on the "lips" in "Luce Irigaray's 'Contradictions': Poststructuralism and Feminism", *Signs* 17(1) 1991, pp. 50–70. See also Berg's "Escaping the Cave: Luce Irigaray and her Feminist Critics" in *Literature and Ethics: Essays Presented to A.E. Malloch*, Gary Wihl and David Williams eds (Montreal: McGill-Queen's University Press, 1988, pp. 62–76). Also of interest are: Diana Fuss, " 'Essentially Speaking': Luce Irigaray's Language of Essence", *Hypatia* 3(3) 1989 esp. p. 63, reprinted in *Revaluing French Feminism: Critical Essays on Difference, Agency, and Culture*, Nancy Fraser and Sandra Lee Bartky eds. (Bloomington: Indiana University Press, 1992, pp. 94–112) and Jane Gallop, *Thinking Through the Body*, *op. cit.*

96 Carolyn Burke, "Romancing the Philosophers: Luce Irigaray", *the minnesota review* 29 (Winter) 1987, p. 112. She suggests that this writing is deliberately unstable and slippery and that it "refuses the demand for fixed philosophical positions" (*ibid.*)

97 Irigaray, "When Our Lips Speak Together", *op. cit.*, p. 209.

8 MOTHERS AND DAUGHTERS: SPEAKING

1 Susan Rubin Suleiman, "Pornography, Transgression, and the Avant-Garde: Bataille's *Story of the Eye*" in *The Poetics of Gender*, Nancy Miller ed. (New York: Columbia University Press, 1986, p. 131). See also: Nancy Vickers, "The Mistress in the Masterpiece", pp. 19–41 in the same volume.

2 See: Melanie Klein, Paula Heimann, Susan Isaacs and Joan Rivière, *Developments in Psycho-Analysis*, Joan Riviere ed. (London: Hogarth Press, 1952) and D.W. Winnicott, *The Family and Individual Development* (New York: Basic Books, 1965); *Playing and Reality* (New York: Basic Books, 1971). For an overview of feminist work in object-relations theory see: Marianne Hirsch, "Mothers and Daughters", *Signs* 7(1) 1981, pp. 200–22; Judith Kegan Gardiner, "Mind Mother: Psychoanalysis and Feminism", in *Making a Difference: Feminist Literary Criticism*, G. Greene and C. Kahn eds. (London: Methuen, 1985, pp. 113–45). Feminist "classics" in object-relations include: Jessica Benjamin, "The Bonds of Love: Rational Violence and Erotic Domination", *Feminist Studies* 6(1) 1980, pp. 144–74; Nancy Chodorow, *The Reproduction of Mothering: Psychoanalysis and the Sociology of Gender* (Berkeley: University of California Press, 1978); Dorothy Dinnerstein, *The Mermaid and the Minotaur: Sexual Arrangements and Human Malaise* (New York: Harper and Row, 1976).

3 Marianne Hirsch's work on maternal anger uncovers some interesting ideas regarding the

NOTES

feminist use of psychoanalytic theory that may be pertinent here. Her reading of Alice Walker's essay "One Child of One's Own" offers a critical look at white feminist psychoanalytic discussions of mothering. Hirsch contends that a (white) psychoanalytic framework silences certain questions that we might ask about maternal subjectivity and its relation to anger; that "it colludes in silencing and repressing any form of maternal anger which is not restricted to the protection of children but is directed *at them* ". Walker's essay questions the cultural opposition between writing and motherhood, arguing that her own experience of mothering has served to nurture rather than hamper her work. Hirsch suggests that a psychoanalytic perspective closes over the complexities of Walker's position, silencing the ambiguities and ambivalences that her text inscribes. Marianne Hirsch, "Maternal Anger: Silent Themes and 'Meaningful Digression' in Psychoanalytic Feminism", *the minnesota review* 29 (Winter) 1987, p. 82. Alice Walker's essay is published in *In Search of Our Mother's Gardens* (New York: Harcourt Brace Jovanovich, 1983).

4 Michèle Longino Farrell's reading of Mme de Sévigné's *Correspondence* theorises the maternal by way of the mother–daughter bond. Farrell demonstrates how, in this seventeenth-century canonical text, the maternal is performed through the (public) act of writing between mother and daughter (p. 4). She suggests that Sévigné's writing inaugurates, as founding text, the literary construction of the mother–daughter relation (p. 253). Farrell's reading of the *Correspondence* attempts to restitute the absent daughter's voice in relation to the body of writing by the mother, in order to offer "a daughter's view of a writing mother" (p. 22). She points out that, in contrast to Sévigné's work, twentieth-century literary inscriptions of the mother–daughter relation in France are written by daughters. See: Michèle Longino Farrell, *Performing Motherhood: The Sévigné Correspondence* (Hanover, NH: University Press of New England, 1991). See also: Marie de Rabutin-Chantal, Mme de Sévigné, *Correspondance*, edited by Roger Duchêne. 3 vols (Paris: Gallimard, Bibliothèque de la Pléiade, 1972–8).

5 Hirsch, "Mothers and Daughters", *op. cit.*, p. 214. Hirsch provides an extensive overview and analysis of mother–daughter literary representations. She suggests that three readings of this literature can be identified: (i) *Psychobiographical analyses*: where the (pre)historic sources of a writer's literary motifs are sought; (ii) *Sociological analyses*: where private family relations are interpreted in their social context; and (iii) *Alternative literary analyses*: where the traditions of oral literature, autobiography and ethnic literature are explored. See also her *The Mother–Daughter Plot: Narrative, Psychoanalysis, Feminism* (Bloomington: Indiana University Press, 1989). Also of interest is: Judith Kegan Gardiner, "The New Motherhood", *North American Review* 263(2) 1978, pp. 72–6. For a discussion of the mother–daughter relation in film see: E. Ann Kaplan, "Motherhood and Representation: From Post World War II Freudian Figurations to Postmodernism", *the minnesota review* 29 (Winter) 1987, pp. 88–102.

6 Marianne Hirsch, "A Mother's Discourse: Incorporation and Repetition in *La Princesse de Clèves*", *Yale French Studies* 62 1981, p. 73.

7 Adrienne Rich, *Of Woman Born: Motherhood as Experience and Institution* (London: Virago, 1979, p. 200).

8 Alice Ostriker, "The Thieves of Language: Women Poets and Revisionist Mythmaking" in *The New Feminist Criticisms: Essays on Women, Literature and Theory*, Elaine Showalter ed. (London: Virago, 1986, pp. 314–38). See also Ostriker's *Stealing the Language: The Emergence of Women's Poetry in America* (Boston, MA: Beacon Press, 1986). Rachel Du Plessis' "Eurydice" is published in *Wells* (New York: Montemora Foundation, 1980, pp. 319–20).

9 Margaret Atwood, *Surfacing* (New York: Popular Library, 1972).

10 Susan Gubar, "Mother, Maiden and the Marriage of Death: Women Writers and an Ancient Myth", *Women's Studies* 6 1979, p. 309.

11 Susan Suleiman, "(Re)Writing the Body: The Politics and Poetics of Female Eroticism" in *The Female Body in Western Culture*, Suleiman ed. (Cambridge, MA: Harvard University

Press, 1986, p. 17). Suleiman is discussing, in particular, Cixous' text *Souffles*. See: Hélène Cixous, *Souffles* (Paris: des femmes, 1975).

12 Phil Powrie,"A Womb of One's Own: The Metaphor of the Womb-room as a Reading-effect in Texts by Contemporary French women writers", *Paragraph* 12(3) 1989, pp. 197–213.

13 Luce Irigaray, *Speculum of the Other Woman*, trans. Gillian C. Gill (Ithaca, NY: Cornell University Press, 1985, p. 41).

14 See Irigaray's "The Bodily Encounter with the Mother", trans. David Macey, in *The Irigaray Reader*, Margaret Whitford ed. (Oxford: Basil Blackwell, 1991, pp. 34–46) for her discussion of a genealogy of women.

15 It is worth noting at this point that the *maternal* writing of the mother–daughter bond can in fact be very centred on the daughter, i.e. a writing which ultimately eclipses the mother in the daughter's desire to write. We need to distinguish writing *from* and *about* the mother. Susan Rubin Suleiman discusses the way motherhood can be and often is reduced to the child's drama in her "Writing and Motherhood" in *The (M)other Tongue: Essays in Feminist Psychoanalytic Interpretation*, S. Nelson Garner, C. Kahane and M. Sprengnether eds. (Ithaca, NY: Cornell University Press, 1985, pp. 352–77).

16 Jahan Ramazani offers an interesting critique of the "continuity" of women's attachment to others, focusing on the daughter's relation to the father. Ramazani uses this as a starting point for a discussion of Sylvia Plath's rewriting of the elegy. See: " 'Daddy, I Have Had to Kill You': Plath, Rage, and the Modern Elegy", *PLMA* 108(5) 1993, pp. 1142–56.

17 The focus on the mother–daughter relation provides us with an approach that celebrates the mother in a positive sense. In opposition to theories that mutilate the mother's body, it offers an expression of her as sexual and desiring. Here she is depicted beyond her phallocentric inscription as perversion and lack. Another way to celebrate the mother is to figure her in humorous terms. Susan Rubin Suleiman, for example, calls for feminist inscriptions of the playful (laughing) mother. She contends that the Surrealist repudiation of the mother by major male avant-garde artists has been reproduced by some feminists who reduce the mother to a (unconscious) defender of patriarchal law. Against this dismissal Suleiman celebrates those rare texts (e.g. Leonora Carrington's *The Hearing Trumpet*) that figure the mother as the irreverent subject of play. See Suleiman's "Feminist Intertextuality and the Laugh of the Mother" in *Subversive Intent: Gender, Politics, and the Avant-Garde* (Cambridge, MA: Harvard University Press, 1990, pp. 141–80). Given Suleiman's insistence on laughter it is interesting to find Irigaray writing the following:

> Isn't laughter the first form of liberation from a secular oppression? *Isn't the phallic tantamount to the seriousness of meaning?* Perhaps woman, and the sexual relation, transcend it 'first' in laughter? … Besides, women among themselves begin by laughing. To escape from a pure and simple reversal of the masculine position means in any case not to forget to laugh.
> See: Luce Irigaray, "Questions" in *This Sex Which Is Not One*, trans. Catherine Porter (Ithaca, NY: Cornell University Press, 1985, (pp. 119–69), p. 163).

18 It seems an odd accusation for Kristeva to make, given her own work on intertextuality.

19 Gilles Deleuze, *Logique du Sens*, p. 302, quoted in (and translated by) J. Hillis Miller, *Fiction and Repetition: Seven English Novels* (Oxford: Basil Blackwell, 1982, pp. 5–6).

20 For a detailed discussion of these various repetitive (mimetic) structures see: Joel Black, "Idology: The Model in Artistic Practice and Critical Theory" in *Mimesis in Contemporary Theory Vol. 1: The Literary and Philosophical Debate*, Mihai Spariosu ed. (Philadelphia, PA: John Benjamins, 1984, pp. 172–200). Black attempts to demonstrate the inter-dependence of these seemingly antagonistic structures. He notes, following Panofsky, that Classical and Neoclassical theory operates with a distinction between imitation and copying. Renaissance theorists interpret this opposition in the following way. Imitation (*imitare*)

involves a positive difference while copying (*ritrarre*) merely *repeats* or *reproduces* its model (p. 176). There is a distinction drawn here between the creative gesture of the imitative arts and the repetitive or reproductive efforts of portraiture. Panofsky's distinction between *imitare* and *ritrarre* is drawn from Vincenzo Danti's *Il primo libro del Trattato delle perfette proporzioni* (1567). See: Erwin Panofsky, *Idea: A Concept in Art Theory*, trans. Joseph J.S. Peake (Columbia, SC: University of South Carolina Press, 1968).

21 J. Hillis Miller traces the subversive mimesis of the repetitive structure in recent times as follows:

> The modern history of ideas about repetition goes by way of Vico to Hegel and the German Romantic, to Kierkegaard's *Repetition*, to Marx (in *The Eighteenth Brumaire*), to Nietzsche's concept of the eternal return, to Freud's notion of the compulsion to repeat, to the Joyce of *Finnegans Wake*, on down to such diverse present-day theorists of repetition as Jacques Lacan or Gilles Deleuze, Mircea Eliade or Jacques Derrida.
>
> (Hillis Miller, *op. cit.*, p. 5)

Likewise, William Spanos traces the deconstructive gesture of repetition-as-difference through Kierkegaard and Heidegger. He argues that this repetition subverts the notion of a circular continuity that recuperates the same. William V. Spanos, "Overture in the Recursive Mode" in *Repetitions: The Postmodern Occasion in Literature and Culture* (Baton Rouge: Louisiana State University Press, 1987, p. 4).

22 Sigmund Freud, *Beyond the Pleasure Principle* (1930), trans. James Strachey (New York: W.W. Norton, 1961, pp. 12–13, emphases added). Also published in *The Standard Edition of the Complete Psychological Works,* Vol. XVIII, James Strachey ed. (London: Hogarth Press, 1955, pp. 3–64).

23 In "Mourning and Melancholia" Freud sets up a similar distinction between the repetitive (pathological) state of melancholia and the process of mourning. He suggests that melancholia involves an unconscious, ambivalent position that cannot be worked through by the (normal) work of mourning. It is a repetitive state linked to "an unconscious loss of a love-object" (p. 155). See: "Mourning and Melancholia" (1917) in *Collected Papers Vol. IV*, Ernest Jones ed. (London: Hogarth Press, 1949, pp. 152–70). Luce Irigaray suggests that Freud's depiction of melancholia closely resembles his discussion of the girl's reaction to knowledge of her "castration". This is interesting, for it seems that Freud (unconsciously) links *Repetition-as-same* with women. See: Irigaray, *Speculum of the Other Woman, op. cit.*, pp. 67f. Margaret Whitford argues, with Irigaray, that the melancholic (repetitive) state of the girl is a consequence of the prohibition placed on symbolising or representing her bond with her mother. See: Whitford, "Maternal Genealogy and the Symbolic" in *Luce Irigaray: Philosophy in the Feminine* (London: Routledge, 1991, pp. 86–7).

24 Søren Kierkegaard also links repetition and remembrance, though not in the manner that Freud's articulation suggests. For Kierkegaard repetition and recollection form a continuous movement. See: *Repetition: An Essay in Experimental Psychology*, trans. Walter Lowrie (New York: Harper and Row, 1964, p. 33). For a further elaboration of Freud's position on repetition and recollection see: Sigmund Freud, "Remembering, Repeating and Working Through" (1914), *Standard Edition of the Complete Works*, Vol. XII, pp. 147–55.

25 Sigmund Freud, "The 'Uncanny' "(1919) in *Collected Papers Vol. IV* (London: Hogarth Press, 1949, p. 399).

26 *Ibid.*, p. 394.

27 Simone de Beauvoir, "The Nomad" in *The Second Sex*, trans. H.M. Parshley (Harmondsworth: Penguin, 1984, pp. 94–7 emphases added).

28 Gilles Deleuze and Félix Guattari, *Nomadology: The War Machine*, trans. Brian Massumi (New York: Semiotext(e), 1986, pp. 36–7). Originally published as "Traité de nomadologie: la machine de guerre" in *Mille Plateaux* (Paris: Minuit, 1980).

29 Vincent Descombes writes: "Repetition should therefore cease to be defined as the return of the same through the reiteration of the identical; on the contrary, it is the *production* (in both senses of the word: to bring into existence, to show) of difference." See: *Modern French Philosophy*, trans. L. Scott-Fox and J.M. Harding (New York: Cambridge University Press, 1980, p. 154).

30 Ellen Friedman questions the sexual specificity of Deleuze's nomadism in an article on women modernist writers. She claims that male texts of modernity typically repeat an Oedipal preoccupation with fathers, and one profoundly nostalgic, while female modernist texts, nomadic in the true sense of the term, "show little nostalgia for the old paternal order, little regret for the no longer presentable." Friedman argues that female texts more usually evoke the unpresentable as "the not yet presented" (p. 242). She concludes: "One wonders what Deleuze and Guattari would conclude from a study of the nomadic patterns of women writers" (p. 250) See: Ellen G. Friedman, "Where are the Missing Contents? (Post)Modernism, Gender, and the Canon", *PMLA* 108(2) 1993, pp. 240–52.

31 Elizabeth Grosz, *Sexual Subversions: Three French Feminists* (Sydney: Allen and Unwin, 1989, p. 231).

32 In employing the term *Imaginary* here I am returning to and drawing from Le Doeuff's discussion of the philosophical imaginary. Le Doeuff's Imaginary hovers somewhere between the sites of rhetoric, philosophy and psychoanalysis and in so doing refuses to be fixed by any certain theoretical terrain. We might say that in this sense her use of the term is *nomadic*. For Le Doeuff the Imaginary is the site of a curious masculine production which functions to say, often through images and metaphor, what cannot be said or articulated conceptually within philosophical discourse. The Imaginary functions in this way as a *conceptual excess*, producing a reading effect which potentially destabilises the apparent stability and coherence of philosophical discourse. In my use of the term the Imaginary serves as the complex site of a series of denials, displacements and disavowals enacted by philosophy in relation to the maternal body. See: Meaghan Morris, *The Pirate's Fiancée: Feminism, Reading, Postmodernism* (London: Verso, 1988, p. 72). Elizabeth Grosz discusses Le Doeuff's Imaginary as "a reading that absorbs the imaginary into the theoretical problems of the system", a "conceptual excess" which exists in the liminal relations of rhetoric, philosophy and psychoanalysis. Grosz, *op. cit.*, p. 185.

33 Luce Irigaray, "Women-Mothers, the Silent Substratum of the Social Order", trans. David Macey in *The Irigaray Reader, op. cit.*, p. 50.

34 Luce Irigaray, "And the One Doesn't Stir Without the Other", trans. H.V. Wenzel, *Signs* 7(1) 1981, pp. 60–7; "When Our Lips Speak Together", in *This Sex Which Is Not One, op. cit.*, pp. 205–18.

35 Irigaray, "And the One Doesn't Stir Without the Other", p. 61.

36 *Ibid.*, p. 60.

37 *Ibid.*, p. 62, 65.

38 *Ibid.*, p. 66.

39 Luce Irigaray, "The Limits of the Transference", trans. D. Macey and M. Whitford in *The Irigaray Reader, op. cit.*, p. 105.

40 *Ibid.*, p. 107.

41 *Ibid.*, pp. 110, 111.

42 *Ibid.*, p. 112.

43 In conversation Melissa White has spoken of the mother-daughter bond as a slow death or gradual draining that exists in contrast to the out and out murder of the Oedipal battle between father and son.

44 Whitford describes Irigaray's claim in the following way: "women (in the symbolic) are in a kind of continuous present; they *represent* the death drives, but cannot sublimate their own, because their own relationship to the passing of generations is unsymbolized." Margaret Whitford, "Maternal Genealogy and the Symbolic" in *Luce Irigaray: Philosophy in the Feminine, op. cit.* (pp. 75–97), p. 87.

45 *Ibid.*, p. 86.

46 Irigaray, "And the One Doesn't Stir Without the Other", *op. cit.*, p. 61.
47 *Ibid.*
48 *Ibid.*, p. 66.
49 *Ibid.*, p. 67.
50 *Ibid.*, p. 66.
51 *Ibid.*, p. 67. Jane Gallop suggests that in this text Irigaray's mother is phallic because she is constructed by the daughter (Irigaray) as the silent interlocutor, the subject presumed to know, the object of transference and the one controlling life, death, meaning and identity. See: "The Phallic Mother: Fraudian Analysis" in *Feminism and Psychoanalysis: The Daughter's Seduction* (London: Macmillan, 1982, pp. 115, 117).
52 Carolyn Burke first introduced her translation of this text suggesting that the dialogue between the *indefinite ones* is between either female lovers or two aspects of the self. Maggie Berg, writing some time after Burke's translation, argues that it is equally important that we read this text as "an ironical rebuttal to Lacan's theory of the phallus, or to his declaration that the clitoris is 'autistic' (i.e. it cannot communicate: it is impotent in the Symbolic)" (pp. 64–5). Berg goes on to show that Irigaray's concerns in this piece revolve around constructing a *lipeccentrism* that attempts to both laugh at and avoid Lacan's pretentious phallic claims. See Berg's "Luce Irigaray's 'Contradictions': Poststructuralism and Feminism", *Signs* 17(1) 1991, pp. 50–70. Also Carolyn Burke, "Introduction to Luce Irigaray's 'When Our Lips Speak Together', " *Signs* 6(1) 1980, pp. 66–8 and "Irigaray Through the Looking Glass", *Feminist Studies* 7(2) 1981, pp. 288–306. Elizabeth Berg comments on the "lover's discourse" Irigaray writes to Lacan in a paper published in 1982. She writes: "All of Irigaray's work is in some sense to be understood as a dialogue with Lacan, although his name is spectacularly missing from her books" (p. 16). See: "The Third Woman," *Diacritics* 12 1982, pp. 11–20.
53 Irigaray, "When Our Lips Speak Together", p. 209.
54 *Ibid.*, pp. 208, 218.
55 *Ibid.*, p. 210.
56 *Ibid.*, p. 214.
57 *Ibid.*, p. 215.
58 *Ibid.*
59 *Ibid.*, p. 217.
60 Luce Irigaray, *Le Corps-à-corps avec la mère* (Montreal: Les editions de la pleine lune, 1981). See: "Body Against Body: In Relation to the Mother" in *Sexes and Genealogies*, trans. Gillian C. Gill (New York: Columbia University Press, 1993, pp. 7–21).
61 Irigaray, 'The Limits of the Transference', *op. cit.*
62 *Ibid.*, p. 109. Carolyn Burke suggests that this piece represents the final text of Irigaray's "transitional stage", a stage encompassing "When Our Lips Speak Together" and "And the One Doesn't Stir Without the Other". Burke argues that Irigaray advocates "a close combat between mother and daughter that may allow both to regain the primary narcissism that is the precondition for the love of another" (p. 106). See: "Romancing the Philosophers: Luce Irigaray", *the minnesota review* 29 (Winter) 1987, pp. 103–114.
63 Burke, *op. cit.*, p. 106.
64 Irigaray's more recent work takes up these concerns in her pursuit of an elemental philosophy, one that strives to regain a link with the repressed world of pre-Socratic thought through the figure of the mother. See: Luce Irigaray, *Elemental Passions*, trans. Joanne Collie and Judith Still (New York: Routledge, 1992, p. 1). Irigaray begins her elemental philosophy in a series of books attempting to engage more recent philosophers with their pre-rational, elemental context. These include: *Marine Lover of Friedrich Nietzsche*, trans. Gillian C. Gill (New York: Columbia University Press, 1991); "The Fecundity of the Caress", trans. Carolyn Burke in *Face to Face with Levinas*, R.A. Cohen ed. (Albany, NY: SUNY Press, 1986, pp. 231–56); *L'Oublie de l'air chez Martin Heidegger* (Paris: Minuit, 1983). Irigaray's elemental works can be read as embodying an eco-feminist sensibility. Throughout them there are myriad references in our sensuous bonds with the earth. See also her more recent work

I Love To You: Sketch of a Possible Felicity in History, trans. Alison Martin (London and New York: Routledge, 1996).

CONCLUSION: SPEAKING WITH(IN) THE SYMBOLIC

1 Françoise Collin, "Polyglo(u)ssons", *Les Cahiers du Grif* Juin 1976, pp. 8–9, cited in Phil Powrie, "A Womb of One's Own: the Metaphor of the Womb-room as a Reading-effect in Texts by Contemporary French Women Writers", *Paragraph* 12(3) 1989, p. 211.

2 Jacques Lacan, "Guiding Remarks for a Congress on Feminine Sexuality" in *Écrits* (Paris: Seuil, 1966, pp. 725–36). Reprinted in *Feminine Sexuality: Jacques Lacan and the École Freudienne*, Juliet Mitchell and Jacqueline Rose eds. (London: Macmillan, 1982, p. 87).

3 For a discussion of this resumed/exhumed imaginary field see: Rosi Braidotti, "The Politics of Ontological Difference" in *Between Feminism and Psychoanalysis*, Teresa Brennan ed. (London: Routledge, 1989).

4 Maggie Berg puts it this way: "The child accedes to language in the 'Name-of-the-Father' – by acknowledging paternity, which depends on signification – and by transcending or barring the imaginary unity with the mother's body. Lacan thus relegates the maternal woman's body to the 'real' of biological reproduction that lies outside of culture or the symbolic." See: "Luce Irigaray's 'Contradictions': Poststructuralism and Feminism", *Signs* 17(1) 1991, p. 58.

5 According to Anika Lemaire the father/symbol replaces or stands in metaphorically for the mother. See: *Jacques Lacan* (London: Routledge and Kegan Paul, 1977, p. 87).

6 Jacqeline Rose, "Introduction – II" to *Feminine Sexuality, op. cit.*, p. 37f.

7 *Ibid.*, p. 38.

8 Berg reads Lacan as suggesting that the mother represents a retreat from the symbolic. Berg, *op. cit.*, pp. 58–9.

9 Rose, *op. cit.*, p. 55.

10 Berg, *op. cit.*, p. 62. See: Luce Irigaray, *This Sex Which Is Not One*, trans. Catherine Porter (Ithaca, NY: Cornell University Press, 1985, p. 88).

11 Elizabeth Grosz suggests that Lacan's notion of *jouissance* positions woman outside articulation. See: *Jacques Lacan: A Feminist Introduction* (Sydney: Allen and Unwin, 1990, p. 139).

12 In the light of Lacan's silencing gesture, Grosz writes: "There are, there must be, other discourses and forms of possible representation capable of speaking of/as women differently." Grosz, *op. cit.*, p. 146. In Elizabeth Wright's analysis of the place of women's language she argues that we have traditionally posed the problem in terms of choice between "submitting to the public language of patriarchy or of inventing a private language which keeps [them] marginalized" (p. 141). Wright believes, however, that contemporary feminist criticism creates a space between these boundaries; she labels this space postmodern. See her "Thoroughly Postmodern Feminist Criticism" in Brennan, *op. cit.*, pp. 141–52. Rosi Braidotti calls for a redefinition of the female subject in terms which would legitimise a female symbolic. Her politics of ontological difference takes woman's sexual difference as its starting point. See: Braidotti, *op. cit.*, p. 102. In a somewhat similar vein Juliet Flower MacCannell writes of the symbolic that: "It is time to redraw its form, its shape." (p. 16). See her "Introduction: Women and the Symbolic" in *The Other Perspective in Gender and Culture: Rewriting Women and the Symbolic*, MacCannell ed. (New York: Columbia University Press, 1990, pp. 3–19).

13 Kelly Oliver, *Reading Kristeva: Unraveling the Double-bind* (Bloomington: Indiana University Press, 1993, p. 10).

14 *Ibid.*

15 Allison Weir approaches the question of a non-homogeneous symbolic in Kristeva's work through the figure of the singular or non-phallic mother. Her reading of Kristeva's divided mother (the phallic and non-phallic mother) allows us to position (at least part of) the mother within the symbolic, and thus as a speaking subject. It is clear from this that Weir

is not operating with Oliver's reconceptualised spatial relation between symbolic and semiotic within the Symbolic. In order to deal with the problem of the mother's subjectivity Weir opts for the dual identity or positioning offered by the figure of the divided mother. What is probably more interesting here than the question of whether Oliver or Weir is right is the motivation behind both accounts to demonstrate that Kristeva's work offers us a mother who speaks. See: Allison Weir, "Identification with the Divided Mother: Kristeva's Ambivalence" in *Ethics, Politics, and Difference in Julia Kristeva's Writing*, Kelly Oliver ed. (New York: Routledge, 1993, pp. 79–91).

16 For a discussion of this point see: Maggie Berg, *op. cit.*, pp. 62f; Margaret Whitford, "Maternal Genealogy and the Symbolic" in *Luce Irigaray: Philosophy in the Feminine* (London: Routledge, 1991, pp. 75–97). By placing the symbolic in quotation marks Hélène Cixous imagines the possibility of one that would be women's. See: Morag Shiach, " 'Their "Symbolic" Exists, It Holds Power – We, the Sowers of Disorder, Know It Only Too Well' ", in Brennan, *op. cit.*, pp. 153–67.

17 Cf. Braidotti on Irigaray's tactical intervention. Braidotti, *op. cit.*, p. 99.

18 Luce Irigaray, "Così Fan Tutti" in *This Sex Which Is Not One, op. cit.*, pp. 94, 95.

19 Whitford, *op. cit.*, p. 85. Whitford writes: "Since the symbolic has a structuring effect upon the otherwise unrepresentable drives, this is a rather important distinction."

20 See Whitford, *ibid.*, p. 84.

21 Luce Irigaray, "The Blind Spot of an Old Dream of Symmetry" in *Speculum of the Other Woman*, trans. Gillian C. Gill (Ithaca, NY: Cornell University Press, 1985, p. 71).

22 Cf. Luce Irigaray, *Divine Women*, trans. Stephen Muecke (Sydney: Local Consumption Publications, 1986). Originally published as "Femmes divines", *Critique* 454 1985. See also: Elizabeth Gross, *Irigaray and the Divine* (Sydney: Local Consumption Publications, 1986).

23 See chapter three of this book for an elaboration of this point.

24 Luce Irigaray, "The Gesture in Psychoanalysis" in Brennan, *op. cit.*, p. 132. Originally published as "Le geste en psychanalyse" in *Sexes et parentés* (Paris: Minuit, 1987).

25 Cf. Irigaray *ibid*, p. 132 for a discussion of this point.

26 *Ibid.*, pp. 132–3.

27 *Ibid.*, p. 133.

28 Nancy Fraser makes some criticisms of Lacan's symbolic that seem relevant here. She claims that feminists should resist Lacan's work because its structuralist orientation eclipses any pragmatic considerations of language and subjectivity. By this she means that Lacan's symbolic operates as an enclosed system that cannot be theorised in terms of conflict, agency or opposition. This system (or space?) conscripts the child into a phallocentric order that requires its submission to the father's law. See: "The Uses and Abuses of French Discourse Theories for Feminist Politics" in *Revaluing French Feminism: Critical Essays on Difference, Agency, and Culture*, Nancy Fraser and Sandra Lee Bartky eds (Bloomington: Indiana University Press, 1992, pp. 177–94).

29 A very rich example of a specific instance has been investigated by Michèle Longino Farrell in her study of the Sévigné correspondence. Farrell demonstrates how Sévigné fashioned a continuing place for herself in French letters through her literary performance of maternity. See: Michèle Longino Farrell, *Performing Motherhood: The Sévigné Correspondence* (Hanover, NH: University Press of New England, 1991).

BIBLIOGRAPHY

Adorno, Theodor W., *Negative Dialectics*, trans. E.B. Ashton (London: Routledge and Kegan Paul, 1973).

Adorno, Theodor W. and Max Horkheimer, *Dialectic of Enlightenment*, trans. J. Cumming (London: Verso, 1979).

Althusser, Louis, "Ideology and Ideological State Apparatuses (Notes towards an Investigation)" and "Freud and Lacan" in *Lenin and Philosophy: And Other Essays*, trans. Ben Brewster (New York: Monthly Review Press, 1971, pp. 127–86, 189–219).

—— *"L'Avenir dure longtemps" suivi de "Les Faits": Autobiographies* (Paris: Stock, 1992).

Althusser, Louis and Etienne Balibar, *Reading Capital*, trans. Ben Brewster (London: Verso, 1979).

Aronowitz, Stanley, *The Crisis in Historical Materialism: Class, Politics and Culture in Marxist Theory* (New York: Praeger, 1981).

Atwood, Margaret, *Surfacing* (New York: Popular Library, 1972).

Badinter, Elisabeth, *The Myth of Motherhood: An Historical View of the Maternal Instinct* (London: Souvenir Press, 1981). Originally published as *L'Amour en plus* (Paris: Flammarion, 1980).

Bakhtin, Mikhail, *Problems of Dostoevsky's Poetics*, trans. R.W. Rotsel (Ann Arbor, MI: Ardis, 1973).

Balbus, Isaac, *Marxism and Domination: A Neo-Hegelian, Feminist, Psychoanalytic Theory of Sexual, Political, and Technological Liberation* (Princeton, NJ: Princeton University Press, 1982).

Barker, Francis, *The Tremulous Private Body: Essays on Subjection* (London: Methuen, 1984).

Barthes, Roland, *S/Z*, trans. R. Miller (New York: Hill and Wang, 1974). Originally published as *S/Z* (Paris: Seuil, 1970).

—— *The Pleasure of the Text*, trans. R. Miller (New York: Hill and Wang, 1975). Originally published as *Le Plaisir du texte* (Paris: Seuil, 1973).

—— "The Death of the Author", "From Work to Text", "Research: The Young" in *The Rustle of Language*, trans. R. Howard (New York: Hill and Wang, 1986).

Baruch, Elaine Hoffman and Perry Meisel, "Two Interviews with Julia Kristeva", *Partisan Review* 51(1) 1984, pp. 120–32.

Bataille, Georges, "The Notion of Expenditure" in *Visions of Excess: Selected Writings 1927–1939*, trans. and ed. A. Stoekl (Minneapolis: University of Minnesota Press, 1985).

Baudrilland, Jean, *Symbolic Exchange and Death* (London: Sage, 1993). Originally published as *L'Échange symbolique et la mort* (Paris: Gallimard, 1976).

—— *The Mirror of Production*, trans. M. Poster (St. Louis, MO: Telos Press, 1985).

Originally published as *Le Miroir de la production, ou, L'illusion critique du materialisme historique* (Paris: Galilée, 1985).

Baynes, Kenneth, James Bohman and Thomas McCarthy eds, *After Philosophy: End or Transformation?* (Cambridge, MA: The MIT Press, 1987).

Beauvoir, Simone de, *The Second Sex*, trans. H.M. Parshley (Harmondsworth: Penguin, 1984). Originally published as *Le Deuxième Sexe* (Paris: 1949, Vintage, 1974).

Benjamin, Andrew ed., *The Lyotard Reader* (Oxford: Basil Blackwell, 1991).

—— ed., *Judging Lyotard* (London: Routledge, 1992).

Benjamin, Jessica, "The Bonds of Love: Rational Violence and Erotic Domination", *Feminist Studies* 6(1) 1980, pp. 144–74.

Benjamin, Walter, "Theses on the Philosophy of History" in *Illuminations: Essays and Reflections*, trans. Harry Zohn (New York: Schocken Books, 1969).

Bennington, Geoffrey, *Lyotard: Writing the Event* (Manchester: Manchester University Press, 1988).

—— "'Ces petits différends': Lyotard and Horace" in *Judging Lyotard*, Andrew Benjamin ed. (London: Routledge, 1992, pp. 145–67).

Benveniste, Emile, *Problems in General Linguistics*, trans. M.E. Meek (Coral Gables, FL: University of Miami Press, 1971).

Benvenuto, Bice and Roger Kennedy, *The Works of Jacques Lacan: An Introduction* (London: Free Association Books, 1986).

Berg, Elizabeth, "The Third Woman", *Diacritics* 12 1982, pp. 11–20.

Berg, Maggie, "Escaping the Cave: Luce Irigaray and her Feminist Critics" in *Literature and Ethics: Essays Presented to A.E. Malloch*, Gary Wihl and David Williams eds (Montreal: McGill-Queen's University Press, 1988, pp. 62–76).

—— "Luce Irigaray's 'Contradictions': Poststructuralism and Feminism", *Signs* 17(1) 1991, pp. 50–70.

Bernheimer, Charles and Claire Kahane, eds, *In Dora's Case: Freud/Hysteria/Feminism* (London: Virago, 1985).

Black, Joel, "Idolology: The Model in Artistic Practice and Critical Theory" in *Mimesis in Contemporary Theory Vol. 1: The Literary and Philosophical Debate*, Mihai Spariosu ed. (Philadelphia, PA: John Benjamins, 1984, pp. 172–200).

Braidotti, Rosi, "The Politics of Ontological Difference" in *Between Feminism and Psychoanalysis*, Teresa Brennan ed. (London: Routledge, 1989, pp. 89–105).

—— *Patterns of Dissonance: A Study of Women in Contemporary Philosophy*, trans. Elizabeth Guild (Oxford: Polity Press, 1991).

Brecht, Bertolt, *Brecht on Theatre: The Development of an Aesthetic*, J. Willet ed. (London: Methuen, 1964).

Brennan, Teresa, ed., *Between Feminism and Psychoanalysis* (London: Routledge, 1989).

—— *The Interpretation of the Flesh: Freud and Femininity* (London: Routledge, 1992).

Brodribb, Somer, *Nothing Mat(t)ers: A Feminist Critique of Postmodernism* (Melbourne: Spinifex Press, 1992).

Burke, Carolyn, "Introduction to Luce Irigaray's 'When Our Lips Speak Together,'" *Signs* 6(1) 1980, pp. 66–8.

—— "Irigaray Through the Looking Glass", *Feminist Studies* 7(2) 1981, pp. 288–306.

—— "Supposed Persons: Modernist Poetry and the Female Subject", *Feminist Studies* 11(1) 1985, pp. 131–48.

—— "Romancing the Philosophers: Luce Irigaray", *the minnesota review* 29 (Winter) 1987, pp. 103–14.

Butler, Judith, *Gender Trouble: Feminism and the Subversion of Identity* (New York: Routledge, 1990).

Carroll, David, *The Subject in Question: The Language of Theory and the Strategies of Fiction* (Chicago: University of Chicago Press, 1982).

—— "Rephrasing the Political with Kant and Lyotard: From Aesthetic to Political Judgments", *Diacritics* (14(3) 1984, pp. 74–88.

—— *Paraesthetics: Foucault/Lyotard/Derrida* (New York: Methuen, 1987).

Chanter, Tina, "Kristeva's Politics of Change: Tracking Essentialism with the Help of a Sex/ Gender Map", in *Ethics, Politics and Difference in Julia Kristeva's Writing*, Kelly Oliver ed. (New York: Routledge, 1993, pp. 179–95).

Chesler, Phyllis, *With Child: A Diary of Motherhood* (New York: Thomas Y. Crowell, 1979).

Chodorow, Nancy, *The Reproduction of Mothering: Psychoanalysis and the Sociology of Gender* (Berkeley: University of California Press, 1978).

Cixous, Hélène, *Souffles* (Paris: des femmes, 1975).

—— "Sorties: Out and Out: Attacks/Ways Out/Forays" in *The Newly Born Woman*, with Cathérine Clément, trans. Betsy Wing (Minneapolis: University of Minnesota Press, 1986). Originally published as *La Jeune Née* (Paris: Union Générale d'Editions, 1975).

—— "The Laugh of the Medusa", trans. K. Cohen and P. Cohen, *Signs* 1(4) 1976, pp. 875–93.

—— "Conversations" in *Writing Differences: Readings from the Seminar of Hélène Cixous*, Susan Sellers ed. (Oxford: Open University Press, 1988, pp. 141–54).

—— *The Hélène Cixous Reader*, Susan Sellers ed. (London: Routledge, 1994).

Clément, Cathérine, "The Guilty One" in *The Newly Born Woman*, with Hélène Cixous, trans. Betsy Wing (Minneapolis: University of Minnesota Press, 1986). Originally published as *La Jeune Née* (Paris: Union Générale d'Editions, 1975).

Collins, Jerre, Ray Green, Mary Lydon, Mark Sachner and Eleanor Honig Skoller, "Questioning the Unconscious: The Dora Archive" in *Dora's Case: Freud, Hysteria, Feminism*, Charles Bernheimer and Claire Kahane eds. (London: Virago, 1985, pp. 243–53).

Cornell, Drucilla and Adam Thurschwell, "Feminism, Negativity, Intersubjectivity" in *Feminism as Critique*, Seyla Benhabib and Drucilla Cornell eds (Minneapolis: University of Minnesota Press, 1987, pp. 143–62).

Coward, Rosalind and John Ellis, *Language and Materialism: Developments in Semiology and the Theory of the Subject* (London: Routledge and Kegan Paul, 1977).

Crowder, Diane Griffin, "Amazons and Mothers? Monique Wittig, Hélène Cixous and Theories of Women's Writing", *Contemporary Literature* 24(2) 1983, pp. 117–44.

Dallmayer, Winfried R., "Beyond Possessive Individualism" in *Twilight of Subjectivity: Contributions to a Post-Individualist Theory of Politics* (Amherst: University of Massachusetts Press, 1981).

Daly, Mary, *Gyn/Ecology: The Metaethics of Radical Feminism* (Boston, MA: Beacon Press, 1978).

de Lauretis, Teresa, *Alice Doesn't: Feminism, Semiotics, Cinema* (London: Macmillan, 1984).

Deleuze, Gilles and Félix Guattari, *Anti-Oedipus: Capitalism and Schizophrenia*, trans. Robert Hurley, Mark Seem and Helen R. Lane (New York: Viking Press, 1977). Originally published as *L'Anti-Oedipe* (Paris: Minuit, 1972).

—— *Nomadology: The War Machine*, trans. Brian Massumi (New York: Semiotext(e), 1986). Originally published as "Traité de nomadologie: la machine de guerre" in *Mille Plateaux* (Paris: Minuit, 1980).

Derrida, Jacques, *Of Grammatology*, trans. Gayatri Spivak (Baltimore, MD: Johns Hopkins University Press, 1974). Originally published as *De la grammatologie* (Paris: Minuit, 1967).

—— "From Restricted to General Economy: A Hegelianism without Reserve" in *Writing and Difference*, trans. Alan Bass (Chicago: University of Chicago Press, 1978). Originally published as *L'Écriture et la différence* (Paris: Seuil, 1967).

—— *Dissemination*, trans. Barbara Johnson (Chicago: University of Chicago Press, 1981). Originally published as *La dissémination* (Paris: Seuil, 1972).

—— "Différance" in *Margins of Philosophy*, trans. Alan Bass (Chicago: University of Chicago Press, 1982). Originally published as *Marges de la philosophie* (Paris: Minuit, 1972).

—— *Spurs: Nietzsche's Styles*, trans. Barbara Harlow (Chicago: University of Chicago Press, 1979). Originally published as *Eperons: Les Styles de Nietzsche* (Paris: Flammarion, 1978).

Descombes, Vincent, *Modern French Philosophy*, trans. L. Scott-Fox and J.M. Harding (New York: Cambridge University Press, 1980). Originally published as *Le Même et l'autre: quarante-cinq ans de philosophie française (1933–78)* (Paris: Minuit, 1979).

Dews, Peter, "The Letter and the Line: Discourse and its Other in Lyotard", *Diacritics* 14(3) 1984, pp. 40–9.

Dinnerstein, Dorothy, *The Mermaid and the Minotaur: Sexual Arrangements and Human Malaise* (New York: Harper and Row, 1976).

Dreyfus, Ella, *The Body Pregnant* (Sydney: McPhee-Gribble, 1993).

Duchen, Clare, *Feminism in France: From May '68 to Mitterand* (London: Routledge and Kegan Paul, 1986).

Du Plessis, Rachel, "Eurydice" in *Wells* (New York: Montemora Foundation, 1980, pp. 319–20).

Farrell, Michèle Longino, *Performing Motherhood: The Sévigné Correspondence* (Hanover, NH: University Press of New England, 1991).

Felman, Shoshana, *Jacques Lacan and the Adventure of Insight: Psychoanalysis in Contemporary Culture* (Cambridge, MA: Harvard University Press, 1987).

Féral, Josette, "Antigone or the Irony of the Tribe", trans. Alice Jardine and Tom Gora, *Diacritics* 8(3) 1978, pp. 2–14.

Foucault, Michel, *The Order of Things: An Archaeology of the Human Sciences* (New York: Random House, 1973). Originally published as *Les Mots et les choses* (Paris: Gallimard, 1966).

—— *The Use of Pleasure: The History of Sexuality Volume 2*, trans R. Hurley (New York: Random House, 1985). Originally published as *L'Usage des plaisirs* (Paris: Gallimard, 1984).

Fraser, Nancy, "On the Political and the Symbolic: Against the Metaphysics of Textuality", *Enclitic* 9(1–2) 1987, pp. 100–14.

—— "The Uses and Abuses of French Discourse Theories for Feminist Politics" in *Revaluing French Feminism: Critical Essays on Difference, Agency, and Culture*, Nancy Fraser and Sandra Lee Bartky eds (Bloomington: Indiana University Press, 1992, pp. 177–94).

Freud, Sigmund, *The Interpretation of Dreams* (1900), trans. James Strachey (New York: Avon Books, 1965).

—— "Three Essays on the Theory of Sexuality: No. 1 The Sexual Aberrations" (1905) in *The Standard Edition of the Complete Psychological Works* Vol. VII, James Strachey ed. (London: Hogarth Press, 1953, pp. 135–72).

—— "Psycho-analytic Notes upon an Autobiographical Account of a Case of Paranoia (Dementia Paranoides)" (1911) in *The Standard Edition of the Complete Psychological Works* Vol XII, James Strachey ed. (London: Hogarth Press, 1958, pp. 9–83).

—— *Totem and Taboo* (1912–13), trans. James Strachey (London: Routledge and Kegan Paul, 1950).

—— "Remembering, Repeating and Working Through" (1914) in *The Standard Edition of the Complete Psychological Works* Vol. XII, James Strachey ed. (London: Hogarth Press, 1958, pp. 147–55).

—— "Mourning and Melancholia" (1917) in *Collected Papers Vol. IV*, Ernest Jones ed. (London: Hogarth Press, 1949, pp. 152–70).

—— "From the History of an Infantile Neurosis" (1918 [1914]) in *Three Case Histories* (New York: Collier, 1963, pp. 187–316).

—— "The 'Uncanny' " (1919) in *Collected Papers Vol. IV*, Ernest Jones ed. (London: Hogarth Press, 1949, pp. 368–405).

—— *Beyond the Pleasure Principle* (1920) trans. James Strachey (London: W.W. Norton, 1961). Also published in *The Standard Edition of the Complete Psychological Works* Vol. XVIII, James Strachey ed. (London: Hogarth Press, 1955, pp. 3–64).

—— "Neurosis and Psychosis" (1924 [1923]) in *The Standard Edition of the Complete Psychological Works* Vol. XIX, trans. James Strachey (London: Hogarth Press, 1961, pp. 149–53).

—— "Negation" (1925) in *The Standard Edition of the Complete Psychological Works* Vol. XIX, James Strachey ed. (London: Hogarth Press, 1961, pp. 235–42).

Friedman, Ellen, "Where are the Missing Contents? (Post)Modernism, Gender, and the Canon", *PMLA* 108(2) March 1993, pp. 240–52.

Fromm, Erich, *Man For Himself: An Enquiry into the Psychology of Ethics* (London: Routledge and Kegan Paul, 1949).

—— *Marx's Concept of Man* (New York: Frederick Unger, 1966).

Fuss, Diana J., " 'Essentially Speaking': Luce Irigaray's Language of Essence", *Hypatia* 3(3) 1989, reprinted in *Revaluing French Feminism: Critical Essays on Difference, Agency, and Culture*, Nancy Fraser and Sandra Bartky eds (Bloomington: Indiana University Press, 1992, pp. 94–112).

Gallop, Jane, *Feminism and Psychoanalysis: The Daughter's Seduction* (London: Macmillan, 1982).

—— "Quand nos lèvres s'écrivent: Irigaray's Body Politic", *Romanic Review* 74(1) 1983, pp. 77–83.

—— *Reading Lacan* (Ithaca, NY: Cornell University Press, 1985).

—— *Thinking Through the Body* (New York: Columbia University Press, 1988).

—— "The Teacher's Breasts" in *Jane Gallop Seminar Papers*, Jill Julius Matthews ed. (Canberra: Humanities Research Centre, Australian National University, 1994, pp. 1–12).

Gardiner, Judith Kegan, "The New Motherhood", *North American Review* 263(2) 1978, pp. 72–6.

—— "Mind Mother: Psychoanalysis and Feminism", in *Making a Difference: Feminist Literary Criticism*, G. Greene and C. Kahn eds (London: Methuen, 1985, pp. 113–45).

Gatens, Moira, "Feminism, Philosophy and Riddles without Answers" in *Feminist Challenges: Social and Political Theory*, Carole Pateman and Elizabeth Gross eds (Sydney: Allen and Unwin, 1986).

Gross, Elizabeth, *Irigaray and the Divine* (Sydney: Local Consumption Publications, 1986).

Grosskurth, Phyllis, *Melanie Klein: Her World and her Work* (Toronto: McClelland and Stewart, 1986).

Grosz, Elizabeth, *Sexual Subversions: Three French Feminists* (Sydney: Allen and Unwin, 1989).

—— *Jacques Lacan: A Feminist Introduction* (Sydney: Allen and Unwin, 1990).

—— "The Body of Signification" in *Abjection, Melancholia and Love: The Work of Julia*

Kristeva, John Fletcher and Andrew Benjamin eds (London: Routledge, 1990, pp. 80–103).

—— "Lived Spatiality: Insect Space/Virtual Sex", *Agenda: Contemporary Art Magazine* 26/27 1992–3, pp. 5–8.

Gubar, Susan, "Mother, Maiden and the Marriage of Death: Women Writers and an Ancient Myth", *Women's Studies* 6 1979, pp. 301–15.

Guerlec, Suzanne, "Transgression in Theory: Genius and the Subject of *La Révolution du langage poétique*" in *Ethics, Politics, and Difference in Julia Kristeva's Writing*, Kelly Oliver ed. (New York: Routledge, 1993, pp. 215–37).

Hegel, G.W.F., *Phenomenology of Spirit* (1807), trans. A.V. Miller (Oxford: Oxford University Press, 1977).

Hirsch, Marianne, "Mothers and Daughters", *Signs* 7(1) 1981, pp. 200–22.

—— "A Mother's Discourse: Incorporation and Repetition in *La Princesse de Clèves*", *Yale French Studies* 62 1981, pp. 67–87.

—— "Maternal Anger: Silent Themes and 'Meaningful Digression' in Psychoanalytic Feminism", *the minnesota review* 29 (Winter) 1987, pp. 81–7.

—— *The Mother–Daughter Plot: Narrative, Psychoanalysis, Feminism* (Bloomington: Indiana University Press, 1989).

Hubert, Renée Riese, "Gender, Genre, and Partnership: A Study of Valentine Penrose" in *The Other Perspective in Gender and Culture: Rewriting Women and the Symbolic*, Juliet Flower MacCannell ed. (New York: Columbia University Press, 1990, pp. 117–42).

Hunter, Dianne, "Hysteria, Psychoanalysis, Feminism in the Case of Anna O", *Feminist Studies* 9(3) 1983, pp. 465–86.

Irigaray, Luce, *Speculum of the Other Woman*, trans. Gillian C. Gill (Ithaca, NY: Cornell University Press, 1985). Originally published as *Speculum de l'autre femme* (Paris: Minuit, 1974).

—— "Women's Exile", trans. C. Venn, *Ideology and Consciousness* 1 (Spring) 1977, pp. 62–76.

—— *This Sex Which Is Not One*, trans. Catherine Porter (Ithaca, NY: Cornell University Press, 1985). Originally published as *Le Sexe qui n'en est pas un* (Paris: Minuit, 1977).

—— *Marine Lover of Friedrich Nietzsche*, trans. Gillian C. Gill (New York: Columbia University Press, 1991). Originally published as *Amante marine, de Friedrich Nietzsche* (Paris: Minuit, 1980).

—— "And the One Doesn't Stir Without the Other", trans. H.V. Wenzel, *Signs* 7(1) 1981, pp. 60–7.

—— "The Bodily Encounter with the Mother", trans. David Macey, in *The Irigaray Reader*, Margaret Whitford ed. (Oxford: Basil Blackwell, 1991, pp. 34–46). Originally published in *Le Corps-à-corps avec la mère* (Montreal: Editions de la pleine lune, 1981).

—— "Women-Mothers, the Silent Substratum of the Social Order", trans. David Macey in *The Irigaray Reader*, Margaret Whitford ed. (Oxford: Basil Blackwell, 1991, pp. 47–52). Originally published as "Les Femmes-mères, ce sous-sol muet de l'ordre social" in *Le Corps-à-corps avec la mère* (Montreal: Editions de la pleine lune, 1981).

—— "He Risks Who Risks Life Itself", trans. David Macey in *The Irigaray Reader*, Margaret Whitford ed. (Oxford: Basil Blackwell, 1991, pp. 213–18). Originally published in *L'Oubli de l'air chez Martin Heidegger* (Paris: Minuit, 1983).

—— "The Fecundity of the Caress", trans. Carolyn Burke in *Face to Face with Levinas*, R.A. Cohen ed. (Albany, NY: SUNY Press, 1986, pp. 231–56). Originally published as

"Fecondité de la caresse," in *Ethique de la différence sexuelle* (Paris: Minuit, 1984, pp. 173–99).

—— "Sexual Difference" in *The Irigaray Reader*, Margaret Whitford ed. (Oxford: Basil Blackwell, 1991, pp. 165–77). Originally published in *Ethique de la différence sexuelle* (Paris: Minuit, 1984).

—— "Sorcerer Love: A Reading of Plato's *Symposium*, Diotima's Speech", trans. Eleanor H. Kuykendall in *Revaluing French Feminism: Critical Essays on Difference, Agency, and Culture*, Nancy Fraser and Sandra Bartky eds (Bloomington: Indiana University Press, 1992, pp. 64–76). Originally published as "L'Amour sorcier: lecture de Platon, *Le Banquet*, discours de Diotime" in *Ethique de la différence sexuelle* (Paris: Minuit, 1984).

—— *Divine Women*, trans. Stephen Muecke (Sydney: Local Consumption Publications, 1986). Originally published as "Femmes divines", *Critique* 454 1985.

—— "The Limits of the Transference", trans. D. Macey and M. Whitford in *The Irigaray Reader*, Margaret Whitford ed. (Oxford: Basil Blackwell, 1991, pp. 105–17). Originally published as "La Limite du transfert", *Etudes freudiennes* 19–20 1982; reprinted in *Parler n'est jamais neutre* (Paris: Minuit, 1985).

—— "Women, the Sacred and Money", trans. Diana Knight and Margaret Whitford; *Paragraph* 8 (October) 1986, pp. 6–18.

—— "The Gesture in Psychoanalysis" in *Between Feminism and Psychoanalysis*, Teresa Brennan ed. (London: Routledge, 1989, pp. 127–38). Originally published as "Le geste en psychanalyse" in *Sexes et parentés* (Paris: Minuit, 1987).

—— "The Three *Genres*", in *The Irigaray Reader*, Margaret Whitford ed. (Oxford: Basil Blackwell, 1991, pp. 140–53). Originally published in *Sexes et parentés* (Paris: Minuit, 1987).

—— *Je, tu, nous: Toward a Culture of Difference*, trans. Alison Martin (London: Routledge, 1993). Originally published as *Je, tu, nous* (Paris: Grasset and Fasquelle, 1990).

—— *Elemental Passions*, trans. Joanne Collie and Judith Still (New York, Routledge, 1992).

—— "Body Against Body: In Relation to the Mother" in *Sexes and Genealogies*, trans. Gillian C. Gill (New York: Columbia University Press, 1993, pp. 7–21).

—— *I Love To You: Sketch of a Possible Felicity in History*, trans. Alison Martin (London and New York: Routledge, 1996).

Jacobus, Mary, *Reading Woman: Essays in Feminist Criticism* (New York: Columbia University Press, 1986).

Jaggar, Alison and William McBride, " 'Reproduction' as Male Ideology" in *Hypatia Reborn: Essays in Feminist Philosophy* Azizah Y. Al-Hibri and Margaret A. Simons eds (Bloomington: Indiana University Press, 1990, pp. 249–69).

Jakobson, Roman, "Two Aspects of Language and Two Types of Aphasic Disturbances" in *Fundamentals of Language*, R. Jakobson and M. Halle, (The Hague: Mouton, 1956, pp. 69–96).

Jameson, Fredric, *The Political Unconscious: Narrative as a Socially Symbolic Act* (Ithaca, NY: Cornell University Press, 1981).

—— "Imaginary and Symbolic in Lacan: Marxism, Psychoanalytic Criticism, and the Problem of the Subject" in *Literature and Psychoanalysis: The Question of Reading Otherwise*, Shoshana Felman ed. (Baltimore, MD: Johns Hopkins University Press, 1982, pp. 338–95).

Jardine, Alice A., "Theories of the Feminine: Kristeva", *Enclitic* 4(2) 1980, pp. 5–15.

—— "Pre-texts for the Transatlantic Feminist", *Yale French Studies* 62 1981, pp. 220–36.

—— "Introduction to Julia Kristeva's 'Women's Time' ", *Signs* 7(1) 1981, pp. 5–12.

—— *Gynesis: Configurations of Woman and Modernity* (Ithaca, NY: Cornell University Press, 1985).

—— "Opaque Texts and Transparent Contexts: The Political Difference of Julia Kristeva", in *The Poetics of Gender*, Nancy Miller ed. (New York: Columbia University Press, 1986, pp. 96–116). An abridged version appears in *Ethics, Politics, and Difference in Julia Kristeva's Writing*, Kelly Oliver ed. (New York: Routledge, 1993, pp. 23–31).

Johnson, Barbara, "Mallarmé as Mother" and "My Monster/My Self" in *A World of Difference* (Baltimore, MD: Johns Hopkins University Press, 1987, pp. 137–43, 144–54).

Jones, Ann Rosalind, "Julia Kristeva on Femininity: The Limits of a Semiotic Politics", *Feminist Review* 18, 1984, pp. 56–74.

Jost, Alfred, "Le Développement sexual prénatal" in *Le Fait féminin* (Paris: Fayard, 1978).

Kaplan, E. Ann, "Motherhood and Representation: From Post World War II Freudian Figurations to Postmodernism", *the minnesota review* 29 (Winter) 1987, pp. 88–102.

Kierkegaard, Søren, *Repetition: An Essay in Experimental Psychology*, trans. Walter Lowrie (New York: Harper and Row, 1964).

Klein, Melanie, "The Importance of Symbol Formation in the Development of the Ego", *International Journal of Psycho-Analysis* 11, 1930. Reprinted in *Love, Guilt and Reparation: and Other Works, 1921–1945* (London: Hogarth Press, 1975; New York; Delacorte Press, 1975, pp. 219–32).

—— *The Psychoanalysis of Children* (London: Hogarth Press, 1932).

—— *Love, Guilt and Reparation, and Other Works, 1921–1945* (London: Hogarth Press, 1975; New York: Delacorte Press, 1975).

—— "Contribution to the Psycho-genesis of Manic-Depressive States (1935)" in *Contributions to Psycho-Analysis, 1921–45* (London: Hogarth Press, 1948). Reprinted in *Love, Guilt and Reparation*, pp. 262–89.

—— "Mourning and its Relationship to Manic-Depressive States (1940)" in *Contributions to Psychoanalysis*. Reprinted in *Love, Guilt and Reparation*, pp. 344–69.

—— *Envy and Gratitude: and Other Works, 1946–1963* (London: Tavistock, 1957; New York: Delacorte Press, 1975).

—— "Notes on some Schizoid Mechanisms (1946)", *International Journal of Psycho-Analysis* 27, 1946. Also in *Developments in Psycho-Analysis*, with P. Heimann, S. Isaacs and J. Rivière, Joan Rivière ed. (London: Hogarth Press, 1952). Reprinted in *Envy and Gratitude*, pp. 1–24.

—— "On Identification" in *New Directions in Psycho-Analysis* with P. Heimann, R. Money-Kyrle, *et al.* (London: Tavistock, 1955). Reprinted in *Envy and Gratitude*, pp. 141–75.

Kojève, Alexandre, *Introduction to the Reading of Hegel*, trans. James Nichols (New York: Basic Books, 1969, p. 25). Originally published as *Introduction à la lecture de Hegel*, R. Queneau ed. (Paris: 1947).

Kristeva, Julia, "Phonetics, Phonology and Impusional Bases", trans. Caren Greenberg, *Diacritics* 4(3) 1974, pp. 33–7.

—— *About Chinese Women*, trans. A. Barrows (London: Marion Boyars, 1977). Originally published as *Des Chinoises* (Paris: des femmes, 1974).

—— *Revolution in Poetic Language*, trans. Margaret Waller (New York: Columbia University Press, 1984). Originally published as *La Révolution du langage poétique* (Paris: Seuil, 1974).

—— "The System and the Speaking Subject", in *The Tell-Tail Sign: A Survey of Semiotics*, T.A. Sebeok ed. (Lisse, Netherlands: Peter De Ridder Press, 1975, pp. 47–55).

—— "China, Women and the Symbolic", Interview with Josette Féral, *Sub-Stance* 13 1976, pp. 9–18.

—— "Stabat Mater", trans. Arthur Goldhammer in *The Female Body in Western Culture: Contemporary Perspectives*, Susan Rubin Suleiman ed. (Cambridge, MA: Harvard University Press, 1986, pp. 99–118). Also in *Tales of Love* trans. Leon S. Roudiez (New York: Columbia University Press, 1987, pp. 234–63). Originally published as *Histoires d'amour* (Paris: Denoel, 1983). "Stabat Mater" first published in "Héréthique de l'amour", *Tel Quel* 74 (Winter) 1977.

—— "Oscillation Between Power and Denial", Interview with Xavière Gauthier, trans. M.A. August in *New French Feminisms: An Anthology*, Elaine Marks and Isabelle de Courtivron eds (Cambridge, MA: University of Massachusetts Press, 1980, pp. 165–7).

—— "Woman Can Never Be Defined", Interview with "Psych et Po", trans. M.A. August in *New French Feminisms: An Anthology*, Elaine Marks and Isabelle de Courtivron eds. (Cambridge, MA: University of Massachusetts Press, 1980, pp. 137–41).

—— *Powers of Horror: An Essay on Abjection*, trans. Leon S. Roudiez (New York: Columbia University Press, 1982). Originally published as *Pouvoirs de l'horreur* (Paris: Seuil, 1980).

—— *Desire in Language: A Semiotic Approach to Literature and Art*, trans. Thomas Gora, Alice Jardine and Leon S. Roudiez (New York: Columbia University Press, 1980). Extracts from *Polylogue* (Paris: Seuil, 1977) and *Recherches pour une sémanalyse* (Paris: Seuil, 1969).

—— "Women's Time", trans. Alice Jardine and Harry Blake, *Signs* 7(1) 1981, pp. 13–35.

—— "Psychoanalysis and the Polis", trans. Margaret Waller in *The Politics of Interpretation*, W.J.T. Mitchell ed. (Chicago: University of Chicago Press, 1983, pp.83–98).

—— "Semiotics: A Critical Science and/or a Critique of Science", trans. Sean Hand in *The Kristeva Reader*, Toril Moi ed. (New York: Columbia University Press, 1986, pp. 74–88).

—— "A New Type of Intellectual: The Dissident" in *The Kristeva Reader*, Toril Moi ed. (New York: Columbia University Press, 1986, pp. 292–300).

—— "Psychoanalysis and Language" in *Language: The Unknown: An Initiation into Linguistics*, trans. Anne M. Menke (New York: Columbia University Press, 1989, pp. 265–77).

Kroker, Arthur, "Baudrillard's Marx" in *The Postmodern Scene: Excremental Culture and Hyper Aesthetics*, Arthur Kroker and David Cook (New York: St Martin's Press, 1986, pp. 170–88).

Lacan, Jacques, *Encore: Le séminaire XX, 1972–3* (Paris: Seuil, 1975).

—— "On a Question Preliminary to any Possible Treatment of Psychosis" in *Ecrits: A Selection* trans. Alan Sheridan (New York: W W. Norton, 1977, pp. 179–225).

—— "The Subversion of the Subject and the Dialectic of Desire in the Freudian Unconscious" in *Ecrits: A Selection*, trans. Alan Sheridan (New York: W.W. Norton and Co., 1977, pp. 292–325).

—— "The Mirror Stage as Formative of the Function of the I as Revealed in Psychoanalytic Experience" in *Ecrits: A Selection*, trans. Alan Sheridan (New York: W.W. Norton, 1977, pp. 1–7).

—— "Aggressivity in Psychoanalysis" in *Ecrits: A Selection*, trans. Alan Sheridan (New York: W.W. Norton, 1977, pp. 8–29).

—— "The Agency of the Letter in the Unconscious or Reason since Freud" in *Ecrits: A Selection*, trans. Alan Sheridan (New York: W.W. Norton, 1977, pp. 146–78).

Laclau, Ernesto and Chantal Mouffe, *Hegemony and Socialist Strategy: Towards a Radical Democratic Politics* (London: Verso, 1985).

Lafargue, Paul, *The Right to Be Lazy*, trans. C. Kerr (Chicago: Kerr, 1917).

Le Doeuff, Michèle, "Women and Philosophy", trans. D. Pope, *Radical Philosophy* 17 (Summer) 1977, pp. 2–11.

—— "Operative Philosophy: Simone de Beauvoir and Existentialism", *Ideology and Consciousness* 6 (Autumn) 1979, pp. 47–57.

—— *The Philosophical Imaginary*, trans. Colin Gordon (Stanford, CA: Stanford University Press, 1989). Originally published as *L'Imaginaire philosophique* (Paris: Payot, 1980).

—— "Ants and Women, or Philosophy without Borders" in *Contemporary French Philosophy*, A. Phillips Griffiths ed. (Cambridge: Cambridge University Press, 1987, pp. 41–54).

—— *Hipparchia's Choice: An Essay Concerning Women, Philosophy, Etc.* trans. Trista Selous (Oxford: Basil Blackwell, 1991). Originally published as *L'Etude et le rouet* (Paris: Seuil, 1989).

—— "Women, Reason, Etc.", *differences: A Journal of Feminist Cultural Studies* 2(3) 1990, pp. 1–13.

Leiss, William, *The Domination of Nature* (New York: George Braziller, 1972).

Lemaire, Anika, *Jacques Lacan* (London: Routledge and Kegan Paul, 1977).

Levin, David Michael, "The Body Politic: Political Economy and the Human Body", *Human Studies* 8(4) 1985, pp. 235–78.

Lewis, Ann, *An Interesting Condition* (Garden City, NY: Doubleday, 1950).

Lewis, Philip E., "Revolutionary Semiotics", *Diacritics* 4(3) 1974, pp. 28–32.

Lloyd, Genevieve, *The Man of Reason: "Male" and "Female" in Western Philosophy* (London: Methuen, 1984).

Lyotard, Jean-François, *Libidinal Economy*, trans. Iain Hamilton Grant (Bloomington: Indiana University Press, 1993). Originally published as *Economie Libidinale* (Paris: Minuit, 1974).

—— "One of the Things at Stake in Women's Struggles", trans. D.J. Clarke, W. Woodhill and J. Mowitt, reprinted in *The Lyotard Reader*, Andrew Benjamin ed. (Oxford: Basil Blackwell, 1991, pp. 111–21). Originally published in *Sub-Stance* 20 1978, pp. 9–17.

—— *The Postmodern Condition: A Report on Knowledge*, trans. Geoff Bennington and Brian Massumi, Theory and History of Literature Series, Vol. 10 (Minneapolis: University of Minnesota Press, 1984). Originally published as *La Condition postmoderne: rapport sur le savoir* (Paris: Minuit, 1979).

—— "Theory as Art: A Pragmatic Point of View" in *Image and Code*, Wendy Steiner ed. (Ann Arbor: University of Michigan Press, 1981).

—— "Analysing Speculative Discourse as Language-Game", trans. Geoffrey Bennington, in *The Lyotard Reader*, Andrew Benjamin ed. (Oxford: Basil Blackwell, 1991, pp. 265–74). Originally published in English in *The Oxford Literary Review* 4(3) 1981, pp. 59–67.

—— "The Dream-Work Does Not Think", trans. Mary Lydon in *The Lyotard Reader*, Andrew Benjamin ed. (Oxford: Basil Blackwell, 1991, pp. 19–55). Originally published in *The Oxford Literary Review* 6(1) 1983, pp. 3–34.

—— *The Différend: Phrases in Dispute*, trans. Georges Van Den Abbeele (Minneapolis: University of Minnesota Press, 1988). Originally published as *Le Différend* (Paris: Minuit, 1983).

—— "Interview" with Georges Van Den Abbeele, *Diacritics* 14(3) 1984, pp. 16–21.

—— *Peregrinations: Law, Form, Event,* (New York: Columbia University Press, 1988).

—— "Sensus Communis", trans. Marion Hobson and Geoff Bennington, in *Judging Lyotard*, Andrew Benjamin ed. (London: Routledge, 1992, pp. 1–25). Originally published in *Paragraph* 11(1) 1988, pp. 1–23.

—— "An Interview with Jean-François Lyotard", Willem van Reijen and Dick Veerman, *Theory, Culture and Society* 5 1988, pp. 277–309.

—— "Can Thought Go On Without a Body" and "Representation, Presentation,

Unpresentable" in *The Inhuman: Reflections on Time*, trans. Geoffrey Bennington and Rachel Bowlby (Cambridge: Polity Press, 1991, pp. 8–23, 119–28).

Lyotard, Jean-François and Jean-Loup Thébaud, *Just Gaming*, trans. Wlad Godzich, Theory and History of Literature Series, Vol. 20 (Minneapolis: University of Minnesota Press, 1985). Originally published as *Au Juste* (Paris: Christian Bourgois, 1979).

Macalpine, Ida and Richard A. Hunter, "Observations on the Psychoanalytic Theory of Psychosis", *British Journal of Medical Psychology* 27 1954, pp. 175–95.

McAuliffe, Chris, "Jean Baudrillard" in *The Judgement of Paris: Recent French Theory in a Local Context*, Kevin Murray ed. (Sydney: Allen and Unwin, 1992, pp. 97–111).

MacCannell, Juliet Flower, "Kristeva's Horror", *Semiotica* 62(3–4) 1986, pp. 325–55.

—— ed., *The Other Perspective in Gender and Culture: Rewriting Women and the Symbolic* (New York: Columbia University Press, 1990).

MacKinnon, Catherine A., "Does Sexuality Have a History?" *Michigan Quarterly Review* XXXL(1) 1991, pp. 1–11.

Mao Tse-Tung, "On Practice" in *Four Essays On Philosophy* (Peking: Foreign Language Press, 1968, pp. 1–22).

Marcuse, Herbert, *Eros and Civilization* (New York: Vintage, 1962).

Marks, Elaine and Isabelle de Courtivron, *New French Feminisms: An Anthology* (Cambridge, MA: University of Massachusetts Press, 1980).

Marx, Karl, *Economic and Philosophic Manuscripts of 1844*, in *Early Writings*, T.B. Bottomore ed. (London: Lawrence and Wishart, 1959).

—— *Writings of the Young Marx on Philosophy and Society*, Loyd D. Easton and Kurt H. Guddat eds (New York: Anchor, 1962).

—— *Grundrisse: Foundations of the Critique of Political Economy*, trans. M. Nicolaus (New York: Penguin, 1973).

—— *Capital* Vol. I (New York: International Publishers, 1975). *Capital* Vol. III (Moscow: Foreign Languages Publishing House, n.d.; Harmondsworth: Penguin, 1981).

Marx, Karl and Frederick Engels, *The German Ideology* (Moscow: Progress Publishers, 1976).

Miller, J. Hillis, *Fiction and Repetition: Seven English Novels* (Oxford: Basil Blackwell, 1982).

Miller, Nancy ed., *The Poetics of Gender* (New York: Columbia University Press, 1986).

Mitchell, Juliet, *Women's Estate* (Harmondsworth: Penguin, 1971).

—— *Psychoanalysis and Feminism* (London: Allen Lane, 1974).

Mitchell, Juliet and Jacqueline Rose, eds, *Feminine Sexuality: Jacques Lacan and the École Freudienne* (London: Macmillan, 1982).

Moi, Toril ed., *The Kristeva Reader* (New York: Columbia University Press, 1986).

Morris, Meaghan, *The Pirate's Fiancée: Feminism/Reading/Postmodernism* (London: Verso, 1988).

Mortley, Raoul, *French Philosophers in Conversation* (London: Routledge, 1991).

Muller, John P. and William J. Richardson, *Lacan and Language: A Reader's Guide to Ecrits* (New York: International Universities Press, 1982).

Murray, Kevin ed., *The Judgement of Paris: Recent French Theory in a Local Context* (Sydney: Allen and Unwin, 1992).

Nicholson, Linda, "Feminism and Marx: Integrating Kinship with the Economic" in *Feminism as Critique: On the Politics of Gender*, Seyla Benhabib and Drucilla Cornell eds (Minneapolis: University of Minnesota Press, 1986, pp. 16–30).

Nye, Andrea, "The Hidden Host: Irigaray and Diotima at Plato's *Symposium*", in *Revaluing French Feminism: Critical Essays on Difference, Agency, and Culture*, Nancy Fraser and Sandra Bartky eds (Bloomington: Indiana University Press, 1992, pp. 77–93). Originally published in *Hypatia* 3(3) 1989.

O'Brien, Mary, *The Politics of Reproduction* (London: Routledge and Kegan Paul, 1981).

Oliver, Kelly, "Kristeva's Imaginary Father and the Crisis in the Paternal Function", *Diacritics* 21(2–3) 1991, pp. 43–63.

—— *Reading Kristeva: Unraveling the Double-bind* (Bloomington: Indiana University Press, 1993).

—— ed., *Ethics, Politics, and Difference in Julia Kristeva's Writing* (New York: Routledge, 1993).

Ostriker, Alice, "The Thieves of Language: Women Poets and Revisionist Mythmaking" in *The New Feminist Criticisms: Essays on Women, Literature and Theory*, Elaine Showalter ed. (London: Virago, 1986, pp. 314–38).

—— *Stealing the Language: The Emergence of Women's Poetry in America* (Boston, MA: Beacon Press, 1986).

Panofsky, Erwin, *Idea: A Concept in Art Theory*, trans. Joseph J.S. Peake (Columbia, SC: University of South Carolina Press, 1968).

Paul, Diana Y., *Women in Buddhism: Images of the Feminine in Mahāyāna Tradition* (Berkeley, CA: Asian Humanities Press, 1979).

Pefanis, Julian, "Jean-François Lyotard" in *The Judgment of Paris: Recent French Theory in a Local Context*, Kevin Murray ed. (Sydney: Allen and Unwin, 1992, pp. 113–30).

Pierce, Jennifer L., "The Relation between Emotion Work and Hysteria: A Feminist Reinterpretation of Freud's Studies on Hysteria", *Women's Studies* 16 1989, pp. 255–70.

Plato, *The Symposium*, trans. Walter Hamilton (London: Penguin, 1951).

—— *Phaedrus and Letters VII and VIII*, trans. Walter Hamilton (London: Penguin, 1973).

—— *The Republic*, trans. G.M.A. Grube (London: Pan, 1974).

Plaza, Monique, "The Mother/The Same: The Hatred of the Mother in Psychoanalysis", *Feminist Issues* 2(3) 1982, pp. 75–99.

—— "Ideology Against Women", *Feminist Issues* 4(1) 1984, pp. 73–82.

Powrie, Phil, "A Womb of One's Own: The Metaphor of the Womb-room as a Reading-effect in Texts by Contemporary French Women Writers", *Paragraph* 12(3) 1989, pp. 197–213.

Rajan, Tilottama, "Trans-Positions of Difference: Kristeva and Poststructuralism" in *Ethics, Politics, and Difference in Julia Kristeva's Writing*, Kelly Oliver ed. (New York: Routledge, 1993, pp. 215–37).

Ramazani, Jahan, " 'Daddy, I Have Had to Kill You': Plath, Rage, and the Modern Elegy", *PLMA* 108(5) 1993, pp. 1142–56.

Readings, Bill, *Introducing Lyotard: Art and Politics* (London: Routledge, 1991).

Rich, Adrienne, *Of Woman Born: Motherhood as Experience and Institution* (London: Virago, 1979).

Roudinesco, Elisabeth, *Jacques Lacan and Co: A History of Psychoanalysis in France, 1925–1985*, trans. Jeffrey Mehlman (Chicago: University of Chicago Press, 1990). Originally published in two volumes as *La Bataille de cent ans* (Paris: Ramsay, 1982; Seuil, 1986).

Roustang, François, *Dire Mastery: Discipleship from Freud to Lacan*, trans. Ned Lukacher (Baltimore, MD: Johns Hopkins University Press, 1982).

Salleh, Ariel Kay, "On the Dialectics of Signifying Practice", *Thesis Eleven* 5/6 1982, pp. 72–84.

—— "Contribution to the Critique of Political Epistemology", *Thesis Eleven* 8 1984, pp. 23–43.

Sartre, Jean-Paul, "Existentialism is a Humanism", trans. Philip Mairet in *Existentialism from Dostoevsky to Sartre*, Walter Kauffmann ed. (Cleveland, OH: Meridian, 1956, pp. 287–311).

Scarry, Elaine, *The Body in Pain: The Making and Unmaking of the World* (Oxford: Oxford University Press, 1985).

Schreber, Daniel Paul, *Memoirs of My Nervous Illness*, trans. and ed. Ida Macalpine and Richard A. Hunter (London: W.M. Dawson and Sons, 1955).

Segal, Hanna, *Introduction to the Work of Melanie Klein* (London: Hogarth Press, 1982).

Shiach, Morag, "Their 'Symbolic' Exists, It Holds Power – We, the Sowers of Disorder, Know It Only Too Well", in *Between Feminism and Psychoanalysis*, Teresa Brennan ed. (London: Routledge, 1989, pp. 153–67).

Silverman, Kaja, *The Subject of Semiotics* (Oxford: Oxford University Press, 1983).

—— "Histoire d'O: The Story of a Disciplined and Punished Body", *Enclitic* 7(2) 1983, pp. 63–81.

Singer, Alan, "Desire's Desire: Toward an Historical Formalism", *Enclitic* 8(1–2) 1984, pp. 57–67.

Smith, Barry, "Textual Difference", *American Philosophical Quarterly* 28(1) 1991, pp. 1–12.

Smith, Grafton Elliot, *The Evolution of the Dragon* (Manchester: Manchester University Press, 1919).

Spanos, William V., "Overture in the Recursive Mode" in *Repetitions: The Postmodern Occasion in Literature and Culture* (Baton Rouge: Louisiana State University Press, 1987, pp. 1–12).

Spelman, Elizabeth V., *Inessential Woman: Problems of Exclusion in Feminist Thought* (London: The Women's Press, 1988).

Sprengnether, Madelon, *The Spectral Mother: Freud, Feminism, and Psychoanalysis* (Ithaca, NY: Cornell University Press).

Stanton, Domna, "Difference on Trial: A Critique of The Maternal Metaphor in Cixous, Irigaray and Kristeva" in *The Poetics of Gender*, Nancy K. Miller ed. (New York: Columbia University Press, 1986, pp. 157–82).

Steiner, George, *Language and Silence: Essays on Language, Literature, and the Inhuman* (New York: Atheneum, 1974).

Sturrock, John, "The Paris Strangler", review of *"L'Avenir dure longtemps" suivi de "Les Faits": Autobiographies* in *London Review of Books* 17 December 1992, pp. 6–7.

Suleiman, Susan Rubin, "Writing and Motherhood" in *The (M)other Tongue: Essays in Feminist Psychoanalytic Interpretation*, S. Nelson Garner, C. Kahane and M. Sprengnether eds (Ithaca, NY: Cornell University Press, 1985, pp. 352–77).

—— "Pornography, Transgression, and the Avant-Garde: Bataille's *Story of the Eye*" in *The Poetics of Gender*, Nancy Miller ed. (New York: Columbia University Press, 1986, pp. 117–36).

—— ed. *The Female Body in Western Culture* (Cambridge, MA: Harvard University Press, 1986).

—— *Subversive Intent: Gender, Politics, and the Avant-Garde* (Cambridge, MA: Harvard University Press, 1990).

Thom, Martin, "The Unconscious Structured as a Language" and "Verneinung, Verwerfung, Ausstossung: A Problem in the Interpretation of Freud" in *The Talking Cure: Essays in Psychoanalysis and Language*, Colin MacCabe ed. (New York: St Martin's Press, 1981, pp. 1–44, 162–87).

Valente, Joesph, "Hall of Mirrors: Baudrillard on Marx", *Diacritics* 15(2) 1985, pp. 54–65.

Vickers, Nancy, "The Mistress in the Masterpiece", in *The Poetics of Gender*, Nancy Miller ed. (New York: Columbia University Press, 1986, pp. 19–41).

Walker, Alice, *In Search of Our Mother's Gardens* (New York: Harcourt Brace Jovanovich, 1983).

Walker, Michelle, "Reproduction: Feminist Footnote to Marxist Text?", *Arena* 77 1986, pp. 155–66.

—— "Reason, Identity and the Body: Reading Adorno with Irigaray" in *Reason and its Other: Rationality in Modern German Philosophy and Culture*, Dieter Freundlieb and Wayne Hudson eds (Oxford: Berg, 1993, pp. 199–216).

—— "The Aesthetics of Detail" in *Aesthetics after Historicism*, Wayne Hudson ed. (Brisbane: Institute of Modern Art, 1993, pp. 79–91).

—— "Silence and Reason: Woman's Voice in Philosophy", *Australasian Journal of Philosophy* 71(4) 1993, pp. 400–24.

—— "Unsettling Terrain: Mark Davies and the Problem of (Maternal) Space", unpublished MS.

Warner, Marina, *Alone of All her Sex: The Myth and the Cult of the Virgin Mary* (New York: Vintage, 1976).

Weir, Allison, "Identification with the Divided Mother: Kristeva's Ambivalence" in *Ethics, Politics, and Difference in Julia Kristeva's Writing*, Kelly Oliver ed. (New York: Routledge, 1993, pp. 79–91).

Whitebook, Joel, "Saving the Subject: Modernity and the Problem of the Autonomous Individual", *Telos* 50 (Winter) 1981–2, pp. 79–102.

Whitford, Margaret, *Luce Irigaray: Philosophy in the Feminine* (London: Routledge, 1991).

—— ed., *The Irigaray Reader* (Oxford: Basil Blackwell, 1991).

Winnett, Susan, "Coming Unstrung: Women, Men, Narrative, and Principles of Pleasure", *PMLA* 105(3) 1990, pp. 505–18.

Winnicott, D.W., *The Family and Individual Development* (New York: Basic Books, 1965).

—— *Playing and Reality* (New York: Basic Books, 1971).

Wittgenstein, Ludwig, *Tractatus Logico-Philosophicus*, trans. D. Pears and B. McGuinness (London: Routledge and Kegan Paul, 1961).

Wittig, Monique, "The Point of View: Universal or Particular" and "The Mark of Gender" in *The Straight Mind: And Other Essays* (Boston, MA: Beacon Press, 1992, pp. 59–67, 76–89).

Woolf, Virginia, *A Room of One's Own*, Morag Shiach ed. (Oxford: Oxford University Press, 1992).

Wright, Elizabeth, "Thoroughly Postmodern Feminist Criticism" in *Between Feminism and Psychoanalysis*, Teresa Brennan ed. (London: Routledge, 1989, pp. 141–52).

Young, Iris Marion, "Pregnant Embodiment: Subjectivity and Alienation" in *Throwing Like a Girl and Other Essays in Feminist Philosophy and Social Theory* (Bloomington: Indiana University Press, 1990, pp. 160–74). Originally published in *Journal of Medicine and Philosophy* 9, 1984, pp. 45–62.

Zepp, Evelyn H., "The Criticism of Juila Kristeva: A New Mode of Critical Thought", *Romanic Review* 73(1) 1982, pp. 80–97.

Ziarek, Ewa, "At the Limits of Discourse: Heterogeneity, Alterity and the Maternal Body in Kristeva's Thought", *Hypatia* 7(2) 1992, pp. 91–108.

Žižek, Slavoj, *Looking Awry: An Introduction to Jacques Lacan through Popular Culture* (Cambridge, MA: The MIT Press, 1991).

INDEX

Abelard, P. 21
abject 2, 50, 64–6, 113, 124, 130–1
Adami, V. 73
Adorno, T.W. 111–12, 163
agency 3, 107–8, 146
Althusser, L. 2, 27–8, 33–49, 51, 55, 63,
    66, 88, 90, 175
Archimedes 167
Aristotle 163
art 72, 118
artist 117–8, 157
Artaud, A. 65, 120
Atwood, M. 161
avant-garde 3, 66, 72, 104, 113–16, 121–2,
    124, 128, 129, 134, 154, 163, 176

Bachelard, G. 16
Bakhtin, M. 113
Barker, F. 129
Barthes, R. 65, 104, 116
Bataille, G. expenditure 92; sovereignty
    97–8
Baudrillard, J. reading Marx 89–91;
    symbolic exchange 97–9
Beauvoir, S. de 4, 26; repetition 163,
    165–6, 168, 170, 181
Bellini, G. 118
Bennington, G. 70, 82
Berg, M. 178
birth 32–3, 39, 42, 51, 55, 60, 63, 64,
    146–8, 150, 152, 173, 174; Marx and
    the language of 87–9; phantasies 59–62;
    philosophy of 160; as repetition 165–6;
    and writing 65–6, 139–40, 157, 160–2,
    173

bisexuality 73, 83, 121; of male writer 76;
    and woman writer 120
body: 14–15, 133; asymbolic 122; censored
    139, 161; in crisis 107–13; dead 47;
    fluids 31–33; fragmentation 111; Freud's
    theory of 109; gesture 33, 180; girl's
    180; hysterical 3; maternal 12, 27, 36,
    38, 48, 52, 53, 60–2, 64–6, 88–9, 105,
    113, 116, 129, 135–6, 138–40, 143,
    144, 145, 149–55, 156, 159, 160–1,
    163, 165–6, 169, 177, 180; and nature
    86–9; and loss/expenditure 92, 97; Plato
    views of 29–33; polylogical 111; potent
    female body 61; productive 2; repressed
    28; re-productive 2, 61; self-engendering
    28; semiotic 106, 111, 145; signifying
    105, 108; silenced 83, 84, 179; social/
    political 74; spastic 122; speaking 68;
    suffering 122; theatre of the 130;
    woman's 19, 27, 61, 78, 82, 166; and
    writing 148, 174
borderline: text 108, 114; subject 114, 124
Bréhier 17
Brodribb, S. 45
Burke, C. 124, 154
Butler, J. 124

Cardinal, M. 162
castration 52–53, 54, 58–62, 110, 145, 149,
    172, 177; and phallic mother 117–18,
    127, 128, 136, 137, 144, 146, 147, 155,
    170–1, 173, 175
Céline, L-F. 65, 114, 130
Chawaf, C. 162
chiasma 19

231